PLATO'S *CRATYLUS*

Studies in Continental Thought

PLATO'S *CRATYLUS*
The Comedy of Language

S. Montgomery Ewegen

Indiana University Press

Bloomington and Indianapolis

This book is a publication of

Indiana University Press
Office of Scholarly Publishing
Herman B Wells Library 350
1320 East 10th Street
Bloomington, Indiana 47405 USA

iupress.indiana.edu

Telephone orders   800-842-6796
Fax orders   812-855-7931

♾The paper used in this publication meets the minimum requirements of the American National Standard for Information Sciences—Permanence of Paper for Printed Library Materials, ANSI Z39.48-1992.

Manufactured in the United States of America

Library of Congress Cataloging-in-Publication Data

Ewegen, S. Montgomery.
  Plato's *Cratylus* : the comedy of language / S. Montgomery Ewegen.
    pages cm. — (Studies in Continental thought)
  Includes bibliographical references and index.
  ISBN 978-0-253-01044-5 (alk. paper) — ISBN 978-0-253-01051-3 (eb)
  1. Plato. Cratylus. 2. Language and languages—Philosophy. I. Title.
  B367.E94 2013
  184—dc23

                                                                    2013010885

    1 2 3 4 5 18 17 16 15 14

*For the Bear, the Platypus, the Cat, and the Magpie
and in memory of Waldo and Søren*

Αἰὼν παῖς ἐστι παίζων, πεσσεύων· παιδὸς ἡ βασιληίη·
Eternity is a child playing, moving pieces in a game. Kingship to
the child.

—Heraclitus, Fr. 52; trans. Kahn, slightly modified

"Big things, child of Hipponicus, you ask. But there is a serious
way of talking about the names of these gods and a playful way.
So ask some others for the serious way; but there is nothing to
prevent us from passing through the playful way. For even the
gods are lovers of play."

—*Cratylus,* 406b–c (my translation)

CONTENTS

PREFACE

A book such as this does not require an extensive and ponderous preface: rather, a short and ponderous preface will suffice. Far from being an exhaustive treatment of Plato's *Cratylus,* this book hopes to show the impossibility of exhausting the Platonic dialogue. Even after this work there is much that remains concealed in Plato's *Cratylus,* and shall perhaps forever remain concealed. My hope is that this present work will inspire new and creative research into this exquisite and tremendously complex dialogue. To all those future interpreters of Plato's challenging work, I offer you the same self-serving words that Socrates offers Cratylus at the end of the dialogue that bears his name: "You must continue to consider [these matters] courageously and thoroughly and not accept anything carelessly—for you are still young and in your prime; then, if after investigating, you find the truth, please share it with me" (440d).

A cold day in Boston—January, 2013

ACKNOWLEDGMENTS

Too many to count have brought the fire to me, always selflessly, never tiring, superabundant. The inadequacy of offering mere words in gratitude for such overflowing warmth is a burden that those who have benefited from others must bear. But gratitude is neither a currency nor a form of compensation: rather, it is an acknowledgment of the impossibility of paying back the gifts that one has received. I offer my limitless, yet forever insufficient, gratitude to John Sallis, Jerry Sallis, Robert Metcalf, Marina McCoy, Drew Hyland, Mary Troxell, and Yvonne and Robert Ewegen. I thank also Dee Mortensen and Indiana University Press for their help and support, and Emma Young for her invaluable assistance. I am grateful, too, to Joe Sachs for his excellent and timely translation of the *Cratylus*. I offer endless gratitude to Maggie, who has had to live with me during the creation of this book and will, hopefully, be living with me for the creation of many more. Finally, I offer this book to Søren, the greatest cat in the universe, who sat on it at every stage of its creation. May the finished product be as comfortable to you as were the many drafts leading up to it—and may there be hardbound books, potent catnip, and buttery croissants in kitty heaven.

NOTE ON TRANSLATIONS

No translation of the *Cratylus* is perfect—a hermeneutical fact owed not to the failures of any particular translator, but to the richness and essential ambiguities of the *Cratylus* itself. In what follows I have made extensive use of Joe Sachs' excellent translation, as well as that of the great H. N. Fowler. In order to emphasize certain themes or correct what I perceive to be misleading phrases, I have occasionally modified the translations. (In particular, I have opted for the more common "correct" over Sachs' "rightness" for interpretive reasons that will become clear.) Occasionally I offer my "own" translations (whatever that means), though even in these cases, I often use the generally superior translations of Sachs and Fowler for orientation and verification.

It is recommended, but by no means necessary, that one keep the Greek text handy as one reads the following book, even if one does not read Greek. As will be seen, the principle behind Socrates' view of language entails the material (which is to say visible and audible) similarities between words. It is therefore exceedingly helpful for understanding the text to be able to look upon these similarities as they occur. *It is impossible to do so with any translation, no matter how good.* The *Cratylus*, perhaps more than any other Greek text, demands *to be looked at.*

LIST OF TEXTUAL ABBREVIATIONS

The following is a list of the abbreviations used within the present work when referring to Plato's texts. Note that if a Stephanus number is cited *without* being preceded by one of the following abbreviations, the citation is from the *Cratylus*.

Ap.   (*Apology*)
Epist.   (*Letters*)
Euthd.   (*Euthydemus*)
Euthr.   (*Euthyphro*)
Hipp.   (*Hipparchus*)
Lg.   (*Laws*)
Phd.   (*Phaedo*)
Phdr.   (*Phaedrus*)
Phil.   (*Philebus*)
Prot.   (*Protagoras*)
Rep.   (*Republic*)
Stat.   (*Statesman*)
Symp.   (*Symposium*)
Tht.   (*Theaetetus*)

PLATO'S *CRATYLUS*

Introduction

This inquiry wishes to let Plato's *Cratylus* voice its own proper matter and, to the extent that is possible, articulate its own interpretative horizons. In order to accomplish this, the *Cratylus* must be read as it shows itself in its own light: as a comic dialogue. Such a reading, rather than attempting to circumscribe the *Cratylus* within a broader theory of Plato's thought "as a whole"—if it even makes sense to speak of such a thing—will attempt to allow the dialogue to announce its own themes and chart its own course, neither forcing it into a preconceived theoretical framework called "Platonism" nor striving to locate it within the development of such a framework. In a word, an attempt will here be made to *receive* Plato's *Cratylus* in the dialogically rich and exorbitantly funny manner in which it presents itself.

The purpose of this attempt is two-fold. To begin with, it wishes to stage an encounter with the dramatic and literary aspects of the *Cratylus* which, although essential to its philosophical trajectory, have tended to be downplayed or ignored within scholarship. In order to do this, strict attention must be paid to the *play* of the text, where this nebulous expression wishes to name those phrasings and dramatic moments of the text that are irreducible to the arguments they comprise. In other words, attention must be paid to the *way* of the *Cratylus,* the manner by which it both presents and obscures itself.[1] This shall, among other things, require attending to the comedic tenor of the *Cratylus.*

Secondly, an attempt will be made to let the *Cratylus* itself say what it has to say about the question of the *correctness of names* that is central to its pages.[2] Throughout the history of its reception the *Cratylus* has been read as Plato's *serious* attempt at offering a positive philosophy of language.[3] As will be seen shortly, such a reading misses the *play* of the text and the manner in which such play informs and determines the philosophical movement of the *Cratylus*. To foreshadow what can only develop through this inquiry as a whole, the *Cratylus* offers a *comic view* of λόγος—that is, a view that is itself comic in a manifold sense that will become clear, one that serves to situate humankind with respect to its proper limits.[4] Only by attending to this comic view, and the comic manner in which it is expressed, can one let the *Cratylus* say what it wishes to say about λόγος and the manner in which λόγος situates the human being in its proper place and defines the human condition.

To truly *receive* the *Cratylus* is thus to let the play of the text play itself out in all of its various and rich aspects. In order to accomplish this seemingly simple task one must first prepare oneself to receive the *Cratylus* in the excessively playful way that it presents itself. Such reception is only made possible by first bracketing and interrogating a number of interpretive presuppositions that have historically served to dampen the play of the *Cratylus*. In order to undertake such preparations, the following section shall strive to understand how the *Cratylus* has been interpreted throughout the millennia and the major presuppositions that have guided those interpretations. Only through such a historical review can one hope to free oneself from certain interpretive decisions that have disallowed the *Cratylus* from playing itself out to its fullest (comic) capacity.

Historical Reception

R. M. van den Berg has given a comprehensive and rigorous account of the history of the reception of the *Cratylus* from Aristotle through middle-Platonism and into Proclus, and his narrative shall be followed closely here. Through a compendium of van den Berg's account two general tendencies at work in the scholarship on the *Cratylus* shall become clear: 1) the tendency to read the *Cratylus* anachronistically in terms of Aristotle's philosophy of language, and 2) the general tendency to resist the *playfulness*—or what I shall call the *comedy*—of the *Cratylus*.[5]

Arguably, the earliest known commentator of the *Cratylus* is Aristotle. As Deborah Modrak has argued, Aristotle's Περὶ Ἑρμηνείας (*On Interpretation*) is responding to the challenges regarding the problems of language raised by the *Cratylus,* if not to the *Cratylus* itself.[6] Against this view, van den Berg argues that while the topic of Περὶ Ἑρμηνείας bears certain similarities to that of the *Cratylus,* its primary concern is fundamentally different, and that Aristotle did not intend it as a criticism of Plato's thought in the *Cratylus* (van den Berg 2008, 24). Whether or not Aristotle's Περὶ Ἑρμηνείας is responding directly to the *Cratylus*—likely an insoluble debate—is for our purposes immaterial. What matters is that, from at least the middle-Platonists on, it was *presumed* that it was, and this presumption has decisively informed the way in which the *Cratylus* has been understood by those who read it.

Chronologically, the next known commentator of the *Cratylus* is the Stoic Alcinous.[7] In his work *Handbook of Plato's Doctrines,* written sometime during the first three centuries AD, Alcinous argues that the *Cratylus* is preeminently concerned with logic and dialectic as they relate to etymology.[8] As van den Berg has observed, the designation of the *Cratylus* as "logical" is likely based on the passage in it in which Socrates considers words to be the tools of the dialectician (van den Berg 2008, 38)—a passage which, as we shall see in chapter 5, there is good reason to take as exceedingly playful and critical. However, as van den Berg notes, Alcinous takes such passages utterly seriously, despite strong textual reasons not to. The designation of the *Cratylus* as logical is representative of Alcinous's general attempt, as John Dillon writes, "to attribute to Plato without reservation the whole system of Peripatetic logic as worked out by Aristotle, and further elaborated by Theophrastus and Eudemus" (Dillon 1993, xvi). As a result, Alcinous' handbook, while certainly interesting in its own right, amounts to little more than "a most *useful* exposition of later Peripatetic logic, presented in such a way as to make it *seem* essential Platonism" (Dillon 1993, xvi; my emphasis). Useful, perhaps, but certainly anachronistic and violent to the *Cratylus*. Rather than receiving the *Cratylus* on its own terms, Alcinous read Aristotelian logic *back into* it, forcing upon it considerations and formulations that do not necessarily belong to it.

Such retrograde readings of the *Cratylus* were characteristic of the middle-Platonists. Through an appropriation of Aristotle, the middle-Platonists in general brought a pseudo-Aristotelian theory of words as symbols (σύμβολα), as well as various Stoic theories concerning etymology, to bear upon the *Cratylus* "in order to construct a clear-cut doctrine concerning names . . . and their function in philosophical inquiries" (van den Berg 2008, 32). While such an attempt surely finds partial justification through a certain reading of the *Cratylus,* it will be shown that such a reading is ultimately belied by the playful and ironic tone of the text as a whole, a tone that the middle-Platonists routinely overlooked.

While it was common amongst the middle-Platonists to treat the *Cratylus* as a "logical" work—a term whose formation, it must be stressed, finds its full philosophical articulation well after Plato[9]—Plutarch is the first on record to consider it as a theological text. Guided by a thoroughly Stoic appreciation for etymology, Plutarch took the *Cratylus* to be an effort on Plato's part to discover the nature of the gods through an inquiry into their names.[10] However, like those before him, Plutarch failed to heed Socrates' warning within the *Cratylus* that one should attend not to the names of things, *but to the things themselves* (see 439b; van den Berg 2008, 51). Plutarch further failed to observe the generally comedic tone of the inquiry and the decidedly comedic timbre of the etymologies. Porphyry, too, took etymologies such as those offered in the *Cratylus* seriously "as a source of ancient knowledge which associates the gods with the physical world" (van den Berg 2008, 75). In so doing, just like all those before him, Porphyry missed both the irony and the play of the *Cratylus*.[11]

The attempt to read the *Cratylus* as a serious theological text reached its ancient pinnacle in Proclus's *Commentary on the Cratylus*.[12] This inexhaustibly rich (if somewhat fragmentary) commentary offers great insight into Proclus's thoughts concerning the philosophy of language. Among other things, Proclus therein offers an interpretation of Socrates' etymologies of the names of the gods that seeks to harmonize them with his own Neo-Platonic theology, which includes a rather robust "theory of the Forms" (a "theory" that, as we shall see in chapter 8, is only broached by the Socrates of the *Cratylus* with the greatest reticence and reserve).

However, despite stressing its theological purpose, Proclus still read the *Cratylus* as logical (λογικός) in character (van den Berg 2008, 136), though in a manner quite distinct from Aristotle (Proclus 2007, 1.10 ff.). In this respect, Proclus remains well within the tradition of middle-Platonism that preceded him even while exceeding it in certain important ways, not the least of which is his sensitivity to the dramatic mode of the text.

For our purposes, the most important general aspect of Proclus's commentary is the manner in which it opposes itself to Aristotle. In his commentary, Proclus interprets the philosophical position of the character Hermogenes as representing a prototype of what comes to be Aristotelian semantic theory (van den Berg 2008, 95). Through a refutation of the supposed position of Hermogenes, Plato (according to Proclus) developed his own theory of the correctness of names that culminates in the utterly serious divine etymologies (van den Berg 2008, 197–198). In developing and endorsing this theory, Proclus rejects an Aristotelian language theory in favor of what he considers to be a positive Platonic one (van den Berg 2008, 133). However, like all those before him, Proclus ignored the many warnings within the *Cratylus* against taking etymology too seriously as a means of philosophical inquiry. As a result, Proclus's interpretation is, according to van den Berg, "a product of his own, deeply religious Neo-Platonism that is as similar to Plato's own philosophy as it is dissimilar" (van den Berg 2008, 199). In a word, through Proclus the *Cratylus* becomes a rigorous, religious, and totally *serious* disputation of Aristotle's language theory.

In the wake of such an interpretation, and the cleft that it left open, many philosophers attempted to reconcile what they considered to be the Aristotelian and Platonic poles. For example, Ammonius Hermiae, and later Simplicius of Cilicia, each attempted to harmonize the positions of Aristotle and Plato in different ways (van den Berg 2008; 204, 207). The specifics of their attempts are well beyond the purview of this inquiry. What must be stressed here is that *any* attempt at a reconciliation of Plato and Aristotle regarding the issue of the correctness of names operates under the supposition that the two philosophers were dealing with the same thing (i.e., a semantic theory) and in the same way. It did not occur to these interpreters that reconciliation might be impossible, not due to the extreme polarity of the positions, but to the dissimilarity of their focus and execution. *Can* one reconcile a dramatic dialogue, which stages a comic inquiry into the correctness of names, with a scientific treatise concerning the nature of words? Or is there a *playful openness* and *epistemological reticence* to the former that is lacking in the latter?

If one believes the *Cratylus* to be the basis of Aristotle's Περὶ Ἑρμηνείας, as the middle and late Platonists evidently did, then any critical reflection on the latter will *a fortiori* bear upon the former, but in a way that imports concerns and formulations that are foreign to Plato's text. Under the sway of such an interpretation the *Cratylus* became a proto-logical or theo-logical text whose purpose is to

present a cogent and well-defined theory concerning the correspondence between words and being(s) and the role of etymology in such correspondence,
despite whatever many textual moments, dramatic or otherwise, might belie this
purpose. What gets left behind in such an interpretation is the *Cratylus* itself, its
internal drama and comic presentation. Such a reading, as van den Berg's analysis has shown, misses the salient playfulness that characterizes the etymologies,
reducing them to a Stoic ideal concerning the veracity of etymological derivations while ignoring the warnings that the Socrates of the text gives about such
pursuits. Rather than attending to the *play* of the text, the Platonists in general
attempted to make the *Cratylus* serious by forcefully aligning it with their own
logical frameworks and theological devotions.

Despite the limits of such an interpretive approach—an approach which, it
will be shown, misses the basic philosophical movement of the text—this reading
has found a resurgence in modern scholarship. A recent and renewed interest in
the *Cratylus* has resulted in many fine articles and books which, in their own
terms and for their own purposes, are exemplary. However, many of these attempts repeat the general tendency to downplay or overlook the obvious playfulness of the text, one of the lacunae that the present inquiry seeks to remedy. To
offer just one example, David Sedley, in a rigorous and thoroughgoing book,
presents a defense of the position that the etymologies of the *Cratylus* are "not a
joke" (Sedley 2003, 39) and that Plato was an adherent to the belief that names are
"encoded descriptions" of reality waiting to be decoded through skillful etymological exegesis (Sedley 2003, 28).[13] Sedley further denies that the etymologies
have any satirical or comic purpose (Sedley 2003, 40).[14] While Sedley is right to
warn against taking the etymologies as *simply* playful, if "playful" equates to
"frivolous,"[15] he goes too far in draining the etymological section in particular,
and the dialogue in general, of its comic vitality.[16] As the reading offered here will
argue, this necessarily drains the text's philosophical vitality as well, for it is
through comedy that the *Cratylus* stages its true philosophical purpose.

Sedley's reading is just one example of how some modern scholars have followed certain ancient interpreters in reading the *Cratylus* as Plato's most sustained
presentation of his philosophy of language, adorned with excessive and sometimes
regrettable literary and comic flair.[17] At their best moments such scholars acknowledge the playfulness of the etymologies: however, all too often they fail to understand the play in terms of the philosophical movement of the text as a whole.[18]

One of the few authors to give the drama and comedy of the *Cratylus* its proper
hearing is John Sallis.[19] In his *Being and Logos*, Sallis offers a rigorous analysis of the
whole of the *Cratylus* which attends carefully to its comedic aspects. Most important in this register is the manner in which Sallis shows how the comedy of the
Cratylus is intimately connected with its philosophical purpose, serving an essentially philosophical and disclosive function (to the more precise operations of which

we shall return below). Most generally, Sallis demonstrates that it is precisely through its comedy that the *Cratylus* enacts a philosophical disclosure of the limits of λόγος and the limits of the human being as a being essentially bound to λόγος. To fail to attend to this comic disclosure, as nearly every other commentator has done, is to miss the basic philosophical accomplishment of the text.

As the present inquiry wishes to show, the almost unanimous tendency within scholarship to overlook or set aside the dramatic and comedic in the *Cratylus* ignores the character of the text itself. Beyond the irony and textual warnings mentioned by van den Berg, the *Cratylus* explicitly argues against an overly serious view of language, or what I will call the "tragic view" of language. It is one of the goals of this present work to show that, over-against this tragic view the *Cratylus* develops what I call a *comic* view of language, both in speech and in deed.

* * *

In light of the above historical review, the question becomes this: why have scholars in general failed to attend to the *comic play* of the *Cratylus,* and thus to the comic view of language presented therein?[20] One possible reason for this neglect is that, when compared to some of Plato's other dialogues, the *Cratylus* contains very little dramatic action. For example, unlike the vividly comedic *Euthydemus*—which has been called one of the more "Aristophanic" of Plato's texts[21]—the *Cratylus* is almost entirely without explicit dramatic action. As an imitative dialogue (in the sense given by Socrates in Plato's *Republic* [see *Rep.* 393c])[22] the *Cratylus* contains no narrated action; rather, we only get the words, the λόγοι, of the speakers as they interact with one another. However, as the reading offered here hopes to demonstrate, what little dramatic action there is in the *Cratylus* bears decisively upon the text as a whole, and therefore should not be overlooked.

The most obvious reason to downplay the comedic in the *Cratylus,* however, is owed to a certain prevalent understanding of Plato's general view on comedy. The notion that Plato views comedy only from the very top of his Hellenic nose is primarily (but by no means exclusively) derived from a certain reading of his *Republic.* In Books III and X, the Platonic Socrates radically censors comedy, finally banishing it entirely from the "city in speech" (see *Rep.* 394d ff.). Because of its potential for deception, as well as its effects on the passions of those who would watch it, comedy is treated as politically pernicious and epistemologically perverse, and, along with its tragic counterpart, is excommunicated, as it were, until someone can come along to offer an adequate apology for it (*Rep.* 608a). Most of all, the Socrates of the *Republic* says, such poetry must not be taken *seriously* (οὐ σπουδαστέον) (*Rep.* 608a).

This picture painted by the *Republic*—a picture which still informs Plato scholarship today—is complicated by the *Theaetetus* (and indeed by the *Republic* itself). In the middle of the *Theaetetus* Socrates offers a description of the character of the philosopher—or, at least, of a certain *type* of philosopher. Such people, Socrates explains, do not know their way around the *agora* or the courthouse, lacking all finesse with the business and perks of such places (*Tht.* 173d). Though the body of such a person dwells amongst others in the city, Socrates continues, "his thinking...takes flight underneath the earth...and above the heavens," engaging in geometry and astronomy (*Tht.* 173e; my translation). Socrates then gives an example of such a person:

> [W]hen Thales was engaged in astronomy and, while looking upward, fell into a well, a certain elegantly witty Thracian maidservant is said to have made fun of him [ἀποσκῶψαι], saying that he was eager to know the things in the heavens but could not notice what was right in front of him and at his feet. The same joke [σκῶμμα] holds for all those who spend their lives engaged in philosophy. (*Tht.* 174a–b; Sachs; trans. modified)

The above passage reveals that philosophy is utterly bound to the laughable, and is in no way separable from it. Any person engaged in philosophy—at least, engaged in it in the manner Socrates has just described—is bound to elicit laughter not just from clever Thracian girls, but from "the rest of the crowd" (τῷ ἄλλῳ ὄχλῳ) (*Tht.* 174c). Characterized by political ineptitude and social helplessness, the philosopher appears laughable, at least from a certain (vulgar) point of view.

Yet the philosopher does not only *appear* laughable. Due to his lack of malice toward others, and his derision of the small but seemingly mighty accomplishments of humankind, the philosopher also *laughs*. The philosopher's very being is brought to laughter in the face of the tyrants who, though no better than pigherders, lather each other with praise. And when it becomes obvious to others that he is laughing not as a pretense but in his very being (τῷ ὄντι γελῶν), he is thought to be an idiot (ληρώδης). In the *Theaetetus*, the philosopher does not merely seem to laugh, he is *essentially laughing* and *essentially laugh-inducing*.

This image of the philosopher as both eliciting laughter and actually laughing fits exceedingly well with the *Republic,* despite the prevalent interpretation. In Book VII, after having glimpsed a vision of the open region beyond the cave, the former prisoner is compelled to descend once more into the world of shadows, a world which now, thanks to the sojourn above, looks utterly different. Regarding such a person, Socrates asks: "do you imagine it is anything surprising...if someone coming from contemplation of divine things to things of a human sort is awkward and looks extremely ridiculous [γελοῖος] while his sight is still dim...?" (*Rep.* 517d; Sachs). The one returning to the cave thus appears laughable to the denizens therein, and precisely because he has just glimpsed the divine things above.

Socrates goes on to describe two ways in which such a person could appear laughable, corresponding to the two ways by which someone can become blind: "when they're removed from light into darkness as well as from darkness into light"

(*Rep.* 518a; Sachs). The denizens of the cave, when laughing at this ridiculous stumbling person, must consider which of these transitions accounts for his ridiculousness. If the transition is one from lightness to darkness, the denizen would pity such a person for having returned from the lighted region above to the realm of shadows below; if from darkness to lightness, the denizen would congratulate the person for undertaking the ascent to the lighted region above. Socrates then explains that if the denizen *did* wish to laugh at the one ascending out of darkness and into brightness, such a laughing person "would be less laughable [ἧττον ἂν καταγέλαστος] for laughing at him than someone who laughed at the one coming out of the light above" (*Rep.* 518b; Sachs; trans. modified).

Thus, though the one descending is laughable, she is less laughable than the one ascending. Those in the cave who are laughing *well* (i.e., reasonably [*Rep.* 518a7]) are laughing because they see a person about to embark upon a great ascent into the shining region above, an ascent away from the dark shadowy region below. *But such a laughing spectator can only know this if they themselves have also ascended,* that is, if they themselves have visited the region above and are aware of what such a sojourn entails. (Otherwise, like those who have never left the cave, they would want the recently returned prisoner dead [*Rep.* 517a].) Thus, those in the cave who are laughing *well* recognize that the person on their way up is in the same condition that they themselves have been: they are laughing because they understand themselves, like the ascending prisoner, *to be laughable*.[23] To undertake to glimpse the Good, as a philosopher does, is a laughable thing.

There is thus something *essentially laughable* about philosophy according to the *Republic*, not simply to those who observe it from the outside, but to those who practice it well. When one overlooks this laughable aspect of philosophy— what might be called its comedic aspect—one risks overlooking something about the very essence of philosophy. One must rather strive to let what is laughable in philosophy show itself as such and play itself out in its own laughable terms. Phrased otherwise, philosophy, which essentially involves laughter, should not be taken *too seriously*.

Comedy, too, must be allowed to present itself in its own comic terms, and not simply be judged in terms of the serious. In Plato's *Laws* there is a comment made by the Athenian Stranger that mitigates his otherwise severe position regarding comedy. During his condemnation of comedy—indeed, precisely during that moment when he seems to have cast comedy most decisively from the city— the Stranger suddenly creates a safe space for comedy, but only under a certain condition:

> Those who were earlier said to have permission [to comically ridicule others] . . . may do so to one another without spirited anger but in *play* [παιδιᾶς], but may not do so in seriousness [σπουδῇ] or in spirited anger [θυμουμένοισιν]. (*Lg.* 936a; Pangle, my emphasis)

Comedy is thus allowed in the city after all, but only if it is presented *playfully*. To phrase this otherwise, one could say that comedy has a secure place within the city so long as it is *practiced comically*. Comedy, like philosophy, must not be taken too seriously. But this is not to say that comedy is frivolous.[24] Rather, it is to suggest that there is something about the play of comedy that is lost when comedy is reduced to serious purposes, something *uplifting* that is damaged or dragged down. Further, it is to suggest that comedy only becomes dangerous in this situation of excessive seriousness.[25] There is thus good textual reason to question the position that holds that Plato's texts offer a simple condemnation of comedy. At best, one could claim that they offer a condemnation of reducing the comic to the serious, or of too hastily and harshly measuring the former by means of the latter.

Of course, none of this evidence, as compelling as it might be, bears upon the *Cratylus* directly. Why ought this text in particular be read as a comedy?

To put it simply, the *Cratylus* ought to be received as a comedy because it *gives itself as such*. If we engage with the text appropriately—that is, with the reticence and attentiveness the text demands—the *Cratylus* shows itself to be a comedy: it begins with a joke and undertakes an absurd task, pursued in a comic way. The text is replete with comic innuendo and wordplay, and the etymological section is as peerless an example of Plato's comic (and philosophical) ability as one could ever wish to find. To receive the *Cratylus* is to let this comic character play itself out.

The essentially comic character of the *Cratylus* is indicated by Socrates himself at various points. Most striking in this regard is the way in which Socrates disparages what he calls "the tragic life" (τὸν τραγικὸν βίον) (408c) with regard to the problem of the correctness of names, that is, a life which entails an understanding of language as essentially tragic. Over against this tragic view of language, Socrates throughout the text both argues for and enacts a comic view, most obviously in the etymological section. Through this enactment the real philosophical movement of the *Cratylus* takes place. In other words, what the *Cratylus* accomplishes—and it accomplishes much—it does through a comic ascent.

But what *is* comedy? Or, less generally, what is comedy in the *Cratylus?* In order to have any hope of letting ourselves be commanded by the comedy of the *Cratylus,* we must first come to some clarity regarding the nature of comedy as it operates within the text. To that end, in what follows I will articulate four distinct but interrelated elements of comedy in Plato: abstraction, disclosure, ridicule, and the laughable.

Comedy

a) Abstraction

To begin with, the *Cratylus* is a comedy in the sense in which Leo Strauss used the term. In *The City and Man*, Strauss observes a certain way in which Plato's texts in general tend toward the "ridiculous or, as we are in the habit of saying, the comical" (Strauss 1964, 62).[26] Each Platonic text, Strauss suggests, engages in an operation whereby it abstracts away from some important matter that, given the purported or even stated purposes of the dialogue, cannot be abstracted away from.[27] (Strauss also astutely notes that, in this way, "the Platonic dialogue brings to its completion what could be thought to have been completed by Aristophanes" [ibid.], thereby noting the [albeit complicated] affinity between Plato and the comic playwright.) As a result of this unwarranted abstraction, the philosophical undertaking of any particular Platonic text is shown to be impossible in a manner that is ridiculous.[28]

In his *Being and Logos*, John Sallis applies a similar conception of comedy to the *Cratylus*, noting that it omits something that cannot in good sense be omitted. The *Cratylus* is developed in such a way that the very *path* of the inquiry—that is, λόγος—is itself the *object* of the inquiry. In other words, the inquiry into the nature of λόγος, which is itself undertaken *through* λόγος, recoils upon itself—a point to which we shall return. The characters, by never drawing attention to this rather obvious and potentially vicious circle, commit a kind of comic avoidance which tints the color of the inquiry to come. Focusing on this latter element, Sallis extends Strauss's understanding of comedy by stressing the manner in which such abstraction involves a moment of radical (self-)forgetfulness. The characters, by continually forgetting this self-reflexive recoil of λόγος, run the risk of failing to accomplish what they set out to, resulting in a "fundamental incongruity between what one takes [oneself] to be accomplishing and what one, in fact, does accomplish" (Sallis 1975, 185). This incongruity is the basis of the comedy.[29]

Such comic self-forgetfulness, as Sallis further argues, serves to disclose something essential about the undertaking of the *Cratylus*. Within the very space of this comic incongruity, something comes to light about the relationship of the human being to λόγος (Sallis 1975, 185): namely, that the human being is essentially bound to λόγος in such a way that it can never wholly free itself from it. Through a comic exhibition that plays out as an attempted inquiry *into* λόγος *through* λόγος—as if λόγος could somehow be rigorously separated from itself—the manner in which the human being essentially dwells in λόγος is made manifest. The comedy thus discloses an essential truth about the human condition: namely, that the human being dwells within λόγος in a manner that is extraordinary. Such comedy brings our human condition with respect to λόγος into focus.

These considerations show that the comedy of a Platonic text, through voicing its own incongruities and the self-forgetfulness of the characters, effectively marks its own *limits*. In the case of the *Cratylus*, the limits of any inquiry into λόγος that proceeds by way of λόγος—and thus any inquiry into λόγος at all (436a)—are brought to light. In general, the movement of abstraction at play in the *Cratylus*, and the continual forgetfulness (and thus concealment) of the abstraction, serve to bring the limits of the inquiry to the fore.

b) Disclosure

It was suggested above that comedy in the Platonic text performs an essentially disclosive function. In other words, comedy is one way by which the Platonic text makes something manifest.[30] The comic play of the dialogue—its comic *ergon*—discloses something about the λόγος of the dialogue, and in a comic manner, no matter how serious that λόγος may occasionally appear.

The λόγος of a text—where λόγος is understood narrowly as 'argument'—cannot reveal on its own what the complex *interplay* of a dialogue with its dramatic context can reveal. Through the comedic play of the text as a whole something about the inquiry comes to light that would otherwise remain hidden. Most often what is brought to light through the comedy are the parameters and constraints of the inquiry itself. For example, as seen above, it is precisely the comic failure to call attention to the self-reflexive character of the inquiry into λόγος through λόγος that brings the limitations of the inquiry into clarity. Thus, comedy is a way of bringing into the open what would otherwise remain hidden. In a word, comedy is a way of *showing* something, a means of exhibition. Rather than simply stating something (i.e., offering some λόγος), comedy, precisely through its performed *ridicule,* demonstrates something about that which it ridicules. So understood, comedy makes a *demonstration* of something that exceeds simple articulation.[31]

c) Ridicule

A Platonic text may also be thought of as comedic insofar as it comes to *parody* or *ridicule* someone or something. The *Cratylus* has a widely acknowledged parodic and satirical aspect.[32] One argument is that Socrates (or Plato) is ridiculing the very use of etymology as a legitimate philosophical or epistemological enterprise.[33] Regardless of whom in particular Socrates is ridiculing, there is general agreement among scholars that some such satirical operation is taking place. As a satire of certain philosophers, sophists, and/or poets, the *Cratylus* certainly shares much with the comedies of Aristophanes, and with Attic comedy in general.

Such satire, so understood, serves a precise *critical* function. Through it there opens a free space wherein a certain philosophical position (either explicit or implicit) is imitated and criticized in terms of the context of the dialogue's philosophical purpose. For example, within the *Cratylus* Socrates will come to *perform,* as if in comic imitation, what he considers to be the Homeric view of names and their correctness (see chapter 6). Through the staging of a comic scene Socrates brings out the absurdities implicit in the Homeric position, and all those who hold it explicitly or implicitly. Such absurdities *only* come to light through Socrates' performance of the Homeric position, his testing of it in deed (e.g., his first set of etymologies) (see 391d ff.). In other words, by performing a parody of Homer, Socrates brings the limits of the Homeric position into clarity in a ridiculous way. It is thus precisely the comic performance of the Homeric position, and the hilarity it brings about, that serves also as the critique of that position.

Of course, Socrates does not only ridicule Homer. There are any number of other thinkers whom Socrates may be ridiculing, most obviously Hermogenes, Protagoras, Euthydemus, Euthyphro, Heraclitus, and Cratylus (i.e., those characters who are mentioned within the pages of the *Cratylus* itself). Each of these thinkers is subjected to a certain criticism by Socrates which brings to light, and makes light of, the absurdities implicit in their positions. Further, as chapter 5 will show, Socrates also comes to ridicule Hermogenes' position that humans have mastery over words, offering a devastating criticism of what has come to be called "the tool-analogy." Most of all, Socrates will come to ridicule the tragic view of language as it is developed within the *Cratylus*, thereby subjecting it to the measure of comedy.

However, most important of all is the manner in which Socrates brings *himself* under such criticism and ridicule. As Baxter has noted, one of the groups that Socrates ridicules is the so-called μετεωρολόγοι, or "those who offer accounts of the things aloft" (Baxter 1992, 140). The term, as Baxter notes, often carried with it a certain disparaging quality, as Socrates' association of the term with "chattering" (ἀδολέσχαι) indicates (401b7). However, Socrates himself, in other contexts, is associated with this term. In the *Apology*, Socrates reports a certain pernicious rumor about him that he is a "thinker of the things aloft" (τά τε μετέωρα φροντιστὴς) (*Ap.* 18b), a rumor traced back to Aristophanes' *Clouds,* wherein Socrates is comically depicted as a swaggering sophist (*Clouds,* 359) and as concerning himself immoderately with the things aloft (τὰ μετέωρα πράγματα) (ibid., 229). Thus, in referring to the μετεωρολόγοι in the *Cratylus,* Socrates could be referring to himself (or, more precisely, a certain popular view regarding him).[34] In this case, to the extent that he comes to ridicule the μετεωρολόγοι, Socrates would be ridiculing himself.

Regardless of whether or not this term constitutes a self-reference, it is textually clear that Socrates finds his own method of procedure in the *Cratylus* ridiculous, and at one point even calls his "swarm of wisdom" (i.e., the etymologies) laughable (γελοῖον) (402a1). Later, after offering the hypothesis that letters and syllables are imitations of beings, Socrates likewise calls that hypothesis laughable (γελοῖα), though perhaps necessary (425d1). Shortly thereafter he claims that he himself thinks such "notions about the earliest words are quite hubristic and laughable" (ὑβριστικὰ εἶναι καὶ γελοῖα) (426b6; my translation). Though we shall have more to say about the "laughable" character of Socrates' procedure in the chapters to come, it suffices here to note that such remarks indicate a certain reticence that Socrates holds toward the inquiry, and serve as a kind of jolly criticism of his own part in the comic play.

Insofar as Socrates ridicules his own performance in the *Cratylus,* his inquiry serves, in addition to everything else, as a kind of *self*-criticism or -critique that operates as an evaluation of himself with respect to the knowledge of the correctness of names. By calling his own efforts "laughable," and thereby making himself into a comic hero, Socrates is calling his own behavior into question, drawing himself into the space of critical inquiry. Considered in this way, the sort of self-reflexive ridicule undertaken within the *Cratylus* is not radically different from Socrates' general pursuit of self-knowledge (as, for example, it is articulated in the *Apology*) (see *Ap.* 21d). What such critical self-ridicule (or ridiculous self-critique) shows above all is that one's pretensions to knowledge are not in fact knowledge, and that one therefore does not know what one thought one knew. In other words, self-ridicule, as critique, marks the limits of one's own knowledge. Thus, the critical operation of ridicule, like that of comic abstraction, is a means of marking limits, perhaps most of all one's own.

However, to ridicule oneself—to mark one's own limits by subjecting oneself to critique—is to extend oneself some measure beyond them. As Socrates calls attention to the laughable character of his inquiry, he raises himself above those others who occupy their philosophical position with austere zeal, such as Cratylus (427e). To recognize one's own ignorance is to transcend the situation of those who are no less ignorant but who have yet to acknowledge their ignorance. To phrase this in terms of our earlier analysis of laughter in the *Republic,* to laugh at one's own limited philosophical position is to enact a certain *ascent* beyond the limitations of that position, an ascent characterized precisely by laughter.

In this register, it should be stressed that, strictly speaking, Socrates does *not* offer his own perspective on the correctness of names within the *Cratylus,* at least not explicitly. He states near the beginning (384b), and repeats later (391a), that he himself does not pretend to hold a position regarding the correctness of names, but is nonetheless willing to investigate (σκοπεῖσθαι) the matter along with Hermogenes. Thus, it is a little misleading to say that Socrates criticizes himself. It would perhaps be more appropriate to say that Socrates, in lending his voice to certain positions, thereby brings those positions into critical ridicule, while always himself maintaining a critical distance from them. Indeed, it is precisely through refusing to offer his own position that Socrates indicates the critical aspect of the *Cratylus* most glaringly. By leaving his own position regarding the question of the correctness of names *open*, Socrates calls the entire enterprise into question, effectively ridiculing it. Socrates' self-critique is so radical as to disallow him from pretending to have knowledge about the correctness of names.[35]

d) The Laughable

There is much that is laughable in the *Cratylus,* from the various ridiculous etymologies to the comic incongruity of the undertaking itself. Most importantly, as will be shown in detail in chapter 3, the text involves an elaborate and persistent joke whose subtlety is exceeded only by its vulgarity: and, although this joke stands at the very head of the *Cratylus*, its full and vulgar character has never been given the prominence it deserves.

Of course, when held against one of Aristophanes' plays, the *Cratylus* surely pales in comparison to the ribald and excessive character of what we have come to understand as Old Greek Comedy. Surely the most austere Plato would not have lowered himself to such devices as explicitly criticized in his most austere book, the *Republic?* Surely the *Cratylus* does not, as the plays of Aristophanes frequently did, contain phallic jokes and tales of castration and sexual innuendo?

Or does it? Are there indeed moments of such comic excess and vulgarity, diluted, perhaps, compared with Aristophanes' *Clouds* or *Birds,* but nonetheless present? As we will see, the *Cratylus* does indeed contain such moments. Further, it shall be argued that such comic moments form an essential part of what the dialogue wishes to accomplish philosophically. From the very beginning of the text, and through its very end, what is foremost in question is the relationship between Hermogenes—"the son of Hermes"—and the god Hermes. It is this question that first opens the dialogue and sets the horizons of the philosophical inquiry to come. At stake in this question is whether and to what extent Hermogenes shares some feature of Hermes such that he could *correctly* (ὀρθῶς) be called his son. As will be argued, the actual feature in question is neither Hermes' role as the god of the *agora* (384c) nor his role as contriver of speech (408a)—or at least not *simply* these—but rather the god's erotic virility and ithyphallic condition. In a word, the *Cratylus* begins with a joke, one calling into question the erotic prowess of Hermogenes, son of Hipponicus. The *Cratylus* thus literally sets its own comic horizons. To truly receive the *Cratylus* is to read it within this horizon.

Thus, the *Cratylus* is comedic in the sense that it brings about laughter; and Socrates, at one point, even admits that it does so (402a).[36] Only by letting the text bring about the laughter it so brilliantly evokes and reflects upon can we hope to hear it in its proper voice. Further, only by letting it evoke our laughter can we let it perform a function essential to the opening of philosophical thought: the provocation of *wonder.*

As Plato's *Euthydemus* makes clear, laughter and *wonder* share a great intimacy. In that dialogue, Socrates and his comrades are given a wondrous display of sophisticated argumentation by the two sophist brothers Dionysodorus and Euthydemus. What comes to light through the drama of the text is that the ridiculous performance of the sophist brothers is only wonderful to the extent that it is laughable. The *Euthydemus* shows that the comic or the ridiculous is such as to induce wonder. Comedy is thus an origin of wonder: that is, it is an origin of the origin of philosophy. Insofar as the *Cratylus* brings about laughter, it invites us into philosophy.

One must recall Thales here, full of wonder, stumbling into the well while pondering the things aloft, and so tickling the Thracian girl with his aloofness. The wonder characteristic of philosophy surely brings about the laughter of others. Yet one must also remember the denizen of the cave as she laughs at the one who ascends to the lighted region above, and must remember that the very condition for the possibility of her well-informed laughter is that she herself has sojourned above. Only because she has been filled with wonder can she recognize the wonder the prisoner is about to undergo: only because she finds herself laughable can the philosopher laugh at the one who undertakes philosophy. Perhaps laugher—at least, the *right kind* of laughter—is nothing other than vocalized wonder, nothing other than the cock-crow of philosophy. One wonders if Thales laughed as he fell.

Gathering these four elements of comedy together, one can say that the *Cratylus* is a comedy insofar as it engages in comic abstractions and comic ridicule, and does so in a way that laughably brings the limits of the inquiry into disclosure, thereby inviting us to wonder about them. To lose sight of these comic operations, as commentators have done all too often, is to lose sight of the horizon of the text, the *limit* of the text, the πέρας from which the text begins and toward which it perpetually tends.

* * *

In her excellent book on the *Cratylus*, Rachel Barney has written that "an entirely new interpretation [of the *Cratylus*] would have to be very strange indeed" (Barney 2001, 3). While the investigation undertaken here cannot pretend to be "entirely new," nor wishes to be, it does perhaps succeed in being "very strange indeed." This, however, is as it should be—for the *Cratylus* itself, as many of its commentators have observed, is exceedingly strange.[37] It is strange in topic with respect to other of Plato's texts, and it is idiosyncratic in the way that it addresses it. In other words, the text *itself* is strange and presents itself to us as such, so long as we allow it to do so. Any interpretation that wishes to let the text show itself in its own terms must therefore itself be strange: but such strangeness is always and only in the service of letting what is strange in the *Cratylus* show itself as such.

And what does the *Cratylus* show? How does it show itself? The *Cratylus* shows itself as an inquiry into the character of words undertaken in a comic manner. In other words, the *Cratylus* is a comedy *of* words, where "of" is taken in the double-genitive. The comedy is of words, it takes place in words, by means of words, and in a manner that is comic. Further, the text is a comedy of words in that it is concerned with nothing other than words. In what follows an attempt will be made to preserve this comedy by letting what is playful in the work play itself out. And why pursue the playfulness? And why turn to comedy in particular to find such playfulness? There can be only one reason: namely, the intimacy of *philosophy* with such play. As John Sallis has written, "whatever else may pertain to it and to its beginning, philosophy is begun in play. It is in play that one begins to philosophize . . . " (Sallis 1975, 21).[38] The play of the Platonic text, if let to play, cannot help but provoke wonder, the initial strivings of philosophy. If play is an origin of wonder and hence of philosophy, such *originary* play, as Sallis further notes, assumes various guises throughout the Platonic corpus, but "is perhaps most apparent in those dialogues which, like the *Cratylus,* most transparently exhibit the form of comedy" (Sallis 1975, 21). For, to extend this thought, comedy is nothing other than *radical* playfulness, a playfulness so radical that it earns its character through threatening transgression of the seriousness to which it would otherwise be bound. Further, comedy, unlike tragedy, is *self-aware:* it draws itself into the parodic critical space that it itself opens up.[39] Insofar as comedy makes playfulness more readily visible, it makes the beginning of philosophy more visible. Comedy, as radical play, facilitates the originating playfulness of philosophy.

Such play is a wondrous invocation, an invocation *to* wonder which, as an invocation, demands a response.[40] It is here supposed that in order to respond *correctly* to this invocation one must sustain the play, one must play it forward. To write on Plato is to play with Plato's plays, to attempt to play *in* the playful situations that Plato, in his own playful writings, opened up. When one acknowledges that philosophy, too, begins in play, then one can see the possible benefits of engaging in such play. To write on Plato is to play at doing philosophy. The risk is that one will come to take oneself *too* seriously, thereby forgetting the cardinal law that binds play, making it lawful: play must *remain* playful.

To forget the play is to forget philosophy.[41]

1 First Words

"Shall we let Socrates here join in our discussion?"[1]
"Suppose that we make Socrates a party to the argument?"[2]
"Do you want us to make our speech a common endeavor with Socrates here?"[3]
"Here is Socrates; shall we take him as a partner in our discussion?"[4]

These four translations of the opening line of Plato's *Cratylus* have been placed beside one another in order to make something manifest. Although the wordings of the four translations differ—though they employ different letters and syllables—they all more or less *say the same*. To use the language of modern linguistics, we could say that although the signifiers differ, the signified remains *more or less* the same in each case, and that despite the material differences of each translation the same formal meaning comes across. To put it colloquially, all four phrasings have more or less the same *gist*. We could even let the opening line of the *Cratylus* be presented in another language, such as German: "Sollen wir auch dem Sokrates da die Sache mitteilen?"[5] Anyone with a German dictionary would see that this more or less *says the same* as its English counterparts, though of course with different semantic nuances, not to mention drastically different graphic and syllabic arrangements. The French translation, too, more or less *says the same*: "Voilà Socrate; veux-tu que nous lui fassions part du sujet de notre entretien?"[6]

Yet, despite this supposed equivalence across tongues, phrasings, and borders—the supposition that these sentences all more or less *say the same*—none of the above translations adequately presents what is most at issue in the opening line of the *Cratylus*. This inability to capture what is at work in the opening line of the *Cratylus* is not due to any deficiency on the part of the particular translations themselves, each of which has its own merits. Rather, it is an inability that belongs to the very act of attempting to translate the *Cratylus* at all. As will become clear though this inquiry, the *Cratylus* presents a certain conflict between language as it is used by human beings (such as translators) and *language itself* insofar as it unfolds from out of itself.[7] More specifically, the *Cratylus* raises the possibility of a human mode of understanding that attends to what language *itself* wishes to say about itself, rather than simply to what certain human beings wish to say about language.[8]

As will be seen, the opening line of the *Cratylus,* understood in light of the dialogue as a whole, subtly draws attention to this possibility. Insofar as the opening line wishes to raise this possibility, *any* attempt to translate it is limited: for in translating the text a translator submits it to his or her own opinions and purposes—or, one might say, to his or her own *wishes.* Through the very act of translation, whatever it is that language itself wishes to say is filtered through what the translator, in accordance with her understanding of the text and her mastery of the particular languages, wishes to say. In making an interpretive decision, as all interpreters must continually do, the interpreter uses language to point the text in a particular direction or toward a particular end (i.e., using "partner" rather than "party," or "argument" rather than "discussion"). Such decisions, *by their very nature,* begin to close off the richness and polysemy that language itself holds in reserve. If it were the case that a text, such as the *Cratylus,* sought as its very philosophical purpose to emphasize the richness and polysemy of language, such interpretive decisions would damage or at least dampen the text's ability to say what it wished to say. The *Cratylus,* as this inquiry will show, indeed wishes to emphasize the richness and polysemy of language.

Of course, one could attempt to avoid these issues of translation by simply returning to the "original" Greek, thereby leaving the text in its "native" tongue: Βούλει οὖν καὶ Σωκράτει τῷδε ἀνακοινωσώμεθα τὸν λόγον; (383a).[9] However, there are two problems with attempting such a return. To begin with, there is a major (and, to a great extent, insurmountable) hermeneutical problem that accompanies the reception of any ancient text. The Platonic texts as they come to us are not hypostatized ideas set eternally unchanged in the clouds: rather, they are *living documents* that change over time, copies of copies (or images of images) which, as dynamic, are subject to the entropic rules of alteration and decay that beset all existent things. How the text was "meant" to appear is an ideal utterly lost to the contingencies of history, though philologists may do their best to speculate upon probable arrangements.[10] In a certain radical sense, then, there is no original to which one could return. Even if we could somehow assure ourselves that we had returned to the original Greek text laid out as Plato had wished it, such a return would in no way relieve us of the labor of translating the text into our own tongues, of interpreting—indeed, one is tempted to say *metaphorizing*— the Greek words into the words of our "own" language. We are all of us—English, Germans, and French alike—barbarians to the Greeks.[11]

The second problem is more specific to the *Cratylus,* and infinitely more abysmal. So many of the words of which the *Cratylus* is comprised are the very words whose meanings are interrogated within Socrates' long series of playful etymologies offered within the *Cratylus* itself. Even if one were somehow to access, across a history of facsimile and linguistic difference, the "original" text of the *Cratylus* in such a way as to have its unadulterated words immediately at hand, one would still have to analyze the *Cratylus* in terms of its *own* rethinking of those words, tracing every instance of them while striving to understand their use in light of the internal etymologies of those terms. One can imagine a scene wherein some scrupulous scholar would set out to accurately trace and record the infinitely complex semantic drift of each of these self-reflexive words, tirelessly striving to present a coherent genealogy of each such word. Yet, such an undertaking would be limitless in scope and Herculean in deed: for without a doubt the very words used to explain one etymology would themselves be words interrogated in another etymology, and so on, and so on.[12] Such an "original" text would thus undermine itself—one is tempted to say "deconstruct" itself—and drag the poor scholar down with it.

Despite all of this, one could argue that even the Greek text more or less *says the same* as its English, French, and German translations; that, despite all the particular (i.e., material) differences in these phrasings, they all for the most part *say the same*. Hermogenes rather famously makes this very point within the *Cratylus* when he, summarizing Cratylus's position, states that "there is a kind of natural correctness [ὀνόματος ὀρθότητα] in names, which is the same for all human beings, both Greeks and Barbarians" (383a; my translation). Whatever the correctness of a name *is*— and this remains to be seen—it is the same for all of us, according to Hermogenes' version of Cratylus's position, despite the idioms of our particular languages. Socrates echoes this when he says that the rare and all-important name-giver, like an iron-smith, might embody the look of a name in different materials (i.e., letter and syllables), but that such materials, whether of domestic or foreign origin, will not alter the ἰδέα that they embody (390a). With such a picture, the phrasings "shall we let," "do you want," "shall we take," "Sollen wir," "veux-tu que nous," and "βούλει" all convey the same idea: they all more or less *say the same*.

It should be observed that this principle, whether or not it is in the end endorsed by any of the characters of the *Cratylus* or its author, is the very condition for the possibility of our reading the *Cratylus*.[13] Without the supposition, flimsy and groundless as it may be, that the Greek words "say the same" as our English words, any attempt to read or understand the *Cratylus* (or any other ancient text) would be laughable to the extreme. It is the unspoken principle of translation that the foreign words we translate must more or less say the same as the words into which we translate them, at least to enough of an extent to allow us to enumerate the differences. To refuse this supposition would be to sever oneself from the possibility of community, of a common term in or around which one could commune with an ancient text. In a word, to refuse it would be to refuse a common λόγος, retreating instead into the realm of private and incommensurable λόγοι, if not into absolute *silence*.

Yet, despite the absolute necessity of supposing a semantic equivalence (without which we would never bother to undertake to read anything at all), none of the above-quoted translations lets the opening of the *Cratylus* say what it itself *wishes* to say (though the translation offered by Joe Sachs arguably gets the closest). If it proved to be true that the *text itself* of the *Cratylus* wished to say something, then the best translations would be those that *let* themselves be guided by the text, not so much translating the text as letting themselves be translated by it. The best translations would be those that hold their own wills and wishes in abeyance *to the extent possible*, thereby letting *the words themselves say what they wish to say*. However, even such reticent translations would still to a great extent be *bound*—in manner that is decidedly *tragic*—to the opinions and wishes of the human beings who constructed them. The best one can do is *play* at letting oneself be transported by the text to whatever strange place it wishes to take us.

* * *

With strict economy Plato has Hermogenes begin the *Cratylus:*

Βούλει οὖν καὶ Σωκράτει τῷδε ἀνακοινωσώμεθα τὸν λόγον;

"You wish that we should gather up in common with Socrates here in the λόγος?" (383a; my translation)

The opening question of the *Cratylus* involves a *wish*. Hermogenes is asking Cratylus if he wishes (βούλει) for Socrates to join them in the λόγος, in what will prove to be a λόγος *about* λόγος, an exchange of words concerned with nothing other than words and the possibility of their meaningful exchange. With the immediate mention of βούλομαι ("I wish") the text is at once oriented toward the operation of human wishing, an operation that will play a decisive role within the philosophical movement of the *Cratylus*. By questioning Cratylus about whether he wishes to bring Socrates in as a mediator in their discussion, Hermogenes is effectively putting wishing itself into question.

As the first word, βούλομαι should be read carefully in light of the dialogue as a whole. There are many occasions where Plato, for dramatically and philosophically significant reasons, uses the first word of the text to mark or foreshadow what is to come.[14] In the case of the *Cratylus,* this first instance of βούλομαι, which occurs some seventy-plus times throughout the text, marks at once one of the most significant and most overlooked elements at play in the dialogue. To overlook this important word, as most commentators have done, is to shunt a vital artery that passes through the very heart of the *Cratylus*. One does well to heed Socrates' statement within the *Cratylus* itself: "Everyone must . . . give great care and great attention to the beginning of any undertaking, to make an inquiry [σκέψιν] about whether it has been laid down correctly [ὀρθῶς] or not" (436d; Fowler; trans. modified). The *Cratylus* begins with βούλομαι, and so, therefore, must we.

What does βούλομαι *mean*—that is, what does it *itself* mean? To begin to answer this we must turn to the lexicons. However, there is a certain irony in undertaking such a turn as a means of deciphering the opening word of the *Cratylus:* for the dialogue, as was seen in the Introduction and will continue to be explored in greater detail, is masterfully derisive of such an etymological turn. In this sense Plato has made us actors in his scene: fools who, due to our historical and linguistic distance from the Greek language, *must* play the role of the very etymologists Plato's play is ridiculing. Indeed, to have recourse to the lexicons one must bracket the problem of the *Cratylus* and proceed shamefacedly as if one can simply rely on the data of the dictionaries, born as they are of a history of etymological and philological research. Plato's play forces us, as barbarians to the Greek tongue, to proceed in such shame: or, perhaps, forces us to mark the shame and proceed *playfully* and *courageously* nonetheless.

Βούλομαι means *to wish, to will,* or *to want*. In Classical Greek, and certainly at the time of Plato, βούλομαι names the will or volition that a person holds toward something. Its meaning is similar to ἐθέλω, *to want*: however, whereas ἐθέλω can have an almost begrudging sense—"if it pleases you, I am willing to do it"[15]—βούλομαι indicates that the agent deliberately wishes for something; it expresses a preference on the part of the agent, that one thing is wished over another.[16] As a so-called deponent verb, βούλομαι has middle/passive endings, though in translation its sense is active. Above all, as a middle-voice verb, what is indicated is that the agent (i.e., the grammatical subject) has some special interest in the action, that the subject is intimately involved in the deed.[17]

Βούλομαι can also sometimes denote *desire*. As Charles Kahn has argued, Plato will often use βούλομαι alongside words like ἐπιθυμέω and ἐράω, each of which, with its own semantic nuances, denotes desire toward something.[18] In Plato's *Protagoras,* for example, Socrates even goes so far as to chide the sophist Prodicus (whom he also mentions in the *Cratylus*) for "distinguishing βούλεσθαι and ἐπιθυμεῖν as not being the same" (*Prot.* 340b), suggesting that, at least within the context of that dialogue, the two terms do more or less *say the same*. For Kahn, "Plato expresses the generic concept of desire not by any single term but by free movement back and forth between a number of different expressions, including *epithumein, boulesthai,* and *eran*" (Kahn 1996, 263). While one must be careful not to simply equate these terms, thereby obfuscating their differences— differences which in other dialogues become explicit[19]—one must be equally careful to hear the kinship between them, and especially between βούλομαι and ἐράω. As it turns out, this kinship will be of the utmost importance to our understanding of the *Cratylus*.

Hermogenes, in using βούλομαι at the beginning of the dialogue, is asking Cratylus if he himself wishes—perhaps even *desires*—for Socrates to come and communicate (ἀνακοινωσώμεθα) with them in their λόγος.[20] "Wishing" is used in this sense throughout the dialogue. Cratylus has a special knowledge of the natural correctness of names, one of which we could avail ourselves "if he wished [βούλοιτο] to state it clearly" (384a; my translation). Socrates later asks Hermogenes where it is he wishes (βούλει) to begin in their pursuit of the correctness of names (397a). The dialogue is peppered with instances where Socrates asks Hermogenes what it is he wishes to do, or whether some action is in accordance with his wishes. In this usage it is clear that βούλομαι and its cognates are used as expressions of the wishes of the interlocutors. It is an expression of the deliberative, volitional, one might even say *fanciful* (386e) drive of the agent. Indeed, given the above-mentioned relationship between βούλομαι, ἐπιθυμέω, and ἐράω, one might even hazard to say that βούλομαι names the *erotic* drive of the agent toward some preferred end or goal. As will be seen, the wishes of the characters, and the erotic drive motivating those wishes, play a decisive role in the development of the structure of λόγος that the *Cratylus* wishes to bring to light.

Although turning shamefacedly to the lexicons has now helped us clarify in general the meaning of βούλομαι, such a turn must be made with the greatest reserve: for βούλομαι is one of the many words for which Socrates offers a playful etymology within the *Cratylus*. Though the definition takes place within the great etymological comedy, and is therefore presented playfully, we cannot simply ignore the meaning which Socrates attributes to βούλομαι. Rather, because the word comes to be interrogated by Socrates, and because the word occupies a privileged place at the beginning of the text, we cannot deny the possibility that the etymology Socrates comes to offer is meant to apply to the word in its general usage throughout the *Cratylus* and to shed light on the greater inquiry. Further, as intimated in the Introduction, the fact that the etymologies are playful in no way undermines their philosophical importance: indeed, such playfulness may precisely underscore their philosophical value.

At the very height of the etymological comedy, just before he runs (θέω) the final lap of his divinely inspired etymologies, Socrates offers the following:

> "Opinion" [δόξα] gets its name either for *pursuing* [δίωξει], in the sense that the soul goes in pursuit of knowing how it stands with things, or else it's for a shot from a *bow* [τοῦ τόξου βολῇ]. The latter looks more likely; at least "supposition" [οἴησις] is in accord with that, since it seems like an indicator of a *motion* of the soul toward all things to get at what each of the beings is like, the same way that a "plan" [βουλή] is a sort of *shot* [βολήν], and "wanting" [βούλεσθαι] and "deliberating" [βουλεύσθαι] signify [σημαίνει] aiming at something. All these various words appear to go along with opinion [δόξῃ] and to be made in the image of taking a *shot* [βολῆς], just as the opposite, "ill-advisedness" [ἀβουλία], on its side, seems to be a *missing* [ἀτυχία], as if on the part of someone who doesn't shoot or hit [οὐ βαλόντος οὐδὲ τυχόντος οὗ τ' ἔβαλλε] what he shot at or wanted [ἐβούλετο] or deliberated about [ἐβουλεύτο] or aimed at. (420b–d; Sachs)

Βουλή is taken to express shooting at something, as with an arrow, and βούλεσθαι (the middle-voice infinitive of βούλομαι) is taken to express the act of aiming at something, the way an archer would aim at a target (420c). Both are associated with δόξα, and are thereby relegated to the realm of human opinion, appearances, and *shadows*.[21] Wishing (βούλομαι) is thusly yoked with opinion (δόξα)—an association that will remain operative throughout the *Cratylus*. This association is perhaps indicated by Cratylus's response to the opening question of the dialogue:

> HERMOGENES: Do you yourself wish [βούλει] that we join up in common with Socrates in (the) λόγος?
>
> CRATYLUS: If it *seems* [δοκεῖ] to you.[22] (383a; my translation)

Human wishing is further shown to consist in an activity of aiming and shooting at something, which carries with it the possibility of failure, or even harm.[23] Socrates makes this latter point by mentioning the possibility of ἀβουλία, the failure to hit that at which one aims (420c). Wishing alone is by no means sufficient to hit upon the truth: rather, wishing always carries with it the possibility of failure, of falling short, of shooting oneself in the foot.[24] This possibility exists precisely because βούλομαι is so decidedly a matter of human opinion, of δόξα.

It could be the case that when we name something—that is, when we use a name in such a way as to call upon the being which the name names—we use a name that is not at all in accordance with the being which we call upon, but rather only in accordance with our own human wishes, or with how that being *seems* to us. To illustrate this with an example that arises within the *Cratylus*, in seeing a human being I could call that human being "horse," either because it seems like a horse to me or simply because I wish to call it thus. In such a case, the name brought about by my own wishes would not correspond to the being which the name names, but only to my *opinions* regarding that being, to how the being *seems* to me, or to how I *wish* for it to be. In such a case, as Socrates says, my speaking would accomplish nothing (387c). The person who, in speaking names, does so only in light of how beings *seem* to him or simply in accordance with his wishes, will accomplish nothing, will fail to hit upon that at which he aimed (i.e., the Being of the thing). In light of this etymology for βούλομαι offered within the *Cratylus*, one must read the text as beginning with an emphasis on the fallibility of human wishing. By emphasizing βούλομαι, the text brings the limits of human wishing to the fore.

The limits of human wishing will haunt the text unto its conclusion. Over the course of the *Cratylus* there will develop a theory of naming in which it is the human name-giver who, through the application of his tool for naming (i.e., names), comes to name things in accordance with how they *seem* to him—that is, in accordance with his wishes. One of the points that the etymological comedy will make clear is the extent to which such a theory fails to hit upon the proper Being of things. By drawing out the consequences of such a theory Socrates will show the manner in which human wishing, bound as it is to the realm of δόξα, cannot help but fall short of a full disclosure of the truth. Socrates marks this risk in his first words of the text by saying that names are difficult (χαλεπά), even dangerous (384b). The act of naming is dangerous precisely because it carries within itself the risk of missing the mark, of failing to hit upon a being by remaining immersed in human wishing. However, Socrates himself intimates quite early on that there is a deeper sense of βούλομαι at play in the text, one quite removed from the human volitional wishing we have seen so far. Just after offering his tool-analogy for names (of which we shall have much to say in later chapters), and as he is considering the proper method of naming, Socrates suggests that "we cannot follow our own will [οὐχ ... βουληθῶμεν], but [rather must follow] the way and the instrument [ᾧ]²⁵ which the nature [πέφυκε] of the things prescribe" (387d; Fowler). It is the job of the artisan to discover the instrument naturally suited to the nature (φύσις) of that which he produces; likewise, it is the job of the name-giver to give the name which is most appropriate to that which he names (389d).

Given this prohibition against simply following one's own wishes, we could say that the name the name-giver gives cannot simply be in accordance with what *he himself* wishes, but rather must be in accordance with the *nature* of the object to be named. If the name stands merely for what the name-giver wants, without concern for the being itself, then it will be ill-suited to perform the function of a name, i.e., to articulate the being in its proper and natural articulations (388c). A certain tension is thus voiced between how a being itself shows its nature and the way a thing appears to the name-giver such that he can name it in accordance with his wishes. In other words, a conflict between βούλομαι (wishing) and φύσις (nature), where φύσις must here be understood in its relationship to Being.²⁶

As it turns out, this conflict plays out within the word βούλομαι itself. In addition to meaning "to wish" or "to will," βούλομαι can also mean "to mean." To offer an example of a construction that occurs on multiple occasions throughout the *Cratylus*, Socrates, during his long string of comic etymologies, at one point suggests that he and Hermogenes look into what precisely the word τέχνη *means* (τέχνην ἰδεῖν ὅτι ποτὲ βούλεται εἶναι) (414b). Socrates then playfully suggests that τέχνη *means* (σημαίνει) possession of mind (ἕξιν νοῦ). This passage reveals that there is a certain synonymy between βούλομαι and σεμαίνω, wishing and meaning.²⁷

Another passage from the etymological section helps clarify this relationship. As Socrates puts it, "γυνή [woman] seems to me to mean [or to wish to be] γονή [womb]" (γυνὴ δὲ γονή μοι φαίνεται βούλεσθαι εἶναι) (414a; my translation). Socrates is playfully suggesting that the word γυνή (woman) means (βούλεσθαι) the same as γονή (womb), thereby indicating its relationship to birth (414a). Though this use of βούλεσθαι as "to mean" seems at first glance far removed from the process of wishing, "to mean" can be understood as a further development of the same basic signification. What Socrates is saying is that the word γυνή *itself* intends its relation to γονή, that it *wishes* to indicate this relationship, that the one word *reaches toward the other*. For a word to mean something is for it to express what it intends,²⁸ what, we might say, it *wishes to be*. That this further sense of βούλομαι is operative within the

Cratylus, and is essential to its philosophical movement, can only be satisfactorily shown through the interpretation of the text as a whole.

This different sense of βούλομαι comes into play through the course of the *Cratylus* and brings about a certain disruption of the human wishing we have just examined. To foreshadow our later analysis in chapter 7, a development occurs in the *Cratylus* whereby an explicit consideration of what a name *means* (βούλομαι) takes place, where this must be understood as an inquiry into what a name itself naturally wishes (βούλομαι) to express over against our merely human wishes. Thus, against the theory of naming that has a name-giver naming things simply as they *appear* to him (i.e., in accordance with his wishes) a more reticent account of naming will unfold in which it is not *human* wishing that imparts meaning through names, but rather *the wishes of the names themselves.* Within the *Cratylus* a great battle will unfold between these two senses of βούλομαι vis-à-vis the question of the correctness of names.

This battle can also be understood in terms of another conflict, one more typically attributed to the *Cratylus*: the conflict between nature (φύσις) and convention (νόμος). As is announced by Hermogenes quite early on, the conflict between nature and convention defines the parameters of the *Cratylus* to a great extent. During his initial appeal to Socrates to come into the λόγος and interpret Cratylus's oracular remarks regarding his name, Hermogenes explains that Cratylus believes "there's a certain natural correctness of names that's the same for all people, Greeks and barbarians alike" (383a; Fowler; trans. modified). A name that is naturally correct is so in a manner that supersedes (or precedes) whatever name a group of people agrees to use. Some dozen lines later Hermogenes asserts his own tentative position regarding the correctness of names: "I'm not able to be persuaded that there's any correctness for a name other than convention and agreement [συνθήκη καὶ ὁμολογία]" (384d; Sachs; trans. modified). Thus, Hermogenes believes that there is a conflict between nature and convention, at least with respect to the correctness of names.

Though we will have occasion to see that the two ostensibly opposed positions of Hermogenes and Cratylus are much more alike than they initially appear, it here suffices to indicate the manner in which this apparent conflict between nature and convention only rearticulates in different terms the conflict mentioned above between the nature (i.e., Being) of things and the way they appear to us (or the way we wish for them to be). At the beginning of the text, Cratylus's position is one in which names are entirely guided by the nature of that which they name (though it has not at all been suggested how such a guiding takes place). As such, it is a position preeminently guided by the nature of the thing, by φύσις. Hermogenes' position, on the other hand, is that names are totally guided by agreement and convention. As such, it is a position utterly dependent upon δόξα, the way that things seem to human beings.

The conflict between nature and agreement is thus one between Being and opinion or, more basically, Being and becoming. Within the *Cratylus*, the realm of human opinion will very quickly be associated with the flow of radical becoming in which all beings—if one can even still call them *beings*—are in flux. Hermogenes' position (which, as noted above, is one that is initially dominated by human opinion) will come to be associated with such radical becoming through the guises of Protagoras, Homer, and eventually Heraclitus, each of whom will be made to hold a position that tends strongly toward the fluctuations of becoming and away from the stability of Being. Over against this, a situation will develop wherein the stability of Being will assert itself against the mere wishes of human opinion. Paradoxically, such an assertion of Being will take place through *names,* indeed, through those very names which seem to indicate that everything is in flux. Despite the best efforts of the name-giver to name things in accordance with his wishes, Being will nonetheless assert itself, will nonetheless express its own wishes, and will do so through names. Words, in the *Cratylus*, will be given the chance to say what they have to say.

* * *

We have now seen the manner in which the opening of the *Cratylus* wishes to put wishing (βούλομαι) at issue. What else does this opening, in which Hermogenes wishes that Socrates come and join them in the λόγος, wish to say? Upon careful reading, a rather complicated tension is already voiced in the opening question of the dialogue. More precisely, a tension between two *directions* appears—a tension which, in no small way, subsists throughout the *Cratylus* and contributes to its fundamental character. To see this tension we must look at two of the words in the opening line of the text, each naming a specific directionality: "Socrates" and ἀνακοινωσώμεθα.

Firstly, the name "Socrates" announces a decisive *downward* trajectory. As has been noted by scholars, Socrates will come to play the role of the god Hermes within the *Cratylus*, serving as a kind of hermetic mediator between Cratylus and Hermogenes.[29] As the messenger of the gods, Hermes traverses the vertical plane between human beings and the divine; however, Hermes is seldom presented as ascending in literature and ceramics, but is rather typically depicted as descending (Suhr 1967, 64). This is no doubt due to his role as psychopomp and his corresponding connection to Hades, the lower realm: as the chaperon of the dead, Hermes bears a decisive relation to Hades and thus to the *down*.[30] Socrates too, then, insofar as he comes to play the part of Hermes within the text, orients us downward—indeed, *deathward*—from the very beginning.[31]

Furthermore, the *Cratylus* arguably takes place at some point during the morning of the same day as the conversations of the *Euthyphro* and the *Theaetetus*.[32]

Thus, as in the case of the other two texts, the *Cratylus* belongs to the long series of dialogues that present Socrates on his way down to the portico of the king to answer to the charges which have been brought against him. Given the eventual trial and death to which this progression leads, the *Cratylus* is haunted from the outset by Socrates' impending death. The very presence of Socrates thus announces a κατάβασις, and in a two-fold sense: Socrates on his way (down) to his (eventual) death, and Socrates as Hermes, the chaperon of the dead, on his way down to Hades, the place of mere *shades*.[33]

Such downward comportment further serves to orient us toward the realm of *opinion* (δόξα). As the messenger of the gods, Hermes has access both to the divine realm (the realm of truth) and the human realm (the realm of opinion). As Hermes descends from the heavens he abandons the divine place of the stability of Being and enters into the human region where opinion reigns. In a sense, then, Hermes is precisely he who offers to human beings the possibility of a communion with the divine, and with the truth of Being. However, Hermes is well known for his mischievous and deceptive nature. As the shifty, deceitful progenitor of λόγος, Hermes imbues λόγος with a certain fatal ambiguity, rendering it capable of both truth and falsity. Insofar as Hermes brings about the possibility for falsity in λόγος, he brings about a situation in which things can *seem* true, and yet not *be* true. In a word, he orients us away from the truth and toward *opinion*, away from certainty and toward ambiguity. Hermes disrupts the communion with the divine truth precisely as he makes it possible. In orienting human beings downward toward falsity and opinion, Hermes brings humans into intimacy with the *tragic*—something Socrates will later make clear (408b ff.). However, in simultaneously signifying the divine and true region above, Hermes represents the possibility of an ascent *beyond* (though forever essentially bound to) the tragic—an ascent which, it shall be argued, must be understood as *comic* in character.

The second word to be considered is ἀνακοινωσώμεθα, above translated as "join us."[34] It is perhaps better rendered as "communicate" or "commune," so long as one is careful to emphasize the sense of communion—a gathering or sharing of many things into one common (κοινός) thing. What needs to be stressed is the manner in which different things come to be unified into one common thing, though without thereby losing their differences. In the case of a disagreement, such as that which evidently stands between Cratylus and Hermogenes at the outset of the text, what would occur would be a gathering together of disparate λόγοι such that they might come together into one common λόγος. Whether or not such a gathering-together in fact occurs within the *Cratylus* remains to be seen.

It is important to note that ἀνα-κοινόω contains the prefix ἀνα- which signifies *back* or, more importantly, *up*. As chapter 7 will develop, it is precisely through a movement *up* (ἀνα) that names—and thereby human beings—are able to overcome the downward pull of human opinion and communicate with (i.e., inherit) the stability proper to Being. We might therefore suggestively translate the word ἀνα-κοινόω as "gather-up-in-common."

There are three points regarding this word that must be observed. First, the instance of this word so early in the text is important—for it announces what proves to be a fundamental theme of the dialogue. The possibility of communication is precisely what is at stake in the very guiding question of the text: for the outcome of the inquiry into the natural correctness of names bears decisively upon our ability to communicate with one another. Without such communication of a common λόγος discourse would be rendered impossible—a contingency perhaps indicated through the silence that Cratylus keeps throughout most of the dialogue.

Second, the notion of communication bears upon the very relationship that names hold to the beings which they name. What will come into question within the dialogue is how a name can communicate with that of which it is the name (i.e., the being), how it can *relate* to it. This question of community between names and Being will become thematized within the *Cratylus* most explicitly through the notion of *inheritance*. The question of the possibility of a communion between names and Being is nothing other than the question of the ability of names to inherit what is proper to the being which they name. This relationship will come up again and again in various guises, and will be examined in detail in chapter 6.

Third, this word ἀνα-κοινόω serves to foreshadow the Hermetic guise that Socrates will assume throughout the discourse. As the messenger of the gods, Hermes is precisely he who brings people together in common: for it is through the delivering of messages that disparate parties are united in something common. Moreover, as the father of λόγος (408d), Hermes is he who begat that which enables people to join their opinions together in common. (However, as already mentioned, it is also Hermes who threatens a disruption of this very function, a point to which we shall return.) Finally, not only does Hermes, father of λόγος, bring people into communion with each other but, as an intermediary between human beings and the gods, he brings human beings into communion with the divine. Phrased differently, one could say that Hermes brings the realms of human opinion and divine truth into communion with one another, allowing passage from the lower region *upward*. Hermes offers both the possibility and the impossibility of a communion between the human and the divine, the apparent and the true. One wonders if all of this is indicated in one of Hermes' epithets, Κοινός Ἑρμῆς.[35]

Thus, the dialogue begins with the voicing of a human wish that Socrates/Hermes—whose name, we have suggested, expresses here a downward comportment—come gather-up-in- common (ἀνακοινωσώμεθα) with Cratylus and Hermogenes in such a way as to himself undertake a gathering-together (συμβαλεῖν) (384a). This double-directionality is perfectly in keeping with the character of the ambiguous Hermes. Socrates (Hermes), himself on his way down to death (Hades), is called into the conversation by Hermogenes in order to undertake a gathering-up into the λόγος whereby he would bring Hermogenes and Cratylus into the λόγος in common. Such a gathering-up must be understood in terms of a movement away from mere opinion and toward Being, away from flux and toward stability: for this is precisely what will occur through the dialogue proper, and the etymological section in particular.

Most of the dialogue will be a testing of Hermogenes' position that names are correct by convention and agreement: that is, that they are correct by human δόξα and wishing. By the testing of this position through a playful analysis of names, Socrates, as Hermes, will undertake a passage away from mere human wishing upward toward the stability of Being. As will be seen in the following chapters, the primary question of the dialogue is whether Hermogenes (and, to a lesser extent, Cratylus) will follow Socrates on this upward path, thereby extending himself beyond mere opinion and into the realm of Being. What will also be in question is Socrates' own ability to maintain an uninterrupted upward path or, more generally, the human ability to undertake such an ascent. Consequent to this question is the further issue of *descent,* and of the extent to which the possibility of a comic ascent is always bound to the threat of a tragic descent. The dual-directionality—one is tempted to say the *dual-nature*—of the beginning of the *Cratylus* marks at once the dynamic intimacy of ascent and descent, of comedy and tragedy, and the way in which this dynamism informs the human condition, "the entire comedy and tragedy of human life" (*Phil.* 50b).[36] Whether the text of the *Cratylus* finally favors comedy over tragedy, as was suggested in the Introduction, can only come to light through this inquiry as a whole.

The *Cratylus* begins with a call, an invocation, to Socrates. Yet, as has already been said, Socrates will come to play the role of Hermes in the text (though not *only* the role of Hermes).[37] The *Cratylus* thus begins with an invocation to Hermes, an invocation to a god, the god who gathers people together in common with the divine. The invocation serves to assert a distance between the human and the divine within the compass of the problem of the correctness of names. Born out of spirited interest (ἕτοιμος) and befuddlement (384e), Hermogenes invokes Socrates so that the latter may interpret Cratylus' oracles, thereby demonstrating his own inability to do so. Hermogenes' invocation of Socrates thus serves to indicate Hermogenes' *limits* with respect to the knowledge of the correctness of names: and his invocation of Socrates—i.e., of Hermes—is a call to the very god of *limits,* to whom we now turn.

2   Marking the Limits

Χαῖρ', Ἑρμῆ χαριδῶτα, διάκτορε, δῶτορ ἐάων.
"Hail, Hermes, giver of grace, guide, and giver of good things!"

—*Homeric Hymn* XVIII.12

The *Cratylus,* perhaps more than any other Platonic text, plays at the limit.

To begin with, the *Cratylus* is *set* at the limit. Though it has been noted by scholars that the text gives no indication of its dramatic setting,[1] this is not in fact entirely accurate. While it is true that we are not given any indication of the specific location of the conversation, we can infer that the conversation takes place within the city of Athens: for Socrates, with rare and notable exception, never left Athens.[2] Further, we are told as the long coversation of the *Cratylus* finishes that Cratylus and Hermogenes go off together into the country (440e), further bolstering the suspicion that they have been conversing within the city's walls. We could say that, given that the end of the *Cratylus* marks a transition from the city to the country, the dialogue takes place at the boundry, or the limit, separating the two.

The city is the place of conventions and laws: it is the τόπος of νόμος. It is within the city that agreements are made to faciliate the coming-together—one might say the *communicating,* the gathering-up-together-in-common (ἀνακοινόω)—of people. In the shadow of such agreements and conventions, which people are made to hold in common, pluralities are unified into communities: that is, pluralities are limited. In the country—the τόπος (or χώρα) not of νόμος, but of φύσις—such formal agreements are wanting, and the fetters of νόμος are looser. A journey to the country would be a journey beyond the walls, and therefore beyond the conventions and agreements, of Athens: it would be a trangression of the limitations placed upon those who remain within the city.[3]

This situation is reflected in the respective positions of two of the characters that comprise the dialogue, Cratylus and Hermogenes. According to Hermogenes, Cratylus mantains that names have a correctness (ὀρθότητα) by nature (φύσει) (383a), while Hermogenes himself considers the correctness of names to be by convention and agreement (ξυνθήκη καὶ ὁμολογία) (384d). On the face of it—but perhaps only on the face of it—these two positions limit one another: for presumably—but perhaps only presumably—the more something is "by agreement" the less it is "by nature," and vice versa. Thus the very placing of the *Cratylus* at the boundary between the city and the country dramatically presents the apparent conflict between Cratylus and Hermogenes regarding the correctness of names.

Interestingly, the positions of the characters are, even at this basic level, limited by the characters themselves. As will be hinted within the *Cratylus*, Hermogenes is a νόθος (bastard) whose rights are not as secure as a full citizen's and whose inheritance is pending.[4] Thus, the character who holds the position that names are correct by convention and agreement is himself not utterly bound by the conventions and agreements of the city in which he lives, though he perhaps wishes to be. Cratylus, on the other hand, is an Athenian citizen with full rights (see 429e),[5] yet it is he who argues for a *natural* correctness of names and who has prepared himself to wander off into the country at the end of the dialogue (440e). There is thus a basic and comic incongruity between these positions and the characters who hold them, an incongruity which will be emphasized in the text in various ways.[6]

This incongruity grows as one examines the positions of the two characters. Though Hermogenes attempts to distinguish himself from Cratylus by claiming that words, rather than having a natural correctness, only come to be correct through convention and agreement, the respective positions of Cratylus and Hermogenes are much closer than they at first appear. To begin with, Hermogenes claims that, if only Cratylus wished (βούλοιτο) to propound his position clearly, he could make Hermogenes agree (ὁμολογεῖν) with him that words are correct by nature and not by convention (384a). Thus, it seems that Cratylus's position, which holds that words are correct by nature and *not* agreement (ὁμολογία) (384d), would itself demand agreement in order to be ratified.

Further, although Cratylus and Hermogenes purportedly hold differing positions at the outset of the text, Cratylus's statement that Hermogenes is not Hermogenes' name "even if the entire world calls him such" indicates that their positions are much closer than they first appear:[7] for Cratylus is suggesting that only he, a *private* person, knows Hermogenes' true name (or, at least, knows what his true name *is not*). But the idea of a *private name* is precisely the position that Hermogenes is about to tentatively endorse over against the position of a natural correctness of names (384d ff.). By asserting that a name of a thing can be changed by anyone, just as the name of a slave can be changed by his master (ibid.), Hermogenes aligns himself with Cratylus, who has done just this to Hermogenes in deed.

Thus, although the positions of Cratylus and Hermogenes seem to limit each other, what in fact comes to light is the manner in which the possibility of a rigorous separation between these two positions is itself limited: and insofar as the inquiry soon to be undertaken within the *Cratylus* appears to operate within the parameters of these two positions, it is itself limited in what it can accomplish. Given that both of these two positions—if it even makes sense to speak of them as two as if they were easily distinguishable—will be to some measure refuted within the dialogue, one wonders if there might be some other third possibility operative between these two poles, one very much at play, but never explicitly mentioned, within the text.[8]

The *Cratylus* operates at the limit in another way. As a so-called "aporetic dialogue," meaning that no definitive answers to the guiding questions of the dialogue are found within the dialogue itself, the *Cratylus* as a whole discloses the limits of its own undertaking. That Socrates, Hermogenes, and Cratylus will all leave the dialogue seemingly without having obtained explicit knowledge concerning the correctness of names (440d ff.) indicates how the dialogue as a whole marks the limits of such a pursuit: for it is shown that the questions asked in the dialogue—or, perhaps, the manner in which the questions are asked—do not admit of knowledge simply or straightforwardly. Furthermore, that the characters remain in *ignorance* with respect to the correctness of names serves to position them with respect to the limits of human knowledge, perhaps suggesting that the inquiry into the correctness of names undertaken within the dialogue seeks, but falls short of, a greater-than-human knowledge. Indeed, Socrates will say explicitly that the knowledge being sought, that of the nature of names, is greater than human (397c; see also 392b).

Moreover, the very object of the *Cratylus*—names (ὄνομα) and, more generally, λόγος[9]—is itself preeminently a matter of limitation: for it is precisely through naming, an operation of λόγος, that beings become delimited, or defined, for human beings. As Socrates will say within the *Cratylus* as he develops the "tool analogy," "a name is a certain kind of tool meant for . . . the disentangling [διακρίνομεν] of being, the same way a shuttle is for a weaver's threads" (388b; Sachs).[10] Names separate beings from one another, setting them apart in their distinction: in a word, naming delimits beings.[11]

Due precisely to its general object—λόγος—the entire dialogue could be said to take place at the very limit of what can be said within a philosophical inquiry. Because the object of the inquiry (i.e., λόγος) is also the medium through which the inquiry will take place, the text teeters at the very limit of speech, of what is possible in human discourse (λόγος): for much will be said within the *Cratylus* about the limits of λόγος, limits which belong to the very medium used to express and expose those limits. In this way, the findings of the inquiry limit the very method by which the findings are found, and anything said within the text about the limits of λόγος will itself be inhibited by those very limits.[12] The risk involved in such a self-reflexive investigation of λόγος is nothing less than the inability of λόγος to ground itself, to measure itself—an inability which threatens to be abysmal.

To push this point farther than prudence might allow, one could say that, insofar as the λόγος on λόγος that is the *Cratylus* is infected by the very limitations of λόγος that will come to be disclosed through the inquiry, the λόγος of the *Cratylus*—its very pursuit, undertaken in words, into the correctness of words—is impossible and laughably naïve. By coming to radically limit the power of human λόγος through a λόγος on λόγος Socrates radically limits the delimitation in which he and his interlocutors are engaged. The impossibility of the task is perhaps dramatically represented through the character of Cratylus, whose continual silence for most of the text discloses the radical danger inherent in any such self-reflexive inquiry into λόγος.[13]

And yet, despite this apparent impossibility of the λόγος of the *Cratylus*, and despite the apparent necessity of silence that such impossibility forces, the silence is broken, continually by Socrates and Hermogenes, and eventually by Cratylus himself. In other words, despite the impossibility of the *Cratylus*, the *Cratylus* nonetheless happens. The pages of the *Cratylus* thus consist of things that should not be said, perhaps *cannot* be said, but are said anyway. The λόγος of the *Cratylus*, which serves to mark the limits of λόγος, is in excess of those very limits. Thus, while one could say that the *Cratylus* takes place at the limit (in the manifold senses enumerated above), one can also say that it, perhaps more than any other Platonic text, transgresses the limit, and in an outrageous way. The very gesture of an attempt to limit λόγος through λόγος without acknowledging the circularity is transgressive, excessive, perhaps even *monstrous*—not to mention comedic (in the manner delimited in the Introduction).

Since it involves a transgression of limits, the inquiry of the *Cratylus* proves to be χαλεπός—both difficult and dangerous—as Socrates himself predicts (384b). The dangers relate to the risk marked above: namely, that λόγος, given the limitations belonging to any inquiry into it, will prove to be impossible. The fact that the characters undertake such a dangerous transgression with neither fearful balk nor copious apology serves to situate the text near the limit that separates the *tragic* and the *comic*. With a task as important and as dangerous as the attainment of knowledge concerning the correctness of names (384b; 427e) the *Cratylus* presents a substantial and noble task whose gravity tilts the text toward the tragic;[14] yet, the aloof and exceedingly playful manner in which the task is pursued tilts the text toward comedy, and more decisively so due to the severity of the undertaking. Whether and to what extent the text ultimately favors comedy over tragedy is something that must come to light through this inquiry as a whole.

To summarize, one could say that the inquiry underway within the *Cratylus*, an inquiry which operates *at* the limit of discourse (λόγος) and whose focus *is* the limits of discourse (λόγος), takes place within the limits of the city, and therefore within the limits of convention. However, as is obvious from the very beginning of the text, the discourse in no way remains within the city, nor within its own proper limits. From the outset the inquiry threatens a transgression of limits, a transgression into the country, the place of nature. The inquiry takes place at, and beyond, the limit between nature and convention. Finally, through the figure of a divinely inspired Socrates, the inquiry will threaten a transgression of *human* limits, a divine transgression that will both allow a resolution of the problem of the limits of λόγος *and* delineate those limits all the more definitively.

All of this—the radically liminal character of the text and the possibility of a transgression of limits, dramatically presented through the tension between country and city, human and divine—is marked from the very beginning through the figure of Hermes, well known in antiquity as the god of borders, thresholds, and crossings. We must therefore turn to an examination of this god and the manner in which he thoroughly pervades and guides the *Cratylus* in order to better understand the parameters of the text as a whole.

* * *

The dialogue gets underway with a report from Hermogenes to Socrates regarding a λόγος in which he and Cratylus have been engaged and which, we learn later (384c), they have had many times before.[15] Hermogenes is the first to speak at length within the dialogue, but only in a sense: he speaks first by speaking *not* for himself, but for Cratylus, relating the latter's position to Socrates—as, say, a messenger would do:

> Socrates, Cratylus here says that for each of the things there are, there is a name [ὀνόματος] of such a nature as to be naturally correct [ὀρθότητα], and this name is not whatever a particular group of people call it when they have agreed to call it that, applying a piece of their own voice to it, but there is a certain natural correctness of names [ὀρθότητά τινα τῶν ὀνομάτων πεφυκέναι] that is the same for all people, Greeks and barbarians alike. (383a; Sachs; trans. modified)

Hermogenes then elucidates Cratylus's position—or, at least, his version of the silent Cratylus's position—by offering a rather comic example:

> So I ask him if "Cratylus" is truly his name and he agrees [ὁμολογεῖ] it is. "And what is Socrates' name?" I said. He said, "Socrates." "And for all other human beings too, the very name we call each one, is that the name of each?" "Well, your name is not Hermogenes, at any rate," he said, "even if all human beings call you that." (383b; Sachs)

Hermogenes then explains that, despite his eagerness to learn what Cratylus means by refusing him his name, the latter will not elucidate his point, offering only ironic dissembling (εἰρωνεύεταί). Hermogenes then invokes Socrates to interpret these ironic oracles.

Two initial points must be made. First, it is important to clarify why Socrates is called into the discussion. Though many commentators have stressed that Socrates is called upon in order to mediate between Cratylus's and Hermogenes' respective and ostensibly incompatible positions regarding the correctness of names, this is in fact the secondary reason for his invocation. The primary reason that Hermogenes calls upon Socrates is so that he might interpret the peculiar oracular pronouncement (μαντείαν) offered by Cratylus that "Hermogenes" is not Hermogenes' name (384a).[16] Only after requesting of Socrates this service does Hermogenes indicate that he would *also* like to learn about Socrates' perceptions (δοκεῖ) concerning the correctness of names, if the latter wishes (βουλομένῳ) to disclose them (384a). Hermogenes' primary concern is thus to have Socrates explain why Cratylus refuses him his name,[17] and it is Socrates who redirects the inquiry toward the correctness of names in general (384c).

Second, it should be noted that Hermogenes' appeal to Socrates intimates the comic tone of the inquiry to follow. It is in an effort to decode Cratylus's ironic utterances that Hermogenes calls upon Socrates: however, the very name "Socrates" is virtually synonymous with irony, for present-day and ancient readers of Plato alike.[18] Hermogenes thus calls upon a master ironist to come and interpret the statements of an unabashed ironist:[19] in this way the text flirts with the ridiculous from the very outset. This is yet another sense in which the inquiry undertaken within the text is limited by the manner by which it is pursued, and with comic results. One wonders how much hope poor Hermogenes—or, indeed, we ourselves—can really have that Socrates will clarify anything at all.

After having been called into the ridiculous inquiry—the comic λόγος on λόγος—and in a manner that only compounds the ridiculousness, Socrates offers a terse and extremely tentative explanation for Cratylus's peculiar claim regarding the truth (τὴν ἀλήθειαν) of the correctness of Hermogenes' name:

> As for the fact that [Cratylus] claims that "Hermogenes" is not truly your name, I suspect he is joking [σκώπτειν], since perhaps [ἴσως] he thinks you're aiming at making money but always failing.[20] But, as I just said, it is difficult [χαλεπόν] to know such things. (384c; Sachs; trans. modified; my emphasis)

As many commentators have observed, the basis of the joke to which Socrates draws our attention seems to be that Hermogenes, whose name literally means "of the race of Hermes,"[21] is poor at making money, and is thus unworthy of the name "Hermes," god of the agora and commercial exchange.[22] We shall return to the precise character of this joke in chapter 3. For the time being, it is sufficient to observe that the primary question of the dialogue—the question which initiates the inquiry and articulates its horizons—involves a joke (τό σκῶμμα).

Three lines after suggesting that Cratylus is making a joke (σκώπτειν), Socrates offers to examine (σκοπεῖν) the matter along with Hermogenes (384c). Socrates' subtle homophonic play on the verbs σκώπτειν (to jest) and σκοπεῖν (to examine) marks the limits of the inquiry to come, suggesting that the examination to follow will not be without its own joviality. This play is reinforced a few lines later when Socrates says "let us examine [σκεψώμεθα] who speaks well" about the correctness of names (385a). With the play between σκώπτειν and σκοπεῖν Socrates is suggesting that the inquiry into the nature of Cratylus's jest will itself be in jest, and indicating the extent to which Hermogenes' appeal to a master ironist has been, to say the least, naïve. Further, Socrates may be suggesting that the inquiry into the natural correctness of names—an august inquiry, to be sure[23]—will involve jesting, a truth which will be borne out by the text as a whole. The verb σκοπεῖν (to examine) occurs with uncanny frequency throughout the *Cratylus*, and, due to its homophony with σκώπτειν (to jest), playfully hinted at here by Socrates, it should always be read within the *Cratylus* as suggestive of a jest. Though this claim cannot but seem fanciful here, it is supported by the *Cratylus* itself: for, as will be seen in later chapters, this type of homophonic play is precisely the sort that structures and supports Socrates' long etymological display and the view of language it is meant to clarify.

What is at stake in Cratylus's refusal of Hermogenes' name is, according to Socrates, a joke which calls into question the relationship between Hermogenes and Hermes, suggesting that the character of the former does not accord with the character of the latter.[24] Simply put, Cratylus is calling Hermogenes' *nature* into question. Yet, calling Hermogenes' nature into question is tantamount to calling upon him with whose nature Hermogenes is, according to Cratylus, in discord: the god Hermes. Calling the veracity of Hermogenes' name into question is equivalent to calling upon the god Hermes, invoking him as an absent object of comparison. Thus, in a concrete (or, perhaps, *monumental*) sense Hermes, though himself seemingly absent from the dialogue, stands at its very head, delimiting the character of what is to come. Further, insofar as Socrates comes to play the role of the great mediator Hermes within the *Cratylus*,[25] and insofar as it is Socrates upon whom Hermogenes calls, it is in effect Hermes who is invoked by Hermogenes at the head of the dialogue.

Hermes thus marks the beginning of the *Cratylus*, like a heap of stones at the head of a trail. In ancient Athens, Hermes was frequently embodied in boundary markers known as "herms," serving to separate the domestic from the foreign, the familiar from the strange, even life from death.[26] In appearance these markers ranged from more archaic vertical heaps of stones piled upon one another (already in use by the sixth century BCE)[27] to the more developed stone herms that pervaded Athens during the fourth century BCE. These latter markers stood at many intersections, crossings, and boundaries in Athens and generally consisted of an upright obelisk crowned with a bust of Hermes, with an erect phallus protruding from his midriff.[28] According to Herodotus, the Athenians were the first Greeks to represent the god Hermes by way of this ithyphallic monument.[29] The ubiquity of the herm in Athens is attested in Plato's (likely spurious) *Hipparchus*, where it is said that the statesman Hipparchus was responsible for erecting a great number of herms.[30]

But how does Hermes mark the beginning of the *Cratylus?* How does he de-limit the text? To be sure, the god Hermes does not appear in the *Cratylus* in the same way that, for example, he appears at the conclusion of Aristophanes' *Clouds* (line 1506);[31] and although the name of the god is explicitly discussed during the long etymological comedy (407e ff.), only with great reluctance does Socrates make him the explicit theme of the investigation. (Indeed, Socrates nearly and quite conspicuously leaves him behind, and Hermogenes is compelled to prompt Socrates to consider him [407d].) Nonetheless, as will be seen, Hermes plays an essential role in the *Cratylus,* setting the horizons of the text as a whole.

There are three questions which the surreptitious invocation of Hermes ini-tially raises. First, the presence of Hermes and the ridiculous comments made by Cratylus regarding the impropriety of Hermogenes' name call into question (in a decidedly comic manner) the relationship between a name and the being it names. More specifically, what is at stake in Cratylus's oracular claim is whether a name *correctly* (ὀρθῶς) names that which it names, whether it properly lets the being it names show itself as what it truly is. It is this question that will soon become explicit (at 384c) and will in some manner guide most of the text that follows. The question of the correctness of names is implicit in Cratylus's joke *as Socrates interprets it.*

Second, with the invocation of Hermes, the relationship between father and son is called into question. In general, this can be thought of as the question of *in-heritance.* Conceived most broadly, this says the same as the first point: for the rela-tionship between a name and what it names can be understood metaphorically as a matter of inheritance, of *how* or *whether* the name inherits what is proper to the being that it names, of whether the nature of the being passes to, and thereby be-comes evident through, the name. The question of inheritance is already implicit in Cratylus's refusal of Hermogenes' name (i.e., "you are not the *son* of Hermes") and is emphasized by Socrates when he refers to Hermogenes as "son of Hipponicus" (384a). Further, the question of the possibility—or, perhaps, impossibility—of in-heritance is already at play in the fact that the historical Hermogenes was a νόθος, a bastard. (This will become explicit at 391c when it is stated that Hermogenes has yet to obtain his inheritance.) The question of inheritance further comes to be themati-cally pursued through the etymologies of Hector and his son (392c ff.). (We shall have much more to say about inheritance in chapter 6.)

Third, at stake in Cratylus's refusal of Hermogenes' name—his calling into question of Hermogenes' inheritance of what properly belongs to the god Hermes— is the relationship between gods and human beings. This relationship will be of the utmost importance to the inquiry and will be explicitly pursued within the ety-mologies: indeed, it is no exaggeration to say that the very possibility of a correct name will depend upon such a relationship. It should further be noted that Hermes, son of immortal Zeus and the nymph Maia, was himself a bastard whose father, ac-cording to the Homeric Hymn about him, abandoned him to his mother (see *Hymn*

IV.4). The very figure of Hermes thus bespeaks abandonment by the father and by the divine, an abandonment of the son to the realm of human beings. Such abandonment should already put us on our guard regarding the possibility of a communion of the human and the divine *via* names.

It is clear that the role of Hermes within the *Cratylus* is monumental. Passing over the role of Hermes and his many significations would be disastrous, for it would pass over the *source* and move directly to the *offspring*; it would pass over the father and move directly to the son. Yet, the move from father to son, from source to inheritor, and from being to name, is precisely what is foremost in question within the dialogue. Further, passing over the character of Hermes (as most commentators have done) would undermine our ability to understand the true stake and import of Cratylus's joke and the manner in which that joke sets the limits of the dialogue as a whole. We must therefore further investigate the character of Hermes in order to prepare ourselves for a full exposition of the joke that begins the *Cratylus*. We shall begin with what is said about the god Hermes in the *Cratylus* itself.

Hermes

Much later in the *Cratylus*, after having offered a long string of etymologies of the gods, Socrates, claiming to be inspired by the superhuman wisdom of a certain Euthyphro, marks the limits of his own temporary wisdom: "Let's get off the gods, for the gods' sake, since I'm nervous about discussing them; toss out any other subjects you want for me, though, 'so you can see what kind of horses' Euthyphro's got" (407d; Sachs).[32] However, before allowing Socrates to stop his inquiry into the gods—an inquiry which has already been said by Socrates to be both playful (παιδικῶς) (406c) and dangerous (χαλεπά) (384b)[33]—Hermogenes requests that Socrates offer one more divine etymology, namely, that for the god Hermes. The fact that Socrates nearly neglected (or deliberately omitted) an account of Hermes' name further indicates the comedy of the inquiry. Given that the very reason Socrates was called into the discussion was to clarify Cratylus's comments about the inappropriateness of Hermogenes' name (and thus the illegitimacy of Hermogenes' association with the god Hermes), it is highly humorous that Socrates would seek to leave the inquiry without commenting upon it.

Following upon Hermogenes' request that they examine (σκέψασθαι) the name "Hermes," Socrates offers the following extended description:

> But surely this name "Hermes" looks like it has something to do with speech [λόγον], something that is interpretive [τὸ ... ἑρμηνέα] and carries messages, while it is also thievish and deceptive in words [τὸ κλοπικόν τε καὶ τὸ ἀπατηλὸν ἐν λόγοις] and adapted to the marketplace,[34] and all that business involves the power of speech [περὶ λόγου δύναμιν]. Now that is exactly what we were saying in the earlier discussion, that discoursing is a use of speech [τὸ ἔρειν λόγου χρεία ἐστί], and then there is something Homer says in many places, "he wrought"

[ἐμήσατο], which is to contrive [μηχανήσασθαί]. So from the two of these together, speaking [λέγειν] and the one who has wrought speech [τὸν λόγον μησάμενον], speaking being discoursing, it is just as if the lawgiver is giving us an injunction about this god, saying "Human beings, he who wrought discoursing [ὅς τὸ εἴρειν ἐμήσατο] would justly be called by you 'Eiremes.'" But nowadays we call him "Hermes," imagining that we're prettying up the name. (407e–408b; Sachs; trans. modified)

There are many significations at work in Socrates' description, and one must pay special attention to each of them. However, there are only four which shall be examined here.[35] To begin with, the relationship between Hermes and λόγος shall be examined. This will naturally open up onto the second point, that pertaining to the relation between Hermes and interpretation (ἑρμηνεία). Thirdly, the erotic power of Hermes will be examined, a power exceedingly important to our reading. Finally, brief mention will be made of Hermes' connection to nature (φύσις). As we proceed we must be vigilant to recall why Socrates has offered this description of Hermes: namely, in order to appease Hermogenes' curiosity about why Cratylus refuses him his name. Thus, our inquiry into Hermes along these four lines is ultimately for the sake of coming to a better understanding of the character of Hermogenes and the nature of Cratylus's joke regarding his name offered at the very outset of the text.

Hermes and λόγος

The first thing that Socrates says is that the name "Hermes" has something to do with λόγος. Sean Kirkland, in an exemplary essay on the *Cratylus,* has argued that the etymology given for Hermes demands special privilege, and for two reasons. First of all, as noted above, Hermes plays an essential role within the *Cratylus* in general and in the opening question of the dialogue in particular. As a result, the *name* "Hermes," when investigated by Socrates, should be of special interest (Kirkland 2007, 1).[36] Second, because the inquiry of the *Cratylus* is concerned with λόγος, Hermes, as having "something to do with λόγος," bears decisively upon that inquiry (ibid.). Insofar as the dialogue is concerned with λόγος, it is concerned with Hermes, "he who wrought" λόγος (408b). The character of Hermes will thus bear immediately upon how one understands λόγος as it operates within the *Cratylus.*

For Kirkland, the association of the divine Hermes with λόγος bespeaks the manner in which λόγος situates the human being into a relation with the divine, and therefore with Being. Because Hermes is the messenger of the gods and he who wrought λόγος, λόγος itself serves as a message from the gods communicating to us certain (albeit limited) divine wisdom regarding Being. As Kirkland puts it, "the language we possess must somehow convey to us the gods' perfect and immediate grasp of things as they are" (Kirkland 2007, 9). Λόγος thus serves as a kind of bridge between human beings and the divine grasp of Being: a bridge which, as any bridge, also inserts a *distance* between its two banks (ibid., 2). Λόγος thus serves both to open us to the gods (and their "perfect and immediate grasp" of beings) and to distance us from them.

On this view, λόγος, as such a gift, is what grants us any access whatsoever to Being. As Kirkland writes, "For Socrates, language is originally the medium in which a human being finds the world disclosed or revealed and, thus, finds him- or herself in an *always prior* relation to 'what is' through language . . ." (Kirkland 2007, 6). In a word, the human being dwells *within* language and thereby has a relation to Being. Λόγος, as Hermes' gift, is that whereby beings can become manifest to humans, can show themselves as they *are*,[37] or, indeed, as they are *not*. It is this latter point—that beings can show themselves in λόγος as they are not—that guides Socrates' second point concerning Hermes, that pertaining to interpretation.

Hermes and Hermeneutics

As Socrates explains, Hermes is "an interpreter [ἑρμηνεία], a messenger [τὸ ἄγγελον],[38] a thief and a deceiver [τὸ κλοπτικόν τε καὶ τὸ ἀπατηλὸν]" (407e ff.; my translation). All of these powers, Socrates continues, involve the power of λόγος (408a). Λόγος is hereby connected by Socrates with the power (δύναμις) for falsity, concealment (see 385b), and deception. Simply put, Hermes the Messenger, "he who wrought λόγος," cannot simply be trusted.

But what is the precise relationship between Hermes and λόγος? A turn to the *Phaedrus* is most instructive. There, Socrates tells a μῦθος about the invention of writing (γράμμα), a μῦθος explored at length by Jacques Derrida in *Plato's Pharmacy*. According to the story (which is apparently contrived by Socrates [275b]), the Egyptian god Theuth presented writing to the king-god Thamus as a means of increasing the memory of the Egyptians, proudly proclaiming that "the *pharmakon* for memory and wisdom has been discovered!" (*Phdr.* 274e; Scully). However, as Thamus rejoins (and as Derrida explores at length), Theuth has in fact invented something that will damage the memories of those who use it: "You, father [πατήρ] of these letters, have in your fondness for them said what is the opposite of their real effect" (*Phdr.* 275a; Scully). Theuth—the Egyptian god with whom the Greeks associated Hermes[39]—is thus not simply the technician of writing, but is its *father* (πατήρ).

This myth occurs in a different dialogue with its own unique context, to be sure, and it is *writing* (γράμμα) and not λόγος as such that is there in question. However, the *Cratylus* itself confirms a filial relationship between Hermes and λόγος. During his etymology of Hermes' son Pan, whom Socrates associates with the power "to signify all [πᾶν], circulate all, and keep all constantly in motion," Socrates offers the following: "And Pan, if he is the son of Hermes, is either λόγος or the brother of λόγος" (408d; Fowler). Hermes is thus the *father* of λόγος. (It should also be noted that this implies that λόγος is alive, i.e., to some extent *natural*, and not some purely human contrivance—a point to which we shall eventually return.) The question thus quickly becomes whether λόγος has inherited the mischievousness characteristic of its father, the capacity for both truth and concealment. Socrates leaves no doubt that it has, stressing the double-nature (διπλοῦς) of Pan. (The dual nature of λόγος is intimated all the way back at 385b.)[40] Λόγος therefore has the capacity for concealment and deception, just like its divine progenitor—like father, like son.[41]

Given its dual capacity for truth and deception, why should λόγος *ever* be trusted? Even if it is the case that the message (i.e., λόγος) or the messenger (i.e., Hermes) is divine in origin (as Kirkland maintains), there is no reason to believe that any of the divinity remains once it has been delivered to human beings: for what is divine in the λόγος could have been utterly obscured during the transport from gods to human beings. Such is the threat that the mischievous Messenger brings. One cannot simply *trust* that λόγος has a divine part, that it is capable of truth: for this supposed property of λόγος could itself be a deception. Or, perhaps it is precisely a matter of *trust*, or a kind of *piety*, over against knowledge: for it is clear that one cannot *know*, in any rigorous sense, whether the message *as delivered* appears as the gods intended. One can only *suppose*—or, perhaps, *hypothesize*—that λόγος has a divine part.[42]

Such trust in the divine part of λόγος would accord with Socrates' comments made in other dialogues regarding the inability of the gods to lie.[43] However, this is complicated by Socrates' claim in the *Cratylus* that Hermes, a god, is a deceiver. It would be strange to claim against this, based on evidence from other dialogues, that Hermes (and therefore λόγος) cannot be a deceiver. Rather, one must humor Socrates' point regarding the potential falsity of λόγος, and admit that there is no self-evident way to tell with certainty that λόγος shows beings as they truly are.[44] The character of Hermes imbues λόγος with a deceptive air whose epistemological consequences are insurmountable. Λόγος is—or, even worse, *may be* in a way that cannot be determined with certainty—a mischievous messenger, a shifty purveyor of beings, a rogue. One cannot help but be at the mercy of the messenger; one can *always* be deceived.[45] The human being thus dwells within λόγος in such a way as never to be sure whether beings are showing themselves as they truly are: the human being is always at the mercy of the concealment inherent in λόγος.[46] Whether and how beings show themselves to us is a matter greatly beyond our control.

But not entirely. Even if λόγος always retains the power to deceive—and it does—it could also be the case that we are mistaken in our interpretations. For example, if we were deceived (by slick etymology) in taking the name "Hermes" to refer to "interpretation" (ἑρμηνεία), then this would mean that some agent—presumably Hermes, Socrates, or λόγος itself—undertook to mislead us about the nature of the being. Yet, it could also be the case that we, as fumbling finite beings, simply misinterpreted the name out of folly; or it could even be that we, for specific purposes (such as euphony or pedagogy), *deliberately* made the name appear in accordance with our *wishes* instead of attending properly to the *being* named, as Socrates claims the tragic poets have done (414c). In other words, the human being, with its wishes and follies, provides an additional and unavoidable hermeneutical layer.

The human being is thereby not merely at the mercy of some divine intermediary (be it Hermes or λόγος itself) but of human intermediaries as well: that is, we are at the mercy of ourselves. Even if a being shows itself in λόγος as it truly is, this λόγος could have been so utterly transformed—that is, *interpreted*—by the whims and wishes of human beings that the original truth has become entirely obfuscated. (This very possibility will be broached by Socrates at 436b.) The human being continually runs the risk of inheriting a misinterpretation of what may or may not be a misinterpretation. Thus, not only is λόγος always *open* to interpretation—it is *doomed* to interpretation. One cannot help but interpret.

There is no way around the hermeneutical abyss that Hermes, as the roguish and deceptive father of λόγος, opens—but there is a way to jump into it well. By becoming aware of this dual nature of λόγος, and the hermeneutical difficulties endemic to it, one can in a sense transcend them (Kirkland 2007, 10). Unlike those living what Socrates will come to call "the tragic life" (τὸν τραγικὸν βίον) (408c)—the life amidst ignorance and deception, the life amongst the shadows[47]—one can raise oneself to a position where one is aware of the deceptive power of λόγος: one can pull oneself out of the cave, as it were, and come to see shadows *as* shadows, no longer living wholly at their mercy.

However, it is not enough simply to become aware of the deceptive power— one must *appropriate* this power. To become aware of the dual nature of λόγος is to become aware of the necessity of always reinterpreting one's world. As one receives λόγοι with the knowledge that they are themselves interpretations (and may be mis-interpretations) one must undertake to interpret them oneself. One must look to the matter anew (438d ff.) and consider whether the words bring the nature of the matter to light, as Socrates and Hermogenes will do during the etymologies. If one wants to ascend beyond the shadows, one cannot simply proceed as if one knows the true nature of the beings the words name: rather, one must continually subject λόγοι to rigorous reinterpretation. As Socrates puts it, "it is necessary *to investigate* [σκοπεῖσθαι] courageously [ἀνδρείως] and well, and not accept anything easily" (440d; my translation).[48]

And yet, recalling Socrates' jest with the words σκώπτειν and σκοπεῖν (384c; see above), it must be asked: is one to *investigate* courageously, or *jest* courageously? Or, when it comes to an inquiry in λόγος about λόγος and in names about the correctness of names, do the two amount to the same? Is it the case that one *must* investigate *playfully*? Now, to investigate purely in earnest would be to lose sight of the deceptive part of λόγος that must always tarry along. Given the deceptive capacity of λόγος, one can only take an inquiry into λόγος so seriously (see

440c). And, as will be seen in chapter 5, over-zealous seriousness is itself a mark of the tragic life, that life lived ignorantly amongst the shadows.

By appropriating the dual nature of λόγος in such a way as to let its utmost possibilities shine, one can *play* at discovering beings through λόγος—one can reinterpret. To relate to λόγος, of which Hermes is the father, is thus to be an interpreter (ἑρμηνεία). Yet, to be an interpreter is to be like Hermes (according to Socrates' interpretation). To relate to λόγος as an interpreter is thus to be like Hermes, to be like the god who *playfully* traverses the distance between humans and gods.[49] This is exactly what Socrates will do with his many etymologies as he comes to play the part of Hermes. By reinterpreting a number of words whose meanings were otherwise commonplace and ossified, Socrates opens the words up into new and creative possibilities, bringing the interlocutors along. Socrates traverses the distance between gods and human beings, the distance that just *is* λόγος, attempting to lead the souls of Hermogenes and Cratylus over the abyss. Socrates enacts a creative reappropriation, or reinterpretation, of names, and does so in a manner that is explicitly playful. To play along with this play is to play at transporting oneself—that is, *translating* oneself—into the realm of the gods. Such play is the safe way into the abyss.

Granting the necessity of such interpretation, and the benefit of engaging it playfully, we must briefly undertake to further interpret the name "Hermes" itself, as Socrates nearly did not (407e). Given the constant threat of deception that λόγος presents, one cannot simply say that "Hermes" is so-called due to his association with interpretation (ἑρμηνεία). To be sure, Socrates himself associates Hermes with interpretation (407e): however, this is within his long series of etymologies which he has already said are playful (παιδικῶς) (406b ff.). Further, the interpretation of "Hermes" as signifying λόγος and interpretation is but one of two distinct interpretations of the god's name offered within the *Cratylus* (384c; 407e). In other words, Socrates himself *reinterprets* the name "Hermes" through the course of the dialogue, thereby stressing the importance of reinterpretation. To simply assert, without further ado, that "Hermes" means "interpreter" is to hypostasize one interpretation among many possible interpretations about the very god who, on this one interpretation, makes interpretation possible.

Additionally, it is said by Socrates that concerning the character and names of the gods, we can know nothing (400d). Thus, the name "Hermes," applied by humans to the god, is itself a human interpretation of the character of the god: that is, it does not necessarily refer to the god "himself," but rather denotes what some name-giving human being (such as Socrates) thought about the god. The name "Hermes" is a human interpretation of the god, an interpretation that Socrates comes to interpret as expressing interpretation. But even if Hermogenes (or Socrates, for that matter) proved to be an excellent contriver of speech, it would in no way indicate that his character was any closer to that of the god Hermes in his nature. Rather, it would only indicate that Hermogenes' character was closer to the character of the god as the person who gave him his name conceived it, whether or not he did so correctly. Further, even if the name-giver did name him correctly, he did so with the words contrived by Hermes, he who wrought λόγος: and yet, we have already seen that Hermes cannot simply be trusted. Here one begins to appreciate just how abysmal the undertaking of the *Cratylus* is.

One is thus bound to a certain ambiguous interpretation of Hermes' name. It is almost as if one can say nothing definitive about Hermes, for there is nothing definitive about him. As Suhr writes, Hermes "seems to have no personality of his own, he seldom speaks his own mind; like a faithful herald, he remains a good mouthpiece for his master" (Suhr 1967, 56). Or, as Derrida more dramatically puts it, "[Hermes] is neither king nor jack, but rather a sort of *joker,* a floating signifier, a wildcard, one who puts play into play. [...] [Hermes][50] is never present. Nowhere does he appear in person. No being-there can properly be *his own*" (Derrida 1981, 93). In other words, "Hermes" is an unstable signifier which we have no choice but to interpret.

Yet, if this is so, then Hermogenes' pursuit of the nature of Hermes will be without limit. He will forever strive to reinterpret the name without ever reaching the end. This act of ceaseless reinterpretation would exemplify the very thing it seeks: Hermogenes would prove that he, like Hermes, is an interpreter. That Cratylus and Hermogenes go off at the end of the dialogue with the promise of continuing to consider (or joke about) the matter (440d) perhaps suggests that Hermogenes is indeed, finally, like his namesake. But this will only be so if Hermogenes ceaselessly reconsiders λόγοι and reinterprets them anew, and if he continually examines (or jests about) the name "Hermes," thus proving himself to be like the (playful) god of interpretation.[51]

Such endless inquiry would amount to a radical pursuit of self-knowledge undertaken through the interpretation of words. By ceaselessly reinterpreting the name "Hermes," Hermogenes ("son of Hermes") is continually calling his own nature into question (i.e., he is asking himself if he is like Hermes). Such radical self-inquiry is nothing other than an instance of radical self-examination as articulated by Socrates in the *Apology* (*Ap.* 21a ff.) and elsewhere. Thus, Hermogenes, through his inquiry into the nature of his namesake, comes to exemplify philosophy understood as the Socratic pursuit of self-knowledge. Given that it is Socrates who plays the mediating role of Hermes in the *Cratylus* (see above), one could say that, insofar as he comes to be a self-interpreter like Socrates (i.e., Hermes), Hermogenes proves himself to be the son of Hermes: that is, proves himself to be himself. By playing the role of interpreter, Hermogenes comes to play the part of the Socratic philosopher. Hermogenes thus in the end takes over the task he himself assigns Socrates, namely, to interpret Cratylus's oracular pronouncements regarding the correctness of his name. (The extent to which this is true shall be examined in later chapters.)

Having now considered the radical hermeneutics that Hermes heralds, we turn to our third strand, that pertaining to the erotic aspect of Hermes' character.

Hermes and Erotics

After suggesting that Hermes is he who wrought discourse (εἴρειν ἐμήσατο) Socrates says the following: "Now that's exactly what we were saying in the earlier discussion, that *discoursing* is a use of speech [τὸ εἴρειν λόγου χρεία ἐστί]" (408a; Sachs). By deriving Hermes' name from εἴρειν, Socrates is hearkening back to his definition of "hero" (398d). There, Socrates suggested that heroes were so called "because they were wise and clever orators and dialecticians, able to ask questions [ἐρωτᾶν], for discoursing [εἴρειν] is the same as speaking [λέγειν]" (398d; Fowler; trans. modified). However, just before offering this explanation, Socrates offered another possibility: namely, that the half-divine heroes were "all born either because a god fell in love [ἐρασθέντος] with a mortal [θνητῆς] or a mortal with a goddess" (398d; Fowler; trans. modified). All of this is evident, Socrates claims, in the relationship between the old Attic dialect form of "hero" [ΗΕΡΟΣ] and desire [ἔρως], "out of which the heroes had their births" (398d; Sachs; trans. modified). Thus, although Socrates is ostensibly alerting us to the connection between εἴρειν and λέγειν, he also indicates the filial connection between heroes and ἔρως. Ἔρως is the procreative source of the heroes.

One could argue that Hermes was born from such an arrangement. According to the *Homeric Hymn* about him, "Maia gave him birth, that nymph whose tresses are fair, having joined in love with Zeus [Διὸς ἐν φιλότητι μιγεῖσα]" (*Hymn* IV.3-4). Maia was a nymph, one of the Pleiades, daughters of Atlas (see Simonides, fr. 555). As a nymph, she was not quite a god, but was somewhat "lower" and at a distance from them (Kerényi 1976, 80). There is some ambiguity about whether such creatures are mortal (that is, capable of dying). According to the *Homeric Hymn* to Hermes, Maia had "deathless limbs" (ἀθανάτων . . . γυίων) (*Hymn* IV.20); however, also according to the *Hymn*, Maia distanced herself from the gods, "shunning [ἠλεύαθ'] the throng of blessed gods and dwelling in a deep-shaded cave" (*Hymn* IV.5). Further, some sources claim that Maia, along with the other Pleiades, committed suicide upon learning of the death of their other sisters, the Hyades.[52] This latter myth suggests definitively that the nymphs, lower than the deathless gods, were mortal.

If Hermes' mother Maia was indeed mortal, then in precisely the sense given to the word in the *Cratylus* Hermes is a *hero,* having been born from the ἔρως between a god and a mortal woman.[53] One of the things this erotic aspect of Hermes indicates is the manner in which he *stands between* gods and the mortal realm, serving as a kind of intermediary between them.[54] Hermes, as a hero, is he who comes about through the communion of mortals and gods: a kind of third term, he is the place or locus in which the mortal and the divine can commune.[55] However, Hermes' heroic birth also indicates a decisive *distance* between mortals and the divine. As previously averred, Hermes was a νόθος, a bastard, in the sense that his father Zeus left him to be raised by his mortal mother in the deep-shaded cave. Hermes thus marks a kind of *withdrawal* of the divine, an abandonment of the mortal realm by the gods. One must leave it to the psychoanalysts to decide if such abandonment accounts for Hermes' roguish behavior.[56] Of course, it is a testament to his character that, precisely due to such behavior, Hermes eventually gained the recognition of his father Zeus.[57] Nevertheless, precisely as the intermediary between gods and mortals, Hermes stands at the threshold of the divine, neither totally in nor totally out—a limitary position implicit in his role as a boundary marker and messenger, and further evident in his potential for both truth and falsity.

Hermes' role as erotic (i.e., heroic) intermediary is further implicated in Socrates' other etymology of "hero": that heroes are so called due to their ability to ask questions (398d). What such ability reveals above all is that such a person is *lacking* in wisdom: for it is precisely due to ignorance, either real or feigned, that one asks questions. More specifically, the ability to ask questions reveals that uniquely human wisdom which knows that it knows nothing: for it is through the informed asking of questions that one demonstrates that one knows nothing. Further, the ability to ask questions well is nothing other than a certain *love* of λόγος.[58] The one who asks questions—the hero in this sense—is one who, precisely out of knowledge of his ignorance, loves λόγος, that is, pursues λόγος in an erotic way. The incessant questioner is one who demonstrates this erotic love of λόγος. Hermes' dialogical ability—his love of λόγος[59]—thus exemplifies the philosophical activity as articulated by Socrates in the *Apology* and elsewhere. It is through the asking of questions that the hero—in this case Hermes—mediates between human ignorance and divine knowledge.

It should also be noted that in the *Apology* Socrates associates such incessant questioning with the labors of Heracles, a hero (*Ap.* 22a), likening his own interrogation of the citizenry with that hero's exploits. In the *Cratylus,* too, Socrates likens himself to the hero Heracles (411a).[60] Socratic questioning is heroic—that is, *erotic*— and Hermes, as a hero, possesses the same ability. Thus, properly understood, the first etymology offered for ἥρος (hero)—that the hero is so called due to the ability to ask questions (ἐρωτάω)—reduces to the second, that pertaining to ἔρως, as the homophonic play between ἔρωτος and ἐρωτᾶν suggests (398d). Ἔρως characterizes both the origin and the activity of the hero. Hermes, as a hero (in the sense given by Socrates), is thoroughly erotic.[61] Whether or not this characteristic was inherited by Hermogenes, "son of Hermes," is precisely what is in question throughout the dialogue, and the answer remains to be seen.

We have now observed the manner in which the erotic side of Hermes bespeaks a distance between the human and the divine, and the (limited) ability to traverse that distance through the asking of questions. However, our analysis of

Hermes' eroticism is incomplete. In a much more concrete and indeed sexual way, Hermes brings ἔρως to the scene.

As already mentioned, by Plato's time Hermes was frequently represented through the ithyphallic stone monument known as the herm.[62] These herms, ubiquitous in Athens, represented the god as having an enormous, if not comically large, phallus. The interpretations of this prominent characteristic are numerous. Most scholars agree that the large phallus marks Hermes' role as a fertility god, thereby associating him intimately with φύσις (to which we shall return below). Suhr, for example, argues that "the presence of the phallus, whenever it was adopted, can hardly be regarded as anything but a fertility symbol" (Suhr 1967, 64). Against this view, Brown argues that in Hermes' case the phallus was never a fertility symbol but was rather an "apotropaic amulet" whose magical powers brought benediction while keeping evil at bay (Brown 1990, 35). Regardless of whether Hermes' large phallus stood for fertility in a broad agricultural sense, it is difficult to perceive it as failing to evoke virility and sexual prowess in general.

One possible reason for Hermes' prominent phallus is his well-documented role as a god of lovers. In addition to being the god of the *agora,* the god of boundaries, and the god of trickery, Hermes was "the patron of another special kind of trickery—the trickery involved in *sexual seduction*" (Brown 1990, 8; emphasis mine). According to Hesiod, it was to Hermes that Pandora owed her "stealthy disposition." As the gods, at Zeus's behest, were outfitting the recently formed Pandora with various accoutrements, Hermes "contrived within her lies and crafty words and a deceitful nature" (Hesiod, *Works and Days,* line 78). As Brown has argued, the "crafty words and deceitful nature" which Hermes bequeaths to Pandora refers to the "*guiles* of women," or "what we sometimes call 'feminine wiles'" (Brown 1990, 9): "Let no strutting dame delude your mind, flattering you with deceitful words, trying to soften your manhood; he who puts his trust in woman puts his trust in tricksters [φηλήτῃσιν]" (*Works and Days,* 373 ff.). For the rabidly misogynistic Hesiod the very notion of trickery is equivalent with feminine sexual beguiling. Indeed, "seduction was, throughout Greek civilization, a magic art [of] employing love-charms, compulsive magic directed at the person desired"; and a person employing such seductive trickery might very well invoke Hermes for assistance (Brown 1990, 14, 35n4).[63] Hermes is thus the very origin of Pandora's seductiveness, and is in general associated with sexual seduction—an association not wholly divorced from his role as god of the *agora.*[64]

This association between trickery and sexual seduction can be seen in Homer. In a passage from the *Iliad* Homer offers a description of Aphrodite's girdle—a charm with which Hera, borrowing the girdle, attempts to trick Zeus into bed with her. As Homer describes it,

> With that she loosed from her breasts the breast-band,
> pierced and alluring, with every kind of enchantment

woven through it . . . . There is the heat of Love [φιλότης],
the pulsing rush of Longing [ἵμερος], the lover's whisper,
irresistible—*trickery* [ἔκλεψε] to make the sanest man go mad. (*Iliad* XIV.214
ff.; translation modified)

Hermes, as a god of trickery (ἔκλεψε), was associated with sexual beguiling, and
thus with Aphrodite:[65] indeed, Aphrodite, Hermes, and Eros all bore the same
epithet "the Whisperer" (Brown 1990, 14). At one point in the *Iliad*, Hermes
voices a certain erotic longing toward Aphrodite. After Apollo asks him if he
would like to bed down with the restrained Aphrodite, Hermes replies: "Oh,
Apollo, if only! [. . .] Archer, bind me down with triple those endless chains! Let
all you gods look on, and all you goddesses too—how I'd love to bed that golden
Aphrodite!" (*Odyssey* VIII.339–42). One sees here clearly Hermes' erotic drive.

The name "Hermes" thus brings with it an air of sexual trickery and sexual
prowess.[66] The name "Hermes" could be said to bring ἔρως to the scene in a double sense. First of all, as a hero born from the ἔρως between gods and humans,
Hermes serves the role of intermediary between them, guiding the souls of the
latter unto the former. Secondly, Hermes brings his sexual virility to the scene,
most obviously in the form of his erect phallus. Of course, these two aspects of
ἔρως are intimately related for Plato, as is seen in the *Symposium* and *Phaedrus*.
In both of those texts, ἔρως of the body (i.e., sexual ἔρως) is precisely that which
leads into the ἔρως of a "higher" sort pertaining to a communion with divine
Being.[67] Even if one argues that sexual desire is "left behind" as one reaches the
higher stages of ἔρως, it is indisputable that sexual desire is initially needed to
enter into the erotic movement toward the beautiful.[68]

Hermes and φύσις

One final, brief point concerning Hermes' character must be made. It has been
mentioned in passing that Hermes, particularly in his connection to the phallus,
bore a certain relationship to φύσις. Suhr, for example, argues that, "Hermes was
originally an agent of fertility, somehow identified with the changing aspects of
the cosmos, including the weather and the seasons, bringing life and prosperity
to the flora and fauna of the earth" (Suhr 1967, 58).[69] According to this view, one
of Hermes' most primitive roles was as a chthonic earth-divinity responsible for
vegetative fecundity and generation (Farnell 1909, 11). Indeed, in Kyllene, reported by some to be his birthplace, Hermes bore the epithet Φαλές, arguably a
derivation of phallus (φαλλός), meant to express his role as a fertility god (Farnell
1909, 11). Such a role he would have inherited from his mother Maia, a nymph-
goddess of vegetable fertility intimately linked to the earth.[70]

Moreover, from very early on Hermes was considered to be the god of herds,
called upon to bring blessings to both flock and shepherd (Farnell 1909, 10). (This
is a role his son Pan will later inherit.) As such, Hermes was frequently associated

with the pasture-lands that lay beyond the city proper, as evident in the following line from Aristophanes: "I pray to Hermes the pasture-god, to Pan and the Nymphs beloved, with fain heart to smile upon our choral dances" (*Thesmophoriazusae*, 977). What should be stressed is the manner in which Hermes' connection to the pasture, and to the pastoral animals therein (Farnell 1909, 10), further orients Hermes toward *nature* (φύσις).[71] Coupled with his roguish tendency to transgress custom—such as when he, only a day old, stole Apollo's bulls (*Hymn* IV.69 ff.)—Hermes' pastoral character serves to orient him away from city and toward the country, toward the wild of nature.

Such an orientation should put us on our guard. Given that a primary conflict at play within the *Cratylus* is between a natural and a conventional correctness of names, Hermes' association with nature should serve to alert us to a certain direction of the text. Although Hermogenes is seen at the beginning to hold that names are only correct by custom and agreement, such a position is threatened by his association with Hermes. In other words, insofar as Hermogenes' relation to Hermes is in question, Hermogenes' relationship to *nature* is in question: and the closer that the son gets to his father, the closer he will come to represent a certain natural attitude with respect to names. Indeed, during the first dialectical exchange between Socrates and Hermogenes, the latter is very quickly brought into an awareness of a certain natural correctness that must belong to names (390d). Of course, given also Hermes' manifest connection to the *polis* (and specifically the *agora*), one suspects that Hermogenes—if he indeed proves to be the son of Hermes—will retain a certain attachment to convention and agreement as well.

Gathering together all that has been said, we have seen that Hermes is a well-endowed lover of λόγος who, due both to his origin in ἔρως and his erotic/heroic ability to ask questions, traverses the distance between the human and the divine, thereby also disclosing that distance. Further, we have seen the extent to which Hermes, as the deceptive father of λόγος, brings about a radical disruption of epistemological certainty and emphasizes the role of radical (self-)interpretation in the attainment of self-knowledge. The *Cratylus* thus begins with a sly invocation to the god of limits and the erotic and hermeneutical transgression of them. By calling Hermogenes' relation to Hermes into question, the text effectively calls upon the mischievous progenitor of λόγος—a call which serves, in the various ways indicated here, to mark the limits and the excesses of the *Cratylus*. In the next chapter, the extent to which this analysis bears upon the character Hermogenes shall be examined.

3   A Question of Inheritance

As mentioned in the preceding chapter, our inquiry into the nature of the god Hermes was undertaken for the sake of clarifying the precise character of Cratylus's joke regarding the correctness of Hermogenes' name that opens the *Cratylus*. It was argued that through calling Hermogenes' name into question the dialogue calls upon the god Hermes (as that to which Hermogenes is being compared). We return now to the joke which, as argued, sets the parameters of the *Cratylus* as a whole.

Near the beginning of the text Hermogenes, like a good messenger, reports to Socrates the following:

> So I ask him if Cratylus is truly his name and he agrees it is. "And what is Socrates' name?" I said. He said, "Socrates."[1] "And for all other human beings too, the very name we call each one, is that the name of each?" "Well, your name is not Hermogenes, at any rate," he said, "even if all human beings call you that." (383b; Sachs)

As Hermogenes will go on to explain, Cratylus has offered only ironic replies (εἰρωνεύται) and has been, through the course of their conversation, "acting like someone who knows about [the correctness of names] as though he himself was thinking something within himself [ἐν ἑαυτῷ] which, if he felt like stating it clearly, would make me agree [ὁμολογεῖν] and say the very things he himself were saying" (384a; Sachs; trans. modified).

Thus, it seems that while the names of both Socrates and Cratylus are correct (ὀρθός) (though it is still unclear at this point what such correctness entails), Hermogenes' name is not. Indeed, it almost seems as if everyone in the world has a correct name and that it is *only* Hermogenes who, in Cratylus's expert opinion, does not. If he wished to (βούλοιτο), Cratylus could share this special knowledge that he holds in himself (ἐν ἑαυτῷ)—but he does not so wish, and poor Hermogenes is left to call upon Socrates for assistance.

Socrates obviously thinks that "Hermogenes" is Hermogenes' name and continually calls him by it throughout the dialogue, occasionally adding the patronymic "Hipponicus," of which more will be said below. Thus, of those present, it is *only* Cratylus who believes Hermogenes' name to be incorrect. One might say that Cratylus has some special knowledge—a knowledge unique to himself, a *private* knowledge—about the efficacy of the name "Hermogenes" to *correctly* disclose Hermogenes' character. To phrase this more suggestively, one might say that there is some feature proper to Hermes which Hermogenes has failed to inherit, a feature about which Cratylus—but *only* Cratylus—has private knowledge.

As we saw in chapter 2, there are many aspects to Hermes' character, any one of which might serve as the reason for Cratylus's refusal of Hermogenes' name, and though the real reason for Cratylus's refusal is a question to which the characters return (408b), it is never satisfactorily answered within the text or within scholarship. The obvious path, and the one most taken by commentators, is to follow Socrates' own initial (but very tentative) suggestion that it is Hermes' role as a god of commerce that is operative within Cratylus's refusal (384c).[2] And yet it is Socrates himself who marks the insufficiency of such an interpretation by explaining, and indeed repeating, that "it is difficult [χαλεπά] to know such things" (384b; 384c).[3] Which feature is it, then, to which Cratylus is referring as he denies Hermogenes his name?

One could argue that the most prominent feature of Hermes, even more so than his roles as god of commerce and divine herald, is his ithyphallic condition, a condition well attested in ancient Greek ceramics. As argued above, this condition can be seen to represent the erotic aspects of Hermes' character, which, among other things, link him to the goddess Aphrodite and, more generally, to ἔρως. Given especially the prominence of the herm in Ancient Athens, most recognizable for its large ithyphallic form, one wonders if it is to this erotic aspect that Cratylus is referring as he refuses Hermogenes his relationship to Hermes.

In claiming that "Hermogenes" is not Hermogenes' name, and thereby claiming that Hermogenes is not (as his name suggests) the son of Hermes, Cratylus could be suggesting that Hermogenes lacks his namesake's erotic ability, or perhaps further still, the prominent physical endowment that often characterizes the god. In other words, Cratylus could be denying that Hermogenes is like Hermes in either ability or appearance. All of this would be Cratylus's personal knowledge about Hermogenes, his private knowledge, which he would share if only he wished.

The fact that *only* Cratylus has this private knowledge regarding the legitimacy of Hermogenes' name raises the question of the nature of the relationship between Hermogenes and Cratylus, a matter never satisfactorily settled within scholarship. Some have suggested that Hermogenes was Cratylus's student.[4] Evidence in support of this claim is to be found both in Hermogenes' eagerness to learn (384a; 384e) and in Cratylus's evident ability to teach (428c; 440e), as well as Socrates' suggestion that Cratylus has pupils (428b). Further, there is evidence that Hermogenes and Cratylus have had this conversation regarding the correctness of names many times before (384c; 427d), a fact which could indicate an academic devotion to a perennial problem. Most obviously, then, the relationship between them seems to be that between a student and teacher.

However, that their relationship is purely academic seems to be excluded from the outset, given that the positions that the two characters hold are seemingly different and, as Hermogenes claims, basically opposed. It would be strange indeed to find the student of Cratylus so resolutely opposed to the position of his teacher: for what sort of disciple considers himself to be *fundamentally* at odds with the philosophical position of his master (at least while *remaining* his disciple)? Furthermore, it is worth noting that Hermogenes is ready (ἕτοιμος) to hear and learn (μανθάνειν καὶ ἀκούειν) not just from Cratylus, *but from anybody else* (ἀλλὰ καὶ παρ᾿ ἄλλου ὁτουοῦν) (384e): thus, he is not solely a devoted student of Cratylus' (384c). Given the apparent opposition of their respective positions, and Hermogenes' stated desire to learn from *anybody* else, it could be the case that they are enemies—but that possibility is precluded by Hermogenes' confessed desire to continue the conversation only for his own edification (384e), and his allusion to the many conversations they have had before (384c). It could also be that they are simply friends, perhaps very good friends, much in the way that Socrates seems to be the friend of both.[5] Yet, if Cratylus and Hermogenes are *simply* friends, one still has to account for Cratylus's *private* knowledge about the efficacy of Hermogenes' name. Whatever knowledge Cratylus has, it is not the sort that is readily available to mere friends: for if it were, Socrates too, as Hermogenes' good friend, would presumably have such knowledge. One is tempted to conclude that Hermogenes and Cratylus are lovers, and that the quarrel between them is thus a *lover's* quarrel. However, there is no definitive textual or historical evidence to support this conclusion, and one may only wonder about the precise character of their relationship.

Whatever the details, I would like to propose that Cratylus' joke at the expense of Hermogenes' name suggests that their relationship is characterized by ἔρως. Specifically, in denying Hermogenes his name, and thus his relationship to Hermes, Cratylus is suggesting that Hermogenes *lacks* ἔρως and, perhaps, the physical manifestation of such ἔρως.[6] Only, rather than delivering such an insult straightforwardly, Cratylus has veiled it in irony, leaving Hermogenes to decipher it on his own (or, finally, with help from Socrates, who in the *Symposium* refers to himself as a "master of erotic matters" [*Symp.* 177e]). Insofar as it is ἔρως that Cratylus thinks Hermogenes is lacking, ἔρως marks the beginning of the text and will be of the utmost importance for the dialogue as a whole.

Indeed, one could interpret Socrates' first words of the dialogue as hinting, with the utmost subtlety, at the importance of ἔρως in what is to come. Prior to offering his tentative interpretation of Cratylus's peculiar pronouncements, Socrates says the following:

> Hermogenes, son of Hipponicus, the ancient proverb that "beautiful things are difficult" [χαλεπὰ τὰ καλά] is the way it is with learning them. And what

has to do with names in particular happens to be no small thing [σμικρόν] to learn. (384b; Sachs; trans. modified).[7]

This statement of Socrates' is exceedingly important, and for at least two reasons. First, taken in the most superficial way, this statement portends the difficult task that lies ahead. The beautiful task of the *Cratylus*, to learn about names, is χαλεπός: difficult, laborious, troublesome, even dangerous. Both the self-referential character of an inquiry into λόγος by means of λόγος and the presence of the mischievous Hermes as the guide of such an inquiry have already suggested that the path ahead will indeed be difficult, if not dangerous.[8] As was seen above, at stake in this difficult path is more than just the veracity of Hermogenes' name, but the very possibility of λόγος and, subsequently, knowledge (see 440a ff.).

Second, in prefacing the inquiry with the words χαλεπὰ τὰ καλά Socrates indicates that names, or the knowledge of them, are καλός, beautiful. In indicating that the inquiry to come is going to be focused (in some unspecified way) on τὰ καλά, beautiful things, Socrates has suggested with typical subtlety that the investigation will be a matter of that which is preeminently concerned with the beautiful: namely, ἔρως.

In Plato's *Symposium*, Socrates relays an account of Diotima's in which she articulates the relationship between ἔρως and the beautiful (τὸν καλόν). She describes the manner in which a lover, beginning with the love of a single beautiful body, eventually "ascends" to a vision of something "wonderfully beautiful" (τι θαυμαστὸν τὴν φύσιν καλόν) (*Symp.* 210e), namely, the beautiful "alone by itself and with itself and always being of one look" (αὐτὸ καθ' αὐτὸ μεθ' αὑτοῦ μονοειδὲς ἀεὶ ὄν) (*Symp.* 211b; my translation). It is this beautiful itself (*Symp.* 211c) that serves as that for the sake of which (ἕνεκεν) erotic matters are undertaken (*Symp.* 210e).[9] In other words, although ἔρως begins with particular beautiful beings, it ends with a glimpse of the beautiful itself in its Being. Or, to phrase this more generally, ἔρως begins amongst sensible beings and, when properly guided, moves toward Being.[10] A similar story is told in Plato's *Phaedrus*, where it is said that beauty (κάλλος), in addition to being the most shining (ἐκφανέστατον), is the most beloved (ἐρασμιώτατον) (*Phdr.* 250e), that is, the most capable of inducing ἔρως.[11] In both cases, the beautiful (κάλλος) itself is that toward which ἔρως is ultimately directed.[12]

Thus, when Socrates says in the *Cratylus* that the inquiry into the knowledge of names is a matter of beautiful things (τὰ καλά), he is suggesting that what is to follow will have something to do with ἔρως. More specifically, Socrates is suggesting that the object of their inquiry to come—names, or the knowledge thereof—deals with beautiful things and must therefore be pursued erotically. By intimating all of this in the wake of Cratylus's joke regarding Hermogenes' name, Socrates is suggesting that the very sense of the joke is somehow intertwined with ἔρως.

In refusing him his name, Cratylus is impugning Hermogenes' erotic ability. On one level this could mean that Cratylus, for whatever reason and in whatever context, finds Hermogenes to fall short of the sexually salacious Hermes.[13] However, on a more philosophical level, this could serve to mark that Hermogenes, at least according to Cratylus, lacks the ability to ascend from beautiful things unto the beautiful itself, to the beautiful in its Being, and is thus unable to follow after those difficult, beautiful things about which he and Cratylus have spoken many times before.[14] In disputing his relationship to Hermes, Cratylus may be suggesting that Hermogenes cannot, as Hermes would, traverse the distance between human beings and gods, opinion and truth, appearances and Being. Perhaps, rather, the un-erotic Hermogenes is stuck in the realm of human opinion (δόξα); and perhaps this is why Cratylus, in responding to Hermogenes' question if he would like for Socrates to join them in the λόγος, says "if it seems [δοκεῖ] to you" (383a), thereby stressing Hermogenes' attachment to δόξα.[15]

However, if this is so, Socrates evidently disagrees, as comes to light through the more sexual sense of Cratylus's joke. This sense is emphasized through Socrates' continual use of Hermogenes' full patronymic designation. Translated literally (while being careful to mark the limits of any attempt at such "literal" translations), Hermogenes Hipponicus's full name is "Son of Hermes, Son of Horse-victor," the first half of which Cratylus disputes. Interestingly, the horse was a common symbol of sexual prowess for the Greeks. Aristotle remarked, in his *History of Animals,* that "the horse is the most salacious of animals after the human species" (*HA*, 575b31).[16] Such salaciousness is seen in the *Phaedrus* precisely during Socrates' account of the ascent of the soul to the Plain of Truth where it gazes upon the beautiful in its Being (*Phdr.* 248b). There, in Socrates' description of the soul as a horse-drawn chariot, one of the two horses which lead us into a glimpse of the beautiful itself (*Phdr.* 250b) is said to be characterized by its excessive desire for sexual intercourse (*Phdr.* 254a). This horse, while initially unbroken and intractable, is nonetheless needed in order for an ascent to the beautiful itself to get underway.[17] In calling Hermogenes by his patronymic Socrates is playfully hinting at Hermogenes' relation to the horse, and thus to his potential to indeed undertake such an erotic ascent (a potential which, it will be seen, is eventually verified).

Such play persists as the dialogue continues. After having listened to Hermogenes' explanation of his own thoughts regarding the habitual and customary correctness of names, Socrates offers to investigate (σκεψώμεθα)—or perhaps, as suggested above, *jest*—into the matter with him (385a). In order to elucidate Hermogenes' claim that any name that we give to something can easily be changed to another name, such as in the case of a master changing the name of his slave (384d), Socrates asks Hermogenes the following:

> Well, then, what if I give a name to any of the things there are, say what we now call a "human being," and I call this a "horse," and what we now call a "horse" I call a "human being?" Will the name of the same thing be "human being" in

public and "horse" in private? Or in the other case "human being" in private and "horse" in public? Is that how you mean it? (385a; Sachs; trans. modified)

The same thing—a human being—will be called a horse in private and a human being in public; or, just as easily, a human being in private and a horse in public. In addition to foreshadowing the utter disintegration of Being that Socrates will soon show to be implicit in Protagoras's claim that "the human being is the measure of all things" (see chapter 4), this example resonates with much of what has come before. To begin with, by calling Hermogenes "Hermogenes," Socrates has been calling Hermogenes something publicly that Cratylus has not been calling him privately. Additionally, in calling Hermogenes by his patronymic "Hipponicus," Socrates has been publicly calling Hermogenes not a horse, but the son of a horse (or, rather, the son of a horse-victor). This play extends in deed what Socrates has just said in speech.[18] Socrates plays with the idea that a man could be called a horse in public by playing with Hermo-genes Hippo-nicus's name.

Horsemanship in general was frequently used in Greek comedy as a euphemism for sexual congress.[19] Hermogenes' father Hipponicus in particular is ridiculed in this register in Aristophanes' Frogs. There, Hermogenes' half-brother Callias, whom we learn a bit about in the Cratylus (at 391c), is targeted by the great comic poet. While poking fun at various infamous Greeks, the chorus sings the following line: "And Callias, we're told, that son of Hippo-coitus ['Ιπποβίνου], fights at sea in a lion-skin made of pussy [κύσθου λεοντῆν ναυμαχεῖν ἐνημμένον]" (Frogs 432).[20] Whatever the precise sense of this insult against Callias, for our purposes what is interesting is that his father Hipponicus is referred to as 'Ιπποβίνου (horse-screwer), or, to put it gently, "one who engages in sexual congress with horses." One can only wonder if Plato had this Aristophanic joke in mind when writing about Hermogenes and Callias Hipponicus in the Cratylus.

It is through emphasizing his relationship to the horse that Socrates playfully indicates Hermogenes' erotic potential, a potential that shall be borne out as the dialogue continues. Near the beginning of the text, after having reported to Socrates Cratylus's oracular pronouncements, Hermogenes says that it would be a pleasure (ἡδέως) for him to hear Socrates' interpretation (συμβαλεῖν) of these oracles (384a) and that, further, it would please him (ἥδιον) to hear about Socrates' own thoughts on the matter. Ἡδέως is arguably related to ἥδομαι, meaning to take delight in something. That Hermogenes delights in such investigations as he and Socrates are currently pursuing becomes clearer when he says that he is eager (ἕτοιμος) to learn (384e),[21] even if it means abandoning his well-weathered and tried position. In a word, Hermogenes presents himself as one who takes delight in the pursuit of truth, as one desirous to follow the λόγος to the truth to which it may lead.[22] Socrates' use of the patronymic "Hipponicus" playfully hints at this desire.[23]

Thus, in calling Hermogenes by his full name, Socrates is alerting us to the issue of desire, or ἔρως.[24] In general, what is brought to our attention through Cratylus's joke is the possibility of a lack of ἔρως within Hermogenes, a lack which Socrates' use of "Hipponicus" puts into question. As will be seen, much of the remainder of the investigation of the *Cratylus* will be a trial of Hermogenes' erotic ability, of his ability to move from beautiful objects toward the beautiful itself, beyond the realm of opinion and unto a vision of Being. As the self-proclaimed master of erotic matters (see *Symp.* 177e) and through his playing of the role of Hermes, Socrates will attempt to guide Hermogenes along the path from the world of sensible things to the divine realm of Being. As will be seen, it will be through *names* (or words: ὄνομα) that this ascent will ultimately occur.

Tangentially, there are indications from another ancient source that Hermogenes did indeed possess great ἔρως. In Xenophon's *Symposium,* while extolling the power of ἔρως as it manifests itself in those present at the party, Socrates describes the sort of ἔρως that characterizes Hermogenes: "As for Hermogenes, who of us does not know that he is pining away with desire [ἔρωτι κατατήκεται] for nobility of character [ἡ καλοκἀγαθία], whatever that may be?" (*Symp.* viii). The lover, Hermogenes, desires above all, according to the Xenophonic Socrates, to be καλοκἀγαθός, that mysterious and noble combination of beauty (καλός) and goodness (ἀγαθός) which the ancient aristocracy so urgently sought. In other words, Hermogenes desired to be beautiful and noble: that is, he desired the καλός.[25] For Xenophon, then, Hermogenes preeminently and erotically desired the beautiful. Of course, as we have seen, the beautiful is nothing other than the proper object of ἔρως. Xenophon's Hermogenes thus serves as a paragon of the erotic posture: he longs for what longing most longs for—the beautiful itself.[26]

Of course, as the Socrates of Plato's *Symposium* suggests, to long for something is to be wanting of it (*Symp.* 199c ff.): Hermogenes thus lacks the beautiful-goodness which he so desires. One recalls that on two occasions in the *Cratylus* Hermogenes' poverty is emphasized: first, when Socrates offers his tentative explanation of Cratylus's joke (i.e., that Hermogenes is poor at money matters [384b]), and second, when it is said that Hermogenes is not in control (ἐγκρατής) of his inheritance (391c).[27] It is precisely this lack, this poverty, that marks Hermogenes' erotic nature most of all.[28] Recalling from Diotima's speech in the *Symposium* that poverty (Πενία) and resource (Πόρος) are the parents of Eros (*Symp.* 203b ff.), one wonders if the emphasis on Hermogenes' poverty within the *Cratylus* highlights his erotic capabilities. It is precisely because he lacks the beautiful that Hermogenes is in a position to comport himself erotically toward it.[29]

To recapitulate, in calling the efficacy of Hermogenes' name (and thus his relationship to Hermes) into question, Cratylus is calling Hermogenes' erotic abilities into question, where this means both his sexual and philosophical prowess. Socrates is called upon by Hermogenes to interpret Cratylus's oracles, and also to offer his own insights regarding the correctness of names. Through the course of his interpretation Socrates will begin to hint, through his use of Hermogenes' patronymic, that the young lover of λόγος is not as lacking in ἔρως as Cratylus's jest suggests. More precisely, it is through playing the role of Hermes that Socrates, as he leads Hermogenes through the inquiry, will bring Hermogenes' erotic ability to the fore.

In light of the erotic character of Hermes which has been brought to light, and given further the erotic sense of Cratylus's joke, it is necessary to consider the precise sense of the word ὀρθός as it is used in the *Cratylus*. Though invariably translated as either "correct" or "right," both of which are perfectly adequate translations, one must be careful to observe the *upward* directionality implicit in the term. Ὀρθός can mean *upright* or even *erect* in the sense of extending upward across the vertical plane, as the well-behaved horse in the *Phaedrus* is said to have an erect posture or form (ὧν τό τε εἶδος ὀρθὸς) (*Phdr.* 253d). Additionally, ὀρθός also had the vulgar meaning which our present day *erect* has. In Aristophanes, ὀρθός is used often to denote an erect phallus;[30] and, most interestingly, Herodotus uses ὀρθά to describe the ithyphallic character of Hermes as he appeared on the herms (*Histories* 2.51.1).

Given the erotic and Hermetic character of the opening joke of the *Cratylus*, it is tempting to translate ὀρθός not as *right* or *correct* but as *erect*. This translation does not mean to stress merely the sexual sense of ὀρθός (though it does intend such a nuance), but also the essentially *upright* or *vertical* directionality of ὀρθός at play. Such verticality can be understood as stressing the movements of Hermes as he moves up and down between the human and divine realms. As will be seen (in chapter 7), many of the etymologies will reflect this upward orientation, this erectness toward the divine and Being. Indeed, the very ascent into a glimpse of Being will be seen to depend upon the upright or erect character of a name and its ability to draw one up away from mere semblance. In translating ὀρθός as *erect*, one captures both the upward directionality and the eroticism at work in the term and through the text as a whole. However, since the word *correct* shares a root with *erect*, the former shall continue to be used here.[31]

Such erotic nuance is important in understanding the *Cratylus*. Returning now to the beginning of the text, when Socrates seemingly redirects the inquiry away from the joke and toward an inquiry into names (384c), we see that Socrates is himself joking, playing on the word ὀρθός and marking this play with a play on σκώπτειν and σκοπεῖν. Socrates undertakes to investigate *and joke about* the *correct-ness* in Hermogenes' name, that is, whether his name accurately captures the nature of Hermes. Further, from out of this inquiry, an examination of the *correct-ness* of names as such, of their ability to ascend the vertical distance between the human and the divine (i.e., the sensible and Being), will occur. What the inquiry as a whole will disclose is whether Hermogenes has the requisite ἔρως to undertake a vertical ascent into a consideration of Being.

Though such erotic play may seem incredible, it is not at all uncommon in the Platonic corpus. As Burt Hopkins has argued, Plato's *Symposium* begins with just such a phallic joke. As the *Symposium* begins, Apollodorus recounts to his nameless comrades an event that took place "just the other day" (*Symp.* 172a). While on his way to Athens from his home in Phaleron, a friend of his (Glaucon, it turns out) came up behind him while playfully calling "Oh, Phalerus!" As Hopkins has argued, there is a homophonic (and, indeed, homosexual) play on Phalerus (Φαλερεύς) and φαλλός, all the more conspicuous given the Glaucon has, for no other specified reason, come up from behind (ὄπισθεν) Apollodorus (Hopkins 2011, 287). In other words, Glaucon is playfully calling Apollodorus a *phallus* or, as Hopkins suggests, a "dickhead" (which is why, as Hopkins argues, Apollodorus is less than joyous to see his friend [ibid.]). All of this play serves to foreshadow the highly erotic character of the gathering (συνουσία)—or intercourse[32]—which Apollodorus relates.

Such play extends into other dialogues. Scully has successfully shown the extent to which Socrates' palinode in the *Phaedrus* utilizes exceedingly erotic language. During his mythic description of the ascent of the soul up to the Plain of Truth Socrates describes the winged soul, as it gazes upon the beautiful, as "swelling, pulsing, throbbing, and sweating"—in other words, as an erect penis (Scully 2003, 107). In further describing the passion that human beings feel, Socrates distinguishes between what such passion is called by human beings and what it is called by the gods:[33] "Verily, mortals call him winged Eros, but gods call him Winged [Πτέρωτα], because he makes things rise" (*Phdr.* 252c; Scully). As Scully observes, "winged" (Πτέρωτα) is slang for an erect penis, to which ancient pottery gives excellent testimony. Scully further notes that it is precisely the suggestion that the gods refer to ἔρως by a slang term for an erect winged penis that Phaedrus laughs (Scully 2003, 33n79). It is worth mentioning in this register that Hermes, herald to the gods, is often presented as winged.[34]

Though there are other examples of such phallic jesting that could be adduced,[35] these two suffice to establish that Plato was in no way bashful about engaging in such play. That the *Cratylus* begins with a similar play has been argued, yet the extent of this playfulness has yet to be fully appreciated. In chapter 6, when we turn to the Homeric scene, both the extent of the play and the manner in which that play bears upon the question of Hermogenes' eroticism will come into greater focus.

4 The Nature of Nature

Just after indicating the ridiculous character of Cratylus's comments regarding Hermogenes' name, and after he has reiterated the difficulty and danger of the inquiry to come, Socrates says that he and Hermogenes must now investigate (σκοπεῖν) in common (εἰς τὸ κοινὸν) into whether Cratylus or Hermogenes is right about the correctness of names (384c). Hermogenes then elaborates upon his previously stated position that naming is a matter of human convention and agreement:

> [I]t seems to me [ἐμοὶ γὰρ δοκεῖ] that whatever name anyone gives [θῆται] to anything is the correct one [τὸ ὀρθόν]; and if one then changes it to something else, and no longer calls it that other name, the later one is no less correct than the earlier one. It's the same way as we change the names of our slaves, for no name is of such a nature [πεφυκέναι] as to belong to any particular thing by nature [φύσει], but only by the custom and habit [νόμῳ καὶ ἔθει] of those who set it down [ἐθισάντων] and call it that [καλούντων]. (384d–e; Sachs; trans. modified)

The correctness of a name, according to this account, depends solely upon the act of conferring it, of setting it down (τίθημι), and the customs or habits that inform that setting-down. In other words, simply by virtue of the activity of conferring a name upon something, that name is correct.

What should immediately be stressed is how Hermogenes' position, which involves a certain *refusal* of nature—that is, a refusal of the position that names are correct *by* nature—in no way abandons nature entirely. Rather, Hermogenes maintains that no name is of such a *nature* (πεφυκέναι) as to be correct by nature (φύσει), saying instead that it is the *nature* of names to be correct by convention.[1] Thus, Hermogenes' position does not so much involve an utter refusal of nature but rather a certain reduction of it to convention, to the machinations of human beings. Phrased otherwise, Hermogenes' position implicitly involves a *doubling of nature* whereby he can simultaneously refuse names a "natural correctness" while still maintaining that their *nature* is such as to be correct by convention. We shall return to this doubling of nature, and the manner in which it pervades and structures the *Cratylus*, below.

It should also be noted that Hermogenes' position—that it is the nature of names to be correct not by nature but by convention—echoes what is said in Hermogenes' first word, indeed, the first word of the *Cratylus*: βούλομαι.[2] In thinking that names are correct by convention, Hermogenes thinks that a name is correct by the actions and machinations of human beings, that is, by virtue of the *will* or *wishes* of the person who gives it. As will be seen in the next chapter, Hermogenes' position as Socrates interprets it reduces naming to a process of human wishing, greatly threatening the relationship between a name and the being it is meant to name.

Despite holding this rather willful position at the outset of the text, Hermogenes indicates a certain epistemological openness, stating that he is ready (ἕτοιμος), even zealous, to listen and to learn "not only from Cratylus but also from anyone else whomsoever" (384e; my translation).[3] In saying this, Hermogenes indicates that he is *open* to inquiry, and is thus eager to be led by another toward a new conception of the correctness of names. Already we can see in Hermogenes the glimmer of an erotic longing toward the truth, a certain philosophical alacrity that makes him particularly suited to follow Socrates (as the Hermetic *psychopomp*) wherever he will lead him. Thus, though holding a position that emphasizes the role of human wishing, Hermogenes himself wishes to learn otherwise, and is eager to be shown.

Socrates begins the inquiry: "let us investigate" (σκεψώμεθα) (385a), perhaps recalling the previously noted play between σκοπεῖν (investigate) and σκώπτειν (jest), thereby subtly hinting that the investigation to come will be to some extent in jest. Socrates then asks Hermogenes if it is the case that "whatever we call [καλῇ] each thing, that is its name," to which Hermogenes replies, "it seems so to me [ἔμοιγε δοκεῖ]" (385a; my translation). This is true, Hermogenes claims, whether it is a city or a private person (ἰδιώτης) who names it (385a). This latter comment serves to reduce Hermogenes' entire position to his example of the slave.[4] There it was said that a master can change the name of his slave as he sees fit, without regard for the nature (or the Being) of the slave in question. In now making the act of naming undertaken by a city equivalent to the act of naming undertaken by a master toward his slave, Hermogenes indicates the extreme extent to which naming is, for him, a matter of individual human caprice. As Socrates will soon put it, "whatever *each particular person* [ἕκαστος] says the name of anything is, that is its name for *that particular person* [ἑκάστῳ]" (385d; my translation). Naming is an operation of the will, or the wishes, of the private individual. What should be emphasized is that such a conception amounts to a certain claim of *mastery* over beings: like slaves, beings can be renamed at the caprice (i.e., the wishes) of a name-giver.[5] As we shall see in the next chapter, such a claim to mastery is at the heart of the so-called "tool analogy" which Socrates will soon analyze.

It should at this point be reiterated that Hermogenes' position articulates in speech what Cratylus, in refusing him his name, has just done in deed. Hermogenes is the slave, and Cratylus is exercising his lordly power, his κράτος, to refuse his name. Here again we see an element of the comic incongruity at play in the *Cratylus*, and the manner in which the positions of the two apparent opponents are not as drastically different from one another as they may first appear. Hermogenes, himself being treated like a slave by Cratylus, is shown to hold the position that naming is a matter of mastery over beings. Thus, though resistant to Cratylus's position and corresponding refusal of his name, Hermogenes' position in fact *legitimates* Cratylus's behavior. It should further be noted that Cratylus's very name, which is related to κρατέω (*to be strong, powerful, to rule*), already suggests that his understanding of names too might involve a certain claim to mastery, one which will prove to be more akin to Hermogenes' position than it first appears.[6]

With Hermogenes' reduction of naming to the willful act of the solitary master—already intimated in the first word of the text, βούλομαι—the *unity*, not to mention the *community*, proper to naming has begun to dissolve. Generally conceived, a name is a single word which stands for many different things to which it can be applied: it is a unit which encompasses a multiplicity and which allows for a community of speakers to join together in common.[7] However, under Hermogenes' position, names are not only different for different cities and groups of people, but for *each* individual person. We are thus no longer even talking about *one* singular name—one ὄνομα which, for example, refers to the many different appearances of Hermogenes—but a plurality of *names*. This unraveling of unity is immediately accelerated in the following line, where it is said by Socrates that "however many [ὁπόσα] names anyone says belong to each thing, that is how many there will be at the time when he says so" (385d; Sachs). Not only may each individual person have her own private name for a thing over against the other names that other people hold for it, but each person may have *in herself* many different names for the same thing. In other words, on Hermogenes' view, naming has quickly been seen to involve radical multiplicity at the expense of unity. Not only is there a lack of agreement in names between persons, there is a lack of agreement in names *within oneself*.[8] Such radical multiplicity will itself only multiply as the dialogue continues.

Again it should be stressed that, although Hermogenes ostensibly holds a position opposed to that held by Cratylus, he has in fact just authorized the latter's position. The opening of the dialogue has just dramatically presented a scene wherein two people (Socrates and Cratylus) each have a different name for the same being, i.e., Hermogenes.[9] In now claiming that there are as many names of things as there are people who speak them, Hermogenes has offered a λόγος for what the dialogue has just presented in comic ἔργον. The beginning of the *Cratylus* dramatically and comically enacts the disruption of the unity of naming that is implicit in Hermogenes' position.

It is in the wake of this disruption of unity that Socrates invokes the figure of the sophist Protagoras. Just after Hermogenes reaffirms his position that, with respect to names, it is every man for himself, Socrates asks him if this is true not only for *names* (ὄνομα) but also for *beings* (τὰ ὄντα):

> Come then, Hermogenes, and let us see whether it also appears to you [σοι φαίνηται] to be that way with the beings [τὰ ὄντα], that the being of them is a private matter for each person [ἰδίᾳ αὐτῶν ἡ οὐσία εἶναι ἑκάστῳ], just as Protagoras used to say, claiming that the "measure of all things" is a human being—so that whatever way the things appear to me [ἐμοὶ φαίνηται] is the way they are for me [τοιαῦτα μὲν ἔστιν ἐμοί] and whatever way they appear to you [οἷα δ᾽ ἂν σοί] is the way they are for you [τοιαῦτα δὲ σοί]. Or does it seem to you that they themselves have some stability of being of their own [ἢ ἔχειν δοκεῖ σοι αὐτὰ αὑτῶν τινα βεβαιότητα τῆς οὐσίας]? (385e–386a; Sachs; trans. modified)

Having established that names, for Hermogenes (now aligned with Protagoras), are a matter of opinion, Socrates wants to know if beings themselves (τὰ ὄντα) are a matter of opinion or if they rather have some stability proper to themselves independent of our wishes. It is with this former position—that beings are as they appear to each private person—that Socrates aligns Protagoras.

This alignment itself serves to align the *Cratylus* with the *Theaetetus*. As has been noted by scholars, the *Cratylus* bears many structural and topical similarities to the *Theaetetus* in general.[10] Though the evocation of Protagoras in the *Theaetetus* belongs to a dramatic context distinct from that of the *Cratylus*, and though Socrates' engagement with Protagoras therein thus belongs to its own unique setting and is subject to its own laws of logographic and dramatic necessity, there are several general ways in which the treatment of Protagoras in the *Theaetetus* corresponds to that undertaken in the *Cratylus*. With respect to the figure of Protagoras, the *Cratylus* is a virtual repetition of Socrates' refutation of the sophist in the *Theaetetus*; though, as Mackenzie has noted, the epistemological contexts of the dialogues differ somewhat.[11] John Sallis has offered a concise analysis of Socrates' refutation of Protagoras in the *Theaetetus* as it relates to the question of the dissolution of unity mentioned above. Through a summary of Sallis's argument, the manner in which a similar dissolution occurs within the *Cratylus* will be made more readily visible. Above all, what Sallis's analysis brings to light is the extent to which the arrival of Protagoras in the *Theaetetus* represents a certain interpretation of nature (φύσις), one which, it will be argued, is no less at play within the *Cratylus*.

Theaetetus

Like the *Cratylus*, the *Theaetetus* presents Protagoras as the proponent of a certain doctrine, namely, that "the human being is the measure [μέτρον] of all things" (*Tht.* 152a). For Sallis, there are three conseqences that the Socrates of the *Theaetetus* draws out of this Protagorean doctrine. The first conseqence is what Sallis calls the "dissolution of oneness." If indeed "the human being is the measure" of all that is—that is, if *each* individual human being is such a measure (as, it should be recalled, Hermogenes so supposes within the *Cratylus* with respect to naming [385d])—then human beings are immediately led into radical ontological relativism.[12] In such a case every being would not only *appear* to each individual as something different, but would actually *be* so for that person. Phrased more concisely, under the Protagorean view as Socrates has interpteted it, there is an equivalence between appearance and Being, opinion and reality. Even more precisely, Being is *reduced* to appearance: what you see is what you get.

In such a scenario, what *is* for one person would not *be* the same for another: that is, Being would no longer be the same as itself, but would be multiplicitous. To use an example from the *Theaetetus,* if the wind *seems* hot to me, then the wind *is* hot for me (i.e., the appearance of the being *is* that being); and if it *seems* cold to you, then it *is* cold for you (*Tht.* 152b ff.). The one being which we call "wind" would thus no longer be one being, but would be as many as there are apprehensions of it (in this case, two). Thus, Protagoras's doctrine brings about the dissolution of the oneness (or unity) of Being (Sallis 2005, 185).

The second consequence for Sallis, following immediately upon the first, is for our greater inquiry the most important. Socrates states that, given the dissolution of oneness that has occurred, "you could not name [or *address:* προσείποις] correctly anything of whatever sort" (οὐδ᾽ ἄν τι προσείποις ὀρθῶς αὐδ᾽ ὁποιονοῦν τι) (*Tht.* 152d; my translation). Because, on Protagoras's view, each being *is* something different for each person who perceives it, the very possibilty of *naming* (προσεῖπον)—and, thus, of communication, of λόγος—has been undermined: for what one person calls "hot," the other will call "cold," and so on. In other words, the dissolution of the oneness of Being has brought about a scenario in which two people, each holding a different apprehension and (thus) name for a thing, have nothing in *common.* As Socrates describes the problem, if nothing is one thing by itself, totally the same as itself, then "if you address [προσαγορεύῃς] it as large it will also appear small, if heavy, light, and everything at all in this way, since nothing is either any one thing or of any one sort [ὡς μηδενὸς ὄντος ἑνὸς μήτε τινὸς μήτε ὁποιουοῦν]" (*Tht.* 152d; Sachs). The dissolution of oneness has thus brought about a dissolution of *naming,* of the *address,* and of the common λόγος: for in this Protagorean world of radical flux nothing will stay the same long enough to allow λόγος to attach a single name to it. In such a world speaking (λέγειν), and the gathering-together-in-common (i.e., λόγος) that speaking entails, would be impossible.

The third and final consequence comes about when Socrates, still paraphrasing Protagoras, claims that "all things . . . come to be through rushing around and motion and mutal mixing; for nothing ever is, but everything always becomes [γίγνεται πάντα]" (*Tht.* 152d; Benardete; trans. modified). Because everything is always in radical motion, nothing rests or pauses long enough *to be* anything: rather, everything is always only *on its way* to Being, that is, is only ever *becoming.*

Stated more strongly, things are only ever becoming *becoming,* are *radically* becoming: for, according to the Protagorean picture, nothing ever attains to Being. Thus, the Protagorean discourse has brought about, finally, the utter dissolution of Being (Sallis 2005, 186).

Most generally, Sallis shows how these three consequences can be seen to develop out of a certain general situation at play within the *Theaetetus.* From its very beginning the *Theaetetus* stages a "scene," as it were, wherein nature (φύσις) comes to be understood as consisting of radical flux (Sallis 2005, 178). As made evident at the outset through the figure of Theaetetus, whose character is described as being as smooth and as fluent as a stream of olive oil (*Tht.* 144b), the *Theaetetus* stages an attempt on the part of Socrates and the young mathematician to address the problem of the dissolution of λόγος (and its epistemological consequences) in the face of such radically flowing φύσις. To phrase this otherwise than Sallis does, one could say that the *Theaetetus* deals precisely with the the problem of the *address,* of how it is possible to address something which belongs to such flowing φύσις, of how it is possible to address φύσις *as such,* or if ceaselessly flowing φύσις is such as to escape the *as such* and hence the address.

To extend Sallis's analysis, we can say that the problem of the address is presented dramatically near the beginning of the *Theaetetus,* when Socrates is introduced to Theaetetus for the first time. Immediately after Theodorus has described the flowing nature of Theaetetus, the latter approaches, standing in the middle of at least two other people. Socrates does not yet know the name of the man in the middle. Theodorus knows his name, but cannot recall his *father's* name (*Tht.* 144c). Conversely, upon seeing the young man, Socrates recalls the father but not the son, the absent past but not the flowing present: "the youth's name [ὄνομα] I do not know" (*Tht.* 144c). It is almost as if something has served to disrupt Socrates' ability to name the inheritor of the father's lineage. Socrates, in the face of the man flowing before him, is not able to name what is *present,* but only the absent *source* of what is present. Socrates' confession that he does not know the name of such a nature names the principal problem of naming as such, namely, the problem of the relationship between λόγος and φύσις, the problem of naming things that come into being and waste away. This can be understood as the problem of establishing a *lineage* between a stable being and a name of a fleeting thing, of offering an account of the *inheritance* by a name of that which it names.[13]

Later in the *Theaetetus,* Socrates explicitly addresses this problem. In the wake of the ceaseless flow of radical becoming, one attempting to account for the things of nature would be compelled to discontinue use of the word *being* (τὸ δ' εἶναι). Given the dissolution of oneness, naming, and Being that the Protagorean doctrine has brought about, the human being (through λόγος) cannot simply continue to use "being" and its cognates with any legitimacy, except from out of a certain ignorance and habituation or, perhaps, *custom* (συνηθείας) (*Tht.* 157b). Rather, as Socrates puts it, "one must make utterances [φθέγγεσθαι] *in accordance with nature* [φύσιν]—becomings and makings and perishings and alterings—since if one stops something in one's speech, whoever does so makes it easily refutable" (*Tht.* 157b; Benardete; trans. modified, my emphasis). Precisely because of the dissolution of Being and, correspondingly, λόγος that the Protagorean doctrine has brought about, the human being (in using λόγος) must refrain from using the word "being" and must instead attempt to speak in accordance (κατὰ) with the radical flow characteristic of becoming. Rather than arresting something in speech through application of the word "being," thereby ceasing its fluctuation, one must let one's speech be dragged along by the flow. Under the sway of the Protagorean scene, to speak κατὰ φύσιν would be to speak in such a way as to give λόγος over to radical becoming, to the measure of the flow of φύσις, leaving behind the stability and determinacy otherwise thought to belong to Being.

Though Socrates does not explain exactly what such speaking κατὰ φύσιν would entail,[14] he does offer a word which perhaps describes the character of such speech. As Sallis observes, during this section of the *Theaetetus* Socrates conspicuously avoids words ordinarily used to denote speaking, offering instead the word φθέγγεσθαι (Sallis 2005, 187).[15] This word, which can mean "to make utterances," can also have the sense of an incoherent sound, such as an animal (say, a horse) would make.[16] As Sallis notes, this word is used elsewhere by the philosopher Heraclitus (who plays an important role in both the *Theaetetus* and the *Cratylus*) to describe the mantic manner of the Sibyl's speech: "The Sibyl with raving mouth utters things [φθεγγομένη] mirthless and unadorned and unperfumed, and her voice carries through a thousand years because of the god who speaks through her" (Heraclitus, Fr. D. 92; Sallis 2005, 187). Having made this philological connection—a connection bolstered by the air of Heraclitean flux at play throughout the *Theaetetus*—Sallis asks if such raving/mantic saying is what it would mean to speak along with the flow of nature, to speak κατὰ φύσιν (Sallis 2005, 188).

One wonders if the *Cratylus* does not show us, in excessive detail, what such utterances would look like.[17] One wonders especially if the long etymological section offers a performance of what such λόγος κατὰ φύσιν would entail, as the etymologies flow along ever faster and faster (420d), showing nothing other than the continual (and decidedly Heraclitean) flux of nature (401d; 402a ff.), a flux so disruptive and vacillatory as even to bring about opposing etymologies for the same words (437a ff.). In this register, it is especially relevent that the Socrates of the *Cratylus,* not unlike the Sibyl, makes his utterances from out of a certain mantic state, a divine inspiration contracted from Euthyphro earlier that morning (396d).[18] Perhaps such raving, roving etymologies as Socrates so tirelessly offers are what it would mean to speak κατὰ φύσιν—so long as φύσις is understood here as the unstable flux of nature.

In the *Theaetetus,* the general problem that arises in the face of the ceaseless flow of nature is this: how is a determinate λόγος about such things possible? If all things are always moving, coming into being and passing away, how is one to speak of them, given that λόγος requires a certain determinacy with which to operate? In other words, how is the determinacy proper to λόγος to be possible in the face of the apparent dissolution of determinacy that accompanies the radical flow of φύσις? How is *speech* (λέγειν) about the things of nature to be possible at all?

For λόγος about nature to be possible—possible, that is, beyond the making of incoherent utterances or the neighing of horses—something must grant a certain stability and determinacy to the otherwise unstable and indeterminate realm of becoming. Yet, as Sallis argues, such determinacy cannot simply be superadded to φύσις from something external to it: for, in such a case, what was added to φύσις would not *belong* to φύσις, and would therefore not be a determinacy *of* φύσις (Sallis 2005, 189). Rather, it would be a determinacy quite alien to φύσις, an arbitrary determinacy lacking in any filial connection to φύσις. Were one then to speak about such a superadded determinacy, one would no longer be speaking about φύσις, nor speaking of a determinacy that was κατὰ φύσιν. Whatever determinacy arises such as to render λόγος again possible must arise from out of φύσις itself, must extend from out of the radical flow of nature. Only then would the determinacy belong *to* φύσις, and only then would a λόγος about such determinacy be a λόγος which remained κατὰ φύσιν (Sallis 2005, 190)—a *natural* λόγος.

According to Sallis, though the Protagorean λόγος that "the human being is the measure of all things" has brought about the very dissolution of λόγος, developing into a scene of ceaselessly flowing φύσις, the Socrates of the *Theaetetus* begins to broach the possibility of a renewal of λόγος and a corresponding return to determinacy. Such a return occurs through what Socrates calls "wonderful and laughable things" (θαυμαστά τε καὶ γελοῖα) (154b).[19] As Sallis explains, the wonderful and laughable things involve a way of speaking in the face of φύσις or becoming, through which a certain level of determinacy is attained. To demonstrate this, Socrates offers an example involving dice (ἀστραγάλους), speaking of what it would mean for such dice to suffer increase (αὐξάνω).[20] Though Protagoras and others like him would account for the increase in terms of the dice themselves becoming bigger—that is, in terms of the dice undergoing alteration into something bigger—Socrates raises the "laughable and wondrous" possibility that such increase can come about by some different means. Something (the dice) can become larger through a certain addition, namely, a conjoining with a certain *excess*. If four dice are brought together, six dice becomes relatively large, whereas if you bring forth twelve dice, the group of six becomes relatively small. In other words, the same six dice can be both large and small while not themselves undergoing any physical change. Through the application of a certain excess, the dice grow and shrink without themselves ever suffering alteration.

The manner of such excessive increase becomes clearer through Socrates' next example. Socrates describes a scenario in which he would at one time be bigger than

Theaetetus and then, a year later, be smaller, having himself not undergone any growth or diminution (*Tht.* 155b). In other words, due to something other than becoming (γενέσθαι)—namely, through Theaetetus having grown bigger than Socrates such as to make Socrates smaller by comparison—Socrates is "afterward what [he] was not before, not having come to be [οὐ γενόμενος] that way" (*Tht.* 155c; Sachs; trans. modified).[21] Such a cause of Socrates' alteration, as Theaetetus's response indicates, would be "beyond what is natural" (ὑπερφυῶς) (*Tht.* 155c; Sallis 2005, 190): that is, it is a cause which is *beyond nature*, beyond the merely sensible or physical nature of Socrates.[22] Such a cause must be understood as a certain excess brought to bear upon the thing such as to cause it to increase, without the thing itself undergoing increase.

As Sallis's analysis shows, the excess in question is nothing other than the look that belongs to a thing, the single εἶδος which belongs to the many appearances of a being (Sallis 2005, 192). As Socrates makes clear to Theaetetus, the various perceptions which we have of things do not merely sit inside of us in their unconnected multiplicity, but rather "stretch together [συντείνει] toward some one look [εἰς μίαν τινὰ ἰδέαν]" (*Tht.* 184d; my translation). Such a look (ἰδέα) does not simply belong to what is given in perception—to the many appearances themselves—but is by some measure in excess of them. As Sallis writes, "the look toward which perceptions stretch is something beyond, something that exceeds φύσις; and yet, it is the look precisely of something in φύσις, belong[ing] itself, to this extent, to φύσις. In other words, the look is determined by the logic of excess, of *monstrosity*" (Sallis 2005, 192; my emphasis). Thus, the "laughable and wondrous" things (θαυμαστά τε καὶ γελοῖα) of which Socrates speaks are nothing other than the looks of things which, though exceeding φύσις in a decisive sense, nonetheless belong to it in an imminent way. This look is the common (κοινός) that both belongs to the thing of sense and exceeds it, the common that runs throughout the various appearances of the thing as it shows itself in nature but that is not reducible to those appearances. Given that these commons belong intimately to the very nature which they decisively exceed, such commons, such looks, are *monstrous:* they are that which exceeds nature from within nature (Sallis 2005, 193). The looks are monsters so understood.

How is this excess, this monstrosity, to be apprehended? That is, if it is the case (as Socrates has said) that the common looks are not simply manifest to the senses but are in excess of them (*Tht.* 184e ff.), how is it that the human being can become aware of them? Through (δία) what means does such awareness occur? It is Theaetetus who provides the answer: "The soul itself, through itself [αὐτὴ δι᾽ αὑτῆς ἡ ψυχή] . . . looks upon the common things [τὰ κοινά] about all of them" (*Tht.* 185e; my translation). The human soul is that by which the monstrous looks are apprehended. Precisely by coming to apprehend a determinacy from out of the otherwise indeterminate flow of nature, the soul comes to arrest nature, to *hold* (ἔχειν) it,[23] at least insofar as it grasps the commons which arise out of it. Phrased otherwise, it is by coming to apprehend Being through the flow of becoming (*Tht.* 186b)—that is, through its engagement with the beings that give themselves to the bodily senses—that the soul, by stretching out (συντείνω) toward the looks, is able to attain a certain level of determinacy in the face of the flow of φύσις.

However, it is not just any soul that can so stretch. Rather, it takes a certain kind of soul, one uniquely capable of such extension and excess. Within the context of the *Theaetetus*, it is the soul of the philosopher—or, at least, a certain kind of philosopher—which is able to extend itself through the flow of φύσις and toward the determinacy of Being. This philosopher is none other than the young Theaetetus who, through his excessive wonder in the face of the wonderful and laughable things (θαυμαστά τε καὶ γελοῖα), comes to extend himself *beyond* himself (Sallis 2005, 190).[24]

Through letting himself be drawn into excessive wonder, Theaetetus comes to be drawn into a certain apprehension of Being, one which does not lose its connection to φύσις. In other words, Theaetetus comes to exceed himself *monstrously* beyond himself by apprehending those looks which are, in turn, the monstrous excess of φύσις. Theaetetus thereby exemplifies a monstrous apprehension of monstrosity. Theaetetus's awareness of the looks that arise from out of φύσις is a laughable, wondrous, and *monstrous* thing. In this register, it is worth noting that at one point Socrates calls Theaetetus "laughable" (ὦ καταγέλαστε) (*Tht.* 149a). We can only wonder if he is laughable *in his very being*, like those philosophers whom Socrates will soon describe (*Tht.* 174a ff.), and whom we discussed in the Introduction. For our purposes it is of the utmost importance to keep in mind this *laughable* character of the monstrous ascent presented in the *Theaetetus* as we proceed through the *Cratylus*.

We have now seen that the *Theaetetus* presents not just the radical flow of φύσις, but a certain way *beyond* the radical flow, a means by which to arrest it, if only in a certain sense. Through its monstrous stretching beyond the things of sense, but precisely *through* the things of sense, a certain type of soul is able to attain to the Being which is set beyond the things of sense, yet in such a way as to belong essentially to them. To phrase this differently, one might say that the soul, by stretching *through* nature understood as radical flux, comes to rest in nature understood as Being. So understood, one could say that a certain *doubling of nature* occurs whereby the soul stretches itself toward the nature *beyond* nature, the very nature *of* nature.[25] As we turn back to the *Cratylus,* we shall see both the extent to which the dialogue is dominated by the flow of φύσις and the manner by which such flow is mediated.

* * *

All three consequences of Protagoras's doctrine within the *Theaetetus* as Sallis has enunciated them—the dissolution of oneness, of λόγος, and of Being—bear decisively upon the *Cratylus* and are, to a great extent, reinscribed within its pages. The setting there, under the shadow of Protagoras, is no less a setting of radical becoming, of pure appearances, where the very oneness and stability of Being is threatened and where beings are always in motion. Likewise, the scene is no less one of φύσις, a point to which we shall return below. One wonders if this setting of continual motion and φύσις is not already intimated at the outset through the furtive invocation of Hermes, the always itinerant fertility god.[26]

As we have already seen, the dissolution of oneness has already begun to occur through Hermogenes' position that naming is the act of private persons (ἰδιώτης). Because each person will name (i.e., refer to) a being in terms of how it *appears* to him, there are as many names for a being as there are apprehensions of it. This dissolution of oneness can be seen clearly in Socrates' horse/man example. By obtaining Hermogenes' agreement that the same thing (a human being) can be called both a human being and a horse at the same time by different people (385a), Socrates has brought about a scenario in which the unity of the being is divided against itself and disolves into multiplicity.

Socrates' horse/man example also indicates the extent to which the Protagorean doctrine that "the human being is the measure of all things" brings about a dissolution of naming. Precisely by reducing the Being of things to their appearances, thereby shattering the oneness of Being into multiplicity, Protagoras's doctrine brings about a scenerio in which a single name is no longer taken in common to refer to the same being. Further, it is a scene in which the same thing can be called two different things by two different people: that is, one being can have two different names. The dissolution of naming, and thereby λόγος,[27] thus accompanies the dissolution of oneness. One could say that the *Cratylus* is the full and comic articulation of the second consequence of Protagoras' doctrine that "the human being is the measure of all things" as it is analyzed by Socrates in the *Theaetetus*. The *Cratylus* presents, in vivid and comic detail, the devastating dissolution of λόγος that follows upon the Protagorean position.[28] The extent to which is this so will be seen in the analysis of the etymologies in chapter 7.

Finally, the appearance of Protagoras in the *Cratylus* dissolves Being no less than in the *Theaetetus*. This is most readily visible in the etymologies, where most of the names (as Socrates himself will observe) indicate the nature of reality to be in flux (411c).[29] By showing that beings were interpreted by the original name-givers purely in terms of how those beings *seemed* to them (411b), Socrates offers an image that shows the extent to which Being dissolves under such a scenario. Precisely because everything *seemed* (φαίνεται) to be spinning and racing around, the original name-givers gave names that indicated such motion. As a result, beings, which seemed to them to be in motion, *were* in motion for them. (In other words, they, like Protagoras, reduced Being to appearance.) However, as Socrates stresses, it was only because they themselves were in radical motion that the original name-givers named beings in such a way. What the scenario shows is that under the sway of the Protagorean doctrine that "the human being is the measure of all things," where Being reduces to appearance, the stability otherwise thought proper to Being dissolves. It should also be observed that, within such a scenario, the original act of name-giving is a matter of the opinion, if not the wishes, of the original name-givers.

Hermogenes admits that he has sometimes been so perplexed in the face of the problem of naming things as to have been "carried away" (ἐξηνέχθην)[30] into this doctrine of Protagoras's that would refuse Being any stability (386a). Socrates asks: "Well, have you ever been so carried away [ἐξηνέχθης] as not to believe that any man is bad?" (386a; Fowler; trans. modified). Hermogenes responds, marking his reply with a swear: "Zeus, no; but I have often been [carried away] into the belief that certain men, and a good many of them, are very bad" (386b; Fowler; trans. modified).

This repetition of ἐκφέρω, of being carried away, serves a two-fold function. First of all, it foreshadows what will soon be shown by Socrates during the long etymological comedy, both in speech and in deed, to be the consequence of the Protagorean doctrine: namely, a situation in which all beings lack stability and are carried away in the wake of radical flux. Secondly, and relatedly, the word ἐκφέρω serves to evoke the figure of Heraclitus. In the *Theaetetus*, Theodorus mentions certain "Heraclitean things" (τούτων τῶν Ἡρακλειτείων) which are "carried away" (φέρονται) and refuse to stand still (*Tht.* 179e).[31] The repetition of the word ἐκφέρω in the *Cratylus* heralds the eventual arrival of Heraclitus and the extent to which his notions of extreme flux bring about a carrying-away of beings.

Socrates now draws out the consequence of the Protagorean doctrine: namely, that if what Protagoras says is The Truth,[32] and (each) human is indeed the measure of all that is, then it will come to be impossible to distinguish between the good and bad, or the foolish and the wise (386c). Because each thing would *be* as it appeared to each person, no one person could legitimately be called wise and another foolish: for each person's perception could, with equal rights, be called true. Thus, the Protagorean doctrine brings about the collapse of the distinction between truth and falsity.[33] Truth, like Hermogenes, would be carried away along the flow of radical becoming, flowing effortlessly into its opposite. (It should also be observed that such a collapse of truth and falsity would render Socrates' philosophical pursuit of self-knowledge impossible: for how could one ever come to recognize oneself as ignorant if one could never be wrong?)

Such a collapse of truth and falsity would bring about a certain kind of *immediacy* and, indeed, an eradication of the past. This immediacy is immediately introduced in the dialogue through the figure of Euthydemus:

> SOCRATES: But surely, I imagine, it doesn't seem [δοκεῖ] to you to be the way it is according to Euthydemus, that all attributes alike belong to all things at the same time always [πᾶσι πάντα ὁμοίως εἶναι ἅμα καὶ ἀεί], since in that case there couldn't even be decent and worthless people, if virtue and vice alike belonged to everyone all the time. (386d; Sachs)

The invocation of the sophist Euthydemus brings about a kind of collapse into the present, where all things are the same at the same time, always. As scholars have noted, this doctrine is not explicitly attributed to Euthydemus in the dialogue that bears his name. However, a reading of the *Euthydemus* as a whole indeed reveals the manner in which the sophistry of Euthydemus and his brother Dionysodorus brings about such a collapse. Therein, while providing a demonstration of their purported ability to teach virtue quickly (*Euthd.* 273d), the two sophist brothers are engaged by Socrates in a dialectical exchange during which the brothers continually strive to keep the conversation within the limits of the present by disallowing Socrates recourse to statements he or the brothers have previously made (*Euthd.* 287b). Socrates tries on several occasions to resist this collapse by extending the conversation into the past, but on each occasion is rebuked by Dionysodorus for not playing by the rules. The result of this collapse is the elimination of the possibility for error.[34] In such a setting of radical immediacy, there is no possibility for error; that is, everything is as true as anything else, and anything goes. The mention of Euthydemus in the *Cratylus* thus brings about, in a different way, the same sort of collapse as Protagoras has brought about: everything is as it appears at any given moment, without regard for how it previously appeared. Such immediacy belongs intrinsically to φύσις conceived as radical flow: for if everything is in flux, then the past has no stability such that it could even be the past.

In the *Cratylus*, Socrates has mentioned both Protagoras and Euthydemus only to refute them by suggesting that, over against this backdrop of radical becoming and utter immediacy,

> it is clear that things [τὰ πράγματα] have some fixed stability [βέβαιον] of their own, not in relation [οὐ πρὸς] to us or caused by us: they do not vary, swaying up and down [ὑφ' ἡμῶν ἑλκόμενα ἄνω καὶ κάτω] in accordance with our fancy [φαντάσματι], but exist of themselves in relation to their own being by nature [ἀλλὰ καθ' αὑτὰ πρὸς τὴν αὑτῶν οὐσίαν ἔχοντα ᾗπερ πέφυκεν]. (386e; Fowler; trans. modified, my emphasis)

And yet, one wonders if the radical becoming and utter immediacy is indeed here overcome, or if they rather permeate the dialogue until its very conclusion: such as in the etymologies, for example, during which it will be shown that the original name-givers believed beings to be characterized by such radical motion, or in Hermogenes' continual use of δοκέω when responding to Socrates' questions.

In offering his supposition of a stable reality over against the vacillatory play of things caused by our apprehensions of them, Socrates has suggested that such stability is *by nature* (πέφυκεν). In doing so, Socrates has indicated the extent to which the investigation underway in the *Cratylus* is preeminently concerned with nature (φύσις). After his initial refutation of Hermogenes' Protagorean position, and after his assertion that names do indeed have a natural correctness (τὴν φύσει ὀρθότητα ὀνόματος) (391a), the inquiry becomes explicitly concerned with discovering the precise character of such natural correctness (391b). In other words, the inquiry is not merely concerned with *whether* names are correct by convention or by nature, but what it would *mean* for names to be correct *by nature*. Clearly, then, the meaning of φύσις bears greatly upon the task of the *Cratylus*, and is of the utmost importance in determining its philosophical movement.

What is the character of nature, the *nature of nature*, such that names could be given correctly in accordance with it? In the *Theaetetus*, φύσις is considered in terms of radical becoming and ceaseless flow, and to speak "by nature" is to lend one's speech to this radical flow. Though this sense of φύσις is doubtless at play in the *Cratylus* (as already seen in Socrates' treatment of Protagoras), and though the inquiry at large addresses itself to what it means to speak κατὰ φύσιν, the word φύσις involves a certain ambiguity that results in two seemingly incompatible meanings, each of which plays a role in the text. The polyvalence of φύσις is the semantic locus of the very conflict between flux and stability that takes place within the *Cratylus*.

The first commentator to observe this polyvalence was Proclus. In his commentary on Plato's *Cratylus*, Proclus outlines four ways in which φύσις can be understood within the dialogue. First of all, φύσις (τὸ φύσει) can be used to refer to the whole Being (οὐσίαι) of plants and animals, including their parts; secondly, it can refer to the activities and powers of a thing (αἱ τούτων ἐνέργειαι καὶ δυνάμεις); thirdly, φύσις can mean the shadows and reflections in mirrors (αἱ σκιαὶ καὶ ἐμφάσεις ἐν τοῖς κατόπτροις); and finally, φύσις can mean the fabricated images (αἱ τεχνηταὶ εἰκόνες) which are similar but not identical to the archetypes of which they are the images (Proclus 2007, 7.17 ff.).[35]

For the purposes of our inquiry, what this array of uses shows is that, according to Proclus, φύσις can be understood as referring either to the stable Being of a thing (i.e., its οὐσία) *or* its unstable and temporary appearance (i.e., shadows, reflections, even fabricated images). Phrased otherwise, "the nature of a thing" can both mean its nature thought of with respect to its *Being*, and/or its nature thought of with respect to its *becoming*. Understood in this way, the ambiguity at play in the word φύσις corresponds to that in our English word *nature*. On the one hand, we use *nature* to denote the stable essence or being of a thing: "what is the nature of Justice?" On the other hand, we use the word *nature* to refer to what is temporary and fleeting: "the storm is a natural phenomenon," or "the jungle is unmitigated nature." Like φύσις, our word *nature* sustains both seemingly opposed meanings, referring both to the swirl of worldly appearances and to a stable reality in excess of such a swirl.[36]

What Socrates shows through his engagement with Protagoras is that, for the latter, φύσις in understood solely in terms of the swirl of worldly appearances. Protagoras (as well as Homer and Heraclitus, with whom Socrates associates Protagoras) understands the nature of a thing in terms of its becoming, of its unstable appearance.[37] By understanding φύσις purely in terms of the world of fluctuating appearances—of how things *seem* to each person—Protagoras interprets the Being of things in terms of such radical becoming, in terms of nature understood as the apparent world of flowing appearances. Under the sway of such an interpretation, everything is itself in sway, never attaining to even the slightest stability.

What Socrates will show in general is that any operation that seeks to discover the "natural correctness" of names based on such an understanding of nature comes to conceive names in terms of such radical flux. In other words, under such an understanding of nature, names would be correct *by nature* if they disclosed nature as consisting of radical flux. Such disclosure is, of course, precisely what will occur through the long etymological section, where many of the names will describe nature as consisting of radical flow and will be shown to depend upon the dizzy perceptions of the original name-givers (411b). Over against this, Socrates has broached a hypothesis concerning names and their correctness that is informed by another understanding of nature, nature understood in terms of stability (386e). As will be seen in chapter 7, the long etymological section will *show* Socrates attempting to lead Hermogenes into a glimpse of such stability, more particularly, of nature understood as such stability. In a word, Socrates will try to *arrest* the flow of nature, to *ascend* beyond it, precisely through his presentation of nature as consisting of radical flux: and just as in the *Theaetetus,* the ascent will essentially depend upon a monstrous operation of the human soul (in this case, Hermogenes'). The *Cratylus* will thusly present a turn *away* from nature understood simply as the radical flow of worldly appearances, *toward* nature understood as a certain stability of being: that is, it will enact a certain *doubling of nature.*

This turn *from* nature *to* nature in the *Cratylus* is nothing other than a rearticulation of Socrates' so-called "second-sailing" as he describes it in the *Phaedo (Phd.* 99c ff.).[38] As Sallis has observed, the *Cratylus* as a whole is a certain (re-) enactment of Socrates' second-sailing, of his turn toward λόγος and away from nature understood only with respect to the senses (Sallis 1975, 258).[39] The *Cratylus* as a whole shows Socrates making such a turn, a turn toward the names of things, toward λόγος, and attempting to lead Hermogenes into the turn. By working to lead Hermogenes beyond a preoccupation with appearance (with how things merely *seem* to be) toward a stability of being (how things *are*), Socrates is attempting to turn Hermogenes *away* from nature understood *solely* in terms of radical flux *toward* nature understood in terms of monstrous excess. In a word, he is trying to turn him toward Being as it manifests itself in λόγος.

✳ ✳ ✳

We have now seen that in the *Cratylus,* as in the *Theaetetus,* Socrates' engagement with the radical relativism of Protagoras has intimated a certain determinacy of Being, independent of our fancy, which comes about *by nature.* The question is this: will such determinacy as is found in the *Cratylus* be any less laughable and wonderful than it was in the *Theaetetus*? Will such determinacy simply exceed φύσις so as to lose all connection to it, or will it rather exceed it in such a way as to maintain an essential connection with the things of φύσις? In other words, will such determinacy be any less monstrous?

These questions very quickly transform into another more fundamental question, indeed, into the most basic and primary question of the *Cratylus*: *who is Hermogenes?* Is Hermogenes' nature such as never to extend beyond the things of sense, beyond how things *seem* to him? Or is Hermogenes of such a nature as to have his soul extended beyond the things of φύσις and into a glimpse of determinacy? Is he like Theaetetus, whose excessive nature was such as to be capable of extending beyond itself and into a glimpse of those monstrous looks that arise from out of the things of φύσις? In other words, is Hermogenes a *monster*?

To foreshadow what can only come to light through a sustained analysis of the etymological section, Hermogenes will indeed show himself to be monstrous in the sense delimited here. We have already seen that the basic question of the dialogue is whether Hermogenes is the legitimate offspring of Hermes, himself a bit of a monster. Thus, to a certain extent, the question of Hermogenes' monstrosity is implicit in the guiding question of the dialogue: is Hermogenes, as his name says, the son of Hermes?[40] Further, we have already alluded to Hermogenes' tenuous relationship to his father Hipponicus, and his severance from his inheritance. That Socrates will eventually explicitly raise the question of monstrous progeny (393b ff.)—that is, sons that are not at all like their fathers—should alert us to the extent to which the question of Hermogenes' monstrosity, and his corresponding ability to move beyond the things of sense, is at play.

Though Hermogenes will eventually demonstrate a certain monstrous ability to move beyond the senses, his ascent is still far off. Socrates has now led Hermogenes some measure away from the absurdities of the Protagorean position, but Hermogenes is not yet free of its shadow. In the following chapter, Hermogenes, still led by Socrates, will begin to attempt to access this stability of Being beyond φύσις: that is, he will attempt to gain access to the stability of beings that subsists beyond our mere perceptions of them. And yet, as will be seen, Hermogenes will not entirely free himself from the world of perceptions, but will rather come to radicalize the Protagorean position which he has just ostensibly overcome. Thus, though some progress has seemingly been made beyond Hermogenes' supposition that names are correct by virtue of the machinations of human beings, he is about to show the extent to which he is still very much bound to such an understanding of the nature of words, as perhaps are we all.

5 Technological Language

Shortly after having shown the disruption of λόγος and dissolution of Being endemic to the Protagorean position that the human being serves as the measure of beings, Socrates undertakes a demonstration whose apparent purpose is to establish that beings have a stable Being of their own, independently of our perceptions and wishes. Through his refutation of the extreme relativism of Protagoras, Socrates gets Hermogenes to agree that

> things [τὰ πράγματα] themselves have some stable being [οὐσίαν] of their own about them that's not relative to us or dependent on us [οὐ πρὸς ἡμᾶς οὐδὲ ὑφ' ἡμῶν], dragged up and down by our imagining [ἐλκόμενα ἄνω καὶ κάτω τῷ ἡμετέρῳ φαντάσματι], something that they have in virtue of themselves in relation to their own being [ἀλλὰ καθ' αὐτὰ πρὸς τὴν αὐτῶν οὐσίαν], holding on in the very way they are by nature [πέφυκεν]. (386d–e; Sachs; trans. modified)

In other words, things (τὰ πράγματα) have a stability that is independent of our φαντάσματι, of our fancy[1]—independent, one might hazard, of our wills and wishes. This stability is nothing other than the Being of a thing.

Hermogenes agrees to all of this by saying "it seems so to me" (δοκεῖ μοι) (386e). Such a response indicates that, although Hermogenes evidently agrees with Socrates, his language does not yet fully support this agreement: for such stability, as Socrates has just shown with his dismissal of Protagoras, cannot simply be a matter of *seeming*. If it is the case that beings have stability *independently* of how they seem to us, then their independence cannot be a matter of seeming, of δόξα. Thus, despite himself, Hermogenes—or, perhaps, Hermogenes' *language*—is still very much of the opinion that the Being of things is relative to us, to our opining, despite his having just denied his adherence to Protagoras's doctrine.

Socrates then extends the argument beyond things (τὰ πράγματα) and into the realm of doing (πράττειν): "Well, could things themselves [have a stability of their own] by nature while their actions [αἱ δὲ πράξεις αὐτῶν] were not the same way? Aren't they too, the actions, one type of the beings that are [ἕν τι εἶδος τῶν ὄντων εἰσίν?" (386e; Sachs; trans. modified). The suggestion seems to be that, because actions (αἱ πράξεις) are a kind (εἶδος) of being, the stability proper to the latter will belong no less to the former. However, there is some dispute over Socrates' rather peculiar formulation that actions are a kind (εἶδος) of being. Generally, this statement—which, it should be stressed, is not a statement or a syllogism, but a *question* posed to Hermogenes—is taken to mean that an action, as one kind (εἶδος) of the many things that are (τῶν ὄντων), has the stability proper to a being, to something that *is*.[2] Granting that such a sense is at play in Socrates' formulation, John Sallis has further argued that Socrates is suggesting that actions have a "proper nature [φύσις] in accord with the proper being of that *on which they are exercised*" (Sallis 1975, 204; my emphasis)—an interpretation which is borne out in the Stephanus lines that immediately follow. David Sedley, too, picks up on this deeper sense of Socrates' formulation, understanding Socrates to mean that "any action *which is a way of dealing* with [some object] has its own nature" (Sedley 2003, 57; my emphasis). Understood in this deeper sense, Socrates is making a claim not so much about actions as a kind of being, but about human actions insofar as they are *concerned* with beings.

Thus, on the one hand, Socrates' claim that the actions of beings have stability could mean that the actions belonging to a being—that is, whatever actions are actions enacted *by* that being—have a stability akin to the being which is acting. (In this case, the action would borrow or derive its stability from the agent enacting the action.) However, on the other hand, one could also take this to mean that whatever actions are enacted *upon* a being have a stability akin to the being with which they are concerned (and are indeed guided by that being). Understood in this way, the claim that actions have a stability of their own would mean that a human action concerned with a stable being itself has a certain stability, so long as it is in fact guided by the stable being upon which it acts. By saying that doing (πράττειν), like beings (τὰ πράγματα), has a natural stability, Socrates is seemingly suggesting that a human action ought to be guided by the nature of the being with which it deals if it is to obtain the stability of the latter.

There are three points which must be made regarding this understanding of Socrates' claim that actions have a stability akin to beings. First of all, if it is true that actions, as Sedley puts it, "get their own nature derivatively from the things *in relation to which* the agent acts" (Sedley 2003, 57), then the "nature" of an agent's action depends upon the nature of the *particular* thing with which it is in relation. In other words, the nature of an action would be relative to, and contingent upon, the individual being on which it acts *in each case*. Were a *different* being to be acted upon, the nature of the action—say, cutting—would change along with the being with which it engaged. (For example, the nature of the action of cutting a tree would differ from that of cutting a chicken: thus, the natures of the actions would be different in each case; yet, remarkably, in both cases the name of the action [i.e., cutting] would remain the same.) One could ask whether such a consequence threatens the claim that actions, like the beings on which they operate, have a stability proper to them. The "nature" of actions, so understood, would vacillate depending upon the being with which they are concerned.

Secondly, though it is surely the case that Socrates (in the form of a question) has suggested that actions have a nature relative to the being on which they act, it will soon be seen that it is precisely this idea that Socrates will conspicuously avoid as the argument progresses. Given that Socrates has suggested that actions must be guided by the nature of the beings with which they are concerned, one would expect him to immediately emphasize the importance of attaining access to beings in their *particularity:* for without such access, an action would have no hope of being correctly guided.[3] Yet, as will be seen, Socrates will continually avoid the question of access throughout the argument, leading one to suspect finally that something peculiar is going on beneath the surface of the text.

Thirdly, it must be observed that a certain shift has now taken place in the argument. In saying that the actions of beings (i.e., the human actions concerned with beings) have a stability like those beings with which they deal, Socrates has shifted the emphasis from beings in general to *human* beings in particular. Socrates has reoriented the focus away from beings as they are independent of us and toward beings as they are with respect to our actions (πράττειν) concerning them. This shift could be neither more problematic nor more comedic: for it is made right within an attempt to access the stability proper to beings independent of our wills and wishes—that is, *independent of our actions.* In so reorienting the focus, Socrates has quietly begun to undermine the very purported purpose of the inquiry. Socrates will continue to undermine the inquiry as the text continues, emphasizing human actions at the expense of the independent reality of beings.

Socrates has now suggested that actions, like beings, have a stability independent of our wishes: "Therefore actions too are performed in accord with their own nature, not in accord with our opinion" (κατὰ τὴν αὑτῶν ἄρα φύσιν καὶ αἱ πράξεις πράττονται, οὐ κατὰ τὴν ἡμετέραν δόξαν) (387a; Sachs). Socrates then gives a most curious example of this:

> For instance, if we took it upon ourselves to cut [τέμνειν] something, any of the things there are [τῶν ὄντων], is it appropriate for each thing to be cut by us in whatever way we wish [βουλώμεθα] and with whatever we wish [βουληθῶμεν]? Or, is it that if we wish [βουληθῶμεν] to cut each thing [ἕκαστον] in accord with the nature of cutting and being cut, and with something of such a nature as to cut it, we will cut it and get ourselves something by it and accomplish that correctly [ὀρθῶς], while if we do it contrary to nature we'll go astray and accomplish nothing? (387a; Sachs; trans. modified, my emphasis)

To cut merely according to our wishes, merely according to the way that seems most appropriate to us, would accomplish nothing—it would not even be an action at all. Cutting accomplishes its end only insofar as it is guided by the nature of "cutting and being cut and with the natural instrument" of cutting (τοῦ τέμειν

τε καὶ τέμνεσθαι καὶ ᾧ πέφυκε). Such actions must be guided by their own natures, the natures that belong to the actions as such.

Three elements of this example must be noted. To begin with, although
Socrates has just said that actions (such as cutting) are to be done in accordance
with the nature of the actions (i.e., "cutting and being cut"), it must be stressed
that such actions are nonetheless a matter of wishing (βούλεσθαι). Socrates has
said that *if we wish* (βουληθῶμεν) to cut something correctly (ὀρθῶς), *we must
wish* to cut it in accordance with the actions of cutting and being cut, and the
nature of the instrument (τοῦ τέμειν τε καὶ τέμνεσθαι καὶ ᾧ πέφυκε) (387a). Such
actions are not somehow independent of our opinions and wishes, but are still
very much bound to them: it is just that those wishes must be in accordance with
the nature *of the action* if the action is to be done correctly. Thus, although some
advancement seems to have been made beyond the radical δόξα of Protagoras,
the discussion is still bound to opinion, to how things seem to us, to how we wish
for things to be. To say that a correct action is that action which is done through
wishing to act in accordance with nature (κατὰ φύσιν) in no way frees our actions
from being subject to our opinions and wishes: to the contrary, it underscores the
extent to which we are bound to our wishes, wishes that risk *separating* us from
the independent being of things. This is all the more clear given the fact that
nothing has yet been said about how one is to access the nature of a being such
that one could act κατὰ φύσιν—nor, indeed, will it ever be (439b).

The next analogy to which Socrates turns, that of burning, reiterates that our
actions are decidedly dependent upon our opinions and wishes:

> So if we took it upon ourselves to burn something, we should burn it not in
> accord with any and every opinion [οὐ κατὰ πᾶσαν δόξαν], but with the correct
> one [κατὰ τὴν ὀρθήν], and that's the one by which each thing is of such a nature
> [πέφυκεν][4] as to be burned and to burn, by something of such a nature
> [πέφυκεν] as to burn it? (387b; Sachs; trans. modified)

According to this example it is not sufficient simply to burn something in accordance with any opinion or wish: rather, again, one must burn it in accordance
with the correct opinion (κατὰ τὴν ὀρθήν), and that is the opinion that is in accordance with the nature of the action, in this case burning and being burned.
Nevertheless, it should be stressed that, for Socrates, a correct opinion is not the
same as the truth:[5] there is still a distance between how things truly are, independent of us, and how they appear to us such that we can form opinions about them.
How things truly are is still filtered through how they appear to us, or how we
wish for them to be.

Secondly, there is something curious about Socrates' argument. In arguing
for the stability of actions (in this case cutting) Socrates says that we cannot cut
according to any old opinion, but rather must "cut each thing in accord with the
nature of cutting and being cut, and with something of such a nature as to cut it

[τοῦ τέμειν τε καὶ τέμνεσθαι καὶ ᾧ πέφυκε]" (387a; Sachs; trans. modified). In other words, in order to cut something correctly our cutting must be guided by the nature of the *action* of cutting and being cut and the *tool* with which (ᾧ) we cut. Yet, is it the case that actions must be guided by the nature of the *action* and the *tool*? Or should they rather by guided by the nature of the *object* of the action, the thing being acted upon? For example, in cutting something, should cutting be guided solely by the nature of the action of cutting and being cut, as Socrates says, or rather by the nature of the *thing* that is cut, the specific being, say, a chicken? If one were to undertake to cut a loaf of bread *as if* it were a chicken, one could hardly be said to have cut the bread in a manner appropriate to the nature of the bread. Socrates' account of correct cutting omits this aspect, one elementally important to the success of any given action.[6] Rather than accounting for the particular being that is acted upon, Socrates only accounts for the *actions* and the *instrument* ("the *with-which*," ᾧ) acting upon that being. One wonders if such an omission is deliberate, and is yet another example of the comic tendency for Socrates to omit something that cannot in good sense be omitted.

Finally, there is something suspicious about Socrates' analogies. What is the *natural* way to cut something? Is there not rather something about cutting that is in principle *against* nature? Is it not the case that cutting a chicken irrevocably damages the nature of the chicken by working against how the chicken naturally is? And what of burning? Is burning not the sort of thing that precisely *destroys* or *dissolves* some nature by reducing it to ash?[7] Both of the examples which Socrates has offered, cutting and burning, are violent actions which risk, if not outright entail, the disfiguration or destruction of the thing being acted upon. The operation of dissecting a chicken at its "proper" joints in order to grasp its nature is self-defeating: for the operation kills the chicken, thereby dissolving whatever unity its natural state may have had. Rather than preserving the nature of the thing, or bringing that nature to light in a sheltered way, these actions radically transform the thing's nature, if not utterly destroy it. Both cutting and burning are human actions that do violence to the *unity* of that upon which they operate. One wonders if such violence will remain in Socrates' account of the act of naming.

Having obtained Hermogenes' assent that cutting and burning must be done by way of a correct opinion in accordance with the nature of the actions and the instrument (but not, it should be stressed, the being of the thing acted upon), Socrates extends the argument to apply to speaking (λέγειν). As a kind of action (μία τις τῶν πράξεών) (387b), Socrates explains, speaking is bound by the same rules of acting outlined in the two previous examples. Speaking will be correct (ὀρθῶς) not if it is conducted in whatsoever manner seems (δοκῇ) good to someone, but only if that person speaks "in the way it is natural to say [λέγειν] the things and for them to be said [λέγεσθαι] by the means [ᾧ] of such a nature as to say them" (387c; Sachs). Only by speaking in accordance with the nature of speaking and being spoken (λέγειν τε καὶ λέγεσθαι) will such a speaker truly *speak* (ἐρεῖ). If a speaker were to speak otherwise, *against* nature, he would presumably merely be making incoherent noises, as Cratylus will later suggest (430a).

Hermogenes assents to what Socrates has asked by again saying "it seems so to me" (οὕτω μοι δοκεῖ) (387c). This response again hints that the language of the argument has not yet entirely freed actions from human seeming and wishing. Just as was the case with cutting and burning, speaking—if it is to be speaking—cannot be guided by any old opinion, but must proceed after that opinion which follows the nature of saying and being said. Yet, as noted above, *correct* seeming is still a *seeming*: that is, it is still a matter of human δόξα. This further indicates that, just as was the case with cutting and burning, Socrates does not yet account for the particular being with which the action (in this case speaking) is concerned independently of human δόξα. Rather than being guided by the unconcealed nature of the being, the correct speaking is guided by the nature of the *human action*, that is, of speaking and being spoken. Thus, yet again, the being is reduced to the action, and Socrates does not consider the being itself.

Having thus investigated speaking (λέγειν), Socrates now turns his attention to a *part* (μόριον) of speaking, naming (τὸ ὀνομάζειν) (387c; see also 385c). As a part of speaking, which is an action, naming is itself "an action concerned with things [πρᾶξίς τις ἦν περὶ τὰ πράγματα]" (387c). As a result, Socrates asks,

> is it appropriate too for the naming to be done in the way it is natural to name the things and for them to be named [ὀνομάζειν τε καὶ ὀνομάζεσθαι], and by something [ᾧ] of such a nature [πέφυκε] as to name them, rather than in whatever way we want to [βουληθῶμεν] . . . ? And would we achieve something and name something in that way and not otherwise? (387d; Sachs; trans. modified)

Hermogenes agrees: "It appears to me" (φαίνεταί μοι). Hermogenes' response and his conspicuous use of φαίνεται indicate a tension at work within the text. On the surface, Hermogenes is agreeing that human wishing cannot guide the human act of naming (if it is to be correct). Yet, the very language with which he assents—φαίνεταί μοι—subtly indicates that what has been said is still a matter of human fancy, opinion, and wishing, despite whatever progress has seemingly been made beyond Protagoras's extreme relativism, and despite Socrates' earlier claim that beings must have stability independent of our φαντασία (386e).[8] Naming, like cutting / burning / speaking, is still a matter of human opinion and wishing, which must be in accord with the nature of the action and instrument of naming and being-named, but not as of yet the being (or the nature) of the particular thing named. Hermogenes' language, his λόγος, is underscoring the commitment to seeming that naming is subtly being shown to entail. It is almost as if language is disrupting the access to the stable being that Hermogenes, with Socrates as his guide, is seeking.

Socrates then begins to consider in more detail what it is *with which* (τῷ) actions in general are enacted. Socrates asks, and Hermogenes agrees, that whatever must be cut must be cut *with* (τῳ) something. Further, Socrates adds two new examples by suggesting that whatever is to be shuttled (κερκίζειν) must be shuttled *with* (τῳ) something, and that whatever is to be bored (τρυπᾶν) is to be bored *with* (τῷ) something.[9] Likewise, whatsoever needs to be named (ὀνομάζειν) must be named *with* (τῷ) something. In the case of boring (τρυπᾶν), it is a borer (τρύπανον) with which (τῷ) we bore; in the case of shuttling (κερκίζειν), it is a shuttle (κερκίς) with which we shuttle. Finally, in the case of naming (ὀνομάζειν), it is a name (ὄνομα) with which (ᾧ) we name. Thus, a name, like a shuttle and a borer, is that with which a certain action is performed: in other words, a tool (ὄργανον) (388a).

What should be stressed is that both of these new examples, boring and shuttling, are no less violent than the previous two, cutting and burning. A borer is used to drill into the earth, or perhaps wood: its action is one of piercing or penetrating into a natural element so as to disfigure or disrupt its natural condition. In the case of shuttling, the shuttle, as Socrates explains it, is used to disentangle (διακριτικὸν) the mingled threads of warp and woof (388c) so as to prepare them for weaving. In other words, the shuttle is used to unravel or dissolve whatever unity the skeins had. The shuttle is thus used to undo a unity and alter it into a multiplicity—it is used to separate and set apart (in order to bring back together in a new form). Rather than letting the threads be as they are, the shuttle alters them, dissolving their unity so that they may *then* be woven together into some pattern which will consist of disparate, though intermingled, parts. Given that all of Socrates' examples involve a kind of violence against a being that disfigures or dissolves it, one wonders again whether naming will also involve such violence.

Having now said that a name is a tool like so many others, Socrates then describes in detail—though, as he has throughout this exchange, in the form of a question—what kind of tool a name is and what it is that this tool accomplishes. Favoring the shuttling example in particular, Socrates says that "a name is a certain kind of tool meant for teaching and for the disentangling of being [διακριτικὸν τῆς οὐσίας], the same way a shuttle is for a weaver's threads" (388c; Sachs). A name, like a shuttle, disentangles something. In the case of shuttling, it is the threads that are disentangled. In the case of names, however, it is *Being* (οὐσία). Names disentangle Being. It should be noted that οὐσία is here in the genitive singular, as the τῆς indicates. Socrates is not saying that a disentangling or distinguishing of *beings* is underway, but of *Being*. Presumably this means that a name separates one being from some other being and that, when we name something, we distinguish it from the many other beings with which we might otherwise confuse it.[10] Further, it is presumably by fulfilling this function that a name teaches.[11]

And yet, διακριτικός (disentangle), as noted above, can also mean *dissolve* or *break apart*. Socrates could be saying that naming, as a human action to some extent guided by our opinions and wishes, disentangles or dissolves the Being of a being, destroys what is proper to it, just as carding the wool destroys the unity of the fibers by separating them (in order to then spin a thread, and, ultimately, weave a garment), and just as we destroy something when we cut into it or burn it to ash. Given that Socrates' ostensible purpose is to assert a stable unity over against the apparent multiplicity raised by Protagoras's position, it should make us wary that the power of a name seems to lie precisely in the disentangling, or destroying, of such a unity, and is grouped together with other such violent actions.

To further understand this destructive capacity, a brief turn to the *Phaedrus* is instructive. During an inquiry into the nature of beautiful speeches, Socrates explains to Phaedrus two powers of speech which, if mastered, would bring about an excellent λόγος. The first is a matter of grasping the εἶδος of a thing by gathering together the many different appearances of it into a single form (εἰς μίαν τε ἰδέαν) (*Phdr.* 265d). This, Socrates says, is a matter of delimitation (ὁρισθέν). The second is the power "to cut through [διατέμνειν] a composition, form by form, according to its natural joints [κατ' ἄρθρα ᾗ πέφυκεν] and not to try to hack through any part as a bad butcher might" (*Phdr.* 265e; Scully; trans. modified). The one who held this second power would cut a thing according to its "natural joints," thus dismembering it *according to nature*.[12]

However, there is a problem with Socrates' example. As suggested above, even a good butcher, one who cuts at the "natural joints," destroys the unity of that which he cuts (i.e., he kills the animal). Likewise, even one who burns things expertly does so in such a way as to destroy that which he burns.[13] It is the very nature of such activities as cutting and burning to fundamentally alter if not destroy that upon which they operate, just as it is the very nature of carding to first dissolve a clew of yarn in order to then weave a garment. A good butcher is still a butcher—he still robs the animal of its nature, still alters and destroys what the animal naturally is in order to submit it to some human purpose. The very act of butchering is by nature violent to nature.

Thus, when Socrates says in the *Cratylus* that the purpose of a name is to disentangle Being (διακριτικὸν τῆς οὐσίας) along the lines of his various violent examples, one cannot help but wonder if the act of naming is any less violent to Being and to nature. The violence of naming, and the extent to which it is against nature, is implicit in what we have already seen: that naming, as an action, is always to some extent guided by human opinion and wishing, and often at the expense of the being itself. Despite Socrates' claim that "actions revealed themselves to us as not being relative to us [αἱ δὲ πράξεις ἐφάνησαν ἡμῖν οὐ πρὸς ἡμᾶς οὖσαι], but as having a certain particular nature of their own [ἀλλ' αὐτῶν τινα ἰδίαν φύσιν ἔχουσαι]" (387d; Sachs), we have seen that even when we wish to act κατὰ φύσιν, our actions are still a matter of wishing and opining. All actions still involve our opinions and wishes: consequently, they cannot help but be violent to some extent to the otherwise independent nature of a thing.

There is thus always something arbitrary, in the sense of willful, about actions such as dividing, cutting, weaving, burning, and, indeed, *all human actions as such*. Human actions are always to some extent subject to human opinions and wishes, to βούλεσθαι—and this holds for naming no less, so long as it is understood along the model of other actions. Even when we opine or wish in accordance with the nature of actions, we are still, as acting human beings, opining and wishing. Thus, so long as naming is considered to be an action akin to others, it is no less bound by the arbitrary character of human opinions and wishes.[14] Such is the violence of naming *so understood*, a violence emphasized through Socrates' violent examples. The violence of a name lies in its dependence upon human wishing and its subsequent inability to account for the independent Being of the thing named—an inability which is stressed through Socrates' omission of this crucially important element.

This arbitrary character of human actions is implicit in Socrates' classification of a name as a kind of tool (ὄργανον). To classify a name as a kind of tool is to reduce the activity of naming to an operation of the human will. One only cuts the chicken when one wants to eat it; one only bores the hole into the earth when one wants to drill for water or oil; one only unravels the thread from the skein when one wants to weave a blanket for the coming cold. Each of these actions is undertaken in order to meet some human want, to appease some human wish, to fulfill some human purpose. By designating a name as a kind of tool Socrates has both limited its ability to disclose a being in its natural unity and its ability to operate independently of the will of the human being. Yet, it was precisely in order to discover the independent reality of things that Socrates undertook this part of the inquiry in the first place (386a). Thus, by considering a name as a kind of tool, Socrates has quietly undermined the purpose for which he and Hermogenes had set out.

* * *

It is of the utmost importance to observe that throughout this development of the so-called "tool analogy" Socrates has been proceeding in the interrogative mode. It has been through the asking of questions that Socrates has drawn out the argument, one which is merely an elaboration of Hermogenes' premise that names are correct by agreement and custom (384c), correct, therefore through an operation of the human will. The "tool analogy" is a consequence of Hermogenes' position that names can be changed at will, like the names of slaves (384d). Thus, the argument belongs not to Socrates, who knows nothing of these matters (384c; 391a), but to Hermogenes.[15] Socrates has been developing Hermogenes' thesis that naming is a matter of human agreement and custom, and thus a matter of the human will, precisely in order to mark the limits of such a thesis. By obtaining Hermogenes' agreement that speaking is an action like so many others, and that a name is a tool, Socrates has in fact shown that such a position reduces naming to an action ineluctably dependent upon the human will, one which therefore cannot simply let beings show themselves as they are, but always damages if not destroys them by distorting them through the lens of human opinion. By proceeding in the interrogative mode, Socrates has made the thesis itself questionable, and has distanced himself from its implications.[16]

Socrates continues to test, always in the interrogative mode, this understanding of a name as a kind of tool. In particular, Socrates begins to examine whose work an artisan uses when he uses a particular tool. A weaver (ὁ ὑφάντης), for example, uses (χρήσεται) the work (ἔργῳ) of the skilled carpenter (τέκτονος) when he uses the shuttle: that is, he uses the shuttle which the carpenter made (388c).[17] The borer (ὁ τρυπητής), for his part, uses the work (i.e., the bore) of the skilled blacksmith (χαλκέως) when he undertakes to bore something. Socrates then extends this line of argument to names, neglecting for the moment the discursive function of naming and focusing exclusively on its didactic use:

> SOCRATES: And whose work will someone who can teach be using when he uses a name?
>
> HERMOGENES: I cannot say.
>
> SOCRATES: Can you not at least say this, who gives us the names that we use?
>
> HERMOGENES: No, I cannot.
>
> SOCRATES: Does it not seem [δοκεῖ] to you that custom [ὁ νόμος] is what gives them?[18]
>
> HERMOGENES: Seemingly [ἔοικεν].
>
> SOCRATES: Therefore someone who can teach will be using the work [ἔργῳ] of a lawgiver [νομοθέτου] when he uses a name?[19]
>
> HERMOGENES: It seems that way to me [δοκεῖ μοι].[20] (388d–e; Sachs; trans. modified)

Having stressed in each other case that it is not merely anyone who can make the artifact which comes to be used by an artisan, but only one with the requisite skill (τὴν τέχνην) (388c), Socrates concludes that "giving names does not belong to every man but to a certain 'name-giver' [ὀνοματουργοῦ],[21] and it looks like that person is the lawgiver, the rarest of craftsmen [τῶν δημιουργῶν] who come along among humankind" (389a). Just as with the other crafts, using names depends upon the work of another, the name-giver, the one who makes and sets the names. The name-giver is thus a kind of carpenter, or technician, who makes the tool that those who use names use.

Given Socrates' harsh (albeit exceedingly nuanced) condemnation of carpentry (ὁ τέκτων) in Book X of the *Republic* (*Rep.* 596a ff.), the association of the art of name-giving with carpentry should put us on our guard. Such an association would reduce name-giving to a kind of mimetic art which, as such, would be hindered by the epistemological limitations of *mimesis*.[22] The limitation most relevant to our inquiry is the extent to which *mimesis* forever remains a matter of human opinion, of how something *seems* to a human being. That name-giving is to be thought of as a mimetic art is established in the very next sequence of the *Cratylus,* where it is considered what precisely the name-giver must have in view when making the names.

Again, Socrates proceeds by way of analogy. Just as the carpenter, when making a shuttle, looks to "some sort of thing which would be of such a nature as to comb on the loom" (389a; Sachs)—that is, to the look (τὸ εἶδος) of a shuttle (389b)—so too must the name-giver (here simply called the custom-setter [ὁ νομοθέτης]) fix his gaze upon "the very thing which a name *is* [αὐτὸ ἐκεῖνο ὃ ἔστιν ὄνομα] in order to make and establish *all the names* [πάντα τὰ ὀνόματα], if he's going to be an authoritative giver of names" (389d; Sachs; my emphasis).[23] In other words, the name-giver must look to what a name *is* (ὃ ἔστιν ὄνομα), to the look of Name (τὸ τοῦ ὀνόματος εἶδος) (390a), and not to any given particular name, just as a shuttle maker must look to the look of Shuttle rather than any particular shuttle. Just like any craftsman, the name-giver must first look to the look of that which he makes, in this case the look of Name.

It is important to stress that Socrates is not here saying that such a name-maker should look to the *thing* of which the name is a name, that is, the particular being. Though this would seem to be precisely what is needed in order for a name to bring the being of a thing to language, Socrates instead suggests that the name-giver look to "the look of name" (τὸ τοῦ ὀνόματος εἶδος). The precise sense of this peculiar formulation has been an opaque matter of strenuous debate. By briefly summarizing some of the scholarship on this question, a general truth concerning the passage will become clear, one which bolsters the interpretation being offered here.[24]

Francisco Gonzalez takes the curious phrase "the look of name" to refer to the *form* of a name, over against its syllabic material, where this form is equivalent to its *function* of referring to one stable nature apart from others (i.e., its ability to distinguish some being from another) (Gonzalez 1998, 66). Ultimately, for Gonzalez, this function (or form) reduces to the manner in which a name is *used* (ibid., 67). Sedley, too, takes the "the look of name" to refer to the generic function of a name to serve "as a tool for instructing by separating being" (Sedley 2003, 82).[25] It should be noted that both authors thus interpret "the look of name" as reducing to the *use,* or the function, of a name (though they do so in wildly different contexts). The εἶδος of a name is what a name *does,* its proper function.

Calvert takes "the look of name" to refer to the general function of a name to refer to something—that is, to *mean* something (Calvert 1970, 33). However, Calvert sees a distinction between this general function (called the Form of Name) and a more specific function attributable to the "proper form," a distinction which he traces along mostly philological lines. What should be stressed here is that even if this distinction holds, the fact remains that under such an interpretation the "proper form" is guided not by the particular being in question, but by the task at hand, the particular human project at issue.[26] In other words, the proper form is dependent upon the human being's *use* of the name.

Weingartner similarly takes "the look of name" to refer to the function of a name, just as the "shuttle that is" refers to the function of the shuttle (Weingartner 1970, 19). Weingartner perspicaciously concludes that, so understood, "the measure of the correctness of a name is [thus] not the thing named . . . [but rather] its suitability in the pursuit and communication of knowledge" (Weingartner 1970, 20). In other words, the name is determined *not* by the being of the thing in question as it subsists independently of us, but rather by the *purpose* or end to which the act of naming has been directed (in this case, teaching).[27] Thus, the name is determined in accordance with human actions, and *not* in accordance with the being as it is independent of such actions.

Whereas Calvert takes the ambiguity of the expression "form of name" and the utter inability of Socrates to elaborate upon it to indicate Plato's confusion regarding the precise character of the term (Calvert 1970, 34, 47), such ambiguity could just as well mark a failure of the analogy at work in Socrates' argument. Further, *the ambiguity and peculiarity could be precisely what we, as readers, are meant to dwell on.* As already seen, far from being Socrates' own theory of naming (the having of which he has already disavowed twice), the so-called tool analogy is a deliberately *false* analogy pursued in order to show the absurdities and inconsistencies endemic to it and the Protagorean position from which it arises. The most salient absurdity is the idea of the "form of name," to which we shall return shortly. First, however, we must follow Socrates' own further development of the analogy.

After the craftsman has discovered the correct tool suited to some particular use, Socrates continues, "he needs to impart to the material out of which he is making it not whatever sort of attribute he himself wishes [βουληθῇ], but the sort that naturally belongs" (389c; Sachs; trans. modified). For example, the craftsman of the drill must know how to shape the iron in such a way that it is appropriate to its particular use (389c). Likewise, the craftsman must know how to set the shuttle into wood in accordance with the purpose of the act of weaving (389d). In the case of the name-maker, this would mean that the custom-giver must be able to set the look of the name into sounds and syllables (εἰς τοὺς φθόγγους καὶ τὰς συλλαβὰς) (389d). Further, just as both the look of the drill and the iron into which it is placed will be guided by the intended *use* of the drill, so too, presumably, must the look of a name and the syllables into which it is set be guided by the intended use of the name.

Despite what other commentators have said about this analogy, what it preeminently shows is that, yet again, the name is to be guided not by the *being* of which it is the name, but by the *activity* to which the name will be put to use. What is important for our purposes is that "the Name that is," whatever it proves to be, is not the *being* of whatever being is in question, the being of which the manufactured name would be the name. Rather, "the Name that is" is a kind of paradigmatic Name which, in keeping with the analogy to other τέχναι, serves as the model on which manufactured names are based. Rather than saying that, in naming, one should look to the particular being itself which is to be named, Socrates has now suggested, following the technological model, that one should look to the "Name itself" and to its intended use.[28] This move is a further extension of Socrates' general and comic avoidance of the *particular being* to which the name is to be attached.

What comes to light through such avoidance is that the tool analogy which Socrates has employed does not work.[29] If a craftsman undertakes to build a shuttle, according to Socrates he should look to what a shuttle looks like in general, and to the action for which the shuttle is designed (namely, its purpose, weaving). In the case of a name, Socrates claims, the name-giver should look to the Name in general, "the Name that is," as if "the Name itself" were a paradigm for names analogous to the Shuttle that is a paradigm for shuttles. And yet, if this were so, then the name-giver, in making names, would make all names in accordance with the paradigmatic Name itself (αὐτὸ ἐκεῖνο ὅ ἔστιν ὄνομα), precisely thereby overlooking the individual beings in question. As a result, all names would be copies of the same paradigm: they would all be the same, albeit with eventual differences in (syllabic) material (once they became sounded). In other words, all names, despite their differences, would name (i.e., refer to, indicate) the same: namely, the Name itself.

Yet, it was said by Socrates earlier (in the interrogative mode) that the purpose of naming is to disentangle Being. If this is indeed the function of a name, then a name cannot be made by looking to the ideal Name: for if the name-maker always looked to the same Name itself, then all names would be copies of this same Name and would in no way formally distinguish themselves from each other. In a word, there would be an utter collapse of formal difference, of distinction, the likes of which only a Protagoras or Euthydemus would approve.[30] If the name-maker wanted to make each name in such a way that it accorded with the nature of the particular *being* it named, then the only viable option would be for him to look to the *being* itself, to the being which is to be named in each case—an option which Socrates has so far conspicuously avoided but which, much later, he will insist upon (439a–b).

Considered most generally, Socrates' treatment of naming as one kind of τέχνη among others has alerted us to the limitations that belong to τέχναι as such.[31] All τέχναι are bound to the constraints of the *purposes* toward which they are oriented. It is the very character of a τέχνη to be guided and governed by the purpose or end for which it is employed.[32] For example, the τέχνη of medicine is a type of knowledge governed by the purpose of maintaining or restoring the health of the human body.[33] Insofar as this is the case, human τέχνη is a matter of the human will, of human wishes (i.e., the wish to preserve a human life). A τέχνη is a knowledge concerning the means by which we accomplish what we wish.

Further, as Socrates eventually makes clear, naming understood as a τέχνη is bound by the limitations of *mimesis*. Much later in the dialogue, during his conversation with Cratylus, Socrates draws a curious comparison between naming and *painting* (ζωγραφία) (424d). After Socrates has made it clear that the technological view of naming treats naming as an art (τέχνη) of imitation (423b), he examines how precisely one would bring about such an imitation. Such a procedure would involve matching letters and syllables to that which they image, the same way painters (οἱ ζωγράφοι) match the color of their pigments (φαρμάκων) to that which they paint. Exactly like these painters, Socrates continues,

> we too will apply the letters to the things, one to one to what seems to require it, or several together, making precisely what people call syllables, and in turn putting together the syllables of which the nouns and verbs are composed. And out of the nouns and verbs again we will organize at last something great, beautiful, and whole, like the painting in our example from visual art; here it is speech, due to skill at name-giving or rhetoric or whatever art it is. (424e–425a; Sachs; trans. modified)[34]

What was called the august and most rare art of name-giving (389a; 390d) is now seen to be the same as the mimetic procedure of painting a likeness. Further, though the sort of person in question was earlier called a craftsman (δημιουργός) (389a), a painter is by no means a craftsman in a classical sense. Rather, a painter is an *imitator* (ἡ μιμητής) of that which craftsmen make. By now comparing the name-maker's art to painting, Socrates indicates the mimetic quality essential to it.

The comparison between naming and painting brings to mind Socrates' analysis of painting in Book X of the *Republic*.[35] In his famous three-fold division, Socrates distinguishes a painter (ὁ ζωγράφος) of a couch from the craftsman (δημιουργός) of that couch,[36] and both from the god who produced (ἐργάσασθαι) that couch in nature (*Rep.* 597b). The couch which is *by nature* (φύσει), the couch which *is* (*Rep.* 597c), is produced by the god, whom Socrates calls the "nature-maker" (φυτουργός) of the couch. The human craftsman, looking to this couch "in nature," fashions a copy as he builds his own couch (*Rep.* 596b). Such a copy, *as* a copy, is not the same as the true couch which it copies, and is thus at a certain remove from it. The painter, as making a copy *of* a copy, stands at even further remove from the true couch, the couch which is by nature (*Rep.* 598a). As a τέχνη thoroughly limited by *mimesis*, painting stands at third remove *from nature*: the painter does not imitate the nature, but rather the work of the craftsman (who imitates nature) (*Rep.* 598a).[37]

Socrates' comparison of naming with painting in the *Cratylus*, examined in light of the passage from the *Republic*, serves to raise concerns regarding the limits of any such understanding of naming. If naming is a tool by which a technician names a being, analogous to the manner by which a painter paints a likeness, then a name could at best be considered an image *of* an image which stands thrice removed from the truth. Further, as a likeness brought about by human agency, the name—that is, the *image*—is necessarily filtered through the vision, not to mention the opinions, of the agent. Socrates' comparison of naming to painting thus further underscores the manner in which the technological view of naming *traps* human beings within the realm of semblance and opinion. On this view, the name-maker is nothing other than a kind of painter, a kind of imitator set at third remove from the truth, one who makes a name based solely on how it appears to him. For our purposes, it is especially interesting that in the *Republic* Socrates aligns the *tragedian* (ὁ τραγῳδοποιός) with such an imitator, claiming that he is also at third remove from the truth (*Rep.* 597e). As will soon be seen, the tragedian will also appear in the *Cratylus* as a kind of imitative technician, one no less removed from the nature of beings. Further, it will be precisely a *tragic* understanding of λόγος that Socrates will show to be utterly trapped within the world of mere appearances.

Through Socrates' development of the technological view, there thus arises a certain tension between τέχνη and φύσις. On the one hand, what is needed is an act of naming which is guided not by the wishes of the name-giver, but rather by the nature (φύσις) of the being itself. On the other hand, insofar as the act of naming has been relegated to the spheres of *mimesis* and τέχνη, it remains decisively within the limits of human action and, thus, human wishing. Insofar as naming is a human τέχνη it is limited in its ability to allow the nature of a thing to show itself as it is independently of our wishes. By developing a theory of language along the lines of a τέχνη Socrates has made it all but impossible that naming would let the nature of a being show itself as such independently of our wishes. The technological model of naming, so understood, is fundamentally opposed to nature.[38]

This tension between τέχνη and φύσις merely rearticulates the tension voiced at the very beginning of the *Cratylus* between convention (συνθήκη) and nature (φύσις) (384d). Hermogenes' position that names are correct solely through convention leads (though perhaps not ineluctably) to the position that names are tools under the mastery of the human will, tools to be used in the service of the τέχνη of naming. On such a model, names are not generated naturally—they are *made, set* (τίθημι), established, wrought, and contrived by the wishes of the name-makers. There is no question, then, of there being a pure lineage between a being and its name, an uninterrupted and *natural* inheritance between them. The technological model serves to disrupt the passage from being to name, inserting human τέχνη in between them. Such a model, while purporting to bring us closer to the being of things, in fact severs us from them irremediably.[39]

* * *

Given the reduction of naming to τέχνη, and the connection between τέχνη and a preoccupation with *use*, it is not surprising that Socrates immediately turns to a discussion concerning the use (χρήσεται) of names.[40] In the following pages,

Socrates will subordinate the entire project of name-making to the proper use of names, thereby subjecting the name-maker to the rule (or the measure) of the name-user.

The conversation focuses on who in particular will serve as the judge of whether or not a name has been so constructed as to embody the nature of the Name itself. Socrates still proceeds by way of analogy with other τέχναι. In the case of the shuttle, Socrates suggests that it is the weaver (ὁ ὑφάντης), rather than the shuttle-maker, who is the most qualified to judge whether the shuttle has been properly made (390b). In the case of a lyre, it is the lyre-player, not the lyre-maker, who knows whether it has been well or poorly made (390b). Likewise, it is the navigator (i.e., the one who helms the ship) who is best qualified to superintend the manufacturing of a ship (390c). Finally, as regards "the works of the custom-setter" (τῷ τοῦ νομοθέτου ἔργῳ) (i.e., names) it is the one who *uses* (χρήσεται) words who is best qualified to say whether or not they have been expertly made (390c).

Before proceeding to examine more closely who precisely this name-user is, it must be noted that this section has further emphasized the extent to which Socrates is focusing on action and use, and ignoring the particular being which is acted upon. What has *not* been said is that the name-giver must depend upon the person who best knows the *nature* of the things which are to be named: that is, the person who best knows about Being and beings. Rather, it is the user of names who is to serve as the measure of whether or not a name is correct. In other words, the fruits of the name-maker's art are reduced to the purposes of those who will use them. While it could be true that it is the user who *happens* to know best the nature of beings and Being, this is in no way specified or implicit: all that is said is that they know best how to use (χρήσεται) names.

As it turns out, it is not just any name-user that will serve as the measure of a name, but one exemplary class in particular:

SOCRATES: And is not [the name-user] the person who knows how to ask questions?
HERMOGENES: Very much so.
SOCRATES: And the same person also knows how to answer them?
HERMOGENES: Yes.
SOCRATES: And do you call [σὺ καλεῖς] someone who knows how to ask and answer questions anything other than a dialectician [διαλεκτικόν]?
HERMOGENES: No, just that. (390c; Sachs; trans. modified)

What should especially be observed is the manner in which this section enacts in deed what it says in λόγος. Socrates asks whether or not the name-user knows how to ask questions and answer them, to which Hermogenes answers "yes." What this suggests is that Socrates and Hermogenes are currently involved in a dialectical display of name use.[41] Indeed, it is immediately after this privileging of questioning and answering that Socrates and Hermogenes will turn to a testing of a certain set of names, namely, those given by Homer. (We shall return to this in the next chapter.) Additionally, it must be noted that it is Hermogenes, and not Socrates, who wants such name-users to be called "dialecticians." Socrates asks, "and you call [σὺ καλεῖς] someone who knows how to ask and answer questions a dialectician [διαλεκτικόν]?" It is thus left undecided whether or not Socrates would call such a person a dialectician.[42] It remains to be seen whether Hermogenes' answer was a good one, and whether he does indeed know how to answer questions well.

What this passage discloses above all is that the name-maker, though rare (389a) and exceedingly important, is subservient to the preeminent name-user, whom Hermogenes believes to be the dialectician. The act of name-making is thereby shown to be subservient to the asking and answering of questions. In other words, it is in order to meet the *purposes* and *wishes* of the dialectician that the rare name-maker makes names.[43] Thus, name-making is still subject to human action, here specifically to the projects of the dialectician, and thus to his opinions and wishes.

Socrates' claim—that it is the one who knows how to ask questions and answer them who most knows how to use names—should be examined more closely: for to a certain extent it begins to disrupt the general picture of mastery that the technological view of language has presented. The one who asks questions is in general one who *lacks* mastery over that about which he inquires: that is, he lacks knowledge, failing to grasp the matter at hand. Further, one who knows how to ask questions *well* is one who knows that one does not know that about which he asks: that is, one who is aware of his own ignorance in the face of such questioning. Such a person, knowledgeable only of his ignorance, knows that he does not master that about which he speaks. In other words, the one who knows how to ask questions well—whom Hermogenes, but not Socrates, affirms is the dialectician—is one who knows that he knows nothing: in a word, Socrates.[44]

However, insofar as the figure of the dialectician arises out of an analogy with other users, it remains within the limits of such an analogy.[45] The dialectician, like a steersman, is presented as a user of a product that some other person makes, a user who, in knowing how to best use the product, serves as a kind of supervisor of the process of manufacturing. To the extent that the dialectician remains a user (albeit an exemplary one), his office remains bound by the limitations of human use—by the wishes and wills of human beings. The dialectician supervises the making of names to ensure that they efficiently and efficaciously serve his purposes, his ends (i.e., teaching and delimiting beings). The dialectician ensures the appropriate construction and employment of names: he is a master technician.

The technological view of language, and the extent to which it remains bound to human will and opinion, is most fully illustrated later in the dialogue when Socrates offers an oracle (μαντεύεσθαι) regarding the supposed original name-givers, those "very ancient men" who fashioned many of the first names for the Greeks. Prefacing his description with a swear (by the Dog!),[46] Socrates offers the following:

> [T]hose very ancient human beings who established names [οἱ πάνυ παλαιοὶ ἄνθρωποι οἱ τιθέμενοι τὰ ὀνόματα] were just like a lot of our wise people [οἱ πολλοὶ τῶν σοφῶν] today who get dizzy from turning around repeatedly in circles while searching for the way things are, and then it appears [φαίνεται] to them that the things [τὰ πράγματα] are turning around [περιφέρεσθαι] and shifting [φέρεσθαι] in every way. So they ascribe the cause of this opinion [τῆς δόξης] not to an internal experience [πάθος] of their own, but to the things themselves [αὐτὰ τὰ πράγματα], as being that way by nature, none of them being still or stable but flowing [ῥεῖν] and shifting [φέρεσθαι] and constantly filled with motion and generation of every sort [γενέσεως ἀεί]. (411b–c; Sachs)

Those ancient name-givers, rather than attending to the things themselves, let themselves be misled by their own opinions (δόξα) about things, opinions which informed their naming of the many beings (as is evident in the many etymologies suggestive of motion). The act of name-giving, on this view, is thus decidedly bound and guided by human opinion, and to an extent that reduces beings to the way they appear.

It almost goes without saying that such a scene as Socrates has just described merely rearticulates, now by means of an oracle, the Protagorean scene of radical becoming which was described in the preceding chapter. There, as we saw, a scene developed in which the reduction of Being to appearances brought about the utter disruption of the unity of Being, λόγος, and finally Being itself. Here, Socrates has described a situation in which the original name-givers, guided by how beings *seem* to them, confer names which bespeak just such radical flux and corresponding lack of stability. In both cases, the action of naming, precisely *as* an action, is bound to the realm of human opinion.

Recalling that Socrates has stressed again and again that naming *cannot* be guided by our wishes, if we are to say things how they are, the ridiculous character of the tool analogy comes to the fore. A theory of language that would place names under the mastery and wishes of human beings—what is here being called the technological view—is incapable of letting things show themselves as they are independent of our wishes: for such a theory, as the scene of the original name-givers shows, is ultimately dependent upon how things *seem* to human beings. If one understands naming as a τέχνη, then the best one can do is trace names back to an original *opinion* concerning the being, but *not the being itself* (436b). The technological model thus severs human beings decisively from beings as they are independent of our opinions.

The position which Hermogenes seems to hold—what has often been given the ambiguous title "conventionalism"—has thus been shown by Socrates to lead to a scenario in which names are tools whereby we name things in accordance with the way they seem to us, subject to our projects and tasks, our wills and wishes.[47] To this extent, naming, under such a model, *traps* us in the realm of human opinion, effectively cutting us off from nature, from the divine, and from the truth of Being.

* * *

Somewhat later, during his long string of etymologies, Socrates will offer one in particular that sheds light on what we have just seen. Immediately after offering his description of Hermes' name, Socrates moves from the father to the son. Taking Pan (Πᾶν), the son of Hermes (408b), as a paradigm to better understand λόγος, Socrates offers the following:

> Well, then, the true part [τὸ ἀληθὲς] of [Pan's nature] is smooth and divine, dwelling above amongst the gods [ἄνω οἰκοῦν ἐν τοῖς θεοῖς], while the false part [τὸ ψεῦδος] is below among the multitude of human beings, and is shaggy and tragic [τραγικόν];[48] for this is where most of the myths and falsehoods are [οἱ μῦθοί τε καὶ τὰ ψεύδη ἐστίν], in the tragic life [περὶ τὸν τραγικὸν βίον]. (408c; Sachs; trans. modified)

Pan is thus dual-natured (διφυής): on the one hand, his nature is such as to be immersed within the human realm, where myth and falsity (οἱ μῦθοι τε καὶ τὰ ψεύδη) reign; on the other hand, his nature is such as to be amongst the gods (ἄνω οἰκοῦν ἐν τοῖς θεοῖς), where truth holds sway. This former condition—which is the condition of the multitude of human beings (πολλοῖς τῶν ἀνθρώπων)—is what Socrates calls "the tragic life" (τὸν τραγικὸν βίον). The tragic life is the life which dwells exclusively and unreflectively in the lower part, that rough part utterly pervaded by myth (οἱ μῦθοι) and falsehood (τὰ ψεύδη).

It should be noted that οἱ μῦθοι and τὰ ψεύδη—myths and falsehoods—are not taken by Socrates to be equivalent. Far from being a mode of dissembling, μῦθος operates within Plato's works, alongside other modes of λόγος (argument, dialogue, etc.) as a means of disclosure[49]—that is, as a means of revealing something, of making something manifest.[50] However, μῦθος differs from other such modes insofar as it operates at a more obscure or opaque level[51]—a level often meant to mirror the topic with which it is concerned.[52] Thus, μῦθος tends to make something manifest *in a concealed way*, in a way that lets what must remain concealed so remain. Owing to this commitment to concealment, and insofar as it lacks the clarity and transparency of other modes of λόγος (such as argument or proof), μῦθος stands "closer" to falsity than these other modes.[53] Like Pan and λόγος, myth and falsity, too, are brothers.

In describing the tragic life (τὸν τραγικὸν βίον) as consisting of myth *and* falsity, Socrates is indicating the extent to which the human being, in its *here* (ἐνταῦθα), relates toward the truth in a concealed way. Whereas the gods dwell amongst the truth (408c) and relate directly (if not immediately) to it, the human being's way of relating to the truth takes place, for the most part, either as falsity or as myth. Myth is a mode of disclosure *proper* to the human condition, and though it is by no means the same as falsity, the two tarry alongside one another in the human realm and set the horizons of human experience. Μῦθος, as a way of λόγος, belongs to the human being, and sets the human being apart from the gods. Myth and falsity are what stand *between* gods and humans, serving to connect *and* to separate them.

Continuing, Socrates says that that which reveals all (πᾶν) and keeps it in motion would correctly (ὀρθῶς) be called "Pan the goatherd," "the dual-natured son of Hermes [διφυὴς Ἑρμοῦ ὑός], smooth in his upper parts but rough and goat-like [τραγοειδής] in his lower ones" (408d; Sachs). Then, most importantly, Socrates finishes his description of Pan with the following: "And Pan either *is* λόγος or is the brother [ἀδελφὸν] of λόγος, if indeed he's Hermes' son [εἴπερ Ἑρμοῦ ὑός ἐστιν]— and for brother to be like brother is nothing to be wondered at" (408d; Sachs; trans. modified). This dual-natured son of Hermes is thus either the brother of λόγος or is λόγος itself. If the latter, then λόγος, like Pan, must be seen as dual-natured, as having a nature that is both "smooth and divine" and a nature that is thoroughly pervaded by myth and falsehood. This dual nature, of course, was already attributed to λόγος much earlier, where it was said that λόγος was capable of both truth and falsity (385b). Additionally, we saw in chapter 2 that it is precisely because of its filial connection to Hermes that λόγος has this capacity: for the mischievous Hermes, himself beyond credibility, imbues his son λόγος with its fatal ambiguity. Both the essential ambiguity of λόγος and its connection to Hermes are reiterated in Socrates' description of the great goatherd Pan.[54]

The tragic life, then, is the life which is lived primarily within the lower parts of λόγος. As Sean Kirkland has argued, what makes this particular life tragic is not just its immersion in falsity, but the inability of those living it to recognize the essentially dual nature of λόγος (Kirkland 2007, 10). As Kirkland writes, such people "do not see the divine aspect of the λόγος that opens humans up to divine wisdom, but take the obscuring lower half alone as the sufficient and true whole of Language" (ibid.). It is thus due to their inability to become aware of the upper, divine nature of λόγος that the many remain so decisively in the lower, concealing part. It is precisely because they do not recognize λόγος as having a dual nature that the many remain trapped within the world below, the world of myth and shadows.

So understood, the tragic life is that life wherein the lower part of λόγος presents itself *as the whole,* while in fact being only a part, and the inferior part at that.[55] To phrase this otherwise, the tragic λόγος is the one which presents itself as being the whole truth while it is in fact merely a part, or perhaps an *image,* of the truth. The tragic λόγος thinks that it knows everything, while in fact it knows nothing: it lacks awareness of its concealing character, and it is precisely this lack that makes it tragic. The tragic λόγος is the λόγος that shows itself as having mastered everything, while in fact it has mastered nothing.

With Socrates' description of the dual-natured Pan we are thus given an image of λόγος which presents λόγος as two-fold. If one, with all due reticence, were to compare this image with another image—that of the cave from Book VII of Plato's *Republic*—one would come to understand the tragic life as itself consisting of nothing but *mere images.* Just as in the cave, where concealment and falsity are intimately attached to images, so too are the lower parts of λόγος utterly pervaded by concealment and falsity—that is, by mere images. Those who live the tragic life take the images to which they are accustomed to be the whole truth, utterly unaware of the true beings which the images image.[56] In other words, the tragic life is the life lived amongst images without the awareness *that* they are images, just as in the case of those denizens of the cave who have yet to make the ascent above and corresponding descent below.

In the *Republic,* the image of the cave provides both the occasion for an ignorant immersion in images (i.e., shadows) and for a certain ascent beyond them: the space in which both a slavish attachment to concealment and a certain mediating of concealment by unconcealment can occur. In the *Cratylus,* it is λόγος itself which gives this occasion, providing both the possibility of ascent and the threat of bondage to mere images. By exposing the human being to both concealment and unconcealment, λόγος provides the clearing, as it were, in which the human can extend itself beyond mere images, or stay comfortably enticed by them.[57] As dual-natured, λόγος grants both possibilities. Λόγος is thus the site wherein both an unreflective immersion in images *and* an ascent beyond them can occur.[58]

As was argued above, the technological view of language which Socrates develops binds the human being decisively to the realm of opinion, what we might now call the "lower" region. By treating naming as just another tool by which the human exercises its will over beings, Socrates has shown how such an understanding remains bound to the limits of human wishing and opinion. Further, such a realm—as Socrates has already said, and will *show* much later on during his conversation with Cratylus—is the realm of *falsity,* of concealment, precisely because it lets itself be guided so extensively by mere opinions. By understanding names as subject to human caprice—just as when a master willfully changes the name of his servant—human beings themselves remain slaves to their wills, to their opinions, and thus to the realm of concealment: not unlike certain prisoners in a cave, slaves to false images, without even knowing *that* they are images.

Thus, the technological view, which binds the human being to falsity and images, is nothing other than the *tragic view* characteristic of the tragic life that is bound solely to the lower part of λόγος. Just as the tragedian in the *Republic* is said to be at third remove from the truth, cast asunder in mere images, here the tragic life is presented as that which dwells exclusively amongst the lower parts of λόγος, pervaded by myth and falsity. Such a view is cut off from the smooth upper region, that of the gods, and is bound utterly to the human realm.

Given that such a tragic—and, as I have suggested, technological—life represents only one aspect of the dual nature Socrates has described, one could well wonder in what ways the life in the upper region differs. As Kirkland has intimated, such a life would involve a certain awareness of the dual nature of λόγος, an awareness both of one's tragic condition and one's ability to extend some measure beyond it (Kirkland 2007, 12). The awareness that this other life would offer would be nothing other than an awareness of *ignorance*, of the concealment that belongs essentially to the human condition insofar as it is set within λόγος. Correspondingly, such a life would grant a certain greater access to the unconcealed nature of beings, oriented as it would be toward the gods, who call things by their correct names (if they call them anything at all) (391e). The life of awareness—what one might call the "examined life"—would be the life which, precisely through a certain knowledge of the gods or that which they represent, embraces the finitude that characterizes the human condition.

Such a life as would come to see λόγος as dual-natured would understand that λόγος *always* brings both concealment and unconcealment with itself as intrinsic possibilities. It is not as if the lower parts could simply be left behind in favor of the upper parts, any more that Pan himself could leave his shaggy goat-legs in order to dwell exclusively in his smooth upper body. To the contrary, the essentially dual nature of λόγος necessitates a belonging together of both parts, of the lower and the upper, the human and the divine. The one who comes to recognize the dual nature of λόγος thereby recognizes the ineluctable intimacy of the lower and the upper—the true and the false, the unconcealed and the concealed. To come to know the upper region is thus also to come to know a certain tragic bondage to the lower—just as, perhaps, a recently freed prisoner comes to know that he must, under pain of necessity, descend once more into the cave.

One wonders: given that the "lower" life lived amongst unreflective concealment is the "tragic life," according to Socrates, would one be justified in naming this more self-aware life—the life lived oriented toward the upper region while mired decisively in the lower—"the comic life"? Socrates certainly never calls it such. And yet, given the classical dichotomous intimacy of comedy and tragedy,[59] and the almost *filial* connection between them;[60] given also the salient comedy of the *Cratylus* which we have seen; given finally the fact that this very awareness of the difference between the upper and lower parts—between concealment and unconcealment, becoming and being—will take place through the comedy of the etymologies, which Socrates himself will call "laughable," one wonders if the life guided by this upper region of λόγος, so essentially tied to the tragic, is nothing other than *the comic life*—the life amidst the gods who, Socrates will later insist, *love to play* (406c). One recalls here that the ascent out of the cave in Book VII of the *Republic* is marked by a certain comedy, a certain laughter that accompanies those who are blinded by the light of the Good beyond Being and come to see the true nature—indeed, true *dual nature*—of their human condition. The extent to which the *Cratylus* presents a similar, laughable ascent will become clearer in the final chapter, but only after the comedy at work in the *Cratylus* comes more clearly into focus.

As a final point, one should pay special attention to a further element of Socrates' mention of Pan, son of Hermes. As we have seen, the very guiding question of the dialogue is whether or not Hermogenes is such as to be considered the son of Hermes. Given that Pan, son of Hermes, is here being examined, one could ask: does Hermo-genes, like Pan, have a dual nature (διφυής)? Is he such as to simultaneously walk upon the lower earth while nonetheless remaining attached to the upper divine region? Does Hermogenes, like Pan, stand between the two? Finally, and most strangely, we must ask: given that Pan, son of Hermes, is *either* λόγος *or the brother of* λόγος, is Hermogenes, if indeed the son of Hermes, *also* brother to λόγος? Is there a filial connection between Hermogenes and λόγος?

If so, Hermogenes would have within him the dual capacities pertaining to λόγος: namely, both the capacity for radical concealment, and the capacity for an overcoming of concealment. So understood, Hermogenes *himself*—as son of Hermes, and thus brother of λόγος—would have the capacity both to remain mired in concealment *and* to ascend beyond it into unconcealment. Phrased otherwise, Hermogenes would be able both to be ignorant of his attachment to opinion *and* to become aware of this attachment. Such awareness, if achieved, would be nothing other than an awareness of one's essential concealment: that is, one's essential *ignorance*. If indeed Hermogenes proved to be the son of Hermes—or, in a manner of speaking, the son of Socrates, who plays the role of Hermes in the *Cratylus*—he would prove himself capable of becoming aware of his ignorance, of coming to know that he knows nothing.[61] Further, precisely thereby he would prove himself to be *comic*—that is, he would prove himself capable of extending beyond the tragic life and into the comic life, that life which lives in excess of the lower region. We shall return to such considerations in chapters 7 and 8. But first, we must analyze Socrates' further development of the tragic view of language and the disruption of the stability of Being it threatens.

6 A Homeric Inheritance

In the foregoing chapter we saw that the technological view of language—that view initially held by Hermogenes and traced back, by Socrates, to the sophist Protagoras—has shown itself to be nothing other than the tragic view of language. It could not be more appropriate, then, that Socrates now turns to the tragic poet Homer.[1] In his treatment of Homer, Socrates will offer a series of etymologies involving the most famous tragic family of Ancient Greece, the House of Atreus. Through the development of these etymologies, and the etymologies of certain gods' names, Socrates will further show the disruption of inheritance that was previously foreshadowed. What will be seen above all is the manner in which the Homeric clue to the correctness of names calls the very possibility of inheritance into question, thereby further disrupting the natural relationship between names and beings, as well as between the human and the divine.

Proceeding with the inquiry, Socrates reiterates that he does not himself say that there is a correctness of names, but is happy to investigate (σκεψοίμην) along with Hermogenes (391a). He then summarizes the findings of the inquiry so far, stating that "names hold [ἔχον] a certain correctness by nature [φύσει], and not everyone knows how to set [θέσθαι] the names beautifully" (391a; my translation). Socrates then says that their present task is to attempt to discover what sort (ἥτις) of correctness belongs to names, *if Hermogenes desires* (ἐπιθυμεῖς) *to know about it* (391b), to which Hermogenes replies decisively, "of course *I desire* [ἐπιθυμῶ] to know" (391b; my translation). In indicating that he desires to be moved upward toward the knowledge of the correctness of names, Hermogenes exhibits his erotic comportment toward the matter at hand, thereby displaying a certain kinship with the erotic and vertically oriented Hermes. Whether and to what extent Hermogenes will continue to demonstrate such kinship, thereby proving himself to indeed be the son of Hermes (and thus proving himself to be correctly named), remains to be seen.

Socrates then offers Hermogenes an imperative: "Investigate" (σκόπει) (391b), to which Hermogenes responds inquisitively, "How is it necessary to investigate [σκοπεῖν]?" Socrates then says that the most correct (ὀρθοτάτη) way to investigate (σκέψεως) would be to enlist the help of those who know about such things: namely, "the sophists [οἱ σοφισταί]—and it is by paying them a lot of money that your brother Callias seems to be wise [σοφὸς δοκεῖ εἶναι]" (391b–c; Sachs). Socrates then offers the following: "But since you are not in control [οὐκ ἐγκρατὴς] of your inheritance [τῶν πατρῴων],[2] you need to plead your case with your brother and beg him to teach you what he learned from Protagoras about the correctness [τὴν ὀρθότητα] involved in such matters" (391c; Sachs; trans. modified). The repetition of the word σκοπεῖν, used five times in fifteen lines, should be viewed in light of the previous play between σκοπεῖν and σκώπτειν (384c), and thus understood as emphasizing the comedy of Socrates' suggestion: for given that he and Socrates have just now decisively rejected the doctrine of Protagoras, it would be palpably ridiculous if Hermogenes now begged his brother Callias to teach him that very doctrine. Hermogenes affirms the ridiculousness by saying that such a course of action would be absurd (ἄτοπος) (391c).[3]

Before proceeding, it must be noted that Hermogenes' inheritance (πατρῷος)— or, more specifically, his *lack* of inheritance—has now been thematically brought to the fore. This mention of Hermogenes' lack of inheritance explicitly names what is about to become a predominant theme within the text: the question of inheritance and the manner in which this question bears upon the correctness of names. In commenting upon Hermogenes' lack of inheritance Socrates has suggested that Hermogenes does not have in his possession what is proper to his father: in other words, *that he is not like his father,* that he lacks the *properties,* or the proper *being,* of his father. The question of the dissimilarity between father and son—which, we will soon see, is nothing other than a question of *monstrosity*—will soon be made an explicit theme within the text.

After having listened to Hermogenes' rather forceful rejection of Socrates' suggestion that he beg his brother Callias to teach him the knowledge concerning the correctness of names (391c), Socrates, not without some irony, suggests that Hermogenes look instead to Homer (391d). Claiming that such knowledge is to be found in those passages in which Homer deals with the differences between human and divine names, Socrates offers the following important query: "Do you not think that he says [λέγειν] in those passages great and wonderful words [θαυμάσιον] about the correctness of names?" (391d; my translation). We should here, as perhaps everywhere, hear the philosophical overtones in the word *wonderful* (θαυμάσιος).[4] What is about to occur through the turn to Homer is a wondrous opening into the nature of words, an opening through which an essential truth concerning the Homeric conception of words will come to light.

It should briefly be noted that the turn to Homer is by no means a turn away from Protagoras and the relativism he represents, but is rather an intensification of the latter's position. In the *Theaetetus,* during a discussion concerning perception, a certain philosophical camp is described of which Homer is said to be the general (στρατηγόν) (*Tht.* 153a). This is the camp (to which Protagoras is also said to belong) for whom "nothing ever *is* but is always becoming" (ἔστι μὲν γὰρ οὐδέποτ' οὐδέν, ἀεὶ δὲ γίγνεται), and for whom "all things are offspring [ἔκγονα] generated out of flowing and motion [ῥοῆς τε καὶ κινήσεως]" (*Tht.* 152e; Sachs). In the *Cratylus*, the turn to Homer is thus not a turn away from the philosophical position represented by Protagoras, but is a turn to the very origin of that position. In a word, Homer is the *father* of the position that believes all things to be in flux. The turn from Protagoras to Homer is thus a turn from an inheritor of the flux-position to the very source of that position: or, phrased otherwise, a turn from the son to the father. As Protagoras was seen to represent the technological view of language—which, properly understood, is nothing other than the tragic view—the turn to Homer is the turn to the very origin of the tragic/technological view of language.[5]

In the *Theaetetus* it is said that anyone who offers a counterargument against the position that Homer and Protagoras represent cannot but seem laughable (καταγέλαστος) (*Tht.* 153a). Of course, in the *Cratylus,* it is Socrates and Hermogenes who develop just such a counterargument by broaching the idea of a stable reality beyond the apparent fluctuations of perception. One should thus hardly be surprised to find much that is laughable, much that is comedic, in the text to come. Given that Protagoras's doctrine was seen to amount to the tragic view of language, and recalling that Homer is said to be a tragedian in the *Theaetetus* (*Tht.* 152e), one wonders if the ridiculousness to come does not mitigate or counter the tragic view of language by some measure. As will be seen in chapter 7, this is indeed the case.

Socrates now begins his pursuit of Homer's wondrous knowledge concerning names. The first example to which he turns involves a certain river in Troy which, according to Homer, the gods call Xanthus (Ξάνθον) but men call Scamander (Σκάμανδρον) (391e). This refers to a passage in Book XX of the *Iliad* where the gods are approaching total war with one another. As Socrates observes, the passage describes a fight waged between Hephaestus (the fire god) and the river Xanthus. The full passage from the *Iliad* (only the last line of which Socrates quotes) is as follows:

> There, look, rearing against the lord Poseidon
> Phoebus Apollo loomed, bristling winged arrows,
> rearing against Ares, blazing-eyed Athena,
> rearing against Hera, Artemis with arrow of gold
> and cry that halloos the hunt, the goddess raining shafts,
> Huntress sister of Phoebus the distant deadly archer—
> rearing against Leto, Hermes the running god of luck
> and against the Fire-god rose the great deep-swirling river
> immortals call Xanthus, mankind calls Scamander. (*Iliad* XX.67 ff.)

It is important to observe that the scene described is one where the gods cannot agree with one another. In such a scene, communication has failed and war has come about: unity is lacking, and multiplicity reigns. So understood, this Homeric passage could be said to present, in tragic/poetic terms, the dissolution of one-ness implicit in Protagoras's doctrine that "the human being is the measure of all things." In this Homeric passage the gods, who occupy the realm of true Being, are divided.

Socrates gives another Homeric example: "Or, *if you wish* [βούλει], take the bird of which [Homer] says, 'gods address it as χαλκίδα but men κύμινδιν'" (392a; Sachs; trans. modified; my emphasis).[6] This quotation is from book XIV of the *Iliad*, just before Hera, having borrowed Aphrodite's girdle, lies to Zeus in order to seduce him into having sex with her (*Iliad* XIV.291). Referring to the same section from the *Iliad* to which Socrates refers in the *Theaetetus* (*Tht.* 152d), this passage serves to indicate a certain disruption of λόγος akin to that which was seen to unfold from Protagoras's doctrine. In the Homeric passage, the seductive Hera is shown to be speaking to Zeus with "false lying purpose" (*Iliad* XIV.201, 302). Thus, although the purported intent of this Homeric passage is to illustrate that the gods call things by their correct names (if they call them anything at all [391e]), it actually demonstrates that gods, like human beings, can lie. Thus, from within this tragic view of language, it seems that both human λόγος and divine λόγος can be deceptive.

This consequence is devastating. Given that the stated purpose of the Homeric example is to show that the names gods use are *more* correct than human names (391d-e), the picture of disagreement amongst the gods painted by the extended Homeric passage (to which Socrates' quote alerts us) undermines that very purpose. Given further that Socrates and Hermogenes will soon set out precisely to discover the divine giver of names—one who, as divine, would have named the things correctly (397c)—the suggestion that even the gods can lie has quietly undermined the legitimacy of such a task. If it is indeed the case that even the gods are capable of "false lying purpose," then Socrates' undertaking is over before it begins: for there would be no reason to suppose that the divine names in fact correctly capture the beings that they name. If the gods can lie, then surely they can call beings by their false names. The Homeric quote thus serves to render impossible the very investigation that it is supposed to make possible (i.e., it undermines the very claim it is meant to bolster). Such self-defeat is a further indication of the comic character of the inquiry as a whole, and especially of what is to come.

Claiming that such considerations are too great (μείζω) for them to understand, Socrates suggests that they turn to a more human investigation (ἀνθρωπινώτερον διασκέψασθαι)—or, perhaps, a more human *jest*—regarding Hector's son and whether Σκαμάνδριος or Ἀστυάναξ is his correct name (392b). Presumably the investigation to come will be "more human" because it will deal not with the differences between what the gods call something and what humans call it, as was the case in the previous examples, but between what two classes of humans (i.e., the men and woman of Troy) call the same thing.[7] However, one also wonders if it is more human precisely because it will remain within those *lower* parts of λόγος we encountered in the previous chapter, those hairy goat-like parts characteristic of the tragic life. As the Homeric scene as a whole will show, such examples are decidedly tragic, and remain decisively in the lower parts of λόγος.

Socrates asks Hermogenes if he recalls the Homeric lines to which he is referring in speaking of Hector's son, to which Hermogenes replies "certainly" (πάνυ γε) (392b). Socrates then asks which of the two names Hermogenes thinks Homer regarded as more correct (ὀρθότερον). The ensuing conversation is as follows:

> SOCRATES: Investigate [σκόπει] like this: suppose someone were to ask you whether you think those who are more sensible or more senseless call things by names that are more correct [ὀρθότερον].
>
> HERMOGENES: It's obvious that I'd say the more sensible ones do.
>
> SOCRATES: And in cities, is it the women who seem to you [σοι δοκοῦσιν] to be more sensible, or the men, speaking of a class as a whole?
>
> HERMOGENES: The men.
>
> SOCRATES: And don't you know that Homer says Hector's child was called Ἀστυάναξ by the Trojans? Isn't it obvious that he was called Σχαμάνδριος by the women, since the men called him Ἀστυάναξ?
>
> HERMOGENES: It seems that way [ἔοικέ γε].[8]
>
> SOCRATES: And Homer too, did he not regard the Trojan men as wiser than their women?
>
> HERMOGENES: I suppose so [οἶμαι ἔγωγε].
>
> SOCRATES: Therefore he thought Ἀστυάναξ applied to the boy more rightly [ὀρθότερον] than Σχαμάνδριος?
>
> HERMOGENES: It appears so (φαίνεται). (392c–d; Sachs; trans. modified)

The first thing that must be noted about this reference to Homer is that it is incorrect.[9] It is the townspeople of Troy who refer to Hector's son as Ἀστυάναξ, and it is Hector himself who calls him Σχαμάνδριος (*Iliad* VI.404).[10] Thus, though Socrates concludes that it is more correct (ὀρθότερον) to call him Ἀστυάναξ, the opposite in fact seems to be the case—for surely Hector, who is his son's namegiver, would know the name of his own son. Apparently Hermogenes does not know the Homeric poem as well as he pretends to (392b).

Despite Hermogenes' failure to notice Socrates' playful misquoting of Homer, Socrates continues by considering (σκοπεῖν) (or perhaps jesting about) the reason why Ἀστυάναξ is more correctly called such. Quoting Homer again, Socrates says the reason is that "he [Hector] alone defended their city and long walls" (392e; Fowler). The son of this defender, for a reason not yet fully specified, is to be called Ἀστυάνακτα, ruler of that which his father defended (i.e., the city, ἄστυ). This example could not be more problematic. First of all, Hector did not, finally, protect the walls of Troy: rather, after Hector was rather spectacularly killed at the hands of Achilles (*Iliad* XXII) Troy was ransacked and pillaged, thanks to a certain famous wooden horse (*Odyssey* IV.271 ff.). Secondly, his son, whatever his name is, never had the chance to defend the walls of Troy. Though it is not said in the *Iliad* what happens to him following his father's demise, the later tradition has him being hurled over the walls to his death.[11] Even if he survived the sacking of the city he was only a small child at the time, and could hardly have protected his cradle, let alone the walls of Troy. It is therefore absurd to think that the name Ἀστυάναξ, "lord of the city," is somehow appropriate for the child (i.e., somehow descriptive of his nature). Further, though the point of the example (as Socrates is about to make clear) is to show the manner in which a son ought to inherit his name from his father—provided the son is not some kind of monster (393b)—what it in fact shows is the *death* of the father and the destitution of the son. The example thus brings the *disruption* of inheritance to the fore.

Although Hermogenes claims to understand the thinking behind Socrates' Homeric examples, Socrates marks the absurdity of the discourse by saying "Indeed?! I do not yet myself understand it!" (392e; my translation). Socrates has been spouting insight (or nonsense) which he himself does not understand, and has in no way been offering an account that he *knows* to be true. In an effort to further elucidate the mysterious correctness of names as Homer conceived it, Socrates rounds out the Hector/Ἀστυάναξ example by explaining in greater detail how the name Ἀστυάναξ came about:

> For ruler [ὁ ἄναξ] and holder [ὁ ἕκτωρ] mean pretty much the same thing [σκεδόν τι ταὐτὸν σημαίνει], so that both are kingly [βασιλικά] names, since whatever anyone is a lord [ἄναξ] of, he is doubtless a holder [ἕκτωρ] of as well. For it's clear that he rules it [κρατεῖ] and possesses and holds it [ἔχει]. (393a; Sachs; trans. modified)

Thus, both Ἀστυάναξ and Ἕκτωρ more or less (σκεδόν) say the same, insofar as being a lord (ἄναξ) is the same as being the holder (ἕκτωρ) of something. Both names indicate the kingly (βασιλικά) nature of the one named.

With this further elaboration Socrates thinks he has touched upon (ἐφάπτεσθαι) the principle at work in Homer's conception of naming. Though Socrates will soon elucidate this principle himself, we can already see that it has two elements. To begin with, the principle seems to operate by way of inheritance, demanding that a son, if he be of the same nature as his father, carry a name which expresses that nature. Secondly, and more subtly, we begin to see that a name, under this view of language, is meant to *describe* the nature of the being that holds it. Both of these elements will find fuller articulations as Socrates continues.

However, we must first make a brief detour in order to better understand what precisely is at work behind Socrates' example. Though Socrates has interpreted Ἀστυάναξ as meaning "lord of the city," the name can also be interpreted another way, a *playful* way, one which sheds light upon our interpretation of the dialogue so far. The name Ἀστυάναξ could be analyzed as consisting of three distinct parts, α-, στύω, and ἄναξ. Στύω is the vulgar Greek verb for getting an erection, used occasionally by Aristophanes.[12] Preceded by the alpha-privative, ἀ-στύω means flaccid or limp.[13] With the word ἄναξ (lord) added to it, the name Ἀ-στυ-άναξ would mean something like "Lord of Impotence."[14] If one were to interpret the name in this way—an interpretation that could only arise out of a playfulness characteristic of Socrates' own approach—then in saying that Ἀ-στυ-άναξ is *correct* (ὀρθῶς) (392e), Homer would be saying that "Lord of Impotence" is correct, that is, is more *upright* or more *erect*.[15] In other words, Homer would be saying that that which is not erect is more erect, that which is flaccid is upright.

If this comic play were indeed operative in Socrates' description—something that could never be proved, but only pursued with a playfulness akin to that which Socrates exhibits throughout his etymologies—what would be the point? The most obvious point would be that Homer's notion about the correctness of names would be seen to lead precisely to something basically opposed to correctness understood as uprightness—namely, flaccidity or impotence. The joke would be that "non-erect" is the *erect* (ὀρθῶς) name of Ἀ-στυ-άναξ. A situation would thus develop where, despite looking for the *erectness* of names in Homer, Socrates and Hermogenes would have found an un-erect (i.e., flaccid) name, a name whose very sense is opposed to erectness. Understood in terms of directionality, this would mean that while looking for something *upright* or oriented toward the heavens (i.e., toward the gods who dwell amongst true Being) they have found something that points *downward*, toward the earth, the realm of myth and falsity. In other words, despite seeking an upward passage, they have remained in the shaggy and goat-like lower region of Πᾶν/λόγος. A comic result has thus come about which is the precise opposite of what was intended. Almost as if to mark the absurdity of such a development, Hermogenes swears—not once, but twice (392e; 393b).

Just after Hermogenes' second swear, Socrates finally explains in more precise terms the "clue" to Homer's notion of the correctness of names which the preceding Homeric references were meant to clarify. The clue involves how it is just (δίκαιόν) to call the offspring (ἔκγονον) of a lion a lion, and the offspring of a horse (ἵππος) a horse (393b). (It should not go unnoticed that, although it is said to be *just*, it is not said to be *true*.) In other words, the offspring ought to be called by the same name as its parent: both ought to have names that make their common nature manifest, if that naming is to be *just*. Looking back at the most recent of Socrates' Homeric examples, this would mean that Ἀστυάναξ, as the son of Hector, ought to have a name which expresses the same nature as Hector, just as the offspring of a horse should have the same name as its parent.[16] Insofar as something is of the same sort as its progenitor—insofar as the offspring has inherited the nature of its parent—it ought also to inherit its name. The clue to Homer's *opinion* (δόξης; 393b) concerning the correctness of names has to do with inheritance.

Inheritance, as we saw, is one of the major issues at play in the joke that begins the *Cratylus*. Thus, Socrates' investigation into Homer—and his jesting about him—has led to one of the principles at the very heart of the jest that begins the *Cratylus*. There, what was at stake was Cratylus's oracular claim that Hermogenes has failed to inherit something from Hermes (i.e., whether he is the son of Hermes and whether, therefore, he *is* Hermogenes). Here, in Homer's example, what is at stake is whether Ἀστυάναξ has inherited the character of his father Hector such that he should be referred to by a name with the same meaning. In both cases, it is a matter of whether a son has inherited the properties of his father and thus should carry the same name. Further, in both cases a certain sexual or erotic sense is at play. If one hazards this playful interpretation of Ἀ-στυ-άναξ, one can see that the Homeric example Socrates has broached echoes the beginning of the text and elaborates the comic operations of the opening scene. Regardless if such a playful interpretation is tenable, it is clear that the problem of inheritance is at play within the text from its beginning, and has now become explicit.

* * *

Socrates continues by suggesting that there are some instances where Homer's clue does not seem to hold, and the method of applying the same name to both parent and child does not work. Socrates explains just such an instance:

> I'm not talking about some sort of monster [τέρας]—such as something other than a horse being born from a horse. . . . If a horse, contrary to nature [παρὰ φύσιν], gives birth to a calf, a natural offspring of a cow, it is not appropriate to call it a colt but a calf, and if something that is not the offspring of a human being is born from a human being, I imagine it would not be appropriate to call that offspring a human being; and it is the same way with trees and everything else. (393b–c; Sachs; trans. modified; my emphasis)

Thus, Homer's clue only applies to those legitimate births whereby a member of a species gives birth to another instance of that species, those births which would therefore be called natural. It would not apply to those instances in which a monster (τέρας) is born.

There are several issues which this mention of monstrosity brings to the fore. First of all, Socrates' use, yet again, of a horse (ἵππος) for his example cannot help but bring Hermogenes to mind. The example calls into question whether Hermogenes Hipponicus—who is the son of a horse(-victor)—ought to be called by his father's patronymic, as Socrates in fact occasionally does.[17] In other words, this merely rephrases what was just said regarding Hermogenes' lack of inheritance (πατρῷων). Understood more generally, the idea of monstrosity raises the question of how it is possible for children to come to be *unlike* their parents, the very source of their being. What is it that accounts for such monstrosity? For example, how is it that Callias, son of the wealthy Hipponicus, could himself come to exhibit such wealth, while his brother Hermogenes comes to be so impoverished? Further, how is it that the former could be so attracted to the sophistry of Protagoras while the latter rejects it so completely?[18] Finally, how is it that two brothers from the same father could have different names (i.e., names that do not at all *say the same*), not to mention drastically different οὐσία, especially in light of Socrates' later general comment that "brother is like brother" (408d)?

What the mention of monstrosity begins to put into question is whether or not Hermogenes is the legitimate offspring of his father, or is some kind of monster. To be sure, Hermogenes was born to a different woman than Callias, was thus a bastard, a νόθος, and was in this sense a kind of monstrosity (at least from a political point of view). Yet monstrosity (τέρας) must also be understood in the sense of *wonder, marvel,* and *divinity* that the word carries with it. A τέρας is a wondrous *sign* or portent through which the divine shows itself in some manner. In other words, a τέρας is to be understood as the appearance of something (i.e., the divine) *in* something else to which it does not properly or naturally belong (i.e., the human). Such showing must thus be understood in terms of *excess,* indeed in terms of *eminent excess,* of an excess inhering in the very thing of which it is in excess. A τέρας is a terrestrial sign through which the excessive character of the divine manifests itself. So understood, a monster is precisely the belonging together of a divine excess and the mundane thing through which such an excess shows itself.

If something is born of a horse that is not itself a horse, Socrates has said, it is a monstrosity—it is the appearance of some form excessive of what properly belongs to a horse. Given Socrates' use of "Hipponicus" when referring to Hermogenes, one must ask: what about a human son who is not at all like his father? As Socrates has said, "if something that's not the offspring of a human being is born from a human being, *I imagine it would not be appropriate to call that offspring a human being*" (393c; Sachs; my emphasis). Is there something *excessive* about Hermogenes? Monstrous? More than human? Does Hermogenes stand for the presence of something *in* something else, such as a god *in* a human being?

One recalls here that Hermes was born from the union of mortal nymph and immortal god. As was argued previously, Hermes is therefore to be understood as a hero in the sense given to that term within the *Cratylus.* Insofar as a hero is a hybrid of each of its parents, neither completely one nor the other, one can ask: is a hero a *monster,* in the sense given here? A hero is precisely the appearance of a god in the mortal—it is the divine excess brought to appearance in the human. Hermes the hero is a monster in this excessive sense, the monstrous union of the divine and the mortal, a union which cannot help but be excessive when viewed from the side of the human. As such, Hermes is also a sign (τέρας), a portent, a *message,* a mortal token that points beyond the mortal to the divine. As such a monstrous sign, Hermes occupies the distance that separates the human realm from that of the gods: like so much currency, Hermes stands between the two, belonging to both in *common,* and thus belonging wholly to neither.

Given that the question that begins the inquiry of the *Cratylus* is whether and to what extent Hermogenes is the son of Hermes, one must ask: if it proved to be the case that Hermogenes was in fact the rightful heir to Hermes, would it be appropriate to call Hermogenes a human being? Or would it be more fitting, indeed, more *correct*, to address him by the class by which one would address his namesake? Would it not be more appropriate to address him as a *hero*? Or a *monster*? Is Hermogenes a monstrous hero, like his namesake? If so, Hermogenes would, like Hermes, serve as a sign of the union of the divine with the human. As such a sign, Hermogenes would prove capable of traversing the distance that separates the two—a traversal which, as we have seen, is precisely a matter of desire (ἔρως). If Hermogenes ever lives up to his name, he will thereby show himself to possess the requisite ἔρως to undertake a movement beyond the limits of the human and into the excess of the divine—or, perhaps, beyond the limits of *convention* and into the excess of *nature*.

As we have seen, Hermogenes has already indicated, albeit subtly, that he is indeed erotically oriented toward Being. As the dialogue continues, Hermogenes will show himself to be a hero who, as Socrates said of heroes in general, has his origin and activity in ἔρως (398c). What will come to light through the inquiry that follows is that Hermogenes is indeed able to make the journey beyond the merely human to the divine, beyond mere perception and unto a glimpse of the stability of Being, beyond the *tragic life* and into a life of another sort. More specifically, through the long and comic etymological section, it will be shown that it is through this heroic (i.e., erotic) ability to ask questions leadingly that the philosopher Socrates transports Hermogenes from the flux of becoming into a glimpse of the stability of Being.[19] The question is thus whether Hermogenes will ever inherit this ability, and thereby show himself to be a philosopher, a lover of wisdom, who travels the road between human ignorance and divine wisdom. In this register it is of the utmost importance that Socrates, much later during the very pinnacle of the etymological play, calls the erotic Hermogenes *daimonic* (ὦ δαιμόνιε) (415a).[20]

ж   ж   ж

Just after elaborating the clue to Homer's conception of the correctness of names, Socrates says something most curious. Rather than offering some further elucidation of the Homeric conception, or further bolstering that conception through argument or new evidence, Socrates calls it entirely into question. Just after obtaining Hermogenes' consent to the proposal that an offspring ought to bear the same name as its progenitor, Socrates marks the limits of such a conception with the following: "Watch out that I do not lead you astray [παρακρούσωμαί]—for by the same argument [τὸν αὐτὸν λόγον], if any offspring is born of a king, it is appropriate to call it a king" (393d; Sachs; trans. modified).

Remarkably, this argument (λόγος) that Socrates has just warned against is precisely the argument which served as the clue to Homer's conception of the correctness of names. There, with the example of Ἀστυάναξ, it was said that a son ought to inherit the name of his father, unless he is some kind of monstrosity. Further, it was shown that both ἄναξ and ἕκτωρ are names which, properly conceived, are *kingly* names—that is, they both mean "king" (βασιλικά) despite their different syllabic arrangements. Yet, this is precisely the sort of reasoning that Socrates has just warned Hermogenes against employing, a reasoning which will only lead them astray. (Further, in the specific case of Hector and Ἀστυάναξ, we saw such reasoning to be false.) With this warning, the entirety of the preceding Homeric discussion is cast under suspicion, as well as the many examples to come that employ such reasoning.

But why is it, exactly, that this reasoning would lead us astray? Such a principle of naming would not attend to the being itself, but only to the *father* of that being. In other words, the Homeric clue is unable to account for the being which presents itself, but only for the absent progenitor (or source) of that being. One remembers that moment in the *Theaetetus* where Socrates, seeing Theaetetus for the first time, recalls the absent father while being unable to name the young man present before him (*Tht.* 144c). Likewise, the Homeric clue has now been shown to be incapable of naming what is present, what shows itself to our senses: in a word, it has shown itself incapable of naming that which shows itself from out of φύσις. The Homeric conception cannot name beings as they show themselves in nature, but only in accordance with the absent source of those beings (i.e., the father, understood both literally and figuratively).

This flaw to the Homeric conception structurally recalls the craftsman analogies we saw in Socrates' elaboration of the technological view of λόγος. There it was seen that just as a shuttle-maker ought to look to the look of Shuttle in order to make a shuttle, so too must the name-maker look to the look of Name in order to make a name (389d). However, it was shown that under such a technological model a name would be unable to name the particular being with which it was ostensibly concerned, but would only name the generic function of naming, that is, its didactic and discursive purpose. Here, under the Homeric view, it is being suggested that a name should be made based upon the being of the *father*, but not of the son being named. Yet again we are given a model of naming that proves incapable of accounting for the *particular being* present, that looks rather to the absent source of that being. Such a view *overlooks* precisely what is to be named.

Socrates has now warned Hermogenes against a principle of naming that would state that an offspring ought to inherit the name of its father. What is astonishing, and highly comical, is that this warning is almost immediately disregarded. After explaining to Hermogenes that the proper function of naming is to bring the nature of a being to the fore, regardless of the particular syllables employed, Socrates expands this reasoning to the example of a king:

> And does not the same argument apply to a king? For in any instance, a king will be born of a king, a good man from a good man, a good-looking man from

a good-looking man, and likewise with everything else, another such offspring born of each kind, if no monstrosity is born [ἐὰν μὴ τέρας γίγνηται], so that it is appropriate to call them by the same names. (394a; Sachs; trans. modified)

This argument (λόγος) is precisely the sort against which Socrates just warned. In agreeing to it (394d) Hermogenes demonstrates that he has already forgotten Socrates' warning that such reasoning will only lead us astray. Such forgetfulness adds to the comedy already well under way.

Socrates proceeds to give various examples where two names composed of different syllables bring the same nature (φύσις) to the word. Just as the names Ἀστυάναξ and "Hector" say the same (i.e., lord), while sharing only a single letter ("τ"), so too does "Archepolis" say the same, despite its different arrangement of letters. Likewise, the three names "Agis," "Polemarchus," and "Eupolemos," all mean "general" (στρατηγόν), despite their material differences (394c), just as both "Iatrocles" and "Acesimbrotus" express the ability to heal. The general point, as Socrates emphasizes again, is that "it is appropriate to give the same names to those who are born in accord with nature" (τοῖς μὲν δὴ κατὰ φύσιν γιγνομένοις τὰ αὐτὰ ἀποδοτέον ὀνόματα) (394d; Sachs).

We would do well to meditate momentarily on Socrates' examples. Who are these people to whom Socrates now refers? Were they real historical personages, or are they merely convenient contrivances that Socrates adduces to make his point? Strictly speaking, in order to serve as evidence in support of the Homeric view of language, these names *must* refer to real people, or at least well-known poetic creations: for in order to be correct in the sense now coming to light, these names would need to *describe* the natures of those who hold them. If Socrates were merely fabricating these names on the spot, then the point would be lost, for Hermogenes would in no way be able to test the names against the characters of those they name.

Yet, we cannot know with any certainty to whom these names refer. "Agis" could perhaps refer to either of the two Spartan kings, both military generals.[21] If so, then in this case, Socrates' principle (which, in fact, is *Homer's* principle) would seem to hold: for the name "Agis," meaning "general," would refer to a person who was in fact a general. Nothing of interest is known about anyone named "Eupolemos," "Iatrocles," or "Acesimbrotus," so it is impossible to know whether Socrates' examples ring true.[22]

However, the name "Polemarchus" should give us pause. Though there is no way to know definitively to which Polemarchus Socrates is referring, the name cannot but bring to mind the character from Plato's *Republic*, the precocious son of Cephalus who forcibly draws Socrates into a discussion about the nature of justice. If Socrates were indeed referring to this Polemarchus, then his reference would serve to complicate Homer's clue rather than reinforce it: for this Polemarchus was no general, but a philosopher (*Phdr.* 257b), though perhaps one with a rather bellicose nature.[23] In that case, Polemarchus's name, which "literally" means "warlord," would not adequately describe his nature. If indeed this is the Polemarchus who is meant, then in making reference to him Socrates has begun to subtly call the very principle he just enunciated into question.

Further, the figure of Polemarchus in the *Republic* is himself bound up with the question of inheritance. It is shortly after his father Cephalus talks explicitly about inheritance (πατρώων) that Polemarchus comes to inherit the λόγος from him, taking his place as Socrates' interlocutor (*Rep.* 331d). The Polemarchus of the *Republic,* then, is an inheritor. Socrates' mention of him in the *Cratylus,* following upon a conversation regarding the principle that a son ought to inherit the name of the father, could thus not be more appropriate. However, given that there is some question as to whether and to what extent Polemarchus inherits his father's λόγος in the *Republic* without bastardizing it, we are just as well alerted to the problem of *mis-inheritance*—that is, the problem of monstrosity, of something diverging from its source.

After having mentioned these names as supposed evidence of the Homeric conception of correct naming, Socrates returns to the question of monstrosity (τέρατος). Though it has been said that a son ought to inherit the name of the father, this is only true for those sons who inherit the *nature* of their progenitor. In the case where a son fails to inherit his father's nature, exhibiting instead a contrary nature, the son should be given the name appropriate to his class (τοῦ γένους) rather than to his father's (394d). For example, an impious son born to a pious father ought not to be named "Theophilus" (beloved of god), but should rather be given a name meaning (σεμαίνει) something opposite (τἀναντία). Such monstrous offspring ought to be named in accordance with the class to which they belong, *not* the patron from whom they in part arise.

This discussion of monstrosity has brought several matters to the fore. To begin with, one suspects that this particular point is of special (if not painful) significance to Hermogenes, whose own inheritance of his father's patrimony is in question, and in a double sense.[24] Secondly, Socrates' example of "Theophilus" raises the following question: how is one to ensure that the name one gives a child will accurately express that child's character? Is there not something *willful* about giving children such names before their true character has been given a chance to develop? Simply naming a child in accordance with one's wishes is insufficient to ensure that they will exhibit the same nature as their name suggests: rather, their nature could be such as to be monstrously different from their given name. Such a willful principle of naming overlooks the actual character of the being in question in favor of some ideal, as Socrates makes clear with the example of the impious Theophilus (394e).[25] By willfully attaching a name suggestive of some great character, a name-giver names not in accordance with the nature of the being (i.e., the son) but in accordance only with his own wishes, with how things seem to him.

After having raised the possibility of monstrosity, Socrates continues his demonstration of the Homeric clue regarding the correctness of names. However, quite abruptly, Socrates makes an interesting turn. While his previous examples were ostensibly of real people, Socrates now turns to a series of names from Greek tragedy, beginning with Orestes. In what follows, Socrates will move generally from the son to the father, thereby hinting at the question of inheritance that overshadows the examples. However, as will be seen, what the examples bring to mind most of all is a decisive *disruption* of inheritance and a fatal discontinuity between father and son.

Orestes is so called, Socrates says, due to his "brutality of nature, a savagery in him, and a mountain-like quality" (394e; Sachs). The brutality and savagery to which Socrates refers is doubtless the fact that Orestes, avenging his father Agamemnon's death, killed his own mother and her lover Aegisthus.[26] The first example that Socrates offers thus involves a scene of death—indeed, of *murder,* specifically of the father. As Socrates continues to speak, the instances of patricide will multiply.

Socrates turns to Orestes' father, Agamemnon, offering the following account of Agamemnon's name:

> Agamemnon is likely to be the sort of person to work hard at what seems right to him and endure the bringing to accomplishment of his intentions through virtue. A sign of it is his remaining at Troy in suffering and endurance. So the name "Agamemnon" signifies that this man is admirable for sticking to it [ὅτι οὖν ἀγαστὸς κατὰ τὴν ἐπιμονὴν οὗτος ὁ ἀνήρ]. (395a; Sachs)

Agamemnon was so called due to his "sticking to it." This translates ἐπιμονήν, from the verb ἐπιμένω, meaning to stay, to remain in place, to abide. Agamemnon stayed in place, remaining in Troy during the siege. His name denotes a kind of stability over against what would not abide, what would fail to remain in place.

For reasons that will soon become clear, it cannot go unnoticed that Agamemnon was killed by Aegisthus, the very man whom Orestes returned to murder in vengeance. Given Socrates' description of Agamemnon's name, one could say that the murdering of Agamemnon is the murdering of stability, of that which abides. This peculiar picture echoes what has already happened in the *Cratylus* through the figure of Protagoras, whose doctrine brought about a disruption of stability. We have already seen that the position of this sophist brings about a sort of radical relativism in which all beings are in flux and are ultimately reduced to their appearances. Against such radical relativism Socrates has hazarded a stability (βέβαιόν) that must be proper to beings (386d–e). Here, Agamemnon has come to stand for such stability; and his murder by Aegisthus denotes a murdering of this stability, a dissolution of endurance. Such dissolution will only heighten as the etymologies within this tragic/Homeric scene continue.

The next name Socrates considers is "Atreus," father of Agamemnon. What immediately comes to light is that it is precisely due to his murderous acts that Atreus is so named. As Socrates explains it, Atreus is so called "because of his murder of Chrysippus and also what he did to Thyestes that was so cruel—all of that was ruinous and disastrous to virtue" (395b; Sachs). As seen in Thucydides, Chrysippus was killed by his half-brother Atreus (Book 1.9). Further, as told by Aeschylus, Atreus murdered Thyestes' children and served their cooked bodies to their father (*Agamemnon*, 1243 ff.). Socrates adds to his description that it was because of his stubbornness (τὸ ἀτειρές), fearlessness (τὸ ἄτρεστον), and ruinous acts (τὸ ἀτηρόν) that Atreus was correctly given his name (395c).

Socrates proceeds to offer an account of the name "Pelops," father to both Atreus and Chrysippus (though through different mothers). According to his account, Pelops was so called due to his inability to foresee the terrible consequences that his actions would have upon his family (γένος); he was in this sense near (πέλας) -sighted (395d). The action to which Socrates is alluding is Pelops' murdering of Myrtilus (395c).[27] As Myrtilus died at Pelops' hand, he cursed him—the very curse which, according to some, led to the tragic events that befell the house of Atreus.[28] It is further interesting for our purposes that, according to some accounts, Myrtilus was the son of Hermes, and that it was thus to Hermes that the curse on the house of Atreus was owed.[29]

Socrates then gives an account of the name "Tantalus," father of Pelops, saying that it was given correctly and in accordance with nature (ὀρθῶς καὶ κατὰ φύσιν τεθῆναι) (395d). Only making a general reference to the "many terrible things that happened to him during his life . . . and in Hades," Socrates derives Tantalus's name from the balancing (τανταλεία) of a stone above his head that he endures in Hades and his most wretched (ταλάντατον) state (395e).[30] The extent of Tantalus's wretchedness in life almost goes without saying—and, indeed, does go without saying in the *Cratylus*. In preparing a feast for the gods, Tantalus butchered his son and cooked him into a stew. The gods, aware of Tantalus's unspeakable deed, condemned him to the aforementioned eternal balancing act.

As is by now quite clear, each of the names Socrates has just considered has murder in the background. In particular, Socrates has investigated the names of the members of the tragic house of Atreus so well poeticized in the works of Aeschylus and equally well satirized in Aristophanes' *Frogs*.[31] While it is presumably Socrates' intent to exhibit the manner in which a name correctly describes that which it names, what Socrates' examples have described is a complicated scene in which the murdering of the son or the father is enacted again and again. Needless to say, this Homeric scene—which has shown itself to be a *tragic* scene—bespeaks a disruption of inheritance, an elimination of the patronymic, and a dissolution of lineage.

In the previous chapter, we saw how the technological view of language (which Hermogenes tacitly accepts) equates with the tragic view of language. Such a view, as argued, is so bound by the limits of human opining and wishing as to sever the possibility of a direct lineage between a name and the being it names. Socrates' turn to Homer has been nothing other than a demonstration of this tragic view, one which has found its most obvious expression through the names of the various tragic members of the house of Atreus. These examples express dramatically what has already happened through Socrates' exposition of the Protagorean doctrine that "the human being is the measure of all things": namely, a complete breakdown of the relationship between beings and names.

In that case we saw that by reducing Being to appearance Protagoras (and his adherents) rendered it impossible to offer a name that accords with the nature of the being in question. Rather, such a technological understanding of language can only name beings in accordance with how they seem to those who give the names. There is thus a disruption of the lineage between a being and the name. Here, in the case of Homer, such a disruption has occurred through the reoccurring tragic act of the death of the father or the son. In both cases, the offspring is severed from the source, and inheritance is rendered impossible.

Having explored the name "Tantalus," Socrates now turns his gaze to Tantalus's father, Zeus. It should be noted that with this step Socrates has moved through the human and up into the gods. Socrates' inquiry, still tracing the lineage that began with Orestes, will now focus on the gods who stand at the head of that lineage. What is surprising is that the murderous scene which Socrates has just described will continue to develop as he turns to the gods. While one might expect the gods to be free of such viciousness and vice, Socrates' tragic examples will show the gods to be at least as despicable as human beings.

As Socrates explains it, the cause of the name "Zeus" is two-fold, each description corresponding to the two names for Zeus, Διὰ and Ζῆνα (396a).[32] Διὰ, Socrates says, derives from the fact that Zeus is he *through whom* (δι' ὅν) all things have the gift of life (ζῆν). As Socrates then explains, reinforcing the principle behind Homer's conception of naming, "when [δία and ζῆν] are combined into one they make the nature of the god evident [εἰς ἓν δηλοῖ], which is exactly what we're claiming it is appropriate for a name to be capable of accomplishing" (396a; Sachs).

What Socrates' description fails to mention is that Zeus killed his father Cronus. According to Hesiod it was Zeus who, after all of his brothers and sisters had been eaten by their father, dethroned the vicious Cronus and led him down into deep Tartarus (*Theogony*, 617 ff.). In the *Euthyphro*, the character Euthyphro, relaying this story, claims that "Zeus . . . bound his own father because he gulped down his sons without justice" (*Euthr.* 5e; West and West).[33] Thus, yet again, Socrates' description is quietly haunted by the murdering of fathers and sons and the corresponding disruption of inheritance.

Socrates then moves to consider Cronus's own father, Uranus. Socrates derives the name from the phrase "looking at the things above" (ὁρῶσα τὰ ἄνω), though he also indicates that it is the astronomers (οἱ μετεωρολόγοι) who call him thus. Just after giving this description, Socrates offers the following:

> if I remembered Hesiod's genealogy, with some still higher ancestors than these that he mentions, I would not stop going over how rightly their names apply to them until I had tried out this wisdom that has just now so suddenly come over me, I know not from what source, to see what it will produce, and whether, after all, it fails to make it through or not. (396c–d; Sachs)

If Socrates further remembered Hesiod's *Theogony*, he would recall that Uranus was killed by his son Cronus. In accordance with his mother Gaia's wishes, Cronus one day took a sickle and castrated his father, throwing his member onto the earth and into the sea; it was out of the froth of this severed member that lovely Aphrodite was born (*Theogony*, 154–210, 453–506).[34] Thus, yet again, the name to which Socrates refers is one that emerges against a backdrop of the murdering of the father, the disrupting of inheritance. This example is particularly disruptive of inheritance as it involves the removal of the very organ of patriarchal inheritance, the penis. Cronus removed the source of his own genesis, severing his very origin.

It should here be remembered that such patriarchal inheritance is the core principle of the Homeric conception of names as Socrates conceives it. Earlier, Socrates considered the clue to the Homeric notion of the correctness of names to consist in the idea that a son, provided that his birth is such as to naturally give him the οὐσία of his father, ought to be called by a name which makes that common Being manifest. While the purpose of the inquiry into the names that followed the elucidation of this clue was ostensibly to establish the principle in greater detail, the result has instead been the development of a tragic scene in which the murderous disruption of inheritance is emphasized again and again.

Further, this murderous scene, tracing back the lineage of Atreus, has extended beyond the human realm and into the divine. What Socrates' examples have shown is that under the Homeric (i.e., the tragic) view of language, even the gods are understood tragically (i.e., as being trapped in the lower parts). The gods are understood not as they are, but rather as they seem from the tragic human posture: thus gods, like humans, are capable of both lies and murder. Such a conception of the gods already calls into question the supposition that the gods, unlike humans, call things by the correct names (391e): for the gods, it seems, are entirely as rough and vicious as human beings. Under such a tragic view the very possibility of a true λόγος dissolves along with the virtuousness of the gods, who cannot even agree with one another.

This passage discloses an important truth regarding the technological/tragic conception of naming. In nearly each case, the name Socrates considers refers (albeit subtly) to a case of familial murder, either of the father or of the son. In other words, each name has been seen to describe a person who operates independently and against its source or offspring. The Homeric and tragic view thus presents a severing of the connection between source and offspring, progenitor and inheritor. Applied to the general problematic of naming, this means that the tragic view of language is incapable of adducing a correct connection between a name and the being it names.[35] Rather, the name is severed from that to which it is supposedly bound, utterly disconnected from its dead origin.

This peculiar formulation says nothing more than what was said in the previous chapter: namely, that the technological/tragic understanding of language cannot account for the being of a thing, precisely because it is bound unreflectively within the world of human opining and wishing. The Homeric view perceives the gods, and Being, purely in terms of the "lower" region, the human region, so utterly pervaded by tragic μῦθος and falsehood. Such an account of language can only bring about a scene wherein the sons are disconnected from the fathers, wherein the names are disconnected from the beings. Such is the tragic understanding of names.

* * *

This entire tragic scene is repeated by Socrates with the utmost subtlety later in the dialogue during his explanation of the name "Hermes"—a name which, we have seen at length, bears special significance within the *Cratylus*. By way of reference to Homer's frequent use of the word ἐμήσατο (wrought) Socrates suggests that Hermes is "he who *wrought discoursing*" (τὸ εἴρειν ἐμήσατο) (408b). The word ἐμήσατο (in the conjugation that Socrates cites) occurs only five times in Homer, each time in the *Odyssey*. In its first two instances the word refers to Aegisthus's wicked plan to kill Agamemnon (*Odyssey* III.194, III.303). In its third occurrence it refers to king Antiphates, who wrought (ἐμήσατο) a terrible plan to eat Odysseus's crew for dinner (*Odyssey* X.115). In its fourth instance, the word ἐμήσατο is used by the shade of Agamemnon to tell Odysseus about how Aegisthus and Clytemnestra planned his death, stating that there is "nothing more bestial than a woman set on works like these—what a terrible thing she plotted [ἐμήσατο], slaughtering her own lawful husband" (*Odyssey* XI.429). Finally, ἐμήσατο is used to refer to the vicious work wrought (ἐμήσατο) by the goatherd as he brings armaments to the suitors from Odysseus's storeroom (*Odyssey* XXII.169).

The most obvious point common to all of these examples is that they involve wickedness. The verb μήδομαι primarily means *to intend, to plan, to plot,* and *to contrive*, though it can certainly mean *to invent*. In all of these selections from Homer the verb carries a sense of *evil* contrivance, of *scheming* in order to accomplish something nefarious. Thus, when Socrates explains Hermes' name as deriving from "he who wrought discourse" (εἴρειν ἐμήσατο), one should hear in this a sense of *evil contrivance*. It is thus that Socrates reinforces the point that discourse (εἴρειν)—which *is* λόγος (τὸ γὰρ εἴρειν λέγειν ἐστίν) (398d; see also

408a)—should be considered with the greatest suspicion and reticence, and precisely due to its connection to Hermes.

Further, in four of the five instances, the word is used to refer to a *murderous* deed, and in three of these Aegisthus's murder of Agamemnon is mentioned.[36] Tracing the use of the word ἐμήσατο in Homer thus leads us repeatedly to the murder of Agamemnon, serving to alert us more generally to the dissolution of stability, of that which abides. Given, as we have seen, that it is precisely the independent stability of beings that Socrates and Hermogenes are ostensibly seeking, one sees that the tragic Homeric view of language threatens any such stability.

But what does all of this have to do with the *Cratylus*, whose purported purpose is the investigation of words as a part of λόγος? Why does Socrates, while describing Hermes, subtly alert us yet again to these macabre significations that bespeak the deaths of fathers and sons, and the subsequent disruption of inheritance? We recall here that the question of inheritance has been at work from the very beginning of the dialogue, from that opening scene where the legitimacy of Hermogenes' name is comically called into question. We recall further that the question of inheritance was said to reinscribe, in filial terms, the very relationship that stands between words and the beings they name: that words are to inherit, so to speak, the nature of the beings they name. Finally, we recall that Socrates, during his etymology for the great goatherd Pan, claims that Hermes is the father of λόγος (408d). The very character of λόγος, then, is cast by Socrates within a filial framework, one whose structure is affected by what we have seen here. By briefly examining the connection between Hermes and λόγος—father and son—the extent to which our preceding musings on the Homeric/tragic view of language bear upon the problem of names and λόγος shall come to light.

First, a question of the *father*. In chapter 2 much was said regarding the complicated and mysterious character of Hermes. There it was seen that Hermes, in addition to being a messenger of the gods, is a playful rogue whose very role as messenger casts his credibility in a suspicious light. Further, we have already seen that λόγος has, according to Socrates, inherited its father's capacity for both truth and falsity, concealment and unconcealment. One cannot but wonder what other characteristics λόγος has inherited from its father Hermes, Prince of Thieves (ἀρχὸς φηλητέων).[37]

As previously noted, Jacques Derrida offers a description of Hermes that captures his essence well, and precisely by underscoring the extent to which this essence cannot be captured. Within the context of a reading of Plato's *Phaedrus*, Derrida analyzes the character of the Egyptian Thoth as he appears—or, for Derrida, does *not* appear—in Socrates' (re-)telling of the myth of the origin of writing. It is near the end of the following extended passage that Derrida aligns his description of Thoth with that of Hermes:

[T]he figure of Thoth takes shape and takes its shape from the very thing it resists and substitutes for. But it thereby opposes itself, passes into its other, and this messenger-god is truly a god of the absolute passage between opposites. If he had any identity—but he is precisely the god of nonidentity—he would be that *coincidentia oppositorum* to which we will soon have recourse again. In distinguishing himself from his opposite, Thoth also imitates it, becomes its sign and representative, obeys it and conforms to it, replaces it, by violence if need be. He is thus the father's other, the father, and the subversive movement of replacement. The god of writing is thus at once his father, his son, and himself. He cannot be assigned a fixed spot in the play of differences. Sly, slippery, and masked, an intriguer and a card, like Hermes, he is neither king nor jack, but rather a sort of joker, a floating signifier, a wild card, one who puts play into play. (Derrida 1981, 93)

Derrida, of course, is writing about writing, and we are writing about λόγος; he is writing about the *Phaedrus* and we the *Cratylus*. Yet Thoth/Hermes is not just the origin of writing, but of λόγος, too, both for Derrida (Derrida 1981, 96) and for Socrates in the *Cratylus* (408d). One can thus say, granting Derrida's description, that the father of λόγος, Hermes, is a wild card, a kind of no-kind whose very essence is characterized by a lack of definitive essence. Just like his Egyptian counterpart, Hermes is never present (Derrida 1981, 93) and is always on the move (Kerényi 1976, 32). The very itinerancy of his vocation demands that he never remain in one place for long, nor even long among the living: he is characterized by movements up and down, back and forth, tarrying between the living and the dead and the human and the divine. Hermes lacks a place of his own (Derrida 1981, 93), lacks property, lacks οὐσία. The father of λόγος is thus himself absent in or as his very being: he is essentially withdrawing and self-displacing.

All of which means that λόγος is a bastard, abandoned by the father. Though Hermes is the very source of λόγος, Hermes is such as *to be no source,* or, rather, to be a withdrawing source which can never be brought to presence, which can never *be there.* With the eternally mobile and absenting Hermes as its father, λόγος is always already separated from its source: for to be with Hermes is to be with an operation of absenting. Further, the word (ὄνομα) is the very vessel of this operation. When uttered, the word is released, perhaps forever, from its origin. To speak, to engage in λόγος, is to open up the very difference that stands between the gods and the human, opinion and truth, word and being, *the father and the son.* Understood in terms of the tragic view of λόγος, one could say that human λόγος, wrought by Hermes, always entails the absenting of the divine, the withdrawal of Being, *the death of the father.* Under such a view, the divine realm and the human realm are hermetically severed from one another.

Thus, the character of the relationship between Hermes and his son λόγος is one which mimics the tragic disruption of inheritance we have seen develop from out of the Homeric scene. Or, rather, it is not a matter of mimicry, or of reinscription, but of *origin*. The division between λόγος and its father is the *original division*, the original disruption, the one which ultimately accounts for the very difference between speech and Being, words and beings, humans and gods (the latter of whom speak correctly, *if they speak at all* [391e]). Λόγος names the difference between human and god, earth and heavens, name and Being: an insurmountable difference—a hermetic difference—which cuts the name off from its source, just as Zeus cut the principle of his inheritance off of Cronus. At least, such would be the condition of λόγος when considered from the tragic/technological view which Socrates has developed at length.

The Homeric scene, as the very origin of the Protagorean doctrine that "the human being is the measure of all things," has thus tragically presented the severing of word and Being that was seen in the preceding chapter to follow upon such a doctrine. On the tragic view, words, being tools of human mastery over beings, are relative to the human realm and ultimately bound to it. As a result, words so conceived cannot let the Being of the thing arise as it is independent of human's technological will or its tragic understanding. When a word is uttered under such a view, the word cuts the human irremediably from the being which it names and, indeed, from Being as such. The house of Atreus, whose members Socrates has etymologized, dramatically shows just such an incision.

This Homeric scene has thus given us a clue to the tragic view of language and its limitations. The tragic view, by conceiving words as tools, overlooks the filial connection that must be at work in order for there to be an uninterrupted lineage between a word and a being (or, more generally, language and Being). The tragic/technological view disrupts such a lineage by reducing naming to an operation of the human will executed in the service of human projects. Thus, while Homer's δόξα (393b) concerning the correctness of names was said to involve the principle of inheritance, what the extended Homeric scene has in fact shown is that such a view of language disrupts such an operation, severing the son from the father, or the word from the being. The tragic/technological view is patricidal.

It could therefore not be more appropriate that Socrates attributes this long string of inspired etymologies to a certain Euthyphro (396d). There is little doubt that this is a reference to the same Euthyphro who appears in the Platonic dialogue of that name, though there is substantial debate over the chronology and nature of the reference. Regardless of the precise nature of his mention in the *Cratylus*, it is a matter of hermeneutic necessity that it bring to mind the character Euthyphro from the *Euthyphro*, and all that that character entails.[38] Though the Euthyphro of the *Euthyphro* is well known for his ultimately misguided aspirations toward piety, he is perhaps best known for bringing an indictment of manslaughter against his father for killing a servant (*Euthr.* 4a ff.). The eventual outcome of Euthyphro's indictment is unknown, though there is some doxographical evidence that Euthyphro may have dropped the indictment following the exchange with Socrates represented in the dialogue.[39] Regardless, the Euthyphro of the *Euthyphro* is a man who, contrary to custom and filial responsibility, brought an indictment of murder against his father, the penalty of which could have been death. Thus, the source of Socrates' inspiration in the *Cratylus* that leads him to bring us before the Homeric scene of patricide, is himself a pending patricide whose relation to the gods is, as the dialogue that bears his name shows, highly questionable.[40]

Socrates' reference to Euthyphro thus serves a two-fold function. To begin with, the reference casts Socrates' frenzied wisdom regarding names—especially those of the gods—in a rather poor light: for if the *Euthyphro* shows anything clearly, it is that Euthyphro does not know the nature of the gods, despite his pretensions. Secondly, the reference shows that the person responsible for the wisdom at work in Socrates' etymologies—a wisdom that has shown the gods to be father-killers—is none other than a potential father-killer. In other words, the tragic scene which has presented the murdering of the father again and again is owed to a man whose *opinion* is that father-killing is justified. A world in which gods, like men, kill their fathers is a world set in accordance with the opinion of the pending patricide Euthyphro. Thus, the reference to Euthyphro reinforces Socrates' criticism of the tragic/technological view of language: namely, that it reduces beings to the opinions of humans regarding beings, and not to the beings themselves.

* * *

Finally, a question of the *son*. As we have seen, Hermes is a bastard, a hero, and a monster: half mortal nymph and half god, abandoned by his father to the innermost recesses of a cave. Hermes himself thus seems to have the dual nature which Socrates attributes to his son, Pan, brother of λόγος. If λόγος, like Pan, inherited its father's divinity and coincident capacity for unconcealment, then λόγος, despite being separated from its father, would reassert its father's character, bringing with it the resources of its absent source. It would then stand as a kind of surrogate father, a kind of *doubled* father who stands in for its eternally withdrawing origin. λόγος itself, son of Hermes, would then grant the possibility of a return to the source, of a return to the father which it itself *is*.[41] Yet, in keeping with its dual nature, such a possibility would always come with the price of a bad return, of a windstorm along the way of an odyssey.[42]

In order for λόγος to provide such a resource, one would need to come to know λόγος as having such a divine part. As was previously seen, the tragic view of λόγος remains ignorant of this part and is therefore waylaid within the lower, human part of λόγος. Thus, in order to come to find in λόγος the resources for a certain return *to* the source—a return to Being and the gods—one would need to extend oneself some measure *beyond* the tragic view. Only through such extension could one hope for a return to that which the tragic view cuts off.

If one were to overcome the tragic view, one would also by some measure overcome the original disruption that the tragic view takes to stand at the heart of the human being's relationship to the gods, and the word's relationship to Being. Phrased otherwise, to overcome the tragic view—to extend oneself beyond the lower parts of λόγος—would be to renew the source, to resuscitate the father (through the son), and thereby to gain access to the origin. Through such overcoming, one could gain a certain access to Being.

As suggested above, one such way of overcoming the tragic view would involve a certain engagement of the upper part of λόγος whereby a recognition of the dual nature of λόγος would take place. As also suggested, such engagement would be properly understood as the *comic view* of λόγος. It is appropriate, then, that Socrates now turns to long series of explicitly playful etymologies which serve as the very height of the comedy of the *Cratylus*. In turning now to this play, we will more readily see the character of such a comic view, and the manner in which it overcomes the tragic understanding of language.

7 What Words Will

Although Socrates has been playing with words since his entrance into the discussion with Hermogenes Hipponicus, it is only after his elaboration of the Homeric clue concerning the correctness of names, and the corresponding demonstration of that clue through the tragic scene of the house of Atreus, that Socrates transitions into an earnest display of the etymological prowess he claims to have contracted from Euthyphro earlier that morning (396d). Considered most generally, the long series of etymologies that follows generates a dramatic scenario reminiscent of the scene of radical becoming that arose out of the Protagorean doctrine that "the human being is the measure of all things." As seen in chapter 4, such a doctrine represents an understanding of nature (φύσις) based entirely upon the way it *appears* to the human being: namely, as a vacillatory play of unstable appearances. Under the sway of such an understanding, the stability thought proper to Being is undermined and supplanted by ceaseless *becoming*, and both λόγος and knowledge prove to be impossible.[1] With certain important exceptions (to which we shall return), the extended etymological section *shows* how those who supposedly conferred the original names upon beings were people who, like Protagoras, opined all things to be in flux and named beings in accordance with that opinion.

To the extent that this attachment to apparent flux and opinion is demonstrated throughout the etymologies, and eventually explicitly noted by Socrates (411b), the long series of etymologies foremost exhibits the *failings* of the technological/tragic/Homeric view of language out of which the names arose. Such a view, as Socrates has been at pains *to show*, is unreflectively bound by the limits of human opinion and is utterly trapped within the rough lower part of λόγος, that goat-like part pervaded by myth and falsity. The etymologies present, in vivid detail, the severance from Being characteristic of the tragic view of language.

Yet, as is apparent from even the most cursory reading of the *Cratylus,* the etymologies are preeminently playful, as Socrates himself explicitly notes on two occasions.[2] Consisting of comic mischief and excessive wordplay, the etymologies represent some of the most comedic moments in the Platonic corpus, despite the attempts of some scholars to take them with utter seriousness. How, then, is one to reconcile the tragic view that Socrates presents with the manifestly comic manner in which he presents it?

As was noted in the Introduction, comedy often operates in Plato's texts as a means of marking limits. It is through the comedy of the etymologies in particular that the limits of the investigation underway within the *Cratylus* are most clearly demarcated. Broadly stated, the etymological comedy discloses the manner—the *tragic* manner—in which human beings are bound to human λόγος.[3] Although Socrates and Hermogenes undertake to discover the correct names of things, and although these correct names are supposed by the interlocutors to coincide with the *divine* (and therefore true) names of things,[4] the etymological play eventually reveals the brute fact that human beings are wholly immersed in *human* names, those names made by human beings and informed by their all-too-human opinions (436b, 439c). In other words, Socrates and Hermogenes, being bound to human λόγος, are essentially incapable of accessing the divine names which they seek, though they remain forgetful of this incapacity. It is through a comic etymological display that Socrates reveals this tragic character of human names and the technological view of λόγος from which they arose.

However, the situation is only tragic if λόγος is *only* human in character—that is, if it is so pervaded by falsehood as to be *utterly* severed from the true λόγος of the gods. And yet, as Socrates will soon say in his etymology of the name "Pan" (discussed in chapter 2), λόγος is not *simply* human in nature, but is also divine and set up amongst the gods (θεῖον καὶ ἄνω οἰκοῦν ἐν τοῖς θεοῖς): that is, λόγος is *dual-natured* (διφυῆ/διπλοῦς) (408b–c). When human beings become cognizant of this dual nature of λόγος their ability to access the divine part of λόγος—that part that bears a relation to true Being—is restored, albeit in a limited manner. Through the recognition of the divine part of λόγος a certain (limited) overcoming of the human part takes place and subsequent (limited) access to the divine and the true is obtained. It is through his comic etymological display that Socrates will reveal this other part of λόγος, that part not wholly bound by the tragic and false.

To offer an analogy that helps clarify the character of such overcoming, one can think of those denizens of the cave imagined in Book VII of Plato's *Republic* who overcome their shadow existence precisely through the act of becoming aware *of* their shadow existence. Through learning that what they took for the truth was merely an image of it, the denizens are able to extend some measure beyond the limits of their bondage to images, while simultaneously becoming aware of the adamancy of that bondage. In the *Cratylus,* it is the long etymological section that reveals the tragic nature of human λόγος and the extent to which human beings are bound to images of the truth, and not the truth itself. However, it is precisely through this revelation that an overcoming of this tragic nature takes place. One could say that the etymological section, insofar as it effects this overcoming, enacts an ascent similar to that which takes place in Book VII of Plato's *Republic,* and does it through a comic analysis of names. It is through his comic revealing of the tragic character of λόγος that Socrates shall disclose a means of exceeding, to some extent, the tragic situation, as well as the necessity of a return.

The etymologies thus present Socrates playing, sometimes excessively, at presenting the tragic view of language—that understanding which takes names to be tools with which humans masterfully capture beings—in order to reveal its limits and thereby exceed them. Through playing at this tragic view, Socrates will open a critical distance between himself and the tragic view he is developing, a distance marked most of all by the comic mode of the exposition. It is within this critical comedy that Socrates will move some measure beyond the tragic view, into what I have called *the comic view.* Thus, the exceeding of the tragic view of λόγος will occur through an act of play, through an operation of comedy.

We will see this exceeding take place through the etymologies themselves, and in a double sense. First of all, we will see that the etymological section in general can be understood as enacting a certain ascent to the stability of Being, despite the apparent flux of the etymologies themselves. Secondly, the exceeding of the tragic view will occur through several *particular* names that Socrates will examine, most notably the names ἄνθρωπος (human being), ψυχή (soul), and ἀνδρεία (courage). Despite eventually remarking that most of the names he has analyzed represent the tragic view of λόγος (414c) and the commitment to flux and opinion which that view entails (411b), these specific names will extend—indeed, *ascend*—beyond such a tragic view. These particular names will disclose the manner in which names in general, and the operation of naming *as such,* resist the tragic understanding of λόγος, thus resisting the flux of nature understood as the world of vacillating appearances. Through such resistance these names will open the space for a new understanding of λόγος, one fundamentally at odds with the tragic view.

It is impossible to present an adequate treatment of the long and complex chain of etymologies that Socrates offers. Not only is the overall play so excessive as to defy rational explanation, but the semantic play of the Greek text is so rich, and above all so idiosyncratic to the Greek language, that any attempt to bring it into a different language without dampening the play is bound to fail.[5] This is due in no small part to the method which proves to be at work behind many, if not all, of Socrates' etymologies. Generally speaking, the etymologies of the *Cratylus* develop along a principle of *play.* Most of the words which Socrates treats are shown to derive from descriptions of the phenomenon in question, that is, a word is formed by condensing a phrase or descriptive sentence in some playful way. Because such derivations depend upon the semantic and syllabic play of the Greek language with itself, the richness and even coherence of most of the etymologies are lost to our Barbarian ears.

To offer just one example, recall Socrates' analysis of the word "hero" (ἥρως) (which we saw in chapter 2). "Hero" is said to relate to either desire (ἔρως) or the asking (ἐρωτᾶν) of questions (398d). In either case, what is clear is that the connection drawn by Socrates between the words ἥρως, ἔρως, and ἐρωτᾶν is one of homophony and syllabic play, a connection impossible to adequately express in English (or, for that matter, any other language). For a translator to say that *Heroes* get their name from *Desire* or *Asking* may be substantively correlative to the Greek text, and yet, the very principle behind the connection is lost through the act of translation. What for the Greeks would have been an obvious onomastic connection is for us a peculiar if not baffling relationship. While translators can do their best to convey the *meaning* of the words—while they can try to *say the same* as the Greek text—the very principle of their derivation is obscured through the act of conveyance.

Thus, in a radical sense, many if not all of the etymologies *defy* translation—they are radically untranslatable. As a result, the *Cratylus* itself, comprised of these many etymologies, resists translation.[6] A translator may draw upon the rich resources of her language, seeking accidental assonances and fortuitous homophonies, in an effort to bring the play of the Greek text into a foreign tongue, yet every attempt to do so will be limited by the *differences* that extend between Greek and Barbarian words. Further, any effort to bring the onomastic play of the etymologies into a foreign language is limited by the metaphysical need to express the "sense" of the word in question, almost always at the expense of a play on words. The metaphysical need to *say the same* as the Greek text, to express the same meanings, limits a translator's ability to translate what is most at play in the *Cratylus*: namely, *play itself.* Any attempt to translate the etymologies of the *Cratylus* is bound to leave a remainder, an excess: and this excess is to be understood as nothing other than the *play* which serves as the very principle behind the etymologies.

As an interesting consequence to this, any translation of the *Cratylus,* no matter how good, will fall short of bringing the excess into language. In other words, there can be no perfect translation of the *Cratylus.* As a result, *one must continually retranslate the text,* always attempting to move beyond the limits of one's language, always seeking to approach a state which, due to the differences at play between Greek and any other language, cannot be attained. One must play at approaching this state, while knowing oneself to be forever short. We shall return to this point in the final chapter.

In the face of the sheer excess of the *Cratylus,* it is customary (if not inevitable) among scholars to seek a certain structural order or coherent unity at work behind Socrates' otherwise chaotic and exorbitant etymological display.[7] Despite the specific differences amongst them, all such attempts mark a scholarly tendency to locate (or impose) an order within the Heraclitean flux of Socrates' fanciful etymologies. Scholars attempt to dampen the play of the text by binding it to a hidden law which would "make sense" out of what is, on the surface, nonsensical. However, as has already been suggested, it is precisely by attempting to limit this excess that scholars end up missing the very principle behind the etymologies—namely, the excess itself.

In all such efforts at mastering the play of the etymologies it is common for scholars to privilege certain words over others, finding within them keys by which the hidden order of the etymologies may be unlocked. It is as if we, the readers of the *Cratylus,* cannot help but grasp ahold of certain words, attempting to arrest their flow by attributing some stable meaning to them which we might then use to gain leverage over the other etymologies. Though such an approach cannot but seem arbitrary in execution, one wonders if this tendency to privilege particular words over others as somehow anchoring the otherwise turbulent flow of the etymologies tells us something about our relationship to λόγος, and even about λόγος itself. As will be seen, the long play of etymologies in the *Cratylus* brings the necessity of such attempts at arresting the flow of words to light, and the manner in which such necessity belongs to the human experience of λόγος.

The interpretation of the long etymological section that follows shall thus, as many before it, privilege certain of Socrates' etymologies over others. (Indeed, it shall even exclude some from consideration.) However, this interpretation shall differ insofar as it recognizes that such privileging *must only be done out of a sense of play.* In arresting the sense of a word—in treating it as if its meaning can be stabilized and trusted—one must treat the word not as secure land in the midst of a fluctuating sea of semantic drift, but as a *raft* which, as a human contrivance, must one day take on water and sink. Floating on such rafts, while *knowing* that they are rafts, one can play at broaching stability, while knowing oneself to be slowly sinking. Only through such play—which amounts to nothing other than a knowledge of the limits of one's language, or of language as such— can one avoid simply sinking along with them. Phrased otherwise, one can *only* play at reducing the excessive play of the etymologies to a lawful order. The moment one takes such play too seriously is the very moment that one loses sight of the excessive play that guides the entirety of the etymological section, the *Cratylus* at large, and—as the *Cratylus* is at pains to show—language itself.

* * *

After attributing his inspired performance in the previous etymologies to Euthyphro, Socrates proposes that they make use (χρήσασθαι) of his daemonic wisdom (δαιμονίας σοφίας) in order to finish their investigation (ἐπισκέψασθαι) concerning names (396d). This occurrence of the word χρήσασθαι (to use) recalls our analysis of *use* in chapter 5, alerting us that what is to come will be a matter of *use,* and thus a product of the technological view of language. We are also notified that the etymologies to come are a product of a wisdom that is not Socrates' own. Socrates' attribution of the knowledge of names to Euthyphro and his superhuman wisdom serves a two-fold function. Firstly, and most obviously, it serves to indicate that what is to come is in some way owed to the gods. Secondly, and relatedly, the reference to Euthyphro operates as a deferral which serves to open a critical distance between Socrates and what is to follow. Understood together, the attribution of the wisdom to Euthyphro's inspiration serves to indicate that Socrates himself does not pretend to be in control of the divine wisdom that he is spouting. It is thus that Socrates both announces the advent of divine knowledge *and* indicates his ignorance with respect to such knowledge. All of this is affirmed in Socrates' claim that though they shall use Euthyphro's wisdom today, they shall conjure it away (ἀποδιοπομπησομεθά) and purify themselves (καθαρούμεθα) of it the following day (396e).

Hermogenes agrees with Socrates' proposal that today they should use Euthyphro's inspiration to finish their investigation (or jest) into names, saying that it would be a great pleasure (ἡδέως) to continue to hear about the correctness of names (397a), thereby reaffirming his erotic commitment to the task at hand. Socrates then asks Hermogenes the following:

> So where do you wish [βούλει] for us to start examining [διασκοποῦντες] [words]? For what we have done is embark upon a certain general project, so that we will be able to see whether the words themselves [αὐτα τὰ ὀνόματα] will bear witness to us [ἡμῖν ἐπιμαρτυρήσει] that they are applied to particular things in a way that does not come altogether from chance [τοῦ αὐτομάτου],[8] but has a certain correctness about it [ἀλλ' ἔχειν τινὰ ὀρθότητα]. (397a; Sachs; trans. modified; my emphasis)

Two elements of this passage must be noted. First of all, it should be observed that Socrates has asked Hermogenes where he wishes (βούλει) to start examining the correctness of names, thereby echoing the first word of the text, βούλει (393a). Wishing will be of tremendous importance in the etymological section to come. Indeed, a great conflict is about to arise between what human beings wish for a word to say and what the word itself wishes to say.

Secondly, and relatedly, in articulating their general project Socrates has indicated the true focus of their inquiry (or jest). No longer interested in what any particular person (such as Protagoras) thinks about the correctness of names, Socrates is now concerned with what *the words themselves* (αὐτα τὰ ὀνόματα) can say about the matter. In the etymologies that follow, the words themselves shall be called upon as witnesses to testify (ἐπιμαρτρήσει) to their own correctness. One could say that Socrates is no longer concerned with what certain people *wish to say* about the correctness of words, but rather with what *words themselves* wish to say regarding such correctness. As will be seen, certain of the words Socrates comically investigates will indeed testify to their own correc*t*ness, indeed, to their *uprightness,* while *all words* will testify to a more general correctness whose structure shall come to light as we proceed.

Rather than focusing on the more deceptive names of heroes and human beings, Socrates suggests that they begin by investigating (σκοπουμένους) those things that "always are and are by nature" (τὰ ἀεὶ ὄντα καὶ πεφυκότα) (397b)—that is, the gods (397c)—whose names were surely given with a care befitting their importance. However, the particular gods whom Socrates now investigates are not the Olympian gods of the fourth century BCE (though they will eventually turn to these). Rather, Socrates suggests that they begin with those gods of primitive Greece, the sun, moon, earth, stars, and sky.[9] It is in the names of these eternal and natural gods that Socrates suggests the correctness of names may be found.

There is great humor in this seemingly sober suggestion. As seen in the previous chapter, the Homeric scene which precedes this passage has given us a rather grotesque picture of the gods' viciousness and mendacity. In short, the Homeric scene revealed that, under the Homeric view of language—which is the tragic/technological view—the gods are understood with respect solely to the lower, human part of λόγος: they are understood not as gods but as human beings.[10] The gesture of turning to the names of the gods as if they were more correct is thus laughable in the extreme: for under the tragic view of λόγος the gods, just like human beings, are capable of deception.

Moreover, as is immediately seen, the names of the gods were given not by rare and expert name-setters, but by the primitive people of Greece, whose acts of naming were guided entirely by their perceiving (ὁρῶντες) that all things are in motion (397c–d).[11] Thus, though the gods themselves may be eternal (ἀεί) and by nature (πεφυκότα), their names were given in accordance with how they *appeared* to human beings: namely, as being in continual motion and transformation. These names of the gods thus have little chance of conveying the correctness of names more ably than any other name.

After considering the names of these primeval gods Socrates turns to the names δαίμονες (daimon), ἥρως (hero), and finally ἄνθρωπος (human being). As scholars have noted, the order in which the etymologies now proceed generally follows a *downward* trajectory from the gods (who dwell amongst true Being) toward human beings (and, more specifically, the body [σῶμα]).[12] This descending order serves to underscore the condition of the etymological display itself by revealing that it is trapped on the earth within the realm of human names, despite its aspirations toward the speech of the gods (see Sallis 1975, 239–240). To phrase this otherwise, one could say that the descending order of the etymologies marks the tragic character of the λόγος from which the words themselves arose. Thus, the order of the etymologies here enacts the tragic descent that is at the very heart of the tragic view of λόγος.[13] Under the sway of the tragic understanding of λόγος words remain intractably oriented toward the human realm, where concealment reigns, oblivious of the gods and true Being above.

Most remarkably, precisely in the word for those who live upon the earth beneath the gods—ἄνθρωπος—a certain reorientation takes place which marks a reversal of this downward tendency, initiating an ascent.[14] As Socrates explains it, giving voice to Euthyphro's divine wisdom,

> [T]he name ἄνθρωπος signifies that the other animals do not investigate [οὐδὲν ἐπισκοπεῖ] or gather up [ἀναλογίζεται] or observe [ἀναθρεῖ] the things they see, but a human being, at the same time that he has seen—that's the has seen [ὄπωπε]—also observes [ἀναθρεῖ] and takes account of [λογίζεται] that which he has seen. And that's why a human being, alone among the animals, is rightly named ἄνθρωπος [human being], one who observes what he has seen [ἀναθρῶν ἃ ὄπωπε]. (399c; Sachs; trans. modified; my emphasis)[15]

The human being is such as to observe (ἀνα-θρεῖ) and reckon up (ἀνα-λογίζεται) all things. The human being is thus described as having an essentially upward comportment. In other words, amidst the downward flow of phenomenal appearance (i.e., of φύσις) and the etymological ordering which brings this to light, it is the human being—or, perhaps, a certain kind of human being—who directs its gaze upward beyond the flow in such a way as to reckon about, or gather up, what it has seen.[16]

Of course, it is the gods who are above (ἀνά) the earth. The name ἄνθρωπος thus shows the human being, though occupying the world of phenomenal flux, as being essentially oriented upward toward the gods who dwell amongst Being. Insofar as this is the case, the name ἄνθρωπος bespeaks a certain excess beyond the earth, a movement or transgression into divine Being above, even as it names that being properly situated on the earth. Just prior to offering the etymology of ἄνθρωπος, Socrates marks the excess of the account by claiming that he is in danger of becoming wiser than he ought to (σοφώτερος τοῦ δέοντος γενέσθαι) (399a). Socrates' inspired etymology is thus an excessive display of that being who, in affixing its gaze upon the gods and Being while standing amongst the flux of the earth, extends itself excessively—or, perhaps, monstrously—beyond itself.

This upward orientation of the human being, which works some measure against the downward pull of the world of appearances in which the human being is situated, continues to be emphasized in the further etymologies. Following the discussion of ἄνθρωπος Socrates turns immediately (at Hermogenes' behest) to an etymology of the word ψυχή (soul).[17] Socrates first suggests that the soul is so named because it is what gives life to the body, "giving it the power to breathe and reviving it [ἀνα-ψῦχον]" (399d–e; Fowler), again making use of the prefix ἀνα-.[18] However, Socrates quickly passes beyond this etymology, claiming to have suddenly come into possession of a better account, one more palatable to the tastes of Euthyphro and his followers (400a). After getting Hermogenes to agree that the soul is that which holds (ἔχειν) and carries the body, and, further-more, that the soul orders and holds the nature (φύσιν) of all things (400a), Socrates finally offers his etymology: "There would be an admirable fitness in calling that power which carries and holds nature [φύσιν ὀχεῖ καὶ ἔχει] φυσέχην: and this may be refined [κομψευόμενον] and pronounced ψυχή" (400b; Fowler). The soul is here described as that which *holds onto* (ἔχει) and *carries* (ὀχεῖ) nature (φύσιν)—a nature which, as we have seen, otherwise flows along uninteruptedly. Furthmore, the word ὀχεῖ, above translated as "carry," can also have the sense of *sustaining, enduring,* or *upholding.* So understood, the soul is that whereby the human being, with its *up*-turned gaze, resists and endures the flow of φύσις, *up*-holding it (or holding it up) and arresting its flow.

Just prior to offering this etymology of ψυχή, Socrates tells Hermogenes to "hold still" (ἔχε ἠρέμα) and prepare himself for the etymology to come (399e5). In telling him to hold (ἔχε) still Socrates is telling Hermogenes to hold on and en-dure in the face of the apparent flux of the etymologies: for it is through such holding (ἔχειν) that Hermogenes will enact the ascent away from the flow of na-ture and toward the stability of Being. Further, in telling him to hold *still* (ἠρέμα) Socrates is foreshadowing his etymology of "Hermes" to come (407e–408b). There, after remarking upon Hermes' mischievous relationship to λόγος (408a), Socrates will say that "he who wrought speaking [τὸ εἴρειν ἐμήσατο] would justly be called Εἰρέμης by you—but nowadays we call him 'Hermes' ['Ερμῆν], believing that we're beautifying the name" (408b; my translation). The homophonous play between ἠρέμα and Εἰρέμης serves to suggest that Hermogenes is here showing himself to be like his namesake Hermes. Insofar as he has begun the ascent from the world of appearances to the world of Being, and precisely through a reinter-pretation of words, Hermogenes has shown himself capable of the transport be-tween humans and gods, appearance and Being, that Hermes represents. This ascent to divine Being will only continue. However, as one would expect with Hermes, a certain attachment to descent and deception will tarry close behind.

Hermogenes responds to Socrates' second account of ψυχή by saying that it is more artful (τεχνικώτερον) than the first (400b), indicating that Socrates' ety-mology was born of the technological understanding of language, that under-standing which takes the human being to be tragically trapped within the fluctu-ating realm of appearances. Yet, the word ψυχή itself, as Socrates analyzed it, seems to suggest a certain overcoming of such a realm by indicating the holding and arresting of such flux. How, then, can this etymology of the word ψυχή be *more* characteristic of the technological view if the word itself indicates the over-coming of such a view?

Socrates' reply gives the answer: "Yes, it *is* more [artful/technological]: how-ever, it seems laughable [γελοῖον] that the name was given [ἐτέθη] so truly" (400b; my translation). Of course, it was Socrates who gave the name, and who did so laughably. Socrates has been *playing* at the tragic view by willfully and artfully contriving names out of fanciful descriptions—and it is precisely through such play that Socrates has indicated a movement beyond the tragic view. By claiming that his more technological (τεχνικώτερον) etymology of ψυχή is laughable (γελοῖον) Socrates has supplanted the tragic view with the comic one, submitting the former to comic ridicule and thereby showing that the comic shall here serve as the measure of the tragic. The etymology for ψυχή thus marks a moment where the comic ascent resists and overcomes the tragic descent characteristic of the technological view of λόγος.

Socrates concludes this series of words—a series which, as noted above, has generally followed an order of descent—with an account of the word σῶμα (body) (400b ff.). Claiming that there are many different explanations for this word, Socrates points out that "some say it's a *tomb* [σῆμα] for the soul, as if the soul were buried in its present condition; on the other hand, because it is by means of [the body] that the soul signifies [σημαίνει] whatever it signifies [σημαίνῃ], it is also for that reason correctly called a *sign* [σῆμα]" (400b–c; Sachs; trans. modified). The body, on this interpretation, is understood as a sign—that is, as a *word* that signifies something beyond itself, namely, whatever the soul signifies or intends. Thus, in looking for what "body" signifies, they have found that it signifies the very function of significance, that it signifies signifying. The body, the very object of the physical world, points beyond itself in a gesture of signification to something absent. In chapter 6, we saw that this gesture of signifying what is absent marks the very function of words in general. In an interesting way, then, the etymology for σῶμα (body) raises, at the level of a single word, the entire problematic of naming being considered within the *Cratylus* as a whole.

Showing his hermeneutic commitment to the reinterpretation of signs (σῆμα)—in this case, the body, which just means (σημαίνει) sign (σῆμα)—Socrates goes on to say that it seems most likely to him that it was the Orphic poets (οἱ ἀμφὶ Ὀρφέα), with their understanding of the body as a *safe* (σῆμα) or *prison* (δεσμωτηρίου) for the soul, who gave the body (σῶμα) its name (400c). Insofar as the soul remains trapped in the body (as the Orphic poets contend), it remains on the earth in the lower region of λόγος, and therefore cut off from the gods, truth, and Being. Socrates' suggestion that it was the Orphic poets who gave the body its name thus amounts to the claim that the name σῶμα was given by those who understood the human condition to be one of tragic bondage to the bodily. What the etymology of σῶμα has thus shown is the tragic character, and subsequent downward orientation, of the understanding which gave the body its name. It should further be observed that the very name 'Orpheus,' whose bearer is perhaps best known for descending into Hades to retrieve his dead wife Eurydice, bespeaks descent.[19] The mention here of the Orphic poets indicates unmistakably that it is the tragic understanding of λόγος that Socrates is playfully espousing.[20]

Shortly after this display Hermogenes requests that they turn to the names of the (Olympian) gods to see what kind of correctness they have (400d). In making this request Hermogenes indicates that he is eager to undertake the ascent to the gods that was broached through the etymology of ἄνθρωπος, thereby breaking free of the descent in which they have otherwise been engaged. However, before proceeding, Socrates first offers a caveat about the character of the etymologies to come. In what follows, Socrates explains, the divine and true names of the gods will not be examined (σκοπεῖν), but only the names that human beings customarily use in their prayers (ἐν ταῖς εὐχαῖς) to the gods (400e). Such names, as products of human contrivance, are necessarily informed by human opinions (δόξαν) (401a)—opinions which can, of course, be incorrect. In other words, the analysis that follows will be of the *tragic* names given to the gods, those names fashioned by those beings who dwell amongst the lower, false part of λόγος, and therefore lack an appropriate relationship to the gods.[21] However, as already averred, this analysis will take place as a comedy, and will thereby extend beyond the tragic names to some as yet unspecified extent.

In accordance with custom, the god with whom Socrates begins is Hestia. Socrates explains that the original name-givers derived Hestia's name from οὐσία and ἐσσία: "Hestia" is thus a derivation of the word for Being.[22] In beginning with Being, Socrates is both announcing the ascent away from becoming and toward Being underway and asking the god of Being, Hestia, for safe passage. However, according to Socrates, there is another etymology for Hestia which associates her with ὠσία, which derives from ὠθοῦν (thrusting). Thus, while some associate the goddess's name with stable Being (οὐσία), others (such as Heraclitus [401d]) associate it with fluctuating, thrusting movement. Following upon our analysis in chapter 4, one can surely add Protagoras and Homer to this latter position. Of course, as we have seen, the position which understands all things to be in flux is nothing other than the tragic view of language. It is thus the tragic view which understands Hestia as representing the movement of thrusting. One can only suppose, then, that it is the *comic* view, the one Socrates is currently *enacting* through his ridiculous etymologies, that understands Hestia as signifying Being. This further indicates a tension between the comic and tragic views of λόγος, and that the ascent underway shall occur precisely through the comic view.

Socrates then claims that they ought now to investigate (ἐπισκέψασθαι) the gods Rhea and Cronus. Claiming to have a totally laughable thing to say (γελοῖον μὲν πάνυ εἰπεῖν), Socrates quotes Heraclitus as saying that "all things move along and nothing abides" (πάντα χωρεῖ καὶ οὐδὲν μένει), and that "you cannot step into the same river twice" (402a; my translation). Both Rhea and Cronus, Socrates continues, were given their names to signify flowing streams (ῥευμάτων).[23] Socrates then quotes Homer as evidence of this, saying that "in the same way, Homer also speaks of 'Ocean, the source of the gods, and Tethys their mother'"

(402b; Sachs). This Homeric passage appears twice in Book XIV of the *Iliad*. In each case, it occurs within the context of the goddess Hera speaking with "false lying purpose" in an attempt to seduce Zeus into sleeping with her.[24] One wonders if Socrates himself is speaking with "false lying purpose" in offering these playful and utterly tragic etymologies—and precisely in order to seduce Hermogenes into following him along the erotic ascent toward Being.

Hermogenes does not entirely understand the example and asks that Socrates explain more fully what the name "Tethys" means (βούλεται). Socrates responds by saying that "the name [Tethys] itself almost says [αὐτὸ λέγει] that it is the name of a stream [πηγῆς]" (402c; my translation). This formulation reminds us that Socrates' foremost concern is with what *the words themselves* wish to say (λέγει) about their correctness (397a). It also bolsters the suspicion voiced in chapter 1 that there is a semantic connection between saying (λέγει) and meaning (βούλεται): that is, between *saying* and *wishing*. (We shall return to this connection below.) In this case, the name "Tethys" wishes to voice the propulsion (διαττώμενον) characteristic of a flowing stream, a description which Hermogenes finds very refined (κομψόν) (402d).[25]

After offering an etymology for Poseidon, Socrates turns to the god Pluto. With this etymology for Pluto (i.e., the underworld), Socrates and Hermogenes have descended as far as they can go. After considering the name "Pluto" and its connection to wealth (πλοῦτος), Socrates turns to the other name of this god, "Hades." Claiming now to be speaking in accordance with how things really seem (φαίνεται) to him, Socrates gets Hermogenes to agree that desire (ἐπιθυμία) is the strongest bond for making a living being (ζῴῳ) remain (μένειν) in place (403c). Socrates then asks Hermogenes whether there is any desire stronger than the "one that arises when one believes that by associating [συνὼν] with someone he'll be a better man" (403d; Sachs). Hermogenes swears, "by Zeus, no!" thereby indicating his own intense desire to improve himself through association with the (inwardly) beautiful and good Socrates.

Desire is here understood as an *arresting*—a cessation of movement that keeps things in place. It is for this reason, Socrates explains, that Hades has been able to entice those who come to him (in death) to remain with him. On account of the beautiful words (καλούς . . . λόγους) with which he charms his visitors, Hades, just like a perfect sophist (τέλεος σοφιστής), is able to convince people to remain in his company (403e). Socrates then appends the following to his description of the god:

> Then, too, he refuses to consort with human beings when they have bodies, but only accepts their society when the soul is pure of all the evils and desires [ἐπιθυμιῶν] of the body. Do you not think this shows him to be a philosopher [φιλοσόφου] and to understand perfectly that under these conditions he could restrain them by binding them with the desire of virtue, but that so long as

they are infected with the unrest and madness of the body, not even his father Cronus could hold them to himself, though he bound them with his famous chains? (403e–404a; Fowler)

It is thus suggested that it is the mark of the philosopher to know that only when the soul is without the body and its desires can it be kept in place by "the desire concerned with virtue" (τῇ περὶ ἀρετὴν ἐπιθυμίᾳ) (404a). The philosopher, it seems, should be without body.

One wonders: can desire (ἐπιθυμία) be conceived of without the body? Further, could the most powerful desire—that for virtue through the association (συνών) with better men (ἀμείνων ἀνήρ)—be understood in utter abstraction from the body? Or, rather, is there not a bodily component to *all* desire, and is one not bound to conceive of desire as ultimately and irremediably tied in some way to the body? In this register it should be observed that Socrates has claimed that there is no greater desire than the desire to improve oneself through association (συνών) with another man (ἀνήρ). The word σύνειμι, while certainly meaning "association" or "coming-together," can also denote the being-together characteristic of sexual intercourse.[26] One wonders if Socrates' use of this term here serves to indicate the illegitimate abstraction from the body at work behind the tragic etymology, as well as subtly hint at desire's essential attachment to the body.[27]

Along these lines, one thinks of the *Symposium*, where the body is seen to be an essential component in initiating the erotic ascent from beautiful bodily things toward the beautiful itself (*Symp.* 210a). Without such bodily desire—or, more generally, without the body—the movement of the soul upward toward Being cannot initialize. The understanding that desire—the very motive force driving the philosophical ascent toward Being—is that which keeps one *in place* is thoroughly informed by the tragic view that understands human beings as stuck in the lower part of λόγος. Under the sway of such a view human beings are trapped in Hades amongst the shades with no means of transport beyond. Socrates is here playing at offering a tragic understanding of desire which takes it as basically opposed to the philosophical movement from the bodily toward Being. In a word, the tragic view understands the philosopher in precisely the wrong way, conflating the philosopher with the sophist (403e; 404a). Such an understanding severs the philosopher irreparably from Being, trapping him in the world of shadows, and depriving him of the requisite desire to escape.

After offering etymologies for Demeter, Hera,[28] and Pherephatta (i.e., Persephone), Socrates turns to a god particularly dear to him: Apollo.[29] Socrates begins by noting that many people (πολλοί) are afraid of this god (404e) on account of their interpreting the name as denoting something terrible (τῷ χαλεπῷ) (405e). Most likely, Socrates is referring here to the apparent connection between the name Apollo and certain words denoting *destruction*, such as ἀπολῶ and ἀπόλωλα.[30] Most interestingly, this exact interpretation can be found in Aeschylus's great tragedy *Agamemnon*. As she pounds her chest in lamentation, Cassandra cries the following words: "Apollo, Apollo, god of the Ways, *my destroyer* [ἀπόλλων ἐμός]— for you have destroyed me utterly [ἀπώλεσας γὰρ οὐ μόλις τὸ δεύτερον]" (*Agamemnon* 1080).[31] One wonders if Plato had this tragic scene in mind as he wrote the *Cratylus*.

After Socrates offers accounts for several other gods, Hermogenes asks about the pair Dionysus and Aphrodite. In a certain sense, the etymology for the god Dionysus is the most important in this series—for Dionysus is the very god of tragedy, and Socrates has been playing at displaying (and displacing) the tragic understanding of language. What is pivotal in this etymology is the extent to which Socrates' comic playfulness comes to the fore. Indeed, just prior to offering his comic etymology for the god of tragedy, Socrates draws attention to the comedy that will follow:

> Big things, child of Hipponicus, you ask: but there's a serious way of speaking about the character of these gods' names and also a playful way [ἀλλὰ ἔστι γὰρ καὶ σπουδαίως εἰρημένος ὁ τρόπος τῶν ὀνομάτων τούτοις τοῖς θεοῖς καὶ παιδικῶς]. So ask some other people for the serious way, but there is nothing hindering us from passing through the playful way [παιδικὸν], since even the gods are lovers of play [φιλοπαίσμονες γὰρ καὶ οἱ θεοί]. (406b–c; my translation)

Socrates thus explicitly states that the etymologies to come are to be guided by a principle of play (παιδικός), a mode of operation which is, moreover, said to be loved by the gods. This statement serves to vindicate the etymological comedy already underway and signal its immediate intensification. Further, this passage indicates that Socrates' etymological exercise is not to be taken too seriously, but must rather be seen in its proper comic light (which, again, is not to suggest that it is in any way frivolous). Finally, this passage reveals a certain intimacy between play and the divine, thus intimating a certain overcoming of the separation of the human beings and the gods characteristic of the tragic view. (We shall return to this point below.) Socrates' general point could be phrased as follows: when one deals with the names of the gods, one must interpret playfully.

Socrates' account of the tragic god Dionysus follows immediately upon this affirmation of comedy. Socrates playfully (ἐν παιδιᾷ) associates the name "Dionysus" with the phrase "the giver of wine" (ὁ διδοὺς τὸν οἶνον), condensing this into the word Διδοίνυσος. On this playful account, the god of tragedy is responsible for drunkenness, which makes people believe (οἴεσθαι) that they have wisdom (νοῦς) when in fact they do not (406c). With this etymology Socrates has slyly equated the tragic view of λόγος, of which the god of tragedy is presumably co-responsible, with the state of drunkenness which results in a false claim to wisdom.

Socrates earlier described the original tragic name-givers as supposing the world to be spinning around, when in fact such an understanding is based only upon the name-givers' own dizziness (411b)—dizziness such as results from drunkenness. With the etymology for "Dionysus," Socrates has solidified his comic depiction of the tragic understanding of language as being essentially bound to false opinion. Those who adopt the tragic view are like dizzy and drunken fools who think that they know what they do not in fact know. One wonders if the *comic* view would thus consist precisely in *not* pretending to know what one does not in fact know, thereby reveling a certain sobriety and possession of νοῦς.[32]

Shortly after this comic overthrow of the god of tragedy, Socrates urges that they leave consideration of the gods behind, as he is afraid to talk about them any further (407d). Socrates' fear is no doubt grounded in the fact that he has been playfully reinterpreting the names of the gods—a reinterpretation which, in light of his impending trial, could appear impious.[33] Hermogenes is happy to oblige, provided that Socrates offer one more etymology, that for the name "Hermes" (407e ff.). As previously noted, the very fact that Socrates nearly omitted an account of this god's name marks the comic character of the inquiry: for the name "Hermes" is the most important of all, given that it was precisely in order to assay Hermogenes' relationship to the god that Socrates was brought into the conversation in the first place (383b). Socrates then offers his etymologies for Hermes and his son Pan, with which we are now quite familiar (see chapter 2 and above).

In the many disorderly (415c) etymologies that follow, the full range and play of which are impossible to capture, one general characteristic comes to the fore: namely, that most of the etymologies indicate things to be in radical flux. Socrates himself will observe this tendency when he mentions the condition of the (perhaps drunk) original name-givers (411b–c), and again much later during his conversation with Cratylus. Moreover, the long string of etymologies indicates that those who gave the names did so from out of a preoccupation with their own opinions of things (τῆς δόξης; 411b) and not with the things themselves. Such a condition is, as we have seen, nothing other than the tragic understanding of language, that understanding immersed in the lower parts of λόγος. In the many frenetic etymologies that follow, Socrates wades through the chaos that such a tragic understanding entails.

However, just prior to reinitiating his etymological exercise—one he has now said consists of searching for the words given in accord merely with how things seemed (φαίνεται) to the dizzy original name-givers—Socrates prepares himself for the onslaught to come:

> That is no trifling tribe of words you're stirring up, my friend. All the same, seeing how I have arrayed myself in the lion's skin, it is necessary not to be cowardly [οὐκ ἀποδειλιατέον]. Rather, the thing to do, it seems, is to examine [ἐπισκεπτέον] "good sense," "understanding," "judgment," "knowledge," and the rest of these beautiful words [τὰ καλὰ ὀνόματα] you invoke (411a; Sachs; trans. modified).[34]

As Joe Sachs has noted, Socrates' mention of the lion-skin is certainly a reference to Heracles, well-known for wandering around in the skin of the Nemean lion.[35]

Thus, in addition to playing the role of Hermes in the Cratylus, Socrates is playing the role of the heroic Heracles. As Joe Sachs further notes, this reference perhaps suggests that the Cratylus as a whole can be understood as reinscribing the labors of Heracles.³⁶

Despite this apparent connection, it is difficult to know which labor in particular we are to understand as bearing upon the etymological exercise underway. Given the structure of descent and ascent to which the *Cratylus* has continually had recourse, one wonders if it is Heracles' twelfth labor, and his most famous, that is meant. In accordance with Eurystheus's will, Heracles descended into Hades to fetch the dreaded dog (δεινὸς κύων) Cerberus.³⁷ Most interestingly, according to the shade of Heracles in the *Odyssey*, he was only able to complete this daunting task because Hermes helped him on his way (*Odyssey* XI.623).³⁸ Perhaps verifying that it is indeed this labor being referenced in the *Cratylus*, Socrates swears "by the dog" (νὴ τὸν κύνα) immediately prior to describing the dizzy and drunken name-givers.³⁹ One can almost imagine that these name-givers are like those who dwell in Hades, the realm of the mere shades of things, whose access to true Being has been severed irremediably.⁴⁰

If indeed it is this labor to which Socrates is subtly referring—again, something that cannot easily be determined—what would be the point of the reference?⁴¹ Perhaps we are meant to understand Socrates as engaged in a descent into Hades, the realm of darkness and concealment, the realm no doubt corresponding to that lower part of λόγος. Is Socrates courageously saving Hermogenes from a life spent amongst the shades? Is he trying to save Hermogenes from forgetfulness—indeed, from that forgetfulness that has haunted their investigation from the outset? Earlier it was argued that both Hermogenes and Socrates proceed through their investigation into λόγος through λόγος in a manner oblivious to the dangerously self-reflexive character of their task. Could it be precisely this forgetfulness from which Socrates is now courageously attempting to save Hermogenes?

Even without knowledge of the specific labor to which Socrates is referring it is clear that Socrates is calling for *courage* in the face of the task at hand.⁴² What is needed is the courage to resist the downward pull of the tragic etymologies, the courage to ascend in the face of such a tragic descent. Interestingly, it is not long after the reference to Heracles, and this call for courage, that Socrates turns to an account of the word ἀνδρεία (courage): "ἀνδρεία got its name in battle, and for there to be a battle in what *is* [μάχην δ' εἶναι ἐν τῷ ὄντι], if that is in flux, would be nothing other than to have an *opposing* flow [τὴν ἐναντίαν ῥοήν]" (413e; Sachs; trans. modified). Socrates then adds, decisively, that the words for male (ἄρρεν) and man (ἀνήρ) refer, like ἀνδρεία, "to the upward flow" (τῇ ἄνω ῥοῇ) (414a; Sachs).⁴³ Man is thus named as he who, through his courage, opposes himself to the flow of things (ἐν τῷ ὄντι), redirecting that flow *upward* (ἄνω). Man is engaged in a battle with the flow of φύσις, bringing an opposition (ἐναντίαν) to bear against it. With this etymology the full import of Socrates' earlier mention of Heracles' lion-skin becomes clear (411a).

One recalls here the etymology for the human being (ἄνθρωπος), who was said to be the animal who turns its gaze upward and reckons up. The human being, in its courage, comes to oppose itself to the downward flow of φύσις by holding onto the flow and redirecting it upwards. It is therefore the courageous human soul that undertakes an arresting of φύσις. The conversation of the *Cratylus* has been a testing of Hermogenes' ability to do just this, to move from the Protagorean understanding of things (which had almost carried him away) toward an understanding of the stability of Being. In a word, Hermogenes' *courage* has been tested. Pursuant to this test is the measure of Hermogenes' erotic ability, that is, the ability of his soul to undertake the movement upward toward Being (such as is described by Diotima in Plato's *Symposium* [211c–d]). Ultimately, this is a test of whether or not Hermogenes is like his "father," Hermes, who moves so effortlessly up and down the vertical plain. Finally, it also amounts to a test of whether or not Hermogenes is a *philosopher*, like Socrates, who occupies a mediate position between gods and human beings.[44] (That Hermogenes will soon be called "daimonic" [ὦ δαιμόνιε] by Socrates [415a] indicates that he does, at least in the eyes of Socrates, occupy a mediate position.) It remains to be seen whether and to what extent Hermogenes will show himself to be in possession of such a courageous soul. But first, the playful tragedy of the etymologies must continue.

The tragic character of the etymologies that follow is marked by Socrates at various points. For example, the moon (Σελαναία), Socrates explains, is so called "due to the fact that it always has a new and an old beam" (σέλας νέον τε καὶ ἕνον ἔχει ἀεί) hence its name Σελαενονεοάεια, which has been refined into Σελαναία. Hermogenes responds to this nifty contrivance by saying that it is "quite a rhapsodizer of a name" (409b–c; Sachs). The word Joe Sachs translates as "rhapsodizer" is διθυραμβῶδές. Hermogenes is saying that Socrates' account of the moon is dithyrambic, after the fashion of a dithyramb. As we know from Aristotle's *Poetics*, the Greeks associated the dithyramb with tragedy (*Poet.* 1449a10). Further, as the Athenian stranger observes in Plato's *Laws*, dithyrambs were associated with Dionysus, the god of tragedy (*Lg.* 700a). Hermogenes is thus calling Socrates' account of the moon *tragic*.

Most appropriately, Socrates further indicates the tragic character of the names during his account of the word τέχνη (art). As Socrates explains it, the word τέχνη originally denoted "possesion of mind" (ἕξιν νοῦ)—a contrivance that Hermogenes finds tacky (γλίσχρως). In defence of his account, Socrates offers the following:

> You blessed fellow, do you not realize that the first names that were given have by now been covered over by people who want to turn them into tragic poetry [τραγῳδεῖν] putting in and taking out letters to make them easy on the tongue

and twisting them every which way. . . . But I imagine the people who do that sort of thing have no respect for truth, but only for the shape of their mouths [τὸ δὲ στόμα πλάττοντες],[45] so they keep making lots of insertions into the first names until they end up making it so that no single human being can understand what in the world the names mean. (414c–d; Sachs; trans. modified)

The word τέχνη has been rearranged and distorted by the tragic understanding of language, which is nothing other than the technological understanding. In other words, the word τέχνη has been altered by the very understanding of language that takes language as a τέχνη, as a tool by which the human exerts mastery over beings. One operating under such an understanding of language, who constantly "tragedizes" it (τραγῳδεῖν), cares less about the truth than about the shape (πλάττοντες) of his mouth.

Of course, it is Socrates himself who has been adding and subtracting letters capriciously, though he has been doing so in a state of explicit playfulness. His playful approach to offering such tragically adorned words is clear in his account for the word βλάβερος (harm). As Socrates explains it, this word is a condensed form of the phrase "wishing to fasten the flow" (τὸ βουλόμενον ἅπτειν) (417e). An attempt to willfully fasten the flow of φύσις through λόγος—to arbitrarily arrest the play of significations—is characteristic of the tragic view of language, that technological view that only has recourse to its own opinions and fancy, but not to the things themselves. Hermogenes' own response to Socrates' etymology of βλάβερος labels it a tragic one: "Fancy [ποικίλα] names do roll off your tongue, Socrates. Why, just now when you were enunciating that word βλουλαπτεροῦν, you looked to me as if you were pursing your lips [στομαυλῆσαι] for the flute prelude of the hymn to Athena" (417e–418a; Sachs). The suggestion is that Socrates, like those tragic souls just mentioned (414c), is here concerned only with the shape of his mouth:[46] or, in other words, his etymologies are in no way guided by the truth of the things themselves, but rather by other, more private considerations. In other words, Socrates has been whistlin' Dixie. Finally Socrates himself states outright the arbitrary (i.e., *willful*) character of the etymological exercise he has been conducting: "And if we are permitted to insert and remove any letters we wish [βούληται] in words, it will be perfectly easy to fit any name to anything" (414d; Fowler; trans. modified)— which is, of course, precisely what Socrates has been doing.

Socrates warns Hermogenes not to demand too much precision in what is to follow: "Do not be too strict about it, daimonic one [ὦ δαιμόνιε], 'lest you incapacitate me of my strength'" (415a; Sachs).[47] Socrates then turns to "the loftiest height of the subject," namely, the words ἀρετή (virtue) and κακία (wickedness) (415a).[48] Beginning with the latter, Socrates explains that κακία is to be connected with "going badly" (κακῶς ἰόν), which, in turn, is to be semantically connected with "cowardice" (δειλίᾳ). Remarking that they ought to have examined "cowardice" (δειλίᾳ) back when they analyzed "courage" (ἀνδρεία) (413e),[49] Socrates explains that

[C]owardice in a soul [δειλία τῆς ψυχῆς] signifies something's being a strong set of chains, since "exceedingly" [λίαν] is sort of like "strong" [ἰσχύς]. So the exceedingly greatest set of chains on the soul would be cowardice [ἡ δειλία], just as being at a loss is also a vice, as is, it seems, everything that is an obstruction to going on and making progress. This, then, appears to make it evident that "going badly" [κακῶς ἰέναι] is proceeding haltingly and in an obstructed manner, so when the soul is in that condition it becomes filled with vice. (415c; Sachs)

Thus, the soul that remains in place, or that "goes badly" (κακῶς ἰέναι), is the cowardly soul. This account hearkens back to Socrates' description of the god Hades, who was said to keep men bound to him through the desire for virtue (τῇ περὶ ἀρετὴν ἐπιθυμίᾳ) (404a). There, it was suggested that the philosopher is understood as remaining in place, indeed, as remaining in place in Hades amongst the mere shades of Being. Here, it has been said that cowardice is to be understood as just such a remaining in place. It is thus that the philosopher, according to Socrates' tragic play, is aligned with cowardice.

Ἀρετή (virtue), Socrates continues, would be understood as the opposite (τοὐναντίον) of cowardice, signifying "ease of proceeding" (εὐπορίαν), and indicating that "a free-flowing condition always belongs to a good soul" (τὴν ῥοὴν τῆς ἀγαθῆς ψυχῆς εἶναι ἀεί) (415d; Sachs). Socrates concludes that the name ἀρετή (virtue) refers to "what is *constantly flowing* [ἀεὶ ῥέον] in an unchecked and unobstructed manner" (415d; Sachs). This account of "virtue" as naming a *certain type* of *flow*—one opposed to the flow of φύσις—hearkens back to Socrates' account of ἀνδρεία (courage), where it was said that courage signifies a flow (ῥοή) opposed to (ἀναντίαν) the flow of beings understood as radical flux (413e). Taken together, Socrates has interpreted ἀρετή in such a way as to refer to the soul that has the courage to resist the flow of φύσις by redirecting that flow *upward* toward Being. We see now that it is not just any human being who opposes the flow of φύσις, but rather the *virtuous* human, the *courageous* human—in a word, the *philosopher* differently understood. There is thus a conflict here between two views of the philosopher, a conflict that corresponds to that between the tragic and comic views of λόγος. The tragic view takes the philosopher as arrested within the world of appearances—a sophist stuck in Hades, unable to ascend. The comic view—the view that Socrates is developing through his etymological performance—takes the philosopher as the virtuous human who courageously ascends beyond the world of mere appearances toward the stability of Being.

Most decisively, Socrates offers the following addendum to his account of ἀρετή: "Now maybe you will claim this is another case of my making something up [πλάττειν], but I claim that if what I said before about κακία [evil] is correct [ὀρθῶς], I've got this name ἀρετή [virtue] correct, too" (415d–e; Sachs; trans. modified). Socrates' use of the verb πλάττειν, translated here as "making something up," playfully suggests that *Plato himself* is responsible for contriving these playful accounts.[50] Plato's jesting examination into names has nearly reached its conclusion.

As Socrates nears his final string of etymologies, he—not unlike a horse approaching the finish line (420d)—offers one final burst of speed. After accounting for "necessity" (ἀνάγκη) and the "voluntary" (ἑκούσιον), Socrates asks about "the greatest and most beautiful names" (τὰ μέγιστα καὶ τὰ κάλιστα): namely, ἀλήθεια (truth), ψεῦδος (falsehood), ὄν (being), and ὄνομα (word, name) (421a). Given that these are the most beautiful (τὰ κάλιστα) names, and that "beautiful things are difficult" (χαλεπὰ τὰ καλά) (384b), one imagines that *courage* will be especially necessary in the face of this difficulty. And indeed such courage is immediately necessary: for the flow of nature, which human courage is meant to resist and redirect, is about to reach its highest pitch.

The first word that Socrates now considers is the word ὄνομα (word, name), which Socrates derives from the phrase "a being for which there is an inquiry" (ὃν οὗ μάσμα ἐστίν) (421a). This account makes manifest the self-reflexive and ultimately abysmal character of Socrates' and Hermogenes' inquiry as a whole: for that which they have been seeking all along—knowledge of words—is now seen to refer (and, indeed, *defer*) to nothing other than further inquiry. On Socrates' account, "word" just names the necessity for continually searching for the meaning of "word." This etymology serves to disclose the abysmal relationship that the human being has with language, and the manner in which the human's ability to inquire into language is limited by the linguistic mode of any such inquiry. More generally, the account of the word "word" indicates that, when it comes to words, one must have the courage to *continually* inquire anew. Phrased otherwise, one can only *interpret* and *reinterpret* the meanings of words, *forever* searching for a stable ground beneath the interpretations: a ground which, though intimated by the very character of a word itself, never arises. (We shall return to this below.) Thus, when it comes to words, one must be an interpreter, a ἑρμηνεύς. In other words, one must be like Hermes.

But to be like Hermes is to be like a god. This means that, when one undertakes a reinterpretation of names, one transgresses the tragic human condition and becomes godlike. It is therefore fitting that the next word to which Socrates turns his play is the word ἀλήθεια (truth), which he interprets as denoting a "divine wandering" (θεία ἄλη) (421b). When one inquires into the nature of words—when one looks into them for their truth—one moves upward toward Being and wanders with the gods. By contrast, if one remains unmoved by words—if one simply takes them as true, without subjecting their meanings to analysis—then one remains at rest. Such a state of rest Socrates here interprets as denoting *falsity*: "what is 'false' [ψεῦδος] is the opposite [τοὐναντίον] of motion, for once again what is restrained and forced to be quiet is condemned and likened to those who are *asleep* [καθεύδουσι]" (421b; Sachs). The one who fails to inquire into the meanings of words is the one who remains in Hades, bound to images, as if asleep.

The final word that Socrates here investigates is, fittingly, Being (τὸ ὄν / ἡ οὐσία)—that toward which the inquiry as a whole has been moving ever since the mention of Hestia (401b). As Socrates explains it,

> "Being" [τὸ δὲ ὄν καὶ ἡ οὐσία] . . . is in agreement with the true [ὁμολογεῖ τῷ ἀληθεῖ], with an iota removed, since it signifies something going [ἰόν], and "not being" [τὸ οὐκ ὄν] in turn signifies something not going [οὐκ ἰόν], which is even the way some people pronounce it. (421b–c; Sachs)

A rather complicated double movement has taken place here. On the one hand, with his etymology for Being (τὸ ὄν καὶ ἡ οὐσία), Socrates has brought about a situation wherein Being, whose stability was being sought, is understood precisely as a lack of stability—that is, as motion (ἰόν). Thus, the etymological comedy, which began with an invocation to Being (401c), has resulted in the termination of the stability of Being. The tragic understanding of language that Socrates has been developing has reduced Being to the flow of appearance, just as Protagoras had done. With this reduction Socrates' performance of the tragic view of language reaches its comic culmination.

On the other hand, Being has here been associated not simply with movement, but with a *divine* movement, a movement that moves with the divine and the true. Not-being (τὸ οὐκ ὄν), by contrast, is equated with stasis, with *rest* (οὐκ ἰόν), which is the very opposite of movement. The association of non-Being with rest is reminiscent of Socrates' earlier etymology for the name "Hades," which was shown to interpret desire (ἐπιθυμία) as remaining unmoved (μένειν) within the underworld (see above). The one who is among non-Being is the one who is stuck in Hades among the shades, utterly severed from the truth of Being. Phrased otherwise, the person who lives solely and unreflectively amongst myth and falsehood, who is none other than the adherent to the tragic view of language, rests amidst non-Being. By contrast, the one who reaches upward and *moves* with the gods has some access to Being.

With his etymology for Being Socrates has thus enacted a sort of *double reading*. On the one hand, he has instantiated the tragic view of language through his downward-oriented etymologies, those etymologies guided by the way things *appear* to certain human beings. On the other hand, Socrates has *critiqued* this view of language through his comic mode of exposition (i.e., through the comedy of the etymologies) by showing that it reduces Being to the flow of appearances. Socrates thus both performs the tragic view of language and simultaneously exceeds it: through his flow of etymologies he demonstrates the flow of worldly appearances while simultaneously intimating something stable beyond it. By way of a playful pastiche of the tragic view of language and the commitment to non-Being it entails,

Socrates has moved away from the tragic view and has redirected his movement toward Being. To phrase this in directional terms: as Socrates' etymologies have moved *downward*, toward the world of unstable appearances, Socrates has simultaneously moved, through a comic λόγος on λόγος, *upward* toward Being. Socrates shows the world to consist of radical flow while simultaneously *redirecting* that flow upward toward Being.

Hermogenes' response to Socrates indicates that just such a redirection of the flow has taken place: "You seem to me to have hammered away [διακεκροτηκέναι] at these words in a thoroughly courageous [ἀνδρείως] manner" (421c; Sachs; trans. modified).[51] With his use of ἀνδρείως (courageous), Hermogenes harkens back to the etymology of *courage* (ἀνδρεία), where the word is said to signify a flow *opposed* to the flow of nature (413e) and, more specifically, a redirection of that flow *upward* (ἄνω) (414a). As Socrates there mentioned, there is a battle being waged concerning Being (ἐν τῷ ὄντι)—that is, a battle between Being understood tragically as the flow of appearance and Being understood as denoting a certain underlying stability. With his etymology for Being (τὸ ὄν / ἡ οὐσία) Socrates has brought both sides of this battle to a head, and has defeated the tragic view courageously.

But what, exactly, was courageous about Socrates' etymologies? Nothing other than his ability to redirect the flow of φύσις *upward* toward Being. Socrates, donning his lion-skin cape (411a), has left the shadowy realm of Hades and wandered upward toward Being, toward the gods, toward that upper part of λόγος that participates in the truth. Socrates has resisted the tragic understanding of λόγος and has overcome it through a comic reinterpretation of words.

When one reinterprets the meanings of words—as Socrates has done—one plays at broaching Being: one leaves behind one interpretation of a word in search of another, better interpretation (i.e., one that more ably reveals that which it names). If one simply rests with words in their ossified meanings, one remains stuck, as it were, in the shadow of the name's legacy: one *inherits* an interpretation, an opinion. The risk, as Socrates has made clear, is that the word might fail to correctly disclose the nature of that which it names. In such a case one's inheritance would be a burden, a mere image of the truth. However, if one investigates the words that one inherits—if one *reinterprets* them—then one draws oneself beyond the shadow, so to speak, of the opinions of the benefactors of one's language: one frees oneself from a legacy of error, from a bad inheritance, exceeding, perhaps monstrously, the limits of that legacy. When one reinterprets, *one kills the father.*

However, such a reinterpretation cannot simply be a willful gesture of interpreting phenomena to one's liking: for such a gesture would simply reinscribe the Protagorean/technological/tragic view of language that Socrates has tried so hard to rebut. Rather, the reinterpretation of words must be done in the service of the phenomena which they name (439b) and must be measured by them. As one experiences phenomena one must test one's words against them, and let those words say what they have to say about the phenomena in question and phenomenality as such. Stated most simply, one cannot simply inherit words as if they give knowledge: one must *search* words for the knowledge they purport to give. When one reinterprets, one shows oneself to be enacting the Socratic pursuit of knowledge.[52]

Some time after his etymology for Being, and after Cratylus finally breaks his silence to enter into the conversation, Socrates affirms the necessity of reinterpreting words. After he admits his own uncertainty about the veracity of the preceding etymologies, Socrates says the following:

> So it seems to me we ought to examine what I'm saying all over again [χρῆναι ἐπανασκέψασθαι]. For deceiving oneself, by oneself, is the most troublesome of all things; when the deceiver is never even a little distance away but always present, how could that not be a terrifying thing? So it looks like it's necessary to turn back repeatedly [μεταστρέφεσθαι] to the things said before and try, in the phrase of that poet, to look "forward and backward at once." (428d; Sachs; my emphasis)

Thus, when it comes to words, χρῆναι ἐπανασκέψασθαι—it is necessary to investigate again. Socrates is saying that it is always necessary to return, that one will never have satisfied or completed the investigation into the nature of a word (ὄνομα), that "being for which there is an inquiry" (421a). One must always begin again—one must always reinterpret. It is only through such reinterpretation that the true character of λόγος will show itself.

Two brief philological points regarding Socrates' use of ἐπανασκέψασθαι must be made. First, the aorist infinitive ἐπανασκέψασθαι ("to investigate again") contains the prefix ἀνα-, which, in addition to meaning "again," can mean "up" or "back."[53] In light of our analysis of ἀνα- above, and the ascensional movement that this prefix indicates, one can hear in the word ἐπανασκέψασθαι a comittment to the ascent toward Being underway within the *Cratylus*. It is precisely through the reinterpreting of words, and the measuring of those words against the phenomena that they bring to light, that one undertakes a movement away from mere vacillatory opinion toward the stability of Being. In other words, it is through a reflective engagement of the play of differences—that is, through reinterpretation—that one begins to ascend beyond the *mere* play of differences. By examining words always anew one raises oneself beyond stubborn and blind attachment to the flow of words and undertakes an ascent toward Being. Interpretation is the movement between unstable words and stable meaning.

Secondly, as has been the case with σκοπεῖν throughout the *Cratylus*, the verb σκέπτομαι must be seen in its playful connection to σκώπτειν. In saying that it is necessary to always return to an examination of words (ἐπανασκέψασθαι), Socrates is playfully suggesting that it is always necessary to return to a *jest* of words, to a comedy of words. He is suggesting that if one wishes an examination (σκοπεῖν) of words to be fruitful, it must be pursued playfully (σκώπτειν): for the over-zealous investigation of language—which is tragic in character—is bound to remain in the lowest parts if λόγος, utterly severed from that which it seeks. Only the playful reinterpretation of words, themselves playful, can play at ascending to the truth.

Yet, this gesture of reinterpretation is two-faced—it is *dual-natured*. As Socrates' extended etymological comedy has shown, words, when submitted to arbitrary reinterpretation, can be made to mean anything (414d): that is, they can be used to obfuscate the truth rather than clarify it. *Yet it is precisely through becoming aware of this obfuscating capacity of language that one exceeds it.* Through reinterpreting the meanings of words, as Socrates and Hermogenes have done, one becomes aware of the limits of one's language to disclose the truth. Yet this awareness of the limits of language itself operates as a partial exceeding of those limits. In other words, in order to come to see one's language as riddled with myth and falsity one must have an experience of the true aspect of language as well: to come to know the lower part one must make a sojourn into the upper part. Such a sojourn has taken place through the Socratic inquiry into words, and more specifically through the comic ascent of the etymologies. Through an inquiry into words Socrates has affirmed the shaggy, goat-like character of λόγος, while simultaneously moving *up* into the smooth, divine part. The *Cratylus* itself has through comedy *shown* the dual nature of λόγος.

The *Cratylus* is thus an exercise in comporting oneself correctly toward language. Such an exercise is meant to assay the double-directionality of language, its dual capacity for both truth and falsity. To accomplish this, Socrates interrogates language itself, *with* language, and lets language show itself in its full richness. In other words, Socrates *listens* to language, letting words themselves testify to their own correctness (397a). When allowed to speak, words say something about themselves, about λόγος, and about the human being's relationship to λόγος. What is it, then, that words *say?* In order to answer this question in greater detail, we now turn to Socrates' use of the word βούλομαι within the *Cratylus*, which, recall, is the very first word of the text. This word itself says something about the nature of names and the nature of the relationship that human beings have to λόγος.

* * *

Throughout the etymologies, Socrates has been asking Hermogenes if he *wishes* (βούλει) to do something. For example, Socrates asks with which words he wishes (βούλει) them to begin their inquiry. Or, again, Socrates says that, *if Hermogenes wishes* (εἰ μὲν βούλει), the god Ares is so called due to his virility and courage (407d). There are many instances where Socrates uses this trope to ascertain what Hermogenes wishes.[54] Additionally, Socrates will occasionally use βούλομαι in referring to what some name-giver (be it Homer or some other) intended in giving the name that he did (see 414c). In all of these cases, Socrates uses the word βούλομαι to refer to the *wishes* of an individual, to what an individual *desires*. In this way, as was suggested in chapter 1, βούλομαι can be seen within the *Cratylus* as holding a special connection to the opinion (δόξα) of an individual. In continually indicating that the etymologies are following what Hermogenes *wishes*— rather than, say, the truth of the matter—Socrates is subtly suggesting that the etymologies are pervaded by falsehood and opinion: that is, that they are a product of the tragic view of language.[55]

However, as also suggested in chapter 1, there is another sense of βούλομαι at play in the *Cratylus,* one which runs counter to this human volitional sense and, indeed, one which can only be discovered through a playful engagement with the text. The first instance of such usage occurs during Socrates' etymology for "Atreus": "Now the given form of the name is a little twisted and hidden, so that it does not make the nature of the man evident to everyone, but to those who understand about names it makes evident enough what 'Atreus' *means* [βούλεται]" (395b; Sachs; trans. modified). Socrates goes on to say that the *name* "Atreus" itself indicates that Atreus's nature (τὴν φύσιν) consists of stubbornness (τὸ ἀτειρὲς), fearlessness (τὸ ἄτρεστον), and disastrous recklessness (τὸ ἀτηρὸν) (395c). In other words, the name *itself* wishes (βούλεται) to say something about that of which it is the name.

This deeper sense of βούλομαι develops as the dialogue continues. Socrates draws out the etymologies for "Rhea" and "Kronos" in an attempt to show that they are names given in accordance with the flux doctrine of Heraclitus, and that they are related to the river Tethys (402b). Hermogenes responds by saying that he does not know "what the name 'Tethys' means" (ὄνομα τί βούλεται) (402c5). Though βούλεται gets translated here as *means, wishes* or *wills* is more appropriate given the emphasis on βούλομαι throughout the text and the relation to wishing it has been seen to entail. Hermogenes does not know what the name of Tethys *itself wishes* (to say or express). Socrates verifies his reading by responding that "the name itself almost says" (αὐτὸ λέγει) what it itself intends: in this case, a combination of the words "strained" (τὸ διαττώμενον) and "filtered" (τὸ ἠθούμενον) (402c–d). We recall here that Socrates has explicitly stated that he is no longer interested in what any particular person has to say about the correctness of names, but only about what *the names themselves* have to say about their own correctness (397a). Throughout the etymological section Socrates is trying to let the names themselves testify to their own nature: that is, he is attempting to let λόγος say (λέγει) what it wishes to say about itself.

Later, during his pursuit of the "elemental words" (i.e., those primal words out of which all other words are constructed), Socrates playfully laments that the wills of these original words "have been completely buried by those who wished to dress them up in tragic adornment [ὑπὸ τῶν βουλομένων τραγῳδεῖν]" through the adding and subtracting of letters for the sake of euphony (414c; Fowler; trans.

modified). These people "who care nothing for the truth but only for the shape of their mouths" have altered the names to such an extent that "no human being can understand what in the world the words mean [βούλεται τὸ ὄνομα]"—that is, what in the world the words themselves *wish to say*. Thus, the dialogue highlights a conflict between the human being, who wishes one thing, and words themselves, which wish another thing. This conflict is essentially a further elaboration of the conflict announced at the very outset of the dialogue. Hermogenes' position, which maintains that words are correct through convention, is in conflict with Cratylus's position, which states that words are correct by nature (384c–d). However, this is only a dramatic enactment of the real battle being waged: the one between the will of the human being and the will of names themselves. Names *will* to be as they are, and *wish* to make something about their nature (or the nature of language in general) manifest through their own self-telling. Human beings, on the other hand, seek to temper names to accommodate their particular human interests (such as euphony). There is a tension, then, between what *language* wills and what a person who uses a name or a word wills.

As the dialogue continues, Socrates begins to let his etymologies be affected by the wishes of the words themselves, listening to what it is they wish to say. The word γαῖα, Socrates says, better expresses what the being itself *wishes* (βούλεται) than does the form γῆ (410b). The word τὸ ἀγαθόν (the good), he later claims, "*wishes* to denote the noble in nature" (τοῦτο τῆς φύσεως πάσης τῷ ἀγαστῷ βούλεται τὸ ὄνομα ἐπικεῖσθαι) (412c; my translation). In his treatment of τέχνη (skill) (414b) also, Socrates indicates that his etymologies are being led by what it is that the names themselves wish (βούλεται) to denote, what it is that they themselves wish to say.

Socrates' examples (e.g., γυνή—γονή; 414a) show that what words wish to denote first and foremost is their playful similarity to other words. Words, by virtue of being words, tend toward other words in a playful way. In other words, words, through their material similarity to different words (i.e., their visible or audible similarities), tend toward those differences: or, to put this more provocatively, words play toward difference, putting differences into play. On Socrates' account, words obey a law of play that drives them toward other, different (though similar) words: and it is this principle that is at work behind the entirety of Socrates' etymological display. Words wish to race off toward other words, flowing into them.

If one attends to words—if one lets words say what they themselves have to say—then one first of all becomes privy to their playfulness: one comes to recognize the filial connections between words, and also the filial connection that stands between words and their mischievous father Hermes. Such awareness can easily lead one to suppose that words are excessively, if not exclusively, playful, and that words therefore cannot be trusted to reveal the true nature of things. (Indeed, Socrates himself will soon make this very claim [440c].) If one were to get lost in this pure play of differences, one would never alight upon the stability in search of which

Socrates and Hermogenes began their inquiry. Rather, one would get lost in a realm of pure myth and falsehood, utterly closed off from Being.

However, this would only occur if one took the play too *seriously*: that is, if one *forgot* that it was play. It was said in the Introduction that a principle of forgetfulness is at work in the *Cratylus* and that this forgetfulness accounts, in part, for the comedy of the text. The greatest forgetfulness at work within the *Cratylus* is that of the essentially playful relationship between human beings and language. If one forgets this play then one *loses* oneself in words, in *mere* words, and stays isolated within the world of shadows (without even knowing *that* they are shadows). To remember the play is to awaken oneself to the other half of λόγος, the *higher* half, that allows one a glimpse—but *only* a glimpse—of true Being.

It is precisely through the long etymological comedy that a reawakening of the other half of λόγος occurs. As we have seen, it is through his comic performance of the tragic etymologies that Socrates comes to reveal the limits of the tragic view of language while simultaneously moving beyond it into the comic view, that view that recalls the dual nature of λόγος. This movement occurs most explicitly through the string of words beginning with the ἀνα- prefix (as analyzed above). As we have seen, Socrates used these etymologies to depict the courageous human soul as the vessel through which an ascent beyond the flux of appearances and toward the stability of Being takes place. Of course, Socrates' etymologies of these "uplifting" terms, which served to counteract the downward pull of φύσις and the tragic view of language, are no less arbitrary than those for any other words in the text (as Plato's play on πλάττειν suggests [415d]). It is not the case that these words somehow escaped the tragic understanding of λόγος from which they arose, or can somehow escape the capriciousness at work in Socrates' many other etymologies; to the contrary, they are as willful as the rest, if not more so. However, despite this, these words as Socrates has contrived them show something about the nature of *all* words, of words as such: namely, that it is within the very character of a word to resist the downward flow of φύσις and to orient itself upward away from the flow. Words, by their very nature, serve to arrest the flow of that which they name. What is needed is the *correct comportment* toward words, one that recognizes their dual nature, *listens to it,* and thus sees their essential filial connection to Being. What is needed is a *comic* comportment as we have come to understand it: one must see language both in its connection to mere appearance (i.e., non-being) and in its essential intimacy with Being. Thus, although words playfully tend toward a flow of differences, they also tend toward stability. (By now we should not be surprised by such ambivalence at play in language, but should rather see it as fitting with the ambiguous and playful character of Hermes, father of λόγος.)

Earlier, we saw that the human soul is that which holds onto (ἔχει) and carries (ὀχεῖ) the flow of nature (φύσις), redirecting that flow *upward* (400b). We see now that it is through λόγος that this redirection of the flow takes place. In the face of the flow of appearances, it is the human soul that, through words (i.e., through λόγος) moves upward toward Being.[56] Λόγος is thus the medium in which the human being moves through appearances toward Being. Socrates' long etymological comedy has been a performance of just this movement, the punchline of which is this: one must let oneself be moved *by words* toward the stability which those words promise but which, in the final moment, they cannot fully supply. A word grants both the possibility and the impossibility of achieving stability, and one must have the courage to follow words into the abyss they themselves open up in pursuit of the stability they intimate.[57]

Words thus *flirt* with moving from their vacillatory play toward a set stability, seducing the human being into movement toward stability. There is thus an essentially *erotic* structure to λόγος so understood.[58] In chapter 2 it was argued that the Heroes, seen in their relation to ἔρως, stand between gods and mortals, traversing the distance between the two. It was also argued that Hermes, as such a hero, typifies this erotic movement. Now it is seen that λόγος, the very offspring of Hermes (408d), stands between flux and stability, offering the possibility for both divine ascent and mortal descent. Λόγος, like Hermes, has a dual nature: like father, like son. Whether Hermogenes finally proves himself to be the son of Hermes—thus proving himself to be like λόγος—shall be addressed in the next chapter.

* * *

In his dissection of previous words, Socrates employed the words τὸ ἰόν (going), τὸ ῥέον (flowing), and τὸ δοῦν (chaining) (421c). Hermogenes, demonstrating his erotic longing for the truth, now asks about the correctness (ὀρθότητα) of these words. As we have seen, Socrates' etymological display has followed the principle that certain words are compounds of other words or condensed sentences. However, as Socrates now makes clear, such a principle threatens an infinite regress. Unless some original, "elemental" words (στοιχεῖα) can be discovered—words that are not made up of any further words (422a)—one would keep on cutting (ἀποκρινόμενον) words indefinitely (421e), always finding other words comprised of other words comprised of other words, and so on. It is these elemental words which Hermogenes would like now to investigate, taking ἰόν, ῥέον, and δοῦν as representative cases.

Before they begin their playful investigation into these elemental words Socrates notes that, due to their antiquity (παλαιότητος), they may be impossible to find (421d). Nevertheless, he insists that "the game does not admit of excuses" (προφάσεις ἀγὼν δέχεσθαι) and it is necessary for them "to investigate [διασκέψασθαι] these things vigorously" (421d).[59] In other words, despite the hopelessness of finding these elemental words in a virginal and untarnished state—or, indeed, of finding them at all—it is necessary to *play* at investigating them. Socrates then asks Hermogenes to join him in the investigation (συνεπίσκεψαι)—that is, to join him in the play—to which Hermogenes replies, "I will investigate with you [συνεπισκέψομαι] to the best of my ability" (422c). Hermogenes is here showing himself to be eager for such play.

Again through the interrogative mode, Socrates claims that all names are the same with respect to their function of making things manifest (δηλοῦν), and that this function is nothing other than their correctness (422d). As Socrates goes on to clarify, this ability to make manifest is a matter of *imitation*: "a name is an imitation by voice [μίμημα φωνῇ] of that thing which is imitated [ὃ μιμεῖται], and one who imitates [ὁ μιμούμενος] anything with his voice [τῇ φωνῇ] names [ὀνομάζει] what he imitates [μιμῆται]" (423b; Sachs). However, the manner by which a word imitates is unique amongst τέχναι. Whereas music (ἡ μουσική) imitates sound (φωνή), and painting (ἡ γραφυκή) imitates shape (σχῆμα) and color (χρῶμά), words imitate something else: namely, words imitate *Being* (οὐσία) (423e).

It is important to read this statement—that words imitate Being—in the context in which it appears. As is so often the case, Socrates proceeds in the interrogative mode:

SOCRATES: Doesn't it seem to you [δοκεῖ σοι] that each thing also has a being [οὐσία], just as it has a color and the attributes we were just speaking of . . . ?

HERMOGENES: It seems so to me [ἔμοιγε δοκεῖ].

SOCRATES: What about it, then? If someone had the power to imitate [μιμεῖσθαι] this very aspect of each thing, its being [τὴν οὐσίαν], in letters and syllables, would he not make evident [δηλοῖ] what each thing is? Or is that not so?

HERMOGENES: Very much so.

SOCRATES: And what would you say about someone with this power, the way you said before that one sort of person is skilled in music and another in visual arts? What is this person?

HERMOGENES: This one seems to me [ἔμοιγε δοκεῖ] to be the one we've been inquiring about all along, Socrates—the name-giver [ὁ ὀνομαστικός]. (423e–424a; Sachs; trans. modified)

Socrates has asked Hermogenes if it seems to him (δοκεῖ σοι) that words are imitations of being (οὐσία), and Hermogenes has agreed by saying that it seems (δοκεῖ) so to him. Hermogenes then says that it seems to him (δοκεῖ) that the technician capable of making such imitations ought to be called the name-maker (ὁ ὀνομαστικός). There are two points of interest here. First, in again emphasizing seeming (δοκέω), Socrates is subtly hinting that this line of inquiry is still very much bound to the limits and pitfalls of human opinion (δόξα), and is thus subject to the same criticisms leveled against the technological view of λόγος analyzed in chapter 5. Second, in continually asking Hermogenes how things seem to him, Socrates has characteristically kept his silence about what he himself thinks about such things. In a word, Socrates has kept his own opinion *open*. As will be seen, such openness is exceedingly important, and is characteristic of Socrates' philosophical position regarding λόγος.

Proceeding on the technological and tragic premise that words are imitations of Being (οὐσία), Socrates now proposes that they consider whether the name-maker, in making those elemental words mentioned above (ἰόν, ῥέον, and δοῦν), correctly grasped the being of each with the letters and syllables he employed (424a–b). In order to consider this, Socrates claims that he and Hermogenes must first separate all parts of language (i.e., vowels, consonants, diphthongs, etc.) and examine them thoroughly (424c). Only once this is done will they be able to determine whether all the parts were properly put together by the original name-maker in such a way as to correspond to the things named. It is worth noting that though Socrates claims that such preparations are necessary if one is to have any hope of discovering the efficacy of the original words, both Socrates and Hermogenes in fact fail to undertake these preparations. This failure is, of course, entirely in keeping with the comedy underway.

Socrates then offers the analogy of painting (γραφική) in order to clarify the name-maker's art (τέχνη). Just as each primary pigment in a painting imitates some actual color, each letter and other phonetic unit corresponds to the being it imitates (425a). As Socrates says,

> In exactly that way, we too will apply the letters to the things, one to one to what seems to require it, or several together, making precisely what people call syllables, and in turn putting together the syllables of which the nouns and verbs are composed. And out of the nouns and verbs again we'll organize at last something great [μέγα], beautiful [καλόν], and whole [ὅλον], like the painting in our example from visual art; here it is λόγος, due to skill at name-giving [τῇ ὀνομαστικῇ] or rhetoric [ῥητορικη] or whatever art it is [ἢ ἥτις ἐστὶν ἡ τέχνη]. (424e–425a; Sachs)

Λόγος is hereby presented as a whole (ὅλον) made up out of various parts, a whole which, like a painting, serves as an imitation of beings. It is worth noting that the art capable of compiling this imitation is not said by Socrates to be dialectic or philosophy, but rather "name-giving or rhetoric or whatever art (ἡ τέχνη) it is." Thus, whatever else can be said about them, these original name-givers were not philosophers or dialecticians—that is, they were not those who know about names and about how to ask questions (390c ff.), nor, more importantly, those who know about Being. One already begins to wonder how correct words could be when given by such people.

Socrates now says that, whereas the ancient name-givers (οἱ παλαιοί)[60] are responsible for having put together language (λόγος) in its present state, it will be the job of Socrates and Hermogenes to "cut these words to pieces" (διελομένους) if they are to know with technical specificity (τεχνικῶς ἐπιστησόμεθα) whether the compound words were put together well (425a–b). In other words, the technological view of λόγος requires a technical (τεχνικῶς) analysis in order to reveal whether the words given under such a view are efficacious tools for imitating reality, and the analysis will proceed by way of cutting (διελομένους). We recall Socrates' analogy, discussed in chapter 5, between naming and cutting (τέμειν) (387a). It was there argued that such an analogy, along with those of drilling and burning, bespeaks a certain violence at the heart of naming. More precisely, it was argued that naming, when considered as a τέχνη among others, submits beings to the wishes and wills of human beings, and thus to the world of mere opinion. In the investigation now underway, Socrates wishes to see whether the original name-givers made their words in accordance with the way things really are, or only in accordance with the way things *seemed* to them. In other words, Socrates wants to discover whether they were carving reality at the joints or haphazardly hacking and hawing. In order to discover this, Socrates himself will need to cut words down to their most elemental parts. These incisions will reveal the manner in which the name-givers named beings only in accordance with their opinions. However, it will *also* and above all reveal the arbitrary and willful character of Socrates' own cutting (i.e., his own method of investigation). Both the act of naming (itself a kind of cutting) and the act of cutting up the words to decipher their meanings are violent and willful acts, dependent on the opinions (δόξα) of the agents, and they risk overlooking the true nature of the beings themselves.

Socrates immediately underscores this attachment to δόξα, and the consequent limitations of his proposed course of action:

> Shall we give up then? Or shall we do the best we can and try to see if we are able to understand even a little [σμικρόν] about them, and, just as we said about the gods a while ago—that we knew nothing about the truth but were guessing at the opinions of humans concerning them [τὰ τῶν ἀνθρώπων δόγματα περὶ αὐτῶν]—so now, before we proceed, shall we say to ourselves that if anyone, whether we or someone else, is to make any analysis of names, he will have to analyze them in the way we have described, and we shall have to study them, as the saying goes, with all of our might? Do these things seem [δοκεῖ] good, or what do you say? (425b–c; Fowler; trans. modified)

Socrates has now explicitly claimed that their investigation is concerned not with the truth, but rather with the opinions of human beings (τὰ τῶν ἀνθρώπων δόγματα). Under the present conditions of the inquiry, this could not be otherwise. Given that the technological/tragic view of λόγος elucidated in chapter 5 is irremediably bound to human opinion, Socrates' and Hermogenes' inquiry, insofar as it proceeds on the premises of that view, is no less bound to human δόξα. What follows will thus remain to a great extent within that lower part of λόγος, the rough, goat-like part permeated by myth and falsehood.

Socrates then makes a statement regarding the tragic way in which some would investigate the correctness of names:

> I suppose it must appear ridiculous [γελοῖα], Hermogenes, that things could become clear by being imitated in letters and syllables, but it's a necessity all the same. For we have nothing any better than this that we can fall back upon for truth in the original names, unless, after all, you wish for us [βούλει] to do as tragic poets [οἱ τραγῳδιοποιοί] do when they get stuck over something, and escape it by cranking up gods on mechanical contrivances [ἐπὶ τὰς μηχανὰς καταφεύγουσι θεοὺς αἴροντες]; we too could get out of our difficulty by talking that way, saying that the gods established the original names and that's why they're right. Is that the most powerful account we can come up with? Or that one that says we took them over from some barbarians and the barbarians are more primitive than we are? Or, as is also the case with the barbarian words, that it's impossible to investigate them on account of their antiquity? These would all be evasions, though very refined ones [κομψαί], by someone who doesn't want to give an account of how the original names are rightly applied. (425d–426a; Sachs; trans. modified)

In claiming that recourse to foreign etymologies and temporal distance is nothing more than a tragic contrivance employed to evade giving a full account of the original names, Socrates indicates definitively that it is the tragic view that he has been playfully espousing all along: for he, on several occasions, has employed just these contrivances (see 409d and 412b). As tragic (τραγικός), this view will remain confined to the goat-like (τραγοειδής) part of λόγος.

Socrates then offers an account of the elemental words, insisting that his account will be hubristic (ὑβριστικά) and laughable (γελοῖα) (426b). In his hubristic and laughable performance, he ends up saying most of these elemental words signify radical flux and motion. To mention only a few of his examples, *rho* is said to be a tool (ὄργανον) expressing motion (τῆς κινήσεως) (426c), due to the fact that the tongue is most agitated (σειομένην) when pronouncing the letter *rho* (426e). It is for this reason, Socrates proposes, that words like ῥεῖν (to flow), ῥοῇ (current), τρόμος (quivering), ἐρείκειν (to rend), and ῥυμβεῖν (to whirl) contain the letter *rho* (426d). The letter *lambda*, due to its ability to make the tongue glide (ὀλισθάνει), was used by the original name-makers in words like ὀλισθάνειν itself (to glide), λιπαρόν (oily), and κολλῶδες (gluey) (427b–c). The letter *alpha* was employed to denote largeness (μεγάλῳ) and *eta*, in its turn, was used to signify length (μήκει), due to the fact that both letters are large (μεγάλα) (427c). The name-maker proceeded in this fashion, making the words for each of the beings (ἑκάστῳ τῶν ὄντων) by employing those letters and syllables that mostly closely imitated the beings themselves (427c).

It thus becomes clear that the original name-givers opined all things to be in flux and named beings in accordance with this opinion, as Socrates said much earlier (411b). Socrates is here playing the role of one of the original name-givers, whom he earlier described as dizzy, drunken sorts bound not by the true *nature* of the beings they named (i.e., their οὐσία) but only by their own (misinformed) opinions about those beings, opinions guided entirely by how things show themselves in nature. As Socrates will show during his conversation with Cratylus, Socrates' own ridiculous and hubristic account of the elemental names is no less bound by such misinformed opinions. Just as he did in the previous long string of etymologies, Socrates is once again playing at presenting the tragic view of λόγος (and, as will be seen, precisely in order to indicate the limitations of that view).

One would do well to meditate upon what makes Socrates' account hubristic and ridiculous (ὑβριστικὰ καὶ γελοῖα) (426b). Most obviously, Socrates' present precipitousness in offering an account is both ridiculous and hubristic because Socrates had not yet accomplished the comprehensive dividing and ordering that he insisted to be a prerequisite for any satisfactory account (424c). More importantly, such an account is hubristic insofar as it reaches beyond its limits in attempting to say something about a matter of which it cannot legitimately say anything substantial. For the reasons articulated in previous chapters, λόγος is limited in its ability to account for itself: there is thus a certain hubris, not to mention ridiculousness, in pursuing the correctness of words as if one could achieve pure access to them. In undertaking such a labor, one acts less like a human and more like a god—a dangerous hubris, indeed.

However, the most obvious way in which Socrates' account is ridiculous is in the very view of language it presents. The idea that a particular letter would somehow onomatopoeically imitate something essential about the *being* in question is laughable in the extreme, not to mention manifestly arbitrary.[61] There are dozens of Greek words beginning with a *nu* sound that in no way signify "inwardness"; likewise, there are scores of words containing *lambdas* that in no way signify *gliding* (ὀλισθάνειν). It is ridiculous to imagine that the tongue, in hitting against the palette, somehow captures the *being* of a thing; at best, one might argue that it captures the *sound* that the being makes. The picture of a purely onomatopoeic language is palpably ridiculous, and it is precisely this picture which Socrates paints through his comic sketch of the elemental names.

Socrates distills the fruits of his and Hermogenes' long conversation, making it clear that the principle at work behind the preceding etymologies was one of imitation (ἀπομιμεῖται) (see 427c).[62] To the extent that this is true, the preceding etymologies have presented, as argued in the previous chapter, nothing other than the technological/tragic view of language, yet in such a way as to resist it comically. By offering a comic pastiche of this view, Socrates has been critiquing it and distancing himself from it. Socrates finishes his long comic performance by saying "this, Hermogenes, appears to me [μοι φαίνεται] what is meant to be the correctness of words [ἡ τῶν ὀνομάτων ὀρθότης], unless, that is, Cratylus here says something different" (427d; Sachs; trans. modified). In stressing that this is how the matter *appears* (φαίνεται) to him, Socrates is again emphasizing the extent to which such a view of the correctness of names remains bound to the world of appearances and opinions. In the remainder of the dialogue, Socrates will examine whether Cratylus has some other (ἄλλο) view contrary to the view just elaborated. However, it will be seen that Cratylus' own position remains decisively within the technological/tragic view of λόγος, and is subject to its same limitations. In a word, Cratylus, no less than Hermogenes, will be seen to hold the tragic view of language.

However, it is important to note that, despite the fact that Hermogenes has been shown by Socrates to hold a tragic view of language, Hermogenes shows himself to be eager to leave behind such a view and learn the truth: "Now, then, Cratylus, in front of Socrates, tell me: is the way Socrates is speaking about names to your liking, or do you have some other way to speak more beautifully? And if you have, say it, so you can either learn from Socrates or teach us both" (427d–e; Sachs). Thus, in the wake of Socrates' long and ridiculous inquiry into λόγος Hermogenes, rather than showing fatigue and impatience with Socrates (as Cratylus eventually will [440d]), instead shows eagerness and excitement about continuing the inquiry. In showing his longing to turn back again to the investigation, the jest of words, the daimonic Hermogenes (415a) reveals his erotic commitment to the truth. The extent to which this erotic commitment itself indicates an abandoning of the tragic view shall be explored at the end of the following chapter.

8 The Tragedy of Cratylus

Cratylus's silence rings throughout the *Cratylus,* serving as the very backdrop for Socrates' and Hermogenes' long conversation regarding the correctness of names. Cratylus's single utterance at the beginning of the text—"If it seems so to you" (Εἴ σοι δοκεῖ) (383a)—serves to draw our attention to his long silence that follows, announcing the character Cratylus before immediately drawing him back into silence for the following forty-four Stephanus pages. One might say that, behind the long and difficult λόγος on λόγος that is the *Cratylus, a silence speaks.*

There are, of course, many ways of keeping silent. The Greeks, from at least Euripides on, were aware that sometimes silence can be interpreted as signifying agreement.[1] The Socrates of the *Cratylus* is aware of this type of silence, and at one point infers Cratylus's consent (συνχώρησιν) based upon his silence (435b). One might suppose, then, that in keeping his silence throughout the long etymological comedy Cratylus has indicated his agreement with Socrates' performance and the philosophical position it is meant to expound and clarify. (Indeed, Cratylus will soon voice his approval of the etymologies [428c], thereby finally breaking his silence.)

Of course, silence can just as easily signify disapproval or dissatisfaction.[2] Consider, for example, Plato's *Phaedo,* where Socrates and his interlocutors fall into a long silence (σιγή . . . πολὺν χρόνον) following one of Socrates' discourses on the immortality of the soul (*Phd.* 84c). This silence is far from approbative in character, but instead indicates a general restless concern and doubt amongst the audience, as Socrates himself observes (*Phd.* 84c). Silence, then, can indicate both agreement and lack of agreement; it is ambiguous. Given that the long etymological section was meant to clarify Hermogenes' position regarding the correctness of names, and that Cratylus and Hermogenes allegedly occupy different positions on this issue (see 383a–d), one might suppose Cratylus's silence to indicate discontent rather than approval.

In addition to consent and disapproval, silence can also bespeak a reluctance to speak born out of fear of shame, such as when Theodorus, in the *Theaetetus,* holds his silence after Socrates' suggestion that they each speak in turn regarding the nature of knowledge (*Tht.* 146a–b). This would be silence as a kind of refuge in which one may avoid the dangers of embarrassment or, worse, self-incrimination. One might suppose Cratylus to be exercising this type of silence, using it as a way to mask his ignorance of the matter in question, were it not for Cratylus's insistence that he, at least in his own opinion, does in fact have knowledge of the correctness of names (427e; 440d).

The *Phaedo* reveals another way of keeping silent. After drinking the *pharmakon,* and by way of chastening his tearful and sorrowful interlocutors, Socrates claims to have heard that one ought to meet one's death in *propitious* silence (εὐφημίᾳ) (*Phd.* 117e). Εὐφημία is the sort of honoring silence that yields to something divine, the sort that one would hold toward a god—thus, a *holy silence.* Such silence reveals both reticence and deference in the face of something greater than oneself, a kind of awe that allows that thing to come to pass without vocal interruption. Perhaps it is a silence that recognizes the tendency of human speech to say too much in such moments, thus drowning out whatever it is that something other, in its passing, wishes to say. This sort of silence involves the recognition that *if* one were to speak—if one were to engage in the operation of λόγος, understood as speech, thereby employing words—one would only succeed in covering-over the phenomenon one sought to dis-cover.

Such holy silence is further characterized by a certain reticence to speak born of the awareness of the limitations, in that instance, of speech. Such silence would be most prudent in the face of an investigation *through* λόγος wherein one sought, with all philosophical rigor, to measure and delimit the power *of* λόγος. Such a prudent silence would recognize the hopelessness—or at the very least the absurdity—of attempting to speak about speaking, of attempting to bring λόγος to bear upon itself, without thereby irremediably damaging one's ability to access the subject matter in a manner wholly unaffected by the means of access. Such prudent silence might also serve to acknowledge the *divinity* of λόγος—who is, as Socrates has said, either the god Pan or his brother (408d)—and would thus recognize the difficulties in saying anything definitive about it: for human beings know little or nothing about the gods (400d).

Short of forcing absolute silence in the face of an investigation into λόγος through λόγος, such prudent silence might lead one to seek to displace λόγος, to divide it against itself, to *double* it by distinguishing, at least in deed, one way of speaking from another. For example, in speaking about words and their correctness, one might try to speak about them by employing words suspected of being of a different order than those being investigated; by using, for example, words thought to be divine and thus most appropriately delivered not through simple human speech (λόγος) but through oracles. By so dividing λόγος one might hope to let one aspect of λόγος—say, its smooth, upper, divine part—bear upon another part—say, its rough, goat-like, human part. By keeping silent with regard to the lower part one could perhaps hope to let the upper part speak for itself and its rough, lower counterpart.

One might suppose Cratylus's silence to be a case of this prudent, holy type—a silencing of human λόγος that seeks to let the divine λόγος speak. In this case, Cratylus's reluctance to cross over from his oracular utterances and into the parlance of common λόγος (384a) would represent his awareness of the dangers at work in any attempt to bring human λόγος to bear squarely and simply upon human λόγος, and the subsequent necessity of a turn to divine λόγος. For surely divine λόγος, unlike its human counterpart, would always be correct. Socrates himself seems to make this very point during his exposition of the Homeric view of λόγος: "Clearly the gods call things by the names that are correct [ὀρθότητα] by nature [φύσει]" (391d-e; my translation). And yet it is Hermogenes' response to Socrates' claim that is most provocative in this regard: "I know well that *if* they speak, they speak correctly" (εὖ οἶδα μὲν οὖν ἔγωγε, εἴπερ καλοῦσιν, ὅτι ὀρθῶς καλοῦσιν) (391e; my translation). Hermogenes' use of the conditional (εἴπερ) reveals doubt on his part as to whether the gods in fact speak; he is only confident in supposing that *if* (εἴπερ) they do, they do so correctly. Hermogenes' reticence is forgivable: for in his own immediate experience the gods do *not* speak directly to human beings, but do so by some other means—by oracles, for example, such as those that the all-too-human Cratylus had been spouting prior to the beginning of the text, or that Socrates spouts nearly the whole *Cratylus* through. *If* the gods speak—if they employ λόγος—they do so through oracles, messengers, and signs, a fact which betrays that the gods *themselves* do not speak, do not dwell within λόγος in the same manner as human beings. The very existence of oracles, messengers, and interpreters (τὸ ἑρμηνέα) suggests that the gods are themselves *silent*, that they are without λόγος: or, at the very least, that their λόγος is so utterly different from human λόγος as to be incommensurable with it.[3]

One can suppose that Cratylus hopes, in holding his silence as he pronounces oracles, to approximate the speech of the gods—a speech which, strictly speaking, is not a speech at all.[4] In proffering oracles Cratylus would hope to let the gods speak *through* him by borrowing his speech, his λόγος, in order to let their divine wisdom come to pass. Such oracles, as averred above, would seek to double λόγος (into its divine and human parts) while thereby revealing the impassable distance between the two. In this manner Cratylus would hope to let divine λόγος serve as the measure of normal human speech, revealing the utter inadequacy of the latter.[5] In short, Cratylus would seek to efface his own human λόγος by replacing it with the divine λόγος.

Yet, any such operation of doubling would remain limited in its ability to reveal the true nature of λόγος. Any attempt to divide λόγος against itself, bringing one "part" to bear upon the other and serve as its measure, would be limited in one of two ways. Either λόγος would be so decisively divided against itself (i.e., the human *versus* the divine) that one "part" would no longer have any possibility of communicating with the other, thereby preventing a gathering-together of λόγος with itself; or, the "parts" of λόγος would fail to be sufficiently distinguished and would thus remain essentially conjoined to each other, and λόγος would, through a *feigned* doubling, merely be reflecting upon itself in its own self-contaminated, self-reflexive way (i.e., the snake would eat its tail). In either case the ability of λόγος to articulate its own limits without having that articulation affected *by* those very limits would remain limited.

Such a doubling of λόγος is, of course, exactly what Socrates does throughout the etymological display, which he continually insists is owed to divine inspiration (396d, 399a) and which Cratylus calls oracular (χρησμῳδεῖν) (428c). In emphasizing the inspired and oracular character of his etymologies, Socrates is silencing his human speech to the extent possible and letting *names themselves* testify to their own correctness (397a). Of course, as Socrates' long comedy shows, it is impossible to *wholly* silence the human part of speech, at least so long as one is speaking: for to speak, even about the gods, is to do so from a human perspective (400d, 406c). One cannot entirely free oneself from the lower part, at least, not so long as one remains human. Even the uttering of oracles takes place through human λόγος—thus, even the "speech" of the gods only finds its expression in human speech. The greatest comedy in which one could engage would be to believe oneself capable, through an operation of doubling, of separating oneself entirely from human λόγος in such a way as to be able to inquire into it without using human λόγος as the means of investigation. Or is this, rather, the greatest tragedy?

Such a doubling of λόγος, whereby one sought to let one part of λόγος speak about the other, would only succeed if the divine "part"—that smooth upper part—were shown to *belong* intimately to the rough lower "part," even while transcending it. In other words, such a doubling of λόγος as Socrates has undertaken would succeed only if it revealed that the two parts—divine λόγος and human λόγος—were intimately, or perhaps genetically, connected. The relationship between divine λόγος and human λόγος would need to be like the relationship between father and son. If the son was *utterly* unlike the father then there could be no legitimate lineage between the two; yet, if the two were *simply* alike, then there would be no difference, and the son would be but a copy of the father. Rather, the son must be his own man, and yet belong genetically to the father: he must transcend the lineage to which he essentially belongs. In a word, he must be a *monster*. Likewise, divine λόγος must transcend, and yet belong to, human λόγος. In other words, λόγος must be dual natured: it must be monstrous, both human and divine.

One could suppose that Cratylus's silence is an attempt on his part to let the divine character of λόγος come into the fore, thereby showing itself to human beings. Yet, it remains to be seen in what follows whether Cratylus ever succeeds in fully appreciating the extent to which this divine character of λόγος *belongs* to λόγος as human beings experience it, or if he instead believes this divine part to remain wholly separate from the human part, indeed, from the human condition altogether. It remains to be seen whether Cratylus believes divine λόγος to truly *belong* to human λόγος, whether he, therefore, believes it possible for human beings (*as* human beings) to participate in the divine λόγος and the relationship to Being this entails. In short, it remains to be seen whether Cratylus ever comes to see the true monstrosity of λόγος. Yet, Cratylus's silencing of human λόγος for most of the text, and the silence into which the tradition places him,[6] leads one to suspect that Cratylus will, in the end, fail to fully appreciate the intimacy of human and divine λόγος, insisting instead on their distance and incommensurability. Perhaps Cratylus's holy silence, which rings throughout the long conversation of the *Cratylus,* serves as his pious insistence on the pure divinity, and subsequent inaccessibility, of λόγος.

In this register, it is worth noting that Cratylus's silence heralds, in its way, the very god of heralds, Hermes. As Plutarch recorded, the Greeks, when a sudden silence befell them, would sometimes say "Hermes is passing" (τὸν Ἑρμῆν ἐπεισεληλυθέναι).[7] One can wonder—but perhaps only *playfully*—if Cratylus's silence, which announces itself at the head of the long road of the *Cratylus,* marks his acknowledgment that the father of λόγος, Hermes, in the guise of the approaching Socrates, has arrived. Perhaps it is most prudent to hold holy silence when the father of λόγος is in the vicinity.

* * *

After reiterating his confusion at Cratylus's position regarding the correctness of names (ὀρθότητα ὀνομάτων) (i.e., that they are correct by nature) (383a), Hermogenes urges Cratylus to contribute to the conversation underway. Given the position regarding the correctness of names that he will soon be seen to occupy, Cratylus's response could not be stranger: "What, Hermogenes [τί δέ, ὦ Ἑρμόγενες]: do you think it is an easy matter to learn or teach any subject so quickly, especially so important a one as this, which appears [δοκεῖ] to me to be the most important [μέγιστον]?" (427e; Fowler; trans. modified). It is not Cratylus's insistence on the difficulty of the matter that is strange: for Socrates has already noted the difficulty of their undertaking on several occasions (384b, 384c, 411a). Nor is it all that striking that Cratylus deems the subject of the correctness of names to be of superlative importance: for, as we have seen, the matter of the correctness of names bears immediately upon the possibility of truth and the stability of Being. What is astonishing is that, despite having caused the very occasion of the *Cratylus* by stoutly refusing that "Hermogenes" is Hermogenes' name (383b), Cratylus would now, in response to Hermogenes' invitation to articulate the reasons for this refusal, call upon Hermogenes by using his name (ὦ Ἑρμόγενες). Despite this baffling and highly comedic moment in the text, Cratylus's use of the very name whose efficacy he denies goes unnoticed by both Hermogenes and Socrates and, indeed, most scholars. Cratylus will soon again employ the name "Hermogenes" in calling upon the son of Hipponicus, at which point we shall speculate further upon his reasons. For the time being it is sufficient to mark the first occurrence, and the comic way in which the interlocutors fail to notice it.

Seemingly oblivious to Cratylus's use of his name, Hermogenes exhorts Cratylus to enter into the conversation, despite its difficulty, even if only, citing Hesiod, to contribute "a little on top of a little" (τις σμικρὸν ἐπὶ σμικρῷ) (428a; Sachs). This is doubtless a play by Plato on Cratylus's patronymic (Σμικρίωνος) and is meant to suggest that very little will be accomplished by the addition of Cratylus to the conversation[8]—a suggestion that will be borne out as the dialogue continues. Due to the fact that Cratylus's and Hermogenes' positions will be almost entirely con-fused and intertwined by Socrates,[9] Cratylus's eventual articulation of his position will indeed contribute little (τις σμικρός) to what has been accomplished so far. It also serves to associate him with Hesiod who, as seen in chapter 6, was among those who held a tragic worldview. We can thus anticipate that Cratylus's position, like that initially held by Hermogenes, will be seen to have a decidedly tragic character.

In an effort to draw Cratylus into the conversation, Socrates quite significantly states that he himself would not stoutly maintain (οὐδὲν . . . ἰσχυρισαίμην) any of the things he has said thus far in the inquiry, but rather that he has been "investigating [ἐπεσεψάμην] what appeared [ἐφαίνετο] to [him] along with Hermogenes" (428a; my translation). This statement definitively indicates that Socrates has not been espousing his own views concerning the correctness of names, but has been drawing out the consequences of Hermogenes' rather Protagorean view announced near the beginning of the *Cratylus*.[10] It also indicates that, for Socrates, the correctness of names remains an *open* question which should be continually reinitiated and reengaged, as touched on in the previous chapter. This openness characterizes Socrates' philosophical position toward the correctness of names and, more generally, toward λόγος, as what follows will show.

Eager to have Cratylus finally voice his heretofore silent opinion about the correctness of names, Socrates goads Cratylus by telling him to "be bold and speak" (θαρρῶν λέγε) (428b). The synonymy between θαρρῶν and ἀνδρεία must here be allowed to ring forth. In telling him to be bold (θαρρῶν) Socrates is recalling the earlier analysis of ἀνδρεία (courage), where this was seen to be a matter of redirecting the flow of φύσις upward toward stability (413e). Having already done so with Hermogenes, Socrates is now giving Cratylus a chance to make a showing of himself and of whether he is able to make the movement from things as they seem (i.e., the vacillatory and fluctuating appearance of things) upward toward the stability of things as they are in themselves. In the end, however, Cratylus will show himself to be lacking the requisite courage for such an ascent, and quite incapable of making it.

Nonetheless, Cratylus takes the bait, drawn in perhaps by Socrates' stated (though no doubt ironic) desire to become Cratylus's pupil (428b). After comparing himself to Achilles in the *Iliad* when he is chastened by Ajax to return to battle (and thereby showing himself to be of a Homeric, which is to say tragic, mindset), Cratylus comments that Socrates' oracular uttering (χρησμῳδεῖν) concerning names is very much to his liking (κατὰ νοῦν) (428c). That such oracular utterances are to his liking is not at all surprising, given that it was precisely due to Cratylus's own obscure oracles (τὴν Κρατύλου μαντείαν) that Hermogenes felt obliged to call Socrates into the λόγος in the first place (384a; see also 427d). Socrates uses this compliment regarding the worth of his oracular ravings to reassert his own commitment to openness and reinterpretation:

> My good Cratylus, I've been wondering [θαυμάζω] myself at my own wisdom all along, and I don't trust it [ἀπιστῶ]. So it seems to me we ought to examine what I'm saying all over again [ἐπανασκέψασθαι]. For deceiving oneself by oneself [ἐξαπατᾶσθαι αὐτόν ὑφ' αὑτοῦ] is the most troublesome of all things; when the deceiver [ὁ ἐξαπατήσων] never departs from the spot even a little [μηδὲ σμικρὸν ἀποστατῇ] but always remains present, how could that not be a terrifying thing? So it looks like it's necessary to turn back repeatedly [μεταστρέφεσθαι] to the things said before and try, in the phrase of that poet, to look "forward and backward at once." (428d; Sachs; my emphasis)[11]

Three points in the passage must be noted. First of all, it should be observed that Socrates is in no way satisfied with the wisdom (σοφία) he has been spouting, but rather distrusts it (ἀπιστῶ) and wonders (θαυμάζω) about it. Insofar as wonder (τὸ θαυμάζειν) is the very origin of philosophy (see *Tht.* 155c–d), one could say that Socrates still considers the question of the correctness of names to be an open question worthy of philosophical inquiry, and in no way believes that they have reached any stable truth regarding the matter. As mentioned above, such openness in the face of λόγος indicates something about Socrates' philosophical position regarding λόγος—a point to which we shall return.

Secondly, as argued in the preceding chapter, Socrates' use of ἐπανασκέψασθαι is significant insofar as it indicates a renewal of the investigation/jest. The importance of beginning again, of reinterpreting, is emphasized two lines later with the word μεταστρέφεσθαι (428d). Socrates claims that it is necessary that they turn back *repeatedly* to the task of investigating the correctness of names.[12] This gives philological support for what was suggested above, namely, that the question of the correctness of names remains open and unsettled for Socrates, and thus demands reengagement. One must *always* return to an investigation of λόγος.

Finally, Socrates' point regarding self-deception must be examined. Socrates has claimed that self-deception (ἐξαπατᾶσθαι αὐτόν ὑφ' αὑτοῦ) is the most troublesome (χαλεπώτατον) precisely because the one doing the deceiving (ὁ ἐξαπατήσων)—i.e., oneself—never stirs even a little from the spot (μηδὲ σμικρὸν ἀποστατῇ), but rather always remains present. In other words, wherever one goes, one brings the deception along with oneself, and thus, properly understood, never *moves* at all. As will soon be seen, it is precisely Cratylus who is unable to move beyond himself, and who therefore continues to deceive himself about the nature of words, while remaining wholly unaware of his self-deception. Socrates' phrase "never stirs even a little" (μηδὲ σμικρὸν ἀποστατῇ) is likely another play on Cratylus' patronymic, suggesting again that it is Cratylus, son of Σμικρίωνος, who is failing to move away even a little (σμικρός) from his self-deception.

With Cratylus now engaged, Socrates, always through the interrogative mode, rearticulates the position that Hermogenes has been shown to hold: namely, that "there is a correctness [ὀρθότης] in a name that makes evident [ἐνδείξεται] what the thing is like" (428e; Sachs; trans. modified). In other words, words make something manifest, they demonstrate something. It is presumably this demonstrative function of a word that leads Socrates to then suggest that words are spoken (λέγεται) with a view toward teaching (διδασκαλίας) (428e).[13] By making something manifest a word can instruct somebody about something. However, as Socrates and Cratylus continue to speak, it becomes clear that this ability to make manifest (and thus to teach) is to be understood as an operation of *mimesis* (imitation), and that the view currently being examined by Socrates still remains to that extent well within the technological/tragic view of language explored in chapter 5. That this is the case is immediately made clear by Socrates, who now suggests—again in the interrogative mode—that the making of words is a τέχνη (art) which, as such, has technicians (δημιουργούς) who practice it (428e).[14] Socrates' consideration of name-making as a kind of τέχνη reveals definitively that he is still working out the consequences of the technological view of language, that view which sees words as tools with which human beings attain their ends.

What the following Stephanus pages make clear is that Cratylus, no less than Hermogenes, holds this view, despite the fact that the two ostensibly hold different and opposed positions. More precisely, the remainder of the *Cratylus* shows that *neither* position can entirely break free from the technological/tragic view of λόγος that finds itself ultimately and unreflectively bound to mere images. In a word, both Hermogenes' and Cratylus's beginning positions are *tragic,* where this term must be understood in light of our investigation as a whole. We have already seen that the daimonic Hermogenes, through his playful engagement with Socrates, comes to move some measure away from such a tragic position. The only question that remains is whether and to what extent Cratylus is able to move away from his tragic state and toward something more tenable.

Having obtained Cratylus's assent that name-making is a τέχνη, Socrates attempts to argue that some names are therefore better than others, as is the case for any work brought about by a τέχνη. Just as some painters (ζωγράφοι) do better than others at rendering their imitative works, so too some name-makers (νομοθέται) do better than others at rendering theirs (429a).[15] However, Cratylus resists this conclusion, insisting that in the case of names all names are equal with respect to their correctness: that is, no name is better than any other (429b). Any name that *is* a name, Cratylus contends, is correct; and if it is not correct, then it is not really a name. In other words, all names are tautologically correct (429b).

In an effort to elucidate Cratylus's peculiar claim that all names, by virtue of being names, are correct, Socrates uses the figure of poor Hermogenes, whose name Cratylus has been denying since before the opening of the dialogue. Socrates asks whether Hermogenes can correctly (ὀρθῶς) have the name "Hermogenes" applied to him only if something about the race of Hermes ('Ερμοῦ γενέσεως) belongs to him (429b). Cratylus responds by stating that, because the nature (φύσις) of Hermes is lacking in Hermogenes, the name does not apply (οὐδὲ κεῖσθαι) *at all*: rather, it only *seems* (δοκεῖν) to apply, but *is* in fact the name of someone else, somebody with the appropriate nature (429c). Thus, when one sounds the syllables "Herm-og-en-es" in the direction of the son of Hipponicus, one is neither speaking truly nor falsely, but is not *speaking* at all: rather, one is merely making incoherent noises (429e).

Socrates is quick to observe the consequence of Cratylus's reasoning—namely, that for Cratylus, there is no such thing as falsehood:

SOCRATES: That it is not possible at all to say anything false [ψευδῆ λέγειν]; isn't that the force of your speech [ἆρα τοῦτό σοι δύναται ὁ λόγος]? For there are some throngs of people who do speak the false, my dear Cratylus, now as in ages past [συχνοὶ γάρ τινες οἱ λέγοντες, ὦ φίλε Κρατύλε, καὶ νῦν καὶ πάλαι].[16]
CRATYLUS: Yes, Socrates, for how, when someone is saying the thing he's saying, could he not be saying something that is? Isn't that what it is to say something false, to say things that are not? (429c–d; Sachs; translation modified)

Cratylus denies that it is possible to speak (λέγειν), say (φάναι), or even utter (προσειπεῖν) falsehood. Because saying is always the saying of something (i.e., of something that is) it is impossible for λόγος to bring to speech that which is not. Pursuant to this denial of falsehood is the claim that names cannot be false: for a name, as a part of saying (λέγειν), always relates to something that is.

One recalls that earlier Socrates claimed that a name is a part of λόγος (385c; 387c). Cratylus's claim that a name cannot be false amounts to a claim that λόγος has no false part, that all of λόγος is true.[17] Such a claim overlooks the dual nature of λόγος already elucidated by Socrates through his comic etymology of Pan (408d) and, more generally, through the long series of etymologies as a whole. Insofar as Cratylus overlooks this dual nature, he overlooks the extent to which λόγος must always and necessarily bear a relation to the false (ψευδής). By taking all λόγος to be true, Cratylus in effect takes even those false parts of λόγος (which Socrates has elucidated) either as true or as incoherent noises. In other words, Cratylus mistakes a part of λόγος for the whole of λόγος, effectively denying that λόγος has parts at all

(429e ff.). Further, in taking all λόγος to be true, Cratylus is treating all λόγος (i.e., λόγος as such) as if it were *divine* and therefore incapable of flaw. As a result of this position Cratylus believes that human beings, insofar as they speak (i.e., use λόγος), speak the λόγος of the gods. Thus, although we speculated that Cratylus's silence indicated an extreme and pious recognition of the divinity of λόγος (see above), we now see that his position amounts to the hubristic claim that human beings speak, when they are in fact speaking, the language of the gods.[18] In supposing all λόγος to be true Cratylus forgets the human—that is, *he forgets himself.*

In failing to see λόγος as dual natured (i.e., as capable of both truth and falsity) Cratylus fails to see the *true* nature of λόγος and the human being's relation to it. Phrased otherwise, by falsely holding the view that λόγος has no false part, Cratylus occupies a false position without knowing that it is false. To the extent that this is so Cratylus remains trapped within the lower part of λόγος—that part rife with myth and falsity—without being aware *that* he is trapped, without being aware of the falsity. Insofar as he has shown himself to be trapped in this realm, Cratylus has shown himself to be *tragic* in the special sense developed in the *Cratylus* and delimited in previous chapters. Socrates immediately demonstrates that he finds Cratylus's position tragic, when he responds to the latter's claim that it is impossible for one to speak falsehood by saying that Cratylus's reasoning (ὁ λόγος) is "too clever" (κομψότερος) for him (429d). This word, κομψότερος, was used earlier by Hermogenes to indicate the refined and tragic character of Socrates' etymologies (402d). Socrates' use of it here indicates that Cratylus is espousing the tragic view of λόγος, a view too refined and sophisticated for Socrates himself.

In order to mitigate this tragic view, Socrates offers a humorous counterexample involving a case of mistaken identity:

> If someone were to greet you, [Cratylus,] in a foreign place, grasp your hand, and say, "Welcome Hermogenes, my friend from Athens, son of Smicrion," would he be saying [λέξειεν] that—or asserting [φαίη] or speaking [εἴποι] or addressing [προσείποι]—[19] not to you but to Hermogenes here? Or to no one at all? (429e; Sachs)

This scenario in which some wayward passerby confuses Hermogenes with Cratylus, though at first glance merely explanatory, in fact discloses something essential about the conversation underway. In showing that Cratylus's view of language is based upon the mimetic relationship between a name and the thing it names, Socrates has shown the extent to which it shares its basic structural identity with Hermogenes' view—namely, the tragic/technological view that reduces Being to appearance. Thus, despite having positioned themselves on opposite poles of an argument concerning the correctness of names, the positions of Cratylus and Hermogenes have become entirely confused and, to a great extent, indistinguishable. Though a crucially important difference between the men, Hermogenes and Cratylus, will soon come to light,[20] their philosophical positions are nearly the same, at least with respect to their ability to elucidate the correctness of names. Thus, as Socrates' humorous example suggests, Cratylus might as well be Hermogenes and vice versa. Socrates here is the wayward passerby, though his confusion is owed not to himself but to the ambiguities inherent in Cratylus's and Hermogenes' positions.

Cratylus responds to Socrates' example by saying that such a man would be speaking neither truly *nor* falsely, but would simply be making noise (ψοφεῖν), "producing a meaningless agitation in himself, as if he were agitating some brass pot [τις χαλκίον] by banging on it" (430a; Sachs). Cratylus is thus still resolute in his claim that it is impossible to speak falsely. However, as we will soon see, it is Cratylus himself, in maintaining this position, who is doing little more than banging a brass pot.

Changing the trajectory of the argument, Socrates now gets Cratylus to agree that there is a difference between a name and that which the name names (430a). More specifically, Cratylus agrees that a name is an imitation (μίμημά) of the thing (πράγματος) of which it is the name (430a–b), and is thus not identical to it. In the pages that follow, Socrates delineates more clearly the mimetic structure at work behind Cratylus's view of λόγος. Names, like paintings, are imitations (μιμήματα) of the things of which they are names (430b). Using the analogy of paintings (ζωγραφήματα) Socrates attempts to argue that some likenesses (εἰκόνα) are better than others in imitating that of which they are the likeness (thus harkening back to his earlier attempt to prove that some names are better than others [429a]), to which Cratylus agrees (430c). Despite an overwhelming (and, as will be seen, quite significant) reluctance to *move* from his position, Cratylus finally concedes (συγχωρῆσαι) that it is possible to mistakenly assign a name to the wrong person (431a), thus apparently abandoning his earlier claim that all names are correct. Socrates now elucidates the parameters of this position:

> And what about someone who imitates the being of things [τὴν οὐσίαν τῶν πραγμάτων] by means of syllables and letters? By the same argument, if he renders everything that's appropriate, won't there be a beautiful image [καλὴ ἡ εἰκών]—a name [ὄνομα], that is—but if on occasion he leaves out or adds a little, an image will come about, won't it, but not a beautiful one? And therefore among names there'll be some that are beautifully turned out but others badly? (431d; Sachs; trans. modified)

Names, then, are imitations rendered by people, some better than others. It would seem to follow that some technicians of names (δημιουργὸς ὀνομάτων), otherwise known as law-givers (νομοθέτης), are better than others (431e).

Yet Cratylus, still resolute in his increasingly shaky position, again insists that though this would all be true for any other τέχνη, it is not the case for the giving of names:

> That is so, but you see, Socrates, when we assign these letters *alpha* and *beta* and each of the letters of the alphabet to names by the art of writing, if we leave

out or add or transpose anything, it's not that the name has been written by us but not correctly; instead it hasn't been written at all [ἀλλὰ τὸ παράπαν οὐδὲ γέγραπται]; it's immediately a different name if it has any of those things happen to it. (431e–432a; Sachs; trans. modified)

Thus, despite having now begrudgingly admitted that some names are better than others, and thus that some name-makers are better than others, Cratylus still maintains that a particular name only is that name if it is written or said perfectly, and that a misspoken or misspelled name is not that name at all (431e–432a). Cratylus still denies that falsehood is possible, showing himself still to be unaware of the dual nature of λόγος, despite his apparent progress in that direction.

Socrates understandably finds Cratylus's reasoning ugly and suggests that they, in their investigation, are not investigating beautifully (μὴ γὰρ οὐ καλῶς σκοπῶμεν οὕτω σκοποῦντες) (432a). Given our analysis as a whole, this comment could indicate that the investigation currently underway is not sufficiently *playful,* and is thus disallowing the true nature of λόγος to come to light. In saying that they are not investigating beautifully, Socrates is saying that they are investigating *tragically,* that is, in such a manner as to overlook the dual nature of λόγος. As Socrates is about to show, this amounts to a failure to observe sufficiently the *difference* between a name and the being the name names (and the possibility of error that this difference implies). If they are to proceed beautifully (καλῶς), they will need to proceed in such a way as to open up the difference between how something appears to human beings and how that thing really is in its Being. Along with this, they will need to access the "higher" realm of λόγος, that smooth divine region characterized by true Being. As has been argued, such access can only be obtained through the "comic view" of language, that playful view which acknowledges the dual nature of λόγος. It is precisely this view that Socrates will attempt (in vain) to bring to Cratylus's attention as the dialogue continues.

Socrates now clarifies what it is that is not beautiful (οὐ καλῶς) about Cratylus's reasoning by showing the latter the extent to which he misunderstands the relationship between an image and that which it imitates, and the manner in which this misunderstanding accounts for Cratylus's peculiar view concerning names. As Socrates says, an image "must not render [ἀποδοῦναι] all of the qualities of that which it imitates, if indeed it is to be an image [εἰκών]" (432b; my translation). Otherwise, Socrates continues, an imitation would simply be another version of the thing which it imitates: it would be a *perfect double.* To elucidate this, Socrates gives the humorous example of Cratylus himself, claiming that if some god (τις θεῶν) were able to imitate Cratylus perfectly in every aspect of his being, then the result would not be one Cratylus and one imitation of him (εἰκὼν Κρατύλου), but rather two Cratylus's (δύο Κρατύλοι) (432c). In other words, the moment an imitation becomes perfect in every respect is the moment it ceases to be an imitation. All imitations, by their very nature, are imperfect—that is, all imitations include *false parts.*

Names, as imitations, must therefore include false parts: and it is precisely these false parts that differentiate them from the beings that they name. If this were not the case, Socrates concludes, then "everything would be double [διττά], and no one would have any way to tell about either one of them whether it was the thing itself or its name [ἔστι τὸ μὲν αὐτό, τὸ δὲ ὄνομα]" (432d; Sachs).

In showing this consequence Socrates has exposed the extent to which Cratylus's position entails the dissolution of the unity of Being just as much as the Protagorean position that "the human being is the measure of all things" (see chapter 4). If an image is a perfect imitation of every aspect of that which it imitates—if, therefore, it is a perfect double, a doppelgänger—then it is not an *image* at all, but rather another instantiation of that being. In this scenario, a name would simply *be* another version of the being of which it is ostensibly the name. Such a scenario, no less that the Protagorean position, dissolves the unity that would otherwise belong to a being, bringing about instead a duplicity of Being.[21] It is in light of this consequence that Socrates gets Cratylus to concede that words (τὰ ὀνόματα) are not the same (ὁμοιωθείη) as that which they name (432d).

The point of the preceding discussion has been to get Cratylus to admit that names—or, more generally, λόγος—contain false parts, as Socrates immediately makes clear:

> Then be brave [θαρρῶν], my noble friend [ὦ γενναῖε],[22] and allow one name to be applied well and another not, and don't force it to have every letter in order to be absolutely the same as that of which it's the name, but allow an inappropriate [μὴ προσῆκον] letter to come in too. And if a letter, then also a name in a sentence [λόγῳ]; and if a name, then also allow a sentence in a discussion to be brought in even if it's not appropriate to the things [μὴ προσήκοντα τοῖς πράγμασιν], and allow the thing to be named and spoken of nonetheless, as long as a general impression [ὁ τύπος] of the thing the speech [ὁ λόγος] is about is present in it, as with the names of the letters of the alphabet, if you recall what Hermogenes and I were saying a little while ago. (432e–433a; Sachs; trans. modified)

Socrates is urging Cratylus to be brave (θαρρῶν) and admit that names, and thus λόγος, have false parts. Such an admission requires bravery insofar as it inserts a distance between the way that things truly are and the way that they merely appear: for in admitting that names have false parts Cratylus has admitted that names are not simply identical to the beings which they name. In other words, Cratylus is now beginning to see that human λόγος is characterized by both truth and falsity, that it is therefore dual-natured. Courage is needed here in order to overcome the tragic view of language that misses this duplicity—indeed, this monstrosity—and believes λόγος to be simply divine and true.

For such a view, as was seen above, results in a dissolution of the unity of Being by bringing about a situation in which words, as perfect imitations, cease to be images and become duplicates of the things themselves, thereby bringing about doubles of every being. To believe words to always be true, as Cratylus does, is to believe that there is no *difference* between beings and their names. It is thus precisely by overlooking the duplicity of λόγος that one brings about the duplicity of Being. When one becomes aware of the dual nature of λόγος (i.e., its capacity for both truth *and* falsity) one also becomes aware of the *difference* between a being and how that being appears to the human being (i.e., how it is accessed through human λόγος). Thus, the acknowledgment of the dual nature of λόγος entails an ascent away from a thing as it merely appears to human beings and toward recognition of that being in itself (καθ' αυτό). However, as the conversation continues, Cratylus will show himself to be lacking in the courage necessary to make this ascent.

Though Cratylus has now progressed so far as to admit that names are not perfect imitations of the beings they imitate, but are by necessity different from them, he is still loath to abandon his position that there is no such thing as an incorrect name. Even after Socrates gets him to admit that some names consist of both appropriate and inappropriate letters (i.e., both true and false parts) (433c), Cratylus refuses to concede that a name can be poorly given, though he begrudgingly acknowledges the futility of his adamancy. In reasserting his contention that no name is incorrect, Cratylus is proving himself to be stubbornly unwilling to move from his position, despite the various concessions he has made to Socrates throughout their discussion. In his adamancy, Cratylus shows himself to be unable to abandon the tragic view of language, and thus unable to move upward into an acknowledgment of the dual nature of λόγος. Cratylus just won't budge.

But this does not stop Socrates from trying. Socrates gets Cratylus to recommit to the position that a name makes something clear (δήλωμα). If this is so, Socrates continues, then those elemental names (i.e., those names not themselves composed of any further names) must resemble the things that they imitate as much as possible (μάλιστα) (433d–e). Furthermore, if these elemental names are to be like the beings they name, then the letters (στοιχεῖα) of these names must be "of a nature that's like the things" (434a; Sachs). Relying again upon the analogy of painting (ζωγραφία) Socrates says that just as the basic pigments (φαρμακεῖα) used in a painting must be like that which they imitate (i.e., be a similar color), the basic "elements" (στοιχεῖα) of words (i.e., letters) must be like (ὁμοιότητά) the things they imitate. In other words, if words are to be imitations of things, then the letters of which those words are comprised must basically correspond to the beings they imitate.

Socrates asks Cratylus to recall a claim made earlier with Hermogenes that the letter *rho* signifies passage (τῇ φορᾷ) and motion (κινήσει) (426d), as well as hardness (σκληρότητι), whereas the letter *lambda* expresses smoothness (τῷ λείῳ) and softness (μαλακῷ) (434c). He then proposes they examine whether or not the word σκληρότης employs correct letters. This is no random word choice. Socrates has no doubt chosen the word σκληρότης, meaning *hard* or *stubborn,* in order to underscore Cratylus's stubborn refusal to budge from his position. In any case, Socrates first points out that the word σκληρότης is spelled σκληρότηρ by the Eretrians—that is, it is spelled the same except with a *rho* at the end rather than a *sigma*. Socrates then gets Cratylus to agree that both *rho* and *sigma* signify motion (κίνησις) equally and that, therefore, the words σκληρότης and σκληρότηρ are the same in their ability to signify motion (434d): that is, the two words *say the same*. Thus, two groups—the Athenians and the Eretrians—call the same thing by slightly different names. However, insofar as *rho* and *sigma* signify the same thing, this is only a superficial and unimportant difference.

Socrates then raises a much more difficult hurdle. Given that the letter *lambda* signifies smoothness and softness, it seemingly has no place in a word for hardness (σκληρότης) (434d), if indeed letters and names bear mimetic relations to reality. The very presence of the *lambda* in the word σκληρότης seems to belie Cratylus's thesis.[23] In Cratylus's response to Socrates' objection something momentous occurs, though few scholars have paid this detail sufficient attention. Cratylus, who has been denying the veracity of Hermogenes' name for the entirety of the *Cratylus,* calls Hermogenes by his name again:[24]

> Well, probably it's not correct [οὐκ ὀρθῶς] to insert it, Socrates. [It is] like the letters you were speaking to Hermogenes about just now, for when you were taking them out or putting them in where necessary, you seemed to me correct [ὀρθῶς] in doing so. Now too one probably ought to say *rho* instead of *lambda*. (434d; Sachs; trans. modified)

Plato's decision here to have Cratylus use the name "Hermogenes" serves a twofold function. First of all, given that Cratylus has just claimed that anyone who called Hermogenes "Hermogenes" would not even be speaking falsely but rather just making incoherent noises (429c–e), Cratylus himself, in using the name "Hermogenes," is doing just that: he is banging a brass pot (430a). This dramatically suggests that Cratylus's position amounts to little more than the unintelligible ravings of a madman: or, perhaps, that his words amount to little more than silence. Cratylus might as well have never opened his mouth.

Secondly, Plato's decision to have Cratylus employ the name "Hermogenes" reveals that *even* Cratylus, great despiser of convention (434a), uses convention in a pinch: that is, he uses it for convenience's sake. Thus, there is an element of convention at work in Cratylus's position despite his earnest efforts to the contrary.[25] It also begins to suggest that there may be an element of convention ineluctably at work *in* λόγος, a point that is immediately made explicit by Socrates.

Despite the apparent misspelling of σκληρότης, and the humorous suggestion that it ought to have a *rho* instead of a *lambda*, Socrates asks Cratylus whether they nonetheless understand each other (μανθάνομεν) when uttering the (misspelled) word. Cratylus concedes that they do; however, he insists, quite disastrously, that they do so only by *custom* (ἔθος) (434e). Socrates then shows, to the utter destruction of Cratylus's position, that custom (ἔθος) is just another word for convention (συνθήκης) (434e), that the two words more or less *say the same,* that they have the same *gist.*[26] Cratylus has thus admitted that convention plays a role in human λόγος, thereby revealing himself to be closer to Hermogenes' position than he previously thought. It is striking, perhaps, that Cratylus only concedes this through his silence (434b). He has begun to see the futility of his position or, at least, of vocalizing it.

Socrates now offers an assessment of the fundamental premise of Cratylus's theory of λόγος, namely, that words are imitations of beings:

> Now for my part, I myself am satisfied for names to be like the things [ὅμοια εἶναι τὰ ὀνόματα] as far as that's in their power, but I'm afraid that in truth this affinity of likeness [τῆς ὁμοιότητος] is a tacky [γλίσχρα] sort of thing, to use Hermogenes' word, and that it's necessary also to have recourse to this vulgar thing, convention [τῇ ξυνθήκῃ], for correctness in names. Now probably names would be spoken in the most beautiful possible way when all or as many as possible were used as likenesses, that is, as fittingly appropriate, and the opposite would be the ugliest way. (435c–d; Sachs; trans. modified)

This passage has been taken by many commentators to reveal Socrates' affinity for the imitative theory of language, if only as an impossible ideal.[27] However, nothing could be further from the truth. To begin with, Socrates maintains here that the principle that names and letters are a likeness of beings is a "tacky" sort of thing. The word Joe Sachs translates as "tacky" is γλίσχρα, the very word Socrates previously used to elucidate to Hermogenes the imitative principle at work behind the elemental words (427b). The word γλίσχρα, Socrates there supposed, contains a *gamma,* and is thus meant to represent gliding—that is, it is meant to indicate the basic and essential motion and flux of all things. In now calling the imitative principle γλίσχρα Socrates is playfully indicating the extent to which such a view of language remains unreflectively bound to things as they appear in their vacillatory flux.

Socrates has also said that names would be spoken most beautifully if all or as many as possible were likenesses of the things named, and ugly if the words were not likenesses. However, as he will soon argue, the human being is lacking in any secure means by which to measure the propriety of one name over any other, and is thus incapable of determining whether a name was given in accordance with the *Being* of the thing, or rather merely in accordance with the opinions of those who originally gave the names. Insofar as the appropriateness of the names cannot be determined, the view of language that sees names as imitations of beings is an ugly thing. The ability of such a view to access the truth of names—those beautiful things (384b) of which the interlocutors are in pursuit (421a)—is thus extremely limited.

Socrates now explores in greater detail the didactic (διδάσκειν) function of words which was broached earlier (428e). According to Cratylus, knowing a thing is simply a matter of knowing the word: or, as he puts it, "that one who knows the words, knows the things" (ὃς ἂν τὰ ὀνόματα ἐπίστηται, ἐπίστασθαι καὶ τὰ πράγματα) (435d; my translation). The power (δύναμις) of a word thus lies in its ability to teach (διδάσκειν) by making something manifest (435d). Socrates then asks if there is any *other* means by which teaching can take place, to which Cratylus responds that names are the only and best method (καὶ μόνον καὶ βέλτιστον) of instruction (436a). He further adds that words are the sole means by which to seek and discover (ζητεῖν καὶ εὑρίσκειν) beings (436a). Without words, it seems, one can neither discover beings nor teach others about them.

Socrates immediately tries to make the precariousness of Cratylus's position clear. If one pursues words as the sole means of discovering reality, then one is doomed: for it could simply be the case that those original name-givers had an incorrect (μὴ ὀρθῶς) understanding of reality (436b). In other words, if one believes that a word is a double of the being which it names, and that knowledge of the word is therefore knowledge of the being, then one is ultimately subject to the *opinions* of those who made the words, opinions which, as subject to the wills and wishes of human beings, can be false.

Cratylus believes he can avoid this consequence by pointing out that the words which Socrates and Hermogenes investigated during the long etymological display *consistently* referred to the unrestrained flow of things, thereby serving as proof that the name-giver was correct in his apprehensions (436c). However, Socrates quickly defeats this weak counter-argument (ἀπολόγημα) by stating that the name-giver could simply have committed some original error (σφαλείς) with which he then *forced* (ἐβιάζετο) all other words to accord (436c–d). In other words, such a name-giver could have overlooked the true Being of things, naming them only in accordance with his wishes. Such a scene as now described corresponds to the one previously developed along with Hermogenes, where it was supposed that the original name-givers, dizzy from drunkenness, named things merely according to how things seemed (δόκει) to them (411b). Socrates has thus shown that the same basic problem undermines both Hermogenes' and Cratylus's supposedly opposite positions.

Socrates now presents Cratylus with a definitive proof of the arbitrary (i.e., willful) character of words by reinterpreting several of the words from the long etymological section, this time showing them as bespeaking stability rather than flux. To take just one example, whereas knowledge (ἐπιστήμη) had previously been shown to indicate the following (ἕπομαι) of things in motion (412a), Socrates now claims that this ambiguous (ἀμφίβολος) word rather indicates that our soul is standing still (ἵστησιν) (437a). Socrates' point is, of course, that words can be forced into almost any meaning (including opposite meanings), as his long etymological comedy has vividly shown. So long as words are seen as *imitations* of beings, words—and thus the beings they ostensibly reveal—are ultimately subject to the wills and wishes of those who make the imitations.

Seeing now that no mere *human* names can be trusted, Cratylus makes a new proposal: that the names were, in truth, given by a power greater than human (μείζω τινὰ δύναμιν εἶναι ἢ ἀνθρωπείαν), or, as Socrates appends, by a spirit or a god (δαίμων τις ἢ θεός) (438c). In suggesting this, Cratylus reveals himself to be evoking a tragic contrivance, a *deus ex machina*, as the tragic poets are wont to do (425d). Cratylus is proposing that if a spirit or god gave the names, then surely they could not be false: for *if* the gods speak, as Hermogenes had supposed, then surely they speak correctly (391e). Of course, in the *Cratylus*, Hermes is the god who gave λόγος to human beings. Yet, we have seen at length that Hermes, as "he who wrought λόγος" (408b), cannot simply be trusted. Rather, λόγος, just like its father, is capable of both truth and falsity: it is dual-natured. Cratylus's tragic appeal to a god as the original name-giver does nothing to navigate the difficulties shown to be endemic to the tragic/technological view of language that Cratylus so steadfastly holds. To the contrary, it *compounds* them. However, Cratylus remains tragically unaware of all this.

In his appeal to divine words, Cratylus hopes to sever the divine from the human, and therefore the true from the false. By appealing to those supposed elemental names given by the gods he hopes to purge words of the falsity that belongs to them by virtue of their human influence. However, in making this appeal, Cratylus overlooks the *essential* intimacy that divine λόγος bears to human λόγος, and the fact that the two ineluctably belong together: for even divine words can be spoken only through human speaking (i.e., through oracles). Cratylus seeks here to leave the human behind and speak only the language of the gods. In so doing he overlooks the monstrous nature of human λόγος, the fact that it contains both human and divine parts.

Now that Socrates has shown Cratylus that many words denote flux, while many others denote stability, he raises the issue of how one is to determine which are true:

> Then since the words are divided into factions, with one group of them declaring that they're like the truth and the other group that they are, by what other means are we going to decide? What are we to go back to? Presumably not to other words different from these anyway, since there aren't any. It's obvious that something else besides words has to be sought [ἀλλὰ δῆλον ὅτι ἄλλ' ἄττα ζητητέα πλὴν ὀνομάτων] that will make apparent to us without words [ἡμῖν ἐμφανιεῖ ἄνευ ὀνομάτων] which of these two versions is the true one, by indicating, obviously, the truth about beings [τὴν ἀλήθειαν τῶν ὄντων]. (438d–e; Sachs; trans. modified)

Other words cannot serve as the measure of the truth and falsity of words; first of all, because there are no other words than those that Socrates has mentioned (some of which denote flux, others of which denote stability),[28] and secondly, because any such appeal to words would itself require an appeal to words *ad infinitum*. Rather, some other means must be sought and discovered by which one could measure the correctness of words, lest one fall into a groundless abyss.

And yet, it was said previously by Cratylus that words are the sole (μόνον) means by which beings can be sought and discovered (436a). The situation is decidedly abysmal. Words, Socrates has said, cannot serve as the measure of words (i.e., of themselves); yet, words are the sole means by which we learn and discover beings (εὕρεσιν τῶν ὄντων). Clearly, then, words must be abandoned and some other means of measurement must be sought; yet, equally clearly, any such abandonment of words would entail the abandonment of the sole method of learning and discovering beings. We're damned if we do, and we're damned if we don't.

The apex of the comedy of the *Cratylus* occurs when Socrates finally suggests, in the face of this abyss, that beings (τὰ ὄντα) are to be learned and discovered (μανθάνειν ἢ εὑρίσκειν) through something other than words (439b). This suggestion, given the structure and progression of the *Cratylus* as a whole, can only be playful:[29] for what the inquiry has brought to light is that it is *only* through words—that is, through λόγος—that the human being has relation to beings *as* beings. As the very space wherein a relationship to Being can occur, λόγος is that without which the Being of a being cannot be discovered. It is thus laughable in the extreme to suggest jettisoning words entirely in an effort to better understand beings: for words are the very vehicle of such understanding!

To what would one have recourse if one forsook λόγος as a means of investigation? Perhaps one could have recourse to appearance (φαίνωμαι), to how things show themselves to sensory perception. Indeed, if one were to remain within the parameters of Socrates' analogy between naming and painting, then perception would seem to be precisely that to which one would turn in seeking to know things.[30] Just as the painter *first* looks to things, and only then comes to imitate them in images, so too the name-maker would *first* look to things, *via* perception, and then name them accordingly by use of λόγος. Yet, this conclusion is prohibited given Socrates' long refutation of Protagoras, the very purpose of which was to show the extent to which perception and appearance by themselves are insufficient to lead to knowledge of beings (see chapter 4). If one relies upon perception as the sole means by which to access the Being of a thing, then one risks merely accessing how that being *seems* to oneself, and not how that being truly is in itself. In a word, one risks reducing Being to appearance.

Perhaps, then, one could simply shut one's mouth and seek recourse in some higher, non-linguistic thinking that would make use, somehow, of the pure unutterable forms. Yet, if this were the case, one would condemn oneself to silence, unable to bring the look of a thing into speech: for the moment that one attempted to speak of the thing one would submit it to the very hazards of human λόγος that one was seeking to evade. In such a case, one would be as Cratylus was at the beginning of the *Cratylus*: for although he had knowledge concerning the correctness of words in himself (ἐν ἑαυτῷ), he was unable to communicate it to Hermogenes sufficiently, relying instead upon irony and oracle (384a). Further, the *Theaetetus* (whose intimacy with the *Cratylus* has already been established) raises the possibility that even thought (διάνοια) is a kind of dialogue (διαλέγεσθαι) or speech (λόγος) that the soul has with itself (*Tht.* 190a). Even if one silently pondered the perfect looks of things one would still be conversing *with oneself,* and therefore relating to λόγος. How, then, would one investigate beings in such a way as to free oneself entirely from one's dependence on words and immersion in λόγος?

Socrates himself suggests that it would be best to learn (μανθάνειν) about things (τὰ πράγματα) not through words (δι' ὀνομάτων) but *through themselves* (δι' αὐτῶν) (439a–b). More precisely, Socrates offers a conditional, stating that *if* (εἰ) things can be learned through words or through themselves, *then* it is better to learn about them through themselves (439a).[31] It is thus never stated that beings can in fact be learned through themselves without the aid of words. Further, nothing whatsoever is said about *how* one would investigate a being through itself without having recourse to words. Rather, Socrates claims not to know how one is to learn about or discover beings (μανθάνειν ἢ εὑρίσκειν τὰ ὄντα) if not with words, suspecting that such knowledge is too great (μεῖζον) for Cratylus and Socrates to obtain (439b). This inability, however, is not due to a deficiency on the part of Socrates or Cratylus, but rather follows ineluctably from Socrates' comic dismissal of words: for it is precisely through words that one comes to *know* or *learn* anything at all (438b). The moment one abandons λόγος one simultaneously abandons one's ability to learn or know about beings as beings. Socrates' suggestion that they abandon λόγος precisely in order to discover beings marks the high point of the comedy, as well as the extent to which Cratylus fails to understand that comedy. With his abandonment of λόγος Cratylus abandons *Being* and relegates himself to the silence into which the tradition claims he retreated.

Socrates now attempts, in the face of Cratylus's commitment to a tragic world of Heraclitean flux, to lead Cratylus toward the stability that words themselves bespeak. Even if it were the case, Socrates argues, that the original name-givers gave their names with the belief that all things are in flux, a certain amount of stability must still have been operative. More precisely, even if the name-givers believed everything to be in flux (as Socrates believes they did), they themselves *by necessity* presupposed a certain stability as they engaged in their operation of naming. If all things are continually in flux, as Heraclitus and Protagoras (and Cratylus) suppose, then whenever we speak about something, that thing has already become dissimilar to itself and thus to the word to which it is attached:

> But if it is constantly departing from itself, is it possible to call upon it correctly [προσειπεῖν ... ὀρθῶς] by saying first it is that and then it is this, or is it necessarily, right at the time we are speaking [λεγόντων], becoming something else and getting away from itself and no longer being the way it was? (439d; Sachs; trans. modified)

Thus, if words are to mean anything at all, there must be some stability to what they name. This would be true even for one who, like Protagoras and Heraclitus, would insist that all things are in flux: for in order for such a position to be cogently articulated, the words "all," "things," "are," "in," and "flux" would need to remain stable long enough to correctly express what the speaker intended. In other words, without a certain amount of stability proper to words, all statements (including "all things are in flux") would be in flux—and the very possibility of coherent λόγος would flow away on the waves of such flux.

As Socrates immediately makes clear, this state of affairs—or, this *lack* of a stable state of affairs—would hold no less for knowledge:

> But it is not even plausible, Cratylus, to claim there is knowledge [γνῶσιν] if everything is undergoing change and nothing stays the same. For if that very thing, knowledge, is not undergoing change, it would be staying the same and knowledge would always be knowledge. But if even the form itself of knowledge were undergoing change [αὐτὸ τὸ εἶδος μεταπίπτει τῆς γνώσεως], then at the time it was in transition to another form of knowledge there would be no knowledge, and if it is always undergoing change, there would always be no knowledge; and by this argument there could be neither anyone to know nor anything to be known. (440a–b; Sachs; trans. modified)

The very possibility of knowledge, then, as well as speaking (λέγειν), depends upon a certain stability amongst beings. As we saw in the previous chapter, the greater etymological comedy has revealed that it is within the very nature of words to indicate such stability beyond themselves, and thus to resist the flow of nature.[32] Words, as they are set, themselves bespeak some enduring Being beyond themselves to which they, by nature, *be*-long. The very operation of speaking, of engaging in λόγος, depends upon such stability. To speak without presuming such stability is to do little more than bang a brass pot or, perhaps, neigh like a horse. In such a case one should hardly bother to open one's mouth at all, as Cratylus himself did not for most of the dialogue. Words, therefore, resist the very play of differences that they themselves put into play, seeking against it a stable nature. In a word, names are, like Pan, *dual-natured*.[33]

With this picture we are finally given the answer to the guiding question of the *Cratylus*, the question of the correctness of words. Regardless of the conventional signifiers one uses—regardless, for example, of whether one calls upon the truth by the name "truth," "veritas," "Wahrheit," or ἀλήθεια—the being that one intends must be *supposed* to have a stability such that it *can* be called upon. In other words, "truth" must be supposed to be the same as itself, even if the word that refers to it may change. Furthermore, *one must intend* this stability lest one undermine one's own operation of speaking.[34] The correctness of a word thus lies in its ability to redirect one away from the mere flux of words (in their playful interrelationships) toward the stability that speaking always implies. Thus, despite whatever the original name-givers thought in giving their words, the words *themselves* bespeak stability. The cor-rect-ness (ὀρθῶς) of a word lies precisely in its ability to reveal stability, to *point upward* toward stability, to di-rect or er-ect the speaker upward.[35]

From out of this proof—that all speaking (λέγειν) presupposes stability—Socrates describes a certain dream (ὀνειρώττω) that he often has: namely, the dream of "a beautiful itself and a good itself [αὐτὸ καλὸν καὶ ἀγαθόν] and the same for each one of the beings [ἕκαστον τῶν ὄντων]" (439c; my translation).[36] As Socrates explains the dream, if any of these things *are*—that is, if they are beings and, as beings, remain the same as themselves—then they cannot be character-ized by flux and motion (440b): for if they were they would pass away into some other being the moment one called upon them (439e). To correctly (ὀρθῶς) speak about a being one must *suppose* that the being is the same as itself while one is speaking about it (439d–e). One *must* therefore dream that the beings to which one refers are stable enough to sustain the reference.

Yet, it is of the utmost importance to note—especially for those who would use this passage as an indication of a rigid Platonic theory of forms in any stage of its development—that it is *only* a dream.[37] Socrates' use of dream imagery here indicates that he in no way considers the content of this dream self-evident or rigorously proved: rather, he sees it as a *hypothesis* that must be made whenever one engages in λόγος.[38] The language of dreaming underscores Socrates' acknowl-edgment of the abysmal impossibility of offering a rigorous λόγος about the es-sential stability at work in λόγος, and the necessity of *posing*—but *only* posing—such stability. It is also worth noting that dreams, for the Greeks, were often sent by the gods—indeed, often by the god Hermes (see *Odyssey* VII.137). In employ-ing the language of dreams, Socrates could be suggesting that the dream of the stable ἰδέες was given by a god, perhaps even Hermes. However, as Barney as-tutely observes (citing *Iliad* II.5–36 and *Odyssey* XIX.563 as evidence), dreams are "notoriously untrustworthy" (Barney 2001, 144)—especially, one presumes, those sent by the mischievous Hermes. One can thus understand—though, unfortu-nately, all too easily overlook—the reticence with which Socrates poses this hy-pothesis of the stable ἰδέες, given the roguish nature of Hermes, "Leader of Dreams" (ἡγήτορ' ὀνείρων) (*Hymn* IV.14).

That Socrates is not offering a robust theory of forms, but is only dreaming about such stability, is made immediately clear:

> Now whether these matters are this way, or the other way, as those surround-ing Heraclitus, and lots of other people, assert, would be, I fear, no easy thing to investigate [μὴ οὐ ῥᾴδιον ἦ ἐπισκέψασθαι], but no human being who has any sense would put himself and his soul at the mercy of words to provide for his well-being, trusting in them and in those who established them enough to insist that he knows anything and to pass judgment on himself and on beings saying that there's no soundness in any of them, but that everything drips like a piece of pottery, and literally imagine that things are in the same condition

as people suffering from runny noses, with all things afflicted by flux and running sores.[39] Now maybe that's exactly how it is, Cratylus, and maybe it's not. (440c–d; Sachs; trans. modified)

By no means has Socrates settled the matter, and by no means does he insist upon the stability he has hypothesized. Rather, Socrates claims that the matter is "no easy thing to investigate" (μὴ οὐ ῥᾴδιον ᾖ ἐπισκέψασθαι). Whether being is stable or in flux is not an easy matter to know, but the presence of a stability behind the apparent flux is the hypothesis without which one would not bother to speak with any hope of being understood. What one can know is that if one speaks—if one relates toward beings with λόγος—then one cannot but dream of such stability.

And the human being is *always* speaking: that is, it is always relating toward λόγος. The human being, precisely by virtue of being the human being, always already stands within λόγος. One might suppose that this is what Socrates means when he offers his etymology of the word ἄνθρωπος, claiming there that the human being is the sole animal who gathers up (ἀναλογίζεται) what he has seen and takes account of it (λογίζεται) (399c). To be human, ἄνθρωπος, is to be the animal who participates in the gathering of λόγος. Even when one is silent, as Cratylus was, one does not terminate one's relation to the gathering, to λόγος, but merely relates to it differently. It is only because the human being is always already dwelling within λόγος[40] that Cratylus's silence can indicate consent, disapproval, or, indeed, anything at all. As ἄνθρωπος—as what Aristotle will come to call the ζῷον λόγον ἔχων[41]—the human being ineluctably stands within λόγος.

Thus, as the ζῷον λόγον ἔχων—as the ἄνθρωπος who dwells within λόγος—the human being dwells within a dream of stability. Yet—and this is the issue that proves to distinguish Hermogenes and Cratylus, whose positions have otherwise been confused—what is essential is that *one comes to be aware of this dream*. If one speaks while unaware of the dream, of the stability that *must* be supposed to stand at the heart of λόγος, then one speaks as if beings are simply as they appear, as if beings are reduced to their appearances. It is only through becoming aware of this dream of stability, and the fact *that* it is a dream, that one raises oneself above the flux of appearances. By acknowledging the dream of stability that operates behind any operation of λόγος one comes to recognize the difference between appearance and Being, between nature (as flux) and nature (as essence). It is through this acknowledgment, and the opening of difference that it entails, that one ascends beyond the world of mere appearances. One must *awaken* to one's dreaming condition.[42]

It is thus not the case that one ought to investigate beings without λόγος, as Socrates comically suggested, but rather that one must comport oneself *correctly* toward λόγος in such a way as to observe its essential relationship to Being. If one believes λόγος to be wholly subject to the wills and wishes of human beings (as Hermogenes, through his Protagorean position, at first did) then one traps oneself in the world of mere images, severing oneself irremediably from Being. Further, if one collapses the difference between names and beings (as Cratylus did), failing to observe the distance between them that λόγος opens up, one remains trapped in the lower part of λόγος, that all-too-human part pervaded by myth and falsehood. One must rather come to recognize the filial relationship between Being and λόγος, and the monstrous way that λόγος both opens a passage through which the human being can ascend to Being and threatens to close that passage off. One must come to stand properly in the dual-natured λόγος in which one, as human, already stands.

Yet, such a correct comportment is exceedingly difficult to obtain, as Socrates points out when he says that such matters are no easy thing to investigate (μὴ οὐ ῥᾴδιον ᾖ ἐπισκέψασθαι). One is reminded of Socrates' initial words of the dialogue: "beautiful things are difficult" (χαλεπὰ τὰ καλά) (384a). Λόγος, and its relationship to Being, has proved most difficult to investigate. More importantly—and this is indicative of Socrates' position regarding λόγος—the matter of words and their relation to Being demands *reinvestigation*. One must continually resubmit λόγος to inquiry in order to examine the nature of beings.

Further, one must even submit the necessary supposition of the stability at the heart of λόγος to rigorous investigation, lest one come to rest unduly in one's pursuit of the truth.[43] The necessity of reinvestigation, or reinterpretation, is immediately stressed by Socrates: "It is necessary to examine [σκοπεῖσθαι] the matter courageously [ἀνδρείως] and well and not accept anything easily—since you're still young and in your prime—and once you've examined it [σκεψάμενον], if you find the answer, share it with me too" (440d; Sachs; trans. modified). One must continually reexamine the matter, never simply accepting anything as true. In other words, one must *engage* λόγος again and again: one must continually play with words.

In again urging him to investigate courageously (ἀνδρείως) Socrates is attempting one final time to lead Cratylus's soul upward toward stability: for courage (ἀνδρεία), as its etymology showed, is precisely what is needed in order to make this ascent.[44] However, Cratylus claims that he is not unreflective (ἀσκέπτως) about this matter, and it appears (φαίνεται) to him that things are in flux, as Heraclitus says (440e).[45] In claiming to have resolved the matter Cratylus reveals his lack of commitment to future investigations, and thus his resistance to Socrates's position that, when it comes to names, one must *always* reengage and reinterpret. For Cratylus, the matter is settled: and it is for this very reason that he remains cut off from the true monstrous character of λόγος. Cratylus remains a tragic figure, never becoming fully aware that he is living in a dream without knowing it, and indeed lacking the desire to investigate/jest. As tragic, he remains trapped within the lower part of λόγος, never aware of its fundamentally dual nature. In showing himself to be unwilling to budge from his spot, Cratylus remains bound to the worst sort of deception, *self-deception* (ἐξαπατᾶσθαι αὐτόν ὑφ' αὑτοῦ): "for how can it be other than terrible when the deceiver [ὁ ἐξαπατήσων] is always present and never moves the littlest bit [μηδὲ σμικρόν ἀποστατῇ]?" (428d; my translation). He also shows himself, in adding very *little* (σμικρός) to the conversation (428a) and never moving even a *little* (σμικρός) from his position, to be the genuine offspring of his father, Σμικρίωνος, at least in name.

* * *

Rather than further committing himself to an investigation into λόγος, Cratylus, feeling confident that he and the Heracliteans have it right, prepares to wander off into the country. Socrates, offering no protest at the prospect of Cratylus's departure, bids him farewell: "Well then, my comrade, you'll teach me [about words] some other time, when you get back [ἐπειδὰν ἥκῃς]. But for now, make the journey into the country [εἰς ἀγρόν] that you've prepared for, and Hermogenes here will lead you [προπέμψει]" (440e). As Cratylus moves away from the city and into the country, he moves away from the place of convention and into the place of nature. In moving into the country Cratylus remains precisely where he was at the beginning (see 383a). Thus, though Cratylus *seems* to be in motion throughout his conversation with Socrates, making occasional movements toward a grasp of the stability at work behind λόγος, he has in fact remained in place; and although Cratylus seems to have admitted the role of convention in λόγος, he remains steadfastly committed to nature understood as the world of fluctuating appearances. Cratylus never fully grasps the monstrous duplicity of λόγος.

To truly admit the role of convention (ξυνθήκη) in λόγος is to admit the possibility of falsehood: for if words are subject to the conventions of human beings, then they are subject to the errors and misapprehensions of human beings. And yet, at the same time, to admit the role of convention in λόγος is to admit a certain stability at work within it. For two people to have an agreement it is required that they carry something in common (κοινός), something that, despite whatever differences transpire between them, remains the same. To acknowledge that agreement (ὁμολογία) plays a role within λόγος is to understand that something in λόγος, despite the vicissitudes of language and multiplicities of tongue, remains the same, or common (κοινός), to those who speak (or, at the very least, it is to *dream* of something that remains common). Despite several apparent steps toward recognition of this common agreement that holds between all those who would speak, Cratylus ultimately fails to grasp the commonality of λόγος. Thus, as Cratylus wanders off into nature, he leaves the common λόγος behind, no doubt reentering the silence he had only just finally come to break.[46] One wonders if he banged a brass pot as he went.

Cratylus does not wander off into nature alone, however. Rather, he is led by a guide: "Hermogenes here will lead you [προπέμψει]" (440e). As many scholars have noted, the very fact that Hermogenes is said to lead Cratylus off into the country indicates definitively that he has finally shown himself to be worthy of his name. Hermogenes, like his "father" Hermes, is the guider of souls. Though this is true, we saw in the previous chapter that there is a much richer sense in which Hermogenes has shown himself to be the son of Hermes. This was seen in Hermogenes' erotic commitment to investigate λόγος and reinterpret matters anew (427d–e), and his corresponding courage to make the ascent toward the stability of Being (386e). Above all, Hermogenes' kinship to Hermes was revealed through his willingness to *play* with Socrates in his word games (i.e., his etymologies) (see 406c), to play with language and to be played by it. In showing all of this Hermogenes has shown himself to be capable of moving beyond the tragic view of λόγος.

From the beginning of the *Cratylus* what has been in question is Hermogenes' relation to Hermes and whether he shows himself to be Hermes' son. Further, insofar as λόγος, too, is the son of Hermes (408d), from the beginning there has also been a question of Hermogenes' relation to λόγος: "for brother to be like brother is nothing to be wondered at" (408d; Sachs). The *Cratylus* as a whole examines the relationship between λόγος and Hermogenes, or, more generally, λόγος and the human being. Through the course of the text Hermogenes has come to comport himself *correctly* (ὀρθῶς) toward λόγος. This has entailed an experience of both the deceiving *and* the disclosing character of words, their ability to both obfuscate the truth and reveal it. Most of all, Hermogenes has come to experience the *playfulness* of language, and the manner in which λόγος itself plays with the human being by revealing and concealing the truth.[47] By finally following Socrates into an experience of this playfulness Hermogenes has comported himself correctly toward words, fully grasping their dual nature. In so doing, the daimonic Hermogenes has finally shown himself to be the son of Hermes: and it is only because he has come to know the true dual nature of λόγος that he can lead Cratylus safely into the country. Hermogenes has become aware of the dream of which Cratylus still remains ignorant.

Insofar as Hermogenes shows himself to be aware of the dual nature of λόγος he extends himself beyond the tragic view of λόγος that Cratylus holds so steadfastly. Although the position that Hermogenes initially held was none other than the tragic view, he has allowed himself to be led by Socrates (i.e., Hermes) beyond that view and into one that recognizes the duality at work within λόγος, its truth and falsity, its humanity and divinity, its seriousness *and* playfulness. In other words, he follows Socrates into the comic view of λόγος which overcomes the limitations of the tragic view that the *Cratylus* as a whole assays and criticizes. In following Socrates along this way Hermogenes has shown himself to have the courage to make the ascent from the world of mere appearances toward the stability that *speaking* about such a world implies. Most importantly, in understanding the importance of reinvestigation and reinterpretation (427e), Hermogenes has revealed his awareness of the fact that in order to make such an ascent one must descend into the play of words. One goes up, in other words, precisely by going down. It is only by engaging words, and engaging them in their vacillatory play, that one moves toward the stability that words promise. Hermogenes thus learns that one must *continually* speak about speaking, if one wishes to broach the stability that words themselves bespeak. One must speak *with* words.

One can thus imagine that, although Hermogenes will now lead Cratylus out to the country, to the place of nature, he will soon return to the city, the place of convention, the world of appearances. (Indeed, he will be back in time for Socrates' execution.)[48] Hermogenes will thus only go a little way into the country, not because he is unable to extend himself toward nature, but because he recognizes that the country is bound by its attachment to the city; that nature is bound by its attachment to convention; that Being is bound by its attachment to beings; finally, that the smooth upper part of λόγος is bound to the rough lower part. One lives in the city so that one may sojourn into the country that much more courageously—one dwells with beings, *as beings,* precisely so as to extend oneself toward Being. Hermogenes' excursion into the country—into nature and into Being—is all the more excessive given his acknowledgment of the necessity of a return. One must have the courage to return to the world of appearances precisely as the vehicle through which one can make an ascent to Being. In his erotic commitment to inquiring into the nature of words Hermogenes displays the courage to engage appearances and thereby transcend them. The daimonic Hermogenes shows himself, no less than λόγος, to be a dual-natured monster.[49]

As Cratylus departs, with Hermogenes as his guide, he urges Socrates to continue to think about these matters: "you too should try to ponder [σὺ πειρῶ ἔτι ἐννοεῖν] these matters still more" (440e; Sachs). This closing line suggests that Socrates shall follow his own advice and "consider courageously and thoroughly and not accept anything easily" (440d; my translation). In other words, when it comes to words, Socrates shall keep the matter *open,* shall ponder it again, and shall forever submit words to reinterpretation. By maintaining a commitment to reinterpretation Socrates shows himself to be like Hermes, whose part he has played throughout the *Cratylus.* In his turn, in proving himself to be like Hermes, Hermogenes proves his comittment to the Socratic philosophical position that one should not pretend to know what what does not know, but that one ought to continually examine the matter anew (see 422c and 427e). By showing himself to be like Hermes, Hermogenes shows himself to be like Socrates. Hermogenes has thus shown himself to be the legitimate offspring of the monstrous Socrates.

Conclusion:

The Comedy of the Cratylus

"[I]t is not we who play with words; rather, the essence of language plays with us, not only in this case, not only now, but long since and always. For language plays with our speech—it likes to let our speech drift away into the more obvious meanings of words. It is as though man had to make an effort to live properly with language."

—Martin Heidegger, *What is Called Thinking*

"Die Sprache spricht."

—Martin Heidegger, "Die Sprache" (in *Unterweg zur Sprache*)

In the *Cratylus, language speaks*. The *Cratylus* unfolds as a dialogical event whereby language is given the space to say something about itself and its relationship to Being, as well as its relationship to the human being. Through the course of the *Cratylus,* and the etymologies in particular, what is shown is the extraordinary manner in which the human being dwells within λόγος in such a way as to thereby relate toward beings *as* beings and the Being in relation to which beings *are* beings. It is only because of λόγος—only by virtue of being ἄνθρωπος, the being who gathers up (ἀναλογίζεται) into λόγος what it has seen (399c)—that the human being can hold-after (μετέχω) Being. The *Cratylus* as a whole *shows* λόγος to be the way by which the human relates to Being.

Of course, the *Cratylus* also shows, in vivid comic detail, that it is equally because of λόγος that the human being can relate inappropriately, or incorrectly, toward Being. In particular, the long and exceedingly playful etymological section demonstrates the extent to which λόγος, rather than simply opening an unobstructed pathway to the stability of Being, can close that pathway off, hermetically isolating the human being. Due to the natural and irrepressible playfulness of words—that is, due to the manner in which the meanings of words fluctuate, blend together, and play with our understandings of our world and ourselves—the human being is seduced into following words not into a dream of stable

Being, but rather into a nightmare of unrestrained flux where "everything drips like a piece of pottery, and things are in the same condition as people suffering from runny noses, with all things afflicted by flux and running sores" (440c–d; Sachs). It is because of this latter capacity of λόγος that Socrates says that no person of sense would place his trust in words enough to claim to know anything at all about beings (440c). Or so Socrates *says*.

Λόγος thus serves as the opening wherein a correct *or* incorrect comportment toward Being can take place. Given that λόγος has the dual capacity to lead one toward stability or toward radical flux—that is, given the fact that it is dual-natured—it is of the utmost importance that one come to comport oneself correctly toward λόγος, lest one get carried away by the viscous and unrestrained flow. The *Cratylus* in general serves as an analysis, and a comic performance, of the possibility of a correct comportment toward λόγος.

And yet, how would one ever come to comport oneself correctly? Through his contrived etymologizing Socrates has shown that words can be willed to mean *either* stability *or* flux (or both) and that, more generally, words can be made, through the human will and its techniques of manipulation, to mean anything at all. Words have the capacity to be used like tools by those who would wish to force them into accord with how reality *seems* to them, or with how they *wish* for reality to be. Given this capacity for deception, how could one ever come to trust that words were genuinely leading one upward toward the stability of Being?

One could not, so long as one remained related toward λόγος as if it were a mere instrument by which one conveys one's own private vision of reality. For the *Cratylus* as a whole has attested to the limitations of any such instrumentalist view, and the extent to which that view remains trapped within the world of mere appearances—that tragic, lower world of myth and falsity. So long as one relates to λόγος as the smith relates to the bore or the weaver to the shuttle, one relegates λόγος to the wills and wishes of those who *use* it, to those who make λόγος speak for them.

What is needed, then, is a comportment toward λόγος that does not seek to reduce it to the status of a tool or mere mechanism. It is the *Cratylus* as a whole, and the etymological comedy in particular, that attempts to delineate the parameters of this comportment. What Socrates' etymologies and accompanying analyses show is, first of all, the extent to which the human being, far from mastering language like a tool, is at its mercy; and, secondly, the extent to which language itself, when allowed to speak *for* itself, has something to say *about* itself. In other words, the *Cratylus* reveals that the human being is not the measure of λόγος, but that λόγος is the measure of the human being.[1] One does not own language, but is owned by it.

For if one listens to what λόγος has to say one becomes aware both of the stability of Being toward which λόγος tends and the extent to which the human being stands at a distance from that stability. More specifically, what λόγος itself says is that the human being cannot simply attain such stability through manipulations of λόγος. Rather, when λόγος speaks, it speaks about the finite condition of the human being and the extent to which it fails to master λόγος. By revealing its connection to stable Being, λόγος also reveals the human being's immersion in the world of appearances. In short, by announcing its smooth upper part, λόγος brings into sharp relief its rough lower part—the part in which the human being for the most part dwells. Λόγος, when it speaks, thus serves to measure the human being's relation to Being.

In addition to serving as the measure of the human being, λόγος is shown within the *Cratylus* to be the measure of *itself*. Despite the fact that words can be contrived to convey either flux or stability, what the *Cratylus* has shown is that if one comports oneself toward λόγος correctly—if one *listens* to language rather than speaks for it—λόγος bespeaks the stability of Being that underlies and renders possible its operations. It is only *because* λόγος is dual-natured, participating in both the lower and upper regions, that λόγος can serve as the measure of itself.

If λόγος had two hermetically *distinct* parts, one human and one divine, that had nothing in common with one another, then neither part could be brought to bear fruitfully upon the other: it would be a gathering of utterly disparate elements and thus not a proper gathering at all. If, on the other hand, λόγος were of one nature, utterly the same as itself, it would be unable to reflect upon itself without the difficulties and pitfalls of self-contamination spoken of earlier. It is only because λόγος has two distinct parts that *intimately* belong together that it can reflect upon itself and measure itself. It is only because the true part of λόγος is genetically attached to the false part—a unity of opposites—that the one part can bear upon the other. In a word, it is only because it is *monstrous* that λόγος can bear upon itself in a fruitful way.

Yet, the human being is the site of λόγος, which is to say that it is the human being who *speaks*. There is no operation of measuring that λόγος can perform in a manner entirely removed from the human being. It is not the case that λόγος is some self-caused agent or god that, when left to itself, can serve as its own measure and justification. Rather, because the human being is the site of λόγος—because, therefore, λόγος cannot unfold without the human being—any such measuring requires the participation (μετέχω) of the human being. As the ζῷον λόγον ἔχων the human being contributes to the monstrous engagement of λόγος with itself. More concisely, the human being is the site through which the full monstrosity of λόγος can come to the fore, the opening where λόγος can come to itself.

Given that it is the dual nature of λόγος (i.e., its monstrosity) that allows for it to measure itself, it is of the utmost importance that the human being become mindful of this dual nature. As the being through which λόγος comes to pass, the human being must *let* the dual nature of λόγος come to the fore. This requires that the human being *listen* to what λόγος has to say, listen to the λόγος *of* λόγος, and thereby bring that λόγος *to* λόγος. It is only through such listening that λόγος, in its full monstrosity, is brought into dialogue with itself.

It is essential, therefore, that one come to heed the essential ambiguity of λόγος. It is even more essential that one not attempt to overcome this ambiguity, somehow resolving λόγος with itself. Rather, one must learn to dwell within this ambiguity correctly.[2] To seek to resolve the ambiguity of λόγος by refusing its dual nature, as Cratylus had done, is to fail to assay the true nature of λόγος, and thereby to cut oneself off from the stability that λόγος would offer. One must rather let oneself dwell within the dual nature of language.

This is precisely what Socrates has attempted to accomplish throughout the *Cratylus*. Through a gathering together (συμβαλεῖν) of Hermogenes and Cratylus, Socrates has attempted a gathering-up in common (ἀνακοινωσώμεθα) into the nature of λόγος. More precisely, Socrates has tried to gather his interlocutors around the stability, the common (κοίνος), that stands as the fundamental hypothesis of λόγος: he has tried to awaken them to the dream of stable Being which they, as the ζῷον λόγον ἔχων, must dream. Yet, he has attempted to do this precisely by engaging λόγος in its lower part, in that part most easily bent to the wills and wishes of human beings. It was through an engagement and affirmation of the lower part of λόγος that Socrates has sought to awaken his interlocutors to the upper part.

It is only Hermogenes, by finally grasping the stability that λόγος promises as well as the abyss that λόγος threatens, who finally shows himself capable of standing within the dual nature of λόγος. Most importantly, through indicating his erotic eagerness to continue investigating λόγος, Hermogenes reveals his willingness to stand fast and courageous in face of the monstrousness of λόγος. It is only through such a courageous stance that the upper, divine part of λόγος can be brought into dialogue, διάλογος, with its lower, human part.

When one recognizes the dual nature of λόγος (i.e., its human and divine parts), and when one further recognizes oneself, as human, as the site of λόγος, one thereby recognizes the divine *within oneself*: one comes to know one's own divine part. As a participant in λόγος, the human being is a site through which the divine can show itself. But, as argued in chapter 4, the appearance of the divine in the human is to be understood as monstrosity. Thus, to recognize the dual nature of λόγος is to recognize the dual nature of oneself: it is to see oneself as a monster. To correctly comport oneself toward the monstrosity of λόγος, one must oneself be a monster.

It is thus in recognizing the dual nature of λόγος that Hermogenes truly shows himself to be the son of Hermes, that monstrous offspring of a mortal and immortal. By acknowledging the dual nature of λόγος, the daimonic Hermogenes recognizes the dual nature of himself. He thereby shows himself to be *like* λόγος: for brother to be like brother is nothing to wonder about. So, by showing himself to be a monster, Hermogenes comes to comport himself correctly toward λόγος. It is through recognizing the unstable and vacillatory character of words (what might be called their "conventional" aspect) *and* recognizing the stability that words, precisely through their vacillatory play, bespeak (what might be called their "natural" aspect) that Hermogenes reveals himself capable of a monstrous apprehension of the monstrous character of λόγος. Most significantly, it is through showing himself eager to play at investigating words, while knowing all too well the risks and limitations of such play, that Hermogenes shows himself capable of making the ascent that only such play can initiate.

Attaining this correct comportment toward λόγος has proved to be no easy matter. If nothing else, the *Cratylus* has made clear the difficulties and absurdities at play in any λόγος on λόγος. One recalls Socrates' first statement of the dialogue, that "beautiful things are difficult, and knowledge of names is no small matter" (395b). Perhaps λόγος, of all things, is the *most* difficult and dangerous (χαλεπός) matter to speak of: for λόγος is, precisely, speech. To speak about speaking—to inquire through λόγος into the nature of λόγος in such a way as to make the reach and limitations of λόγος manifest—is to employ the very thing one wishes to investigate. In other words, it is to engage oneself in a circle.

However, this of all circles must not be understood as a vicious circle, but rather as a hermeneutic one. More precisely, this circle must be understood as *the* hermeneutic circle, as the founding and originary circle in which the human being, as the ζῷον λόγον ἔχων, finds itself. The human being always already finds itself *in* language. Phrased otherwise, the human being is always already the recipient of a gift from the god Hermes, "he who wrought λόγος" (408b): and this gift is that with which we come to submit the (same) gift to interrogation when we come to look the gift-horse in the mouth. It is only because of the gift of λόγος that we can bring λόγος itself into the space of inquiry—and yet, when we do so, we bring the snake's mouth ever closer to its own tail. Λόγος is the method of *every* inquiry, most of all an inquiry into λόγος itself: for how could one interrogate language without using language? To discover that one is the recipient of λόγος, gift from the god Hermes, is to find oneself in *the* hermeneutic circle.

The *Cratylus* elucidates three possible ways to comport oneself toward this circle. The first is to charge blindly into such an inquiry without voicing the slightest concern for the legitimacy and efficacy of such a pursuit. (It is this route which Socrates, and especially Hermogenes, take at the outset of the dialogue.) This comportment fails to recognize the circularity, proceeds zealously into an inquiry into λόγος through λόγος, and thereby makes the circle vicious in its blind attempt to accomplish something which, owing to the circle, is impossible. Such a blind pursuit is of the utmost tragic character: it remains trapped within a limited method without knowing *that* it is limited.

The second option is to remain silent, perhaps fully aware of the abyssal dangers that will inevitably overwhelm any λόγος on λόγος. This option, however, demands that one give up λόγος precisely in order to undergo a genuine experience of λόγος, that one give up, therefore, precisely what one would hope to gain.

It is this position that the silent Cratylus occupies: the position that grasps one part of λόγος while losing sight of the other; the position that grants the divinity of λόγος while forgetting its humanity. Such a position is also characteristic of the tragic life as Socrates understands it. Here, one "solves" the circle by stepping out of it, leaving behind λόγος in the process.

The third option is to be aware of the difficulties and dangers involved in any λόγος on λόγος and nonetheless courageously risk an inquiry into it. Such a position requires that one be fully aware of the limits of one's investigation, and yet undertake the investigation anyway. Above all, this position requires a *playfulness* which vigorously investigates λόγος even while insisting on the inadequacy of such an investigation. It is this position—which I have called the comic view of language—which Socrates unfolds throughout the *Cratylus,* and which he, to some measure, brings Hermogenes to hold.

What characterizes this position is that, in the face of a recognition of the duplicity of λόγος, one engages (in) λόγος anyway, one hazards to speak about it. For it is precisely in speaking reflexively about λόγος (i.e., in letting one's immersion and dependency on λόγος come to light) that one discovers the dream of stability that all speaking supposes, and the connection to Being that language therefore entails. Thus, it is by marking the limits of one's λόγος, and by fully appreciating the dual nature of λόγος, that one begins to transcend those limits. Such transcendence can only take place if one plays with words: for only by speaking can one hear what words themselves wish to say. It is only through engaging λόγος that one can come to let the divine part dialogue with the human part, and listen to what that dialogue says.

So long as one knows that one is playing, and remains steadfast in such play, one remains comported toward λόγος correctly. However, the moment that one believes oneself to have finally accessed the truth of beings through words—that is, the moment one's play ceases to be play by becoming overly serious—one fails: for one believes oneself to be accomplishing more than one legitimately can. In this register, one recalls Socrates' proviso as he entered into his inquiry concerning the names of the gods:

> There's a serious [σπουδαίως] way of talking about the names of these gods and also a playful way [παιδικῶς]. So ask some other people for the serious way, but there's nothing preventing us from passing through the playful way: for even the gods are lovers of play. (406b–c; my translation)

The *Cratylus* as a whole has revealed that all words, and therefore λόγος in general, must be examined playfully if λόγος is to come to show its true character. Only the playful engagement of λόγος comports correctly to the circle of λόγος in which the human being always already finds itself.

One might here playfully call upon a certain passage from the *Laws* in which the Athenian distinguishes between serious and playful pursuits:

I assert that what is serious should be treated seriously [χρῆναι τὸ μὲν σπουδαῖον σπουδάζειν], and what is not serious not [τὸ δέ μὴ σπουδαῖον μή], and that by nature god is worthy of a complete, blessed seriousness, but that what is human, as we said earlier, has been devised as a certain plaything of god [θεοῦ τι παίγνιον], and that this is really the best thing about it [αὐτου τὸ βέλτιστον]. Every man and woman should spend life in this way, playing the most beautiful games [καλλίστας παιδιὰς]. . . ." (*Lg.* 803c; Pangle; trans. modified)

The games that the Athenian enumerates are sacrificing, singing, and dancing. Here, in a gesture of play, we might extend these words of the Athenian into the *Cratylus*. We recall that Socrates claims that knowledge of words is a beautiful matter (τὰ καλά) (383a). We recall, too, Socrates' playfulness throughout the etymologies and insistence that such play is not to be taken too seriously. We can thus imagine that the inquiry into words, which is itself a beautiful matter, is among those most beautiful games that human beings, by virtue of being the playthings of the gods, ought to playfully pursue. It is this capacity to play—to be a plaything (παίγνιον), a toy, a jest—that is the best quality (βέλτιστον) of the human.

Why is it that this capacity for play is so grand? It is Socrates, in the *Cratylus*, who gives the answer: "because even the gods are lovers of play" (φιλοπαίσμονες γὰρ καὶ οἱ θεοί) (406c). This could mean that, in playing, we become loved by the gods. This could also mean that, if we come to love play, we become *like* the gods, who themselves love play. For the purposes of our inquiry, this means that when we play with words—when we playfully engage them in their playful ambiguities—we ascend to the higher region characterized by truth and Being. But it is only when the engagement remains playful that such an ascent occurs.

Such willingness to play with words amounts to nothing other than a dedication to the necessity of *interpretation*. The *Cratylus* has shown that it is only through a continual engagement with λόγος—which amounts to a continual reinterpretation of words—that one broaches the stability that λόγος bespeaks. Through his long and comic inquiry Socrates shows that one can never rest simply with how words *seem,* but must continually resubmit them to inquiry, to λόγος.

This commitment to interpretation is characteristic of Socrates' philosophical practice in general, at least insofar as this can be gleaned from Socrates' own exposition of that practice in Plato's *Apology*. There, Socrates speaks of a certain λόγος given by the god Apollo, through the oracle at Delphi, that claimed that no one is wiser than Socrates (*Ap.* 21a). This λόγος was exceedingly puzzling to Socrates, who knew himself "to be wise neither much nor little" (*Ap.* 21b). The difficulty for Socrates is extreme: for, on the one hand, Socrates is adamant in his belief that he is not wise; yet, on the other hand, Socrates is resolute in his belief that the god cannot lie. The human λόγος—Socrates' own λόγος that he is not wise—and the divine λόγος—that no one is wiser than Socrates—are in direct conflict. In a word, they have nothing in *common.* It was in the face of this tension that Socrates set out to test the λόγος of Apollo by measuring himself against the wisdom of others.

It is only through *interpreting* the oracle that Socrates is able to resolve this tension.[3] Through coming to interpret the god's λόγος as meaning that "human wisdom is of little or no worth" (*Ap.* 23b), Socrates brings the divine λόγος and his own human λόγος into harmony, gathering them together in common. More precisely, Socrates' interpretation of this divine λόγος serves to measure his own human λόγος, showing the manner in which the latter harmonizes with the former. In other words, Socrates' interpretation reveals that, despite their apparently oppositional differences, the human λόγος and the divine λόγος in fact belong together: they more or less *say the same.* Thus, in the face of a conflict between human λόγος and divine λόγος, what is needed is interpretation. It is only through such interpretation that the divine λόγος and the human λόγος are able to gather together in common, like two sides of the same coin—or, perhaps, two sides of the same Hermes Koinos.

However, it is of the utmost importance to observe that Socrates does not rest with this interpretation, but continues to test the λόγος of the god: "I am still even now going about and searching and investigating at the god's behest anyone, whether citizen or foreigner, whom I think is wise" (*Ap.* 23b; Fowler). Socrates dedicates himself to the investigation of others, and thus to the testing of the veracity of his interpretation of the god's λόγος. Indeed, Socrates will carry out this act of reinterpretation until the very end of his life, an end hastened by his unwavering commitment to such reinterpretation.

Thus, Socrates' philosophical practice in general can be understood in terms of a resolute commitment to the importance of reinterpretation. It is only to the extent that the Hermogenes of the *Cratylus* comes to approximate Socrates' philosophical dedication to reinterpretation that he shows himself to be the son of Hermes. In demonstrating his alacrity to submit words to reinterpretation Hermogenes reveals his true kinship with Hermes and, therefore, with Socrates, who has played the part of the playful god throughout the *Cratylus.* One can read the *Cratylus* as emphasizing the necessity of reinterpretation and exploring the extraordinary manner in which such reinterpretation, despite its apparent commitment to flux and indecision (i.e., to continually moving from one interpretation to another), leads one to a glimpse of the stability of Being. One can read the *Cratylus,* which begins with a veiled call to Hermes (Ἑρμῆς) (in the guise of Socrates), as a call for the importance of interpretation (ἑρμηνεία).

All of this holds no less for the *Cratylus* itself and those who would undertake to read it. In reading the *Cratylus*—in striving to let the dialogue itself say what it has to say—one must give oneself over to the inadequacy of one's own interpretation and the subsequent necessity for reinterpretation. It follows from this line of thinking that there can be no complete or definitive interpretation of the *Cratylus*. The moment one believes oneself to have "solved" the problems of the *Cratylus* is the moment one becomes like Cratylus, who believed himself to have settled the issue of the correctness of words (440d). Yet, in becoming like Cratylus one would cut oneself out of the conversation, rendering oneself silent in the face of an inquiry into λόγος.

One must rather remain eager for inquiry, even while knowing the limits of all such inquiries. In a word, one must be open to *dialogue*, to the bringing of one λόγος into communion with another, to the bringing of one interpretation to bear upon another in such a way as to reveal something common to both. In a word, one must strive to be like Hermogenes, who has shown himself to be eager to reengage λόγος through the reinterpretation of words. Only in this way can one hope to let the true nature of λόγος come to light.

The *Cratylus* is a playful attempt to bring us, the readers, into an acknowledgement of our own monstrous ability to ascend into a grasp of the monstrous character of language. To comport oneself correctly toward the *Cratylus* is to show oneself capable of responding playfully to the play that the dialogue itself puts into play, with all of the ambiguity and uncertainty that this position entails. So long as one gives oneself over to this playfulness, one shows oneself to be like Hermogenes, son of Hermes, brother to Pan and λόγος.

Notes

Introduction

1. See Sallis 1975, 13.

2. The word "name" translates the Greek ὄνομα, which can be variously translated as "name," "noun," "word," "expression," "phrase," etc. The ambiguity of the word ὄνομα has caused interpreters of the *Cratylus* a great deal of trouble, as it is difficult to know its scope. Although the *Cratylus* begins with an examination of a proper name (i.e., "Hermogenes") it will eventually come to consider not just names but abstract nouns, adjectives, verbs, and participles. As Ademollo notes, "the term ὄνομα generically applies to any word whose function is not primarily syntactic" (Ademollo 2011, 1). I will translate ὄνομα as either "name" or "word," depending on the context. However, it is important to note that in both cases what is meant is a word that *names* something, that calls upon it or addresses it, be it a person, a god, an abstract notion, an action, or other. It is also important to note the danger in trying to narrowly translate the word ὄνομα: for the essential ambiguity of words if precisely what will come to light through the *Cratylus*.

3. See, for example, Barney 2001, 19: "[I]n the case of the *Cratylus* at least, I think it is reasonable . . . to read Socrates' arguments as attributable to Plato in a fairly strong sense. Through Socrates, Plato presents what he takes to be the best arguments available for true and important conclusions, in the hope that we will reflect on and ultimately accept them." Despite this, Barney is extremely sensitive to the parodic aspect of the text. There have also been various attempts to see the *Cratylus* as Plato's attempt at preparing the blueprints for an "ideal language," most notably Baxter 1992. For an excellent refutation of this general attempt, see Gonzalez 1998, 80–81.

4. Given that the *Cratylus* undertakes a rigorous investigation into the meaning and function of λόγος, I have strived to leave the word in its Greek form. However, in many cases "language" has been chosen to translate λόγος, despite the necessary penury of the translation. What Socrates means by λόγος depends, of course, upon context. (It can sometimes mean "language," "word," "argument," "statement," "sentence," "story," etc.) Any general ideas about λόγος as it unfolds through the *Cratylus* can only come to light through a reading of the *Cratylus* as a whole. Stated provisionally, λόγος, seen in its connection to λέγω (understood as a gathering or collecting), refers to the manner by which beings (in their Being) come to be gathered together for the human being in such a way that they can be set apart from other beings. Such a gathering is a fundamental and constitutive phenomenon of the human condition and precedes vocal or symbolic articulation.

5. *Play* and *comedy* are not simply equivalent. As will be clarified at the end of this Introduction, comedy is herein considered as a kind of *radical play.*

6. Modrak 2001, especially 3–4, 13, 19. Modrak remains neutral about whether or not Aristotle was responding to the *Cratylus* in particular or merely to certain philosophical problems that were in the air of the Academy. Regardless, Modrak herself is "satisfied . . . that the *Cratylus* states the problem Aristotle is addressing" (14n1).

7. Or perhaps Albinus. There is debate among scholars about the author of the *Handbook.* For a clear summary of the debate, see the Introduction to Dillon 1993.

8. Diogenes Laertius, too, considers the *Cratylus* to be a logical work (τοῦ λογικοῦ) (*Lives*, III.50 ff.).

9. Although the word λογική appears in Aristotle, it does not come within a semblance of its modern sense until Alexander of Aprodisias's *In Aristotelis topicorum libros octo commentaria,* 74.29, some 500 years after Plato. See Guthrie 1981, 135.

10. See his *Quaestiones Convivales* 9, 14, 746b. See also van den Berg 2008, 38, 47.

11. Though much could be said about the relationship between irony and play in Plato, let it here suffice to say that irony is one of the many ways—but by no means the only way—that Socrates plays with his interlocutors. Play is a more general category of which irony is but one species.

12. See Proclus 2007, 47. Van den Berg argues that those who attempt to develop Proclus's theory of language by having recourse to *In. Cratylus* do so only by overlooking the text's role as a commentary (van den Berg 2008, 93).

13. However, Sedley 2003 also argues that etymology has limited philosophical value for Plato; see his chapter 6.

14. Against this, see Taylor 1960, 77: "it is plain that we are not to find the serious meaning of the dialogue here."

15. See also Baxter 1992, 87: ". . . nothing in Plato is just a joke."

16. To bolster his claim that Socrates' use of etymology is not ironic, Sedley writes that "it is worth recalling . . . that etymology is similarly exploited by Plato's speakers Timaeus and (in the *Laws*) the Athenian stranger, neither of whom shares Socrates' tendency for irony" (Sedley 2003, 41). One can well wonder whether Timaeus indeed abstains from such irony: see Sallis 1999, 85–86. Furthermore, Sedley here leaves it unasked whether the *entirety* of a character's role in a dialogue could serve an ironic or satirical end.

17. See also Schleiemacher 2010, 228.

18. Among the ancients, Proclus offers a notable exception to this interpretive trend. Perhaps more than any other commentator, Proclus attends to the dramatic folds of the *Cratylus.* Yet, despite his sensitivity to the action (and *dramatis personae*) of the text, even Proclus finally reduces the dramatic to his own cosmological theory, interpreting it through his own theological lens. Further, there is absolutely no indication that Proclus took the *Cratylus* as at all playful or comedic, and every indication to the contrary. Thus, while attentive to the dramatic tenor of the text, Proclus was deaf to its comedy.

19. For another excellent reading of the *Cratylus* which is sensitive to the irony of the text, see Rosenstock 1992.

20. Sedley notes that no ancient commentator took it to be a comedy: "if Plato was joking, the joke flopped" (Sedley 2003, 39). However, the inability of an audience to "get" a joke hardly determines whether it is in fact a joke. Further, we have no evidence either way as to how the *Cratylus* was received by those in the academy closest to Plato (with the possible exception of Aristotle—see above).

21. See Lamb 1924, 377.

22. Or, as Taylor puts it, a "directly enacted drama" (Taylor 1960, 75).

23. See Sallis 2008, 144.

24. See Freydberg 1997, 2: "Playfulness in Plato is never frivolous or merely decorative, but always has philosophical content."

25. An example, perhaps, is Aristophanes' caricature of Socrates in the *Clouds,* which became dangerous only once it came to be taken seriously by the general public.

26. The ridiculous character of Platonic comedy shall be addressed below.

27. Strauss's paradigmatic example is the *Republic,* which engages in a number of such comical abstractions. In particular, Strauss shows how Socrates' inquiry into justice abstracts away from procreation (Strauss 1964, 96) and sexual difference, *eros* (which amounts to an abstraction from philosophy itself) (ibid., 112), and nature (ibid., 138). (See also Rosen 1968, 120.) According to Strauss, none of these can properly be omitted from an inquiry into the just city and soul, and Socrates' continual abstraction of them must be understood as ridiculous or comic as Strauss defines the terms.

28. Strauss also contrasts the landscape of Platonic dialogue with the Christian worldview by calling the former "slightly more akin to comedy than to tragedy" (ibid., 61).

29. Sallis elaborates upon this conception of comedy in his *Transfigurements,* where he considers it in terms of the comedies of Shakespeare. See especially his chapter 6.

30. See Sallis 2008, 145: "The comedies in the [Platonic] dialogues are played out alongside more rigorously dialectical passages and often are intimately linked to them in such a way as to show something that bears significantly on the dialectical passages."

31. For reasons that will become clear, one would do well to hear the root *monstrum* (from which we get our *monster*) in *de-monstration.* The comedy of the *Cratylus,* it will be seen, deals extensively with the *monstrous.*

32. Taylor takes the etymologies in particular to be "good-humored satire on attempts to reach a metaphysic by way of 'philology'" (Taylor 1960, 78). Sallis considers the parodic character of the etymologies to be of secondary importance, emphasizing rather the necessity of exhibiting the comic character of the dialogue as a whole and the philosophically disclosive function such comedy serves (Sallis 1975, 234). The parodic quality of Plato's texts in general has been well charted by Andrea Nightingale, who has argued that many of Plato's texts operate as parodies of other literary and philosophical genres, where such parody serves to "criticize, subvert, or co-opt the genre that it represents" (Nightingale 2000, 7). However, Nightingale argues that such parody, while traditionally thought of as comic in character, is by no means bound to the comic (Nightingale 2000, 8). Rather, she argues that parody can be understood as an opening of a critical space in which certain differences between the parodied text and the parody itself can become manifest. Even while granting Nightingale's broader analysis, one could ask whether parody (and the critical space it opens) can indeed be conceived independently of the comedic, or whether parody in its very nature will always involve some aspect of the comic.

33. Scholars have attempted throughout the years to isolate precisely whom Socrates is ridiculing. Steiner, for example, argues that the etymologies Socrates offers are meant to satirize the purported etymologizing of Antisthenes (Steiner 1915; and see also Baxter 1992, 1; Levinson 1958, 32). Some have argued that it is precisely the influence of the historical Cratylus whom Socrates is satirizing; others have suggested Euthyphro; still others Homer or Pythagoras. For an excellent attempt at isolating the many voices which Socrates satirizes within the *Cratylus,* see Baxter 1992, chapter 5.

34. Against this, Baxter argues that Plato is taking pains to separate the Socratic "stargazing" from that practiced by other, more frivolous philosophers (Baxter 1992, 141).

35. According to Aristotle in his *Poetics,* the ridiculous (τὸ γελοῖον) "is a sort of missing the mark [ἁμάρτημά τι] and a deformity that is painless and not destructive" (*Poet.* 1449a35). What will be seen is that much of what takes place within the *Cratylus* involves just this. Indeed, it is no exaggeration to say that almost the entirety of the *Cratylus* performs a certain missing of the mark, disclosing the way in which a certain view of the correctness of names fails. What will be shown is that both Hermogenes and Cratylus, though *wishing* to explain the correctness of names, both miss the mark—and that this missing of the mark occurs precisely *through* such wishing. This missing of the mark is the comic way of the text. Insofar as comedy brings this "missing of the mark" to light, it serves to disclose the limits of that which it ridicules.

36. However, it is worth noting that, unlike some other of Plato's dialogues, there is no laughter in the *Cratylus*—a fact owed in part to its imitated (i.e., non-narrative) structure. However, short of actually laughing, Socrates explicitly calls the inquiry *laughable* on several occasions (402a, 425d, 426b).

37. See Riley 2005, 11: ". . . one of Plato's strangest dialogues."

38. Further, as Bernard Freydberg has argued, play is not only the origin of philosophy, but also its end. See Freydberg 1997, 22, 169.

39. Perhaps the finest illustration of this is the phenomenon of the *parabasis* in Old Greek Comedy, where a member of the chorus (or, in the case of the *Clouds,* the playwright himself) transgresses the dramatic action and speaks directly to the audience. Such a transgression brings the comedy itself into a critical space: that is, it *plays* with the comedy. See *Clouds,* 518 ff.

40. See Sallis 1975, 21: "[The playfulness of the Platonic texts] calls for a responsive play on the part of one who seeks to interpret them."

41. From out of his reading of the *Republic* and the *Laws* in particular, Freydberg has argued for a kind of primal play (which amounts to a pre-logical exposure to the graceful ordering of music) that grounds and makes possible both "serious" and "frivolous" play (Freydberg 1997, 17). According to Freydberg, "[p]hilosophy in the Platonic dialogues is . . . fundamentally playful" (ibid., 21); and, as a result, to pursue the matters of philosophy too seriously is to "transgress the order of philosophical play" (ibid.), thereby diverting oneself from genuine philosophical movement.

1. First Words

1. 383a; translation by C. D. C. Reeve.

2. 383a; translation by B. Jowett.

3. 383a; translation by J. Sachs.

4. 383a; translation by H. N. Fowler.

5. 383a; translation by U. Wolf.

6. 383a; translation by V. Cousin.

7. This is not to imply that language could ever do so without the human being as the very site of this unfolding.

8. In his excellent article on the *Cratylus,* Bruce Rosenstock has also argued that language "says" something about itself within the text: "I believe that, for all its paradoxes and puzzles, [the *Cratylus*] does have something very serious to say. . . . It is that the 'care

for the soul' begins with a confrontation with an unsettling, ironizing voice. In the *Cratylus, this is the voice of language itself*. . . . [L]anguage itself is the vehicle of the ironizing power which Plato typically vests in the words of Socrates, [and] Socrates in turn is represented as a kind of demonic embodiment of the ironic power of language. . . ." (Rosenstock 1992, 396; my emphasis).

9. This is the Greek as it appears in the Oxford Classical Text. (There are two slight variations in the manuscripts, neither of which are relevant here.)

10. For a recent instance of such speculation, see Sedley 2003, 7–14.

11. Compare Tanner 2010, vii.

12. Socrates himself, during the etymological comedy, indicates this abyss: "we have to take it to heart that if someone is going to keep constantly asking for the former words by means of which names are spoken, and again in turn inquires after the words by means of which *they* had been spoken, and doesn't stop doing that, isn't it necessary for the one asking the questions finally to give up[?]" (421d–e; Sachs). To offer just one actual example of this regress as it is performed within the *Cratylus*, ἐπιθυμέω is used in the account Socrates gives of the god Hades (403c ff.). Later, ἐπιθυμέω itself becomes the object of the etymological inquiry (419e).

13. Baxter argues that this principle represents Plato's notion of an "ideal language" (Baxter 1992, 83), a kind of proscription of the way that languages, Greek or otherwise, ought to be.

14. On the first word of the *Phaedo*, see Burger 1984, 15. On the first word of the *Republic*, see Sallis 1975, 313–320, and Brann et al. 2004, 119. On the first word of the *Phaedrus*, see Sallis 1975, 104–109. Suffice it to say, there are many well-argued cases where the first word of a Platonic text is especially significant when read in light of the text as a whole.

15. See 408e: "I am willing [ἐθέλω]." See also 431a6: "I am willing to concede to you [ἐθέλω σοι . . . συγχωρῆσαι]."

16. See Bernal 2006, 338.

17. See Smyth 1920, 107.

18. Kahn 1996, 262–263. See also *Symposium,* 200a ff., where a certain intimacy between βούλομαι, ἐπιθυμέω, and ἐράω can be seen.

19. In the *Phaedrus,* for example, Socrates demarcates certain differences between ἐπιθυμέω and ἐράω (*Phdr.* 237d).

20. Zuckert takes the opening line to show Hermogenes asking Cratylus' *permission* for Socrates to come and join in their conversation, thereby stressing Hermogenes' penchant for agreement (ὁμολογία) (Zuckert 2009, 652–653). However, as context makes clear, βούλομαι here does not have the sense of agreement, but rather of *preference*.

21. See *Republic* 510a.

22. The extent to which the character Hermogenes is connected to the realm of human opinion has been noted by several scholars, though each interprets this connection differently. See, for example, Proclus 2007, 5.15 ff. See also Baxter 1992, 17 ff.

23. The etymology that Socrates offers for βούλομαι hearkens back to the one offered for the word βλαβερόν, in which "wishing" gets associated with "harm" (417d–e). We shall return to this in chapter 7.

24. As mentioned in the Introduction, Aristotle claims in his *Poetics* that such a failure to hit what is aimed for is the mark of comedy (*Poet.* 1449a35).

25. Literally, the "with which."

26. There is an ambiguity to the word φύσις as it is used within the *Cratylus*. On the one hand, φύσις is used to refer to the stability of a being that allows for it to remain the

same as itself. In this signification, φύσις is almost a synonym for οὐσία (386e). On the other hand, φύσις will be used within the *Cratylus* to refer precisely to the instability and flux of natural things, that is, of things which appear in the realm of becoming (see 411c). This ambiguity persists in our present day use of the word *nature*: one speaks both of the nature of a thing (meaning its essence) and of the natural world as the realm of alteration and decay. We shall return to this in chapter 4.

27. See also 414d: "they keep making lots of insertions into the first names until they end up making it so that no single human being can understand what in the world the names mean [ὅτι ποτὲ βούλεται τὸ ὄνομα]" (Sachs).

28. See *Republic* 590e: "The law [ὁ νόμος], which is the ally of everyone in the city, makes it clear that it intends [βούλεται] something of that kind. . . ."

29. See Sallis 1975, 253.

30. See Grant 1980, 206. The character of Hermes and his importance for the *Cratylus* will be addressed at length in chapter 2.

31. See Suhr 1967, 64: "More than any other major divinity . . . Hermes was a frequent visitor to the lower world." See also Kerényi 1976, 104; see also Brann 2004, 119.

32. There is an extensive debate on the dramatic date of the *Cratylus* and whether or not it belongs to the series of dialogues in which I just placed it. Given that I have nothing substantially new to add to this debate, I shall only assert that I generally agree with Allan 1954 and Sallis 1975, both of whom place the *Cratylus* as following *dramatically* upon the *Euthyphro*. However, for the purposes of this inquiry, whether or not the *Cratylus* in fact occurs within that dramatic sequence is largely immaterial: what matters is that Socrates' mention of Euthyphro cannot but bring the dialogue *Euthyphro* to mind, thereby calling upon us to draw certain comparisons. For a similar argument, see Zuckert 2009, 650–652.

33. Contrary to this view, Proclus offers an etymology of Socrates' name that indicates an upward comportment: "'Socrates' is based on the fact that he is a savior of the power of the soul [*sōtêra . . . tou kratous tês psukhês*]—that is, of reason—and is not drawn down by the senses" (Proclus 2007, 15).

34. On the suggestive import of ἀνακοίνοῦσθαι, see Baxter 1992, 15.

35. See Kerényi 1976, 111. See also Cornford 1909, 281–284.

36. This is Seth Benardete's translation of τῇ τοῦ βίου συμπάσῃ τραγῳδίᾳ καὶ κωμῳδίᾳ.

37. Socrates will compare himself to Heracles at 411a. At 428c, Socrates will be compared to Ajax by Cratylus.

2. Marking the Limits

1. See Nails 2002, 312. See also Hyland 1995, 16.

2. See *Crito* 52b.

3. Moreover, as one travelled farther away from Athens, one would encounter new and differing dialects until, finally, one would wander beyond the Greek language entirely. A trangression of the city is a transgressions not just of its laws, but of its *language*.

4. Though there is debate about the precise legal status of a νόθος, it seems clear that there is some legal or at least social difference between a νόθος and a legitimate son; otherwise the designation would serve no function. Nails thinks otherwise, arguing that Hermogenes "enjoyed such citizen rights as he wished to exercise, and such obligations as he was required to bear" (Nails 2002, 163). The emphasis within the *Cratylus* on Hermogenes' lack

of his father's inheritance suggests that a νόθος lacked certain rights and responsibilities, or at the very least the social status, characteristic of a full citizen. See, for example, Aristophanes' *Birds*, where Heracles is accused of being a νόθος who is therefore *forbidden by law* from inheriting his father's wealth (*Birds*, 1648 ff.). See also Davies 1977, 107.

5. See Nails 2002, 105.

6. As Baxter observes, Hermogenes has a certain "fluxy" character about him, insofar as he is eager to be convinced that the truth regarding names is otherwise than he conceives it, whereas Cratylus sticks to his guns (i.e., stays in place) up to the bitter end (Baxter 1992, 96). (We shall return to Cratylus's stubbornness in chapter 8.) In light of this, one could say that the personality of each interlocutor mimics the philosophical position they are seen to hold. Of course, this is complicated by the fact that, in Cratylus's case, the doctrine he steadfastly holds on to is one of flux. There is thus a humorous incongruity *within* the figure of Cratylus himself.

7. Regarding the extent to which Cratylus and Hermogenes come to occupy their opposing positions, see Sallis 1975, 187–188.

8. This will be taken up in chapters 7 and 9.

9. See 385c, where a name (ὄνομα) is said to be the smallest part of λόγος.

10. Socrates also mentions *teaching* (διδάσκω) as part of the purpose of names. However, as Sallis has argued, the pedagogical use of words reduces to their function as a means of articulating beings (Sallis 1975, 208).

11. The limits belonging to the tool analogy itself will be explored in chapter 5.

12. If this regress is wanting of an example, imagine a scientist who, in order to discover what is distorting and perspectival about all microscopes, places a microscope under a microscope in order to better see it. Any causes of distortion that he discovers will now have distorted the very discovery. As will be seen in greater detail, this threat of distortion is endemic to the inquiry underway in the *Cratylus*.

13. The meaning—or, rather, the un-decidable polysemy—of Cratylus's silence will be examined in greater detail in chapter 8.

14. On the role of nobility in Greek tragedy, see Hyland 1995, 119.

15. Sedley has suggested that Hermogenes is annoyed with Cratylus's peculiar statement and inability (or unwillingness) to substantiate it, and that he and Cratylus have been involved in a "heated debate" by the time they come upon Socrates (Sedley 2003, 3–4; see also Keller 2000, 293). Though the "heat" of this debate does not immediately come across in the text (nor, for that matter, does Hermogenes' annoyance), one thing is textually clear: Hermogenes does not understand why Cratylus insists on refusing him his name, and is *eager to learn*.

16. It is appropriate that it is Socrates in particular who is called upon to interpret Cratylus's oracles, for Socrates, as seen in the *Apology*, is already a practiced interpreter of oracles (*Ap.* 21a ff.). See also Sallis 1975, 191.

17. See Kirkland 2007, 1.

18. See *Apology*, 38a; *Symposium*, 216e; *Gorgias*, 489e.

19. Baxter notes Socrates' use of irony in the beginning of the *Cratylus* (Baxter 1992, 30).

20. The tentativeness of Socrates' interpretation is marked through his use of the word ἴσως ("perhaps").

21. One must be careful here. Given that the *Cratylus* deals explicitly with both the problem of the correctness of names in general, and the correctness of Hermogenes' name in particular, one cannot simply proceed as if the dictionary definition of a term satisfies

the semantic nuance at play within the dialogue. The efficacy of "literal" etymologies is one of the major issues at question within the text.

22. See Baxter 1992, 10. For another ancient source testifying to Hermogenes' penury, see Xenophon's *Symposium*. It is interesting to note that Hermogenes claims to have servants at *Cratylus* 384d, suggesting that he is not totally without resources.

23. According to Cratylus, one of the most important (μέγιστον) of inquiries (427e).

24. This is affirmed at 408b.

25. See Sallis 1975, 253.

26. See Guthrie 1950, 88. See also Suhr 1967, 63: "Hermes was very commonly represented in the form of a *herm* on the roads, at gateways and graves." See also Kerényi 1976, 89.

27. See Aesop's *Fables* (translated by Laura Gibbs, 2008), 259: "There was a four-cornered statue of Hermes by the side of the road, with a heap of stones piled at its base."

28. See Martin 1996, 158: "Herms, stone posts with sculpted sets of erect male organs and a bust of the god Hermes, were placed throughout the city as guardians of doorways, boundaries, and places of transition. A herm stood at nearly every street intersection, for example, because crossings were, symbolically at least, zones of special danger."

29. Herodotus, II.51.

30. "Hipparkhos . . . proceeded, with the design of educating those of the countryside, to set up figures of Hermes for them along the roads in the midst of the city and every district town . . ." (*Hipp.* 228d; Lamb). Scholars generally agree that the *Hipparchus* was authored by someone other than Plato; regardless, the dialogue, likely written around the middle of the third century BCE, attests to the presence of herms in Athens.

31. As West and West note in their translation of the *Clouds,* some manuscripts do not have Hermes appearing at the end of the text (West and West 1998, 176n222).

32. As Joe Sachs explains in his translation of the *Cratylus,* this expression seems to refer to the power of Euthyphro's divination: "A modern automotive equivalent might be 'so you can see how many horses he's got under the hood'" (Sachs 2011, 186n47). However, as will be speculated in the next chapter, the role of the horse may serve a slightly different function within the dialogue.

33. One wonders if it is dangerous due especially to Socrates' impending trial. Part of the charge brought against Socrates relates to his alleged inability to believe in the gods of the city (*Ap.* 24b). Many of the etymologies Socrates will later offer involve playful construal of the names of the gods. Such play, *if taken too seriously,* would no doubt appear impious.

34. Note how it is thievery and deception in words that associates Hermes with the marketplace. This adds nuance to Socrates' first interpretation of the meaning of Cratylus's claim, for it suggests that Hermogenes is no good at making money because he is *neither* thievish nor deceptive in speech. This is hardly an insult.

35. In addition to these four, there is a fifth point that will be examined in chapter 6. Socrates makes a rather peculiar reference to Homer, one which is exceedingly important for our interpretation. For now, it suffices to indicate that this subtle reference to Homer emphasizes the extent to which the possibility of *inheritance*—both from father to son, and from a being to a name—is at stake within the dialogue.

36. Kirkland writes that the etymology for "Hermes" offered in the *Cratylus* "demands to be taken seriously" (Kirkland 2007, 1). While I agree entirely with this sentiment, I shall argue below that this name, perhaps more so than any other name, demands to be taken *playfully.*

37. See also Sallis's discussion of the relationship of λόγος to manifestation (Sallis 1975, 10).

38. See *Laws,* 941a.

39. Derrida 1981, 93, 88. See also Faivre 1995, 76.

40. Some scholars dispute the placement of this passage. See Sedley 2003, 11ff.

41. See Rosenstock 1992, 395: "language, Plato will show in the *Cratylus,* is irreducibly ambivalent and, what is more, ironic, tempting us with words that have the appearance of univocity, but giving us not mere polysemy, but words with *antithetic* meanings."

42. We shall return to the all-important role of hypothesis in chapter 8.

43. See, for example, *Republic,* 382a.

44. The capacity for the gods to lie is further emphasized through Socrates' references to Homer. See my chapter 6.

45. Could it not therefore be the case that we are deceived about the deceptive capacity of λόγος? As Sallis has shown, such a situation is untenable: "for then we would be in the impossible situation of being deceived by *logos* into thinking that deception on the part of *logos* is possible" (Sallis 1975, 252). Λόγος cannot deceive us into thinking that deception in possible without thereby showing itself capable of deception. Regardless of whether λόγος truly shows itself as deceptive, or deceptively shows itself to be so, the deceptive power of λόγος remains. Thus, while λόγος cannot establish its own truthfulness, it *can* establish its own deceitfulness: the one thing that λόγος truly discloses is its capacity for deception (ibid.). In the final chapter I shall argue further that λόγος can indeed ensure its own truthfulness, though only in a very particular sense.

46. As Kirkland puts it, "Language [λόγος] determines us, not we it" (Kirkland 2007, 8).

47. Much more will be said about the tragic life in chapters 5–8.

48. As will be seen in chapter 7, *courage* (ἀνδρεῖος) plays an important role in this ascent.

49. Suhr comments on the jurisdiction of Hermes as spanning from the heavens down to Hades (Suhr 1967, 57, 64).

50. Derrida actually writes "Thoth" here; however, he has already made the identification between Thoth and Hermes (Derrida 1981, 88).

51. In a wonderful book, Gregory Dobrov (drawing upon the *Homeric Hymns*) has shown the manner in which Hermes, while still young, comes to interpret *his own* nature and biography, indicating a certain "hermeneutics of self" operative in the young rogue (Dobrov 2001, 3–4.) One might say that Hermes, the god of interpretation, exemplifies the importance of self-interpretation.

52. See Pseudo-Hyginus, *Astronomica* 2.21. The author attributes this story to the Orphic poet Musaeus.

53. Hermes is, of course, a god, and part of the Pantheon. However, he did not begin as such: rather, he began as a baby, abandoned to his mother. Only after his various mischievous exploits (such as stealing Apollo's cattle) does Hermes earn the recognition of his father Zeus.

54. See Sallis 1975, 241.

55. This interpretation fits perfectly with Hermes' role as both herald to the gods and *psychopomp.*

56. Indeed, Hermes' behavior was so roguish as to almost incite his mother to abandon him as well (*Hymn* IV.160).

57. *Hymn* IV.389.

58. See Sallis 1975, 241: "The hero is intermediate . . . by virtue of love and *logos,* as a lover of *logos,* and this corresponds to the fact that the philosopher is not one who is wise but who rather is in search of wisdom, who is intermediate between ignorance and wisdom."

59. Hermes' epithet "Hermes Logios" should be kept in mind. See Kerényi 1976, 59.

60. As Joe Sachs has suggested, the dialogue may be read as an enactment of the labors of Heracles (Sachs 2011, 190n55). Interestingly, the figure of Heracles was a kind of comic archetype frequently employed by ancient Greek comedians (as in, for example, Aristophanes' *Frogs*). See Cornford 1961, 152–156. We shall return to the image of Heracles in chapter 7.

61. Hermes was the god *of* heroes. See Suhr 1967, 55: "Once he was well established as a member of the Olympic family he became one of the busiest of divinities, rushing about between heaven and earth, even into Hades, with old trappings of a fertility god, serving as a guide for heroes and a functionary of Zeus."

62. See Brown 1990, 108: "The characteristic form in which Hermes was represented as god of the *agora* was the herm, which was an Athenian invention." See also ibid., 32.

63. See also Farnell 1909, 13.

64. As Brown argues, the exchanging of wives in Greek marriage customs can be thought of along the lines of the more general exchanging of property. As an overseer of property exchanges, Hermes likewise oversaw marriage: "Thus Hermes came to be the master of the magic art of seduction and a patron god of marriage" (Brown 1990, 42). See also Kerényi 1976, 102, where Hermes is said to bear a connection to the bridal-bed.

65. See Farnell 1909, 12, who notes that the names "Hermes" and "Aphrodite" appear on an inscription in Lesbos. Indeed, much later, in Ovid, the two gods are even sometimes combined in the figure of Hermaphroditus (Brown 1990, 14). See also Kerényi 1976, 83, who argues for a more essential connection between Hermes and Aphrodite. Finally, see Friedrich 1969, 92, who argues that Aphrodite and Hermes "seem closer to each other in overall gestalt than either is to any other deity."

66. See Grant and Hazel 1980, 205, who note that Hermes had many romantic adventures ("hatte viele Liebesabenteuer").

67. See Friedländer 1969, 48–49.

68. Friedländer convincingly argues that the body can never be left behind, but is continually needed for the ascent to the beautiful to occur. See Friedländer 1969, 49, 54, 56. See also Rosen 1968, 121.

69. To mitigate this view, Farnell has noted that Hermes is more associated with animal and human procreation than with raw vegetative fertility (Farnell 1909, 10). More in keeping with Suhr, Kerényi argues that Hermes was an elemental god, calling him "the original begetter" (Kerényi 1976, 98).

70. Maia was considered among many Greeks to be a lower goddess of fertility, a characteristic revealed through her frequent association with Gaia. See Aeschylus's *Libation Bearers,* 30 ff.); see also Kerényi 1976, 39.

71. This also serves to further indicate his procreative function. See Kerényi 1976, 26.

3. A Question of Inheritance

1. For an excellent account, reminiscent of Proclus, of why Cratylus ultimately believes "Socrates" to be Socrates' correct name, see Rosenstock 1992, 412. The correctness, for Rosenstock, has to do with Socrates' inheritance of *phronesis* from his father Sophroniskos.

2. See Proclus 2007, 8.25 ff.; see also Baxter 1992, 50.

3. It is also Socrates who marks the comedy. Socrates could have simply proceeded into the inquiry regarding the correctness of names; instead, he explicitly draws attention to the humorous character of Cratylus's refusal of Hermogenes' name. See Sallis 1975, 192.

4. See Keller 2000, 293. More typically, scholars argue that it was Plato who was Cratylus's student, basing this on a statement made by Aristotle in *Metaphysics A.* Kahn has

disputed such evidence by pointing out the "Peripatetic tendency . . . to construct lines of philosophical succession" where none necessarily exist (Kahn 1996, 83n24). Sedley accepts Aristotle's claim with certain reservations, while also offering a concise summary of the debate (Sedley 2003, 17n36 and 17n37).

5. That Hermogenes and Socrates were friends is evident from Plato's *Phaedo* (*Phd.* 59b). Their friendship is also clear in Xenophon's *Symposium, Apology,* and *Memorabilia.* See Taylor 1960, 75: "Hermogenes is well known to us as a member of Socrates' *entourage.*" See also Baxter 1992, 10.

6. As has been well documented by Kenneth Dover, the ancient Greeks found the small penis more aesthetically beautiful than the large one: "In caricature and in the representation of satyrs a penis of great size, even of preposterous size, is very common, and it is a reasonable conclusion (though not, I admit, an inescapable conclusion) that as a big penis goes with a hideous face and a small penis with a handsome face, it is the small penis that was admired" (Dover 1989, 126). Further, as Martha Nussbaum has argued, the small penis was seen (at least by Aristophanes) as congruent with a tough, "manly" man, who exercised a certain degree of self-control over his desires, whereas a large penis or an erection was "a shameful symbol of need run rampant" (Nussbaum 2005, 156). In light of these two analyses, one might say that the large erect penis (such as Hermes flaunts) is a sign of *unrestrained* ἔρως, a desire so strong as to lead one to transgress custom, a sort of *monstrous* desire.

7. This is likely a play on Cratylus Smicrion's name. For another likely play on Cratylus's name, see 428a.

8. The difficulty of beauty is echoed later in the text. Just before offering an etymology for κάλος, Socrates says: "it is more difficult [χαλεπώτερον] to understand" than some of the others (416b).

9. See Friedländer 1969, 51; see also Kahn 1996, 259.

10. This is not to suggest that the movement is one of pure or uninterrupted ascent. As the sudden interruption of the excessively embodied Alcibiades suggests, such ascent is necessarily accompanied by a bodily descent. For a similar point, see Alan Bloom's *Ladder of Love* (in Benardete 2001, 154).

11. See Friedländer 1969, 196; see also Sallis 2008, 168.

12. As will be seen in chapter 8, it is ultimately a glimpse of the beautiful itself toward which Socrates is leading his interlocutors. See 439c.

13. See *Odyssey* VIII.339.

14. In this register it is worth noting that Cratylus, according to Hermogenes, has the εἶδος in his mind (384a). Perhaps Cratylus, in feeding Hermogenes oracles, is indicating his distrust in Hermogenes' ability to grasp such an εἶδος. Weingartner, in a radically different context, has suggested that part of Socrates' task in the *Cratylus* is to expose the inadequacies of the Athenian educative structure by "exhibiting the muddledness of its most intelligent and well meaning products" (i.e., Hermogenes) (Weingartner 1970, 7n5). Against this, I shall argue that it is precisely Hermogenes' philosophical aptitude, rather than his "muddledness," which is ultimately exhibited throughout the *Cratylus.*

15. As has been noted by various scholars from Proclus on, Hermogenes' continual use of δοκέω throughout the text seems to indicate his immersion in the realm of seeming and opinion (δόξα). See Proclus 2007, 5.15. See also Baxter 1992, 91n26.

16. "The stallion is sexually capable up to the age of thirty-three years, and the mare up to forty, so that, in point of fact, the animals are sexually capable all their lives long" (*HA,* 545b15); "Of female animals the mare is the most sexually wanton, and next in order comes the cow. In fact, the mare is said to go a-horsing; *and the term derived from the*

habits of this one animal serves as a term of abuse applicable to those who are unbridled in the way of sexual appetite" (*HA*, 572a10–14; my emphasis).

17. Though the wanton horse comes eventually to be broken (*Phdr.* 254e), it is precisely his sexual desire that first draws the charioteer toward the beloved (*Phdr.* 254a).

18. As Baxter has observed, "the addition of the patronymic reinforces the fact that the man does bear the name *Hermogenes* and thereby subtly underlines the paradoxical nature of Cratylus' claim" (Baxter 1992, 10). By adding the patronymic, Socrates demonstrates that *this man here* is Hermogenes.

19. See Henderson 1975, 165.

20. Cited from Nails 2002, 73.

21. See Proclus 2007, 11.10.

22. See Keller 2000, 293.

23. Hermogenes' erotic posture is perhaps further indicated in the position of *questioning* (ἐρωτῶ) which he assumes from the outset of the text (383b). See the previous chapter for the relationship between ἔρως and questioning. In this connection, see 398d.

24. It also playfully foreshadows the conversation which takes place later regarding inheritance (to which we shall return in chapter 6). Given that Socrates will there argue that the son of a virtuous man should be a virtuous man *unless he is a monster,* one wonders if Socrates' insistence on using the patronymic does not suggest that Hermogenes is the son of a horse, the most salacious of all the animals.

25. See Proclus 2007, 29.1, where Hermogenes is said to be a mixture of opinion and desire for the Good.

26. One must be careful not to simply conflate the Xenophonic Hermogenes with the Platonic one. However, through a comparison of the two, this common characteristic of ἔρως has come to light. Such a comparison can help guide us in our interpretation of the character of the Platonic Hermogenes.

27. Against this, see Nails 2002, 163.

28. See Pangle 1985, 103–105.

29. It also indicates a certain similarity between Hermogenes and Socrates—an important similarity to which we shall return in chapter 8. See Pangle 1985, 105.

30. See *Lysistrata* 725, 836, 995; *Ecclesiazusae* 916; *Acharnians* 243, 259. See also Plato Comicus, 173.10. For all of this, see Henderson 1975, 112.

31. Both *erect* and *correct* share the Latin root *regere*.

32. Συνουσία can mean both social and sexual intercourse—an ambiguity doubtless at play in the *Symposium*.

33. The difference between human names and divine names will become an explicit part of the inquiry in the *Cratylus*.

34. Hermes is variously presented as having wings on his ankles and helmet.

35. See, for example, *Charmides,* 155d.

4. The Nature of Nature

1. οὐ γὰρ φύσει ἑκάστῳ πεφυκέναι ὄνομα οὐδὲν οὐδενί, ἀλλὰ νόμῳ καὶ ἔθει τῶν ἐθισάντων τε καὶ καλούντων (384d).

2. See chapter 1.

3. Baxter notes Hermogenes' willingness to listen (Baxter 1992, 17, 23). See also Sedley 2003, 51.

4. See Sallis 1975, 194.

5. See Kirkland 2007, 4, 8. See also Gonzalez 1998, 63.

6. On a different interpretation of Cratylus's name, see Proclus 2007, 8.15.

7. See Sallis 1975, 151; see also 309 where Sallis associates, with due reserve, the unity of a name with the distinct being of a thing. In this register, see also the *Parmenides*, 135a ff., where Parmenides insists that, although the looks of things (εἴδη τῶν ὄντων) are unknowable, they are the very precondition for conversation, διαλέγεσθαι.

8. See Weingartner 1970, 7, who argues that such a individualized conception of naming as Hermogenes offers cannot properly be called "conventionalism" (as it so often is), for "when . . . even an individual user of a language may, without being in error, employ different sounds at different times as the name of the very same object, we no longer have convention or agreement in any sense at all." However, as Socrates' analysis has just suggested, we can have or lack an agreement *of* ourselves *with* ourselves.

9. Though, to be sure, we are not told which name Cratylus thinks is correct for poor Hermogenes, only that he finds "Hermogenes" decidedly incorrect.

10. For the many ways in which the two dialogues are similar, see MacKenzie 1986, 126, 129. MacKenzie also does an excellent job of noting the ways that the *Cratylus* and *Theaetetus* differ.

11. MacKenzie 1986, 131.

12. As many scholars have remarked, it is not immediately clear that the historical Protagoras in fact held such a position as Plato here presents him as holding. Nonetheless, as Sedley has observed, "in Plato's hands . . . Protagoras' dictum becomes above all an affirmation of the individual's power to determine truth for themselves at any given time. All truth is relative, in the particular sense of being relative to the judging subject" (Sedley 2003, 54).

13. The reasons for employing the language of inheritance have already been adduced (in chapter 2), and shall be returned to in detail in later chapters, especially chapter 6.

14. See Cornford 1957, 43 ff..

15. See *Theaetetus* 157b6, 162a3, 163b4, and 179d4.

16. Liddell and Scott, 860.

17. It is worth noting that φθέγγεσθαι is used several times throughout the *Cratylus*: 383a7, 394c8, 399b3, 399b4, 417b5, 429e9, 430a2, 434e6, 435a2, and 435a5.

18. Regarding the mantic speaking of the Sibyl, see *Phaedrus*, 244b.

19. Or, as Sachs translates, "astonishing and ridiculous things."

20. "Presumably we say that six dice, if you bring four near them, are more than the four, half as many, while if you bring twelve, they are less, half as many, and no other way of speaking can be upheld" (*Tht.* 154c).

21. A similar example arises at *Phaedo* 102b ff.

22. On this, see Sallis 2000, 220. See also Sallis 1995, 202–203.

23. See Sachs 2004, 8–10.

24. As Sallis argues, this discourse on philosophy that occurs in the middle of the *Theaetetus* presents philosophy as consisting of a certain opening to Being beyond φύσις, an opening expressed through the ascensional orientation of Thales (Sallis 2005, 191). Yet, as Sallis is quick to point out, it is precisely this ascensional gaze that threatens to disconnect such a philosopher from φύσις. As a result of his zealous concern for the things above, Thales loses sight of the things below, the things of the world (*Tht.* 174a), and thus the things of φύσις. One might say that Thales pursues the excess to such an excess as to lose

all connection with the φύσις to which the excess must essentially be bound. And it is precisely due to his excessive pursuit of the excess—his immoderate attachment to Being and corresponding disregard of φύσις (understood as appearance)—that Thales falls that much harder down the well. We are thus given two different images of the philosopher. For Sallis, "What is lacking in the philosopher as he appears in this central scene [i.e., as Thales] is a comportment that, in exceeding φύσις, would at the same time remain bound to φύσις. What the Thales of this scene lacks is the monstrosity that Theaetetus achieves in the moment of wonder" (Sallis 2005, 191).

25. Sallis does not explicitly refer to such a doubling. However, at one point he mentions a certain *displacement* of φύσις which occurs through the ascendency of philosophy (Sallis 2005, 191). He then cites the relevant passage from Socrates, who talks about the philosopher's thought as "exploring everywhere all the φύσις of each whole of the things that are and letting itself down to not one of the things nearby" (*Tht.* 174a; Sallis 2005, 191). This seems to me to bespeak a certain doubling of nature (φύσις) which Sallis has articulated in terms of displacement: on the one hand are the "things nearby," those sensible things of nature; on the other hand are the looks of those things, inherent within the very things of which they are the excess, but not simply reducible to them.

26. See Kerényi 1976, 32–33: "the situation of the journeyer [over whom Hermes presides] is defined by movement, fluctuation. To someone more deeply rooted, even to the [mere] traveler, he appears to be always in flight. . . . He is completely absorbed by movement, but never by a human community that would tie him down. . . . Hermes is constantly underway: he is ἐνόδιος ('by the road') and ὅδιος ('belonging to a journey'), and one encounters him on every path."

27. Or, at least, *part* of λόγος. Cf. 385c.

28. See *Theaetetus,* 207b.

29. Indeed, this will prove true for the very *word* for Being, τὸ ὄν, which will be shown by Socrates during his comedic etymological display to signify constant motion (ἰόν) (421b).

30. Aorist passive of ἐκφέρω.

31. Much later in the *Cratylus,* Socrates will associate such extreme flux with Heraclitus, and will to a certain extent (con)fuse Protagoras with him. In the *Theaetetus,* too, Heraclitus is mentioned during an inquiry into Protagoras, who argues for a sort of "being which is carried along" (*Tht.* 179d).

32. As in the *Theaetetus,* Socrates seems to be playing upon the title of Protagoras' book "The Truth" (ἡ ἀλήθεια).

33. See MacKenzie 1986, 127.

34. See MacKenzie 1986, 128.

35. Aristotle discusses the polyvalence of the word φύσις in *Metaphysics* Δ, chapter 4. There, it is said that φύσις can be understood as 1) the genesis of growing things (ἡ τῶν φυομένων γένεσις), 2) that from out of which something first begins to grow, 3) the source or origin (ὑπάρχει) of motion of that thing, 4) the primary stuff (ὕλη) out of which a thing comes to be, and 5) the thinghood of a thing (ἡ τῶν φύσει ὄντων οὐσία), the latter being the more proper (κυρίως) meaning of φύσις (*Metaph.* 1014b17 ff.).

36. See Sallis 2004, 133.

37. See *Theaetetus,* 152e, where these three thinkers are also grouped together as adherents to the opinion that all is in flux. Empedocles and the comic poet Epicharmus are also mentioned. See also *Theaetetus* 160d.

38. Against this, see Heath 1888, 193.

39. So understood, the second-sailing—the turn to λόγος—amounts to a way of comporting oneself toward the things of nature so as to avoid the soul-blindness that threatens those who look *merely* with the senses, a way that thereby opens up a certain access to the Being, or the nature, of beings. Such a comportment is in no way an absolute turning away from nature, but is rather a *re-turn* to nature, a re-engagement with the monstrous excess that nature itself gives. The re-turn to nature in λόγος is a response to the excess imminent in nature of which nature itself speaks, an excess for which the senses alone cannot account. To turn to λόγος in the face of nature is to let oneself be addressed by this excess—an excess which is nothing other than the looks that belong to things.

40. As we have seen, Socrates plays the role of Hermes in the *Cratylus*, serving as a mediator between Cratylus and Hermogenes and a leader of their souls. Further, it was argued above that insofar as Socrates plays the role of Hermes, the question "is Hermogenes the son of Hermes" equates to the question "is Hermogenes the son of Socrates": that is, does he show himself to practice philosophy as understood by Socrates? This shall be answered in the affirmative in chapter 8.

5. Technological Language

1. Φαντάσματι here, as the context makes clear, has the sense of the creative imagination understood as our ability to drag or draw (ἕλκω) the appearances of things at will (i.e., our ability to exercise a certain mastery over them).

2. Reeve 1998, xvi; Ackrill 1997, 38. See also Sedley 2003, 56. For a more comprehensive analysis of this passage, see Ademollo 2011, 96–97.

3. Sedley argues that Socrates is saying that "the way that it is natural to act on something is identical to the way it is natural for that thing *to be acted upon*. . . . Thus . . . the way in which it is natural for a surgeon to cut his patient's flesh is identical to the way in which it is natural for the flesh to be cut" (Sedley 2003, 57). However, Socrates does not specify his comment to apply to the action of a surgeon cutting a patient, but rather "the nature of cutting and being cut" (τοῦ τέμειν τε καὶ τέμνεσθαι καὶ ᾧ πέφυκε) in general (387a): that is, it applies to cutting *as such*. The unspoken difficulty here is that, if the nature of cutting depends upon the object it cuts, then, strictly speaking, there is no nature of cutting *as such*, for the nature of cutting would depend in each case upon the particular being in question. Socrates' peculiar argument raises this difficulty without explicitly stating it, and it is a difficulty which will haunt the pages to come.

4. Some manuscripts have ἐπεφύκει.

5. See, for example, *Meno*, 97a ff.

6. Many commentators simply assume that Socrates is talking about the being of a thing. Weingartner thinks that the "objective character of the world . . . determines the operations that must be performed," though he also astutely observes that the "the goal [i.e., the desired end] also serves as the measure of adequacy of the operation" (Weingartner 1970, 17). Sallis, too, takes Socrates to be referring to the "nature of what is to be cut or burned" (i.e., the object) (Sallis 1975, 205). Against this, I am suggesting that the Greek— τοῦ τέμειν τε καὶ τέμνεσθαι καὶ ᾧ πέφυκε—rather cleverly omits the being of the thing, claiming instead that one must cut in accordance with the nature of the *action* of cutting and being cut, as well as the insturment with which one cuts. Presumably, these other commentators take "being cut" (τέμνεσθαι) as refering to the being of the particular

thing, whereas I am taking it to refer simply to the passive side of the action *regardless* of the particular being in question. Socrates' language here brings to light to the extent to which the conversation is *avoiding* the being of things in their considerations—which is precisely the one thing that cannot, in good sense, be avoided. This avoidance fuels the comedy already well underway.

7. On the impropriety of burning as an analogue to λόγος, see Sallis 1975, 205. One could say that burning is a means of separating (i.e., purifying) one thing from another, and in this way serves as an appropriate analogue for the discursive function of naming soon to be mentioned. However, even so understood, burning still involves the disintegration or alteration of the object being burned.

8. This is not to say that whatever shows itself (φάντασμα) is simply false. Rather, Hermogenes' statement emphasizes that even the truth shows itself *to humans*, "to me" (μοι), and that such a showing always comes to be mixed, in varying measure, with seeming (φαίνεταί) and opinion (δόξα).

9. As Joe Sachs notes in his translation, Socrates is careful to distinguish between the specific act of disentangling threads *prior* to weaving (κερκίζειν) from the more general act of combining threads through weaving (ὑφαντική), the latter of which he will not mention until 389d. (On the manner in which διακριτικός differs from weaving (ὑφαντική), see *Statesman*, 282b ff.) Ademollo observes this difference, and translates κερκίζειν as "to pin-beat" (Ademollo 2011, 108). For purposes of familiarity I have continued to use the term "to shuttle" to refer to the act of κερκίζειν and the tool associated with it. However, it is of the utmost importance that the disentangling (i.e., dividing) function of κερκίζειν be kept in mind. (As confirmation of this, see Aristotle's *Physics*, 243b3 ff.)

10. Barney 2001, 45. See also Sedley 2003, 61; Gonzalez 1998, 66.

11. Sallis argues that the didactic function of a name reduces to its diacritical function (Sallis 1975, 208). Conversely, Baxter argues that the discursive function of a name is secondary to its pedagogical purpose (Baxter 1992, 41). Barney sees the didactic and the diacritical functions as two sides of the same coin (Barney 2001, 45).

12. In this passage from the *Phaedrus,* Socrates shows a certain uncertainty, if not reticence, about referring to the one capable of this power as the "dialectician." After describing the powers of such a person, Socrates says the following: "And furthermore—god knows whether I've been speaking correctly [ὀρθῶς] or not—up to now I have been calling those who have the capacity to do this 'dialecticians' [διαλεκτικούς]" (*Phdr.* 266b). It thus remains questionable whether Socrates himself truly understands the dialectician as exercising such powers.

13. This seems to be the very sense of burning. Even in medical burning, something (i.e., a disease or symptom) is destroyed.

14. See Taylor 1960, 77.

15. Against this, see Weingartner 1970, 17, 25. See also Thomas 2008, 343–344. Though there are differences among the specific claims of these scholars, both maintain that the tool analogy represents Socrates' view of language within the *Cratylus*.

16. For another criticism of Socrates' tool analogy, see Wood 2007.

17. This line of reasoning threatens an infinite regress, though one to which Socrates does not call attention. Given that it is the carpenter who makes the shuttle, one could ask: who is it who makes the saw with which the carpenter makes the shuttle? And who makes the file with which the iron-worker makes the saw? And so on. Another such regress will be indicated later in the dialogue with respect to the figure of the original name-giver.

18. Νόμος is invariably translated as either *law* or *custom*. However, one should not lose sight of the sense of *song* that νόμος can have. Given that it will be Homer to whom Socrates and Hermogenes will soon turn (391c), and who will be said to be a person who gives (ἔθετο) names (393a), νόμος must be understood both as custom and song in the Greek sense. For an excellent account of νόμος and its role in the *Cratylus*, see Barney 2001, 27 ff.

19. As Nancy Demand has observed, the νομοθέτης is a pun on ὄνομα (Demand 1975, 107).

20. This passage enacts in deed exactly what it says in speech: for Socrates has just taught Hermogenes, who was unable to answer.

21. Sachs translates "craftsman of names." This is good insofar as it captures the thrust of the argument. However, the Greek τίθημι more suggests a name *placer* or *setter*. It should also be noted that in this case, as far as the historical evidence suggests, Plato himself is the name-setter of this ὀνοματουργός, the name-setter's name-setter.

22. Baxter similarly argues for a certain mimetic aspect to the tool analogy (Baxter 1992, 84). Gonzalez disagrees with this, and argues that the mimetic theory of language (offered later in the *Cratylus*) does not grow out of the technical model offered earlier (Gonzalez 1998, 306n28). Against this, I hope to show momentarily that the two sections are intimately connected, though for reasons other than those which Baxter contends.

23. It must be stressed that the name-setter looks to the same single thing, "the name that is," in making *all* the names (πάντα τὰ ὀνόματα). The multiplicity of names is thus referred to a single look.

24. For a more comprehensive review of the scholarship, see Baxter 1992, 43n54.

25. Sedley, like Calvert before him, distinguishes between the "generic" Form of Name and the "specific" Form of Name (Sedley 2003, 82). He goes on to say that the specific "Form of the name . . . is to be understood as, roughly, the function of giving instruction by *vocally* separating" the being of the thing in question (ibid.; my emphasis). However, the Form of name (even its "specific" form) cannot be equivalent to the function of *vocalizing* the being of the thing, but, in accordance with the tool analogy Socrates has set forth, must precede any such vocalization. See Gonzalez 1998, 66.

26. Furthermore, even granting Calvert's distinction, Socrates does not say that the law-maker ought to look to these proper forms, but rather to the Name that is, what Calvert calls the "Form."

27. However, Weingartner takes this to be Socrates' own view of language, if not Plato's (Weingartner 1970, 21), whereas I take it to be an elaboration and criticism of Hermogenes' view. Weingartner argues that Socrates (or Plato) had a vision of a descriptive scientific language such as we find in present-day sciences (i.e., botany, chemistry, etc.). However, Weingartner seems to overlook the rather damning criticism which Socrates brings against this very view with his comments about the supposed original name-giver.

28. The vital distinction, which Socrates leaves unsaid and scholars tend to avoid, is that a woven garment is a manufactured thing, whereas many beings waiting to be named have arisen *naturally*. How a new garment is made depends upon our wishes in making it. How a newly discovered plant (or human being) is named ought to be different, if we are indeed to let the being of the thing come into language.

29. See Sallis 1975, 212n22.

30. As seen in the previous chapter, Socrates shows how the positions of both Protagoras and Euthydemus result in a scenario in which the distinction between truth and falsity is erased.

31. Cf. Sedley 2003, 46.

32. See Sachs 2011, 164n3.

33. Cf. Sedley 2003, 46.

34. Notice that Socrates here does not call this art "dialectic," but rather "name-giving or rhetoric or whatever art it is." This further shows a reticence on the part of Socrates to define the powers of the dialectician.

35. I do not mean to suggest that this account represents Socrates' final views on the mimetic character of painting, nor that one can simply apply without remainder his conception of painting in the *Republic* to that of naming the *Cratylus*. However, Socrates' own comparison of naming to painting can incite us to draw comparisons between the two texts.

36. Such a craftsman is also called, simply, "the couch-maker" (ὁ κλινοποιός) (*Rep.* 597a).

37. For an excellent analysis of this passage of the *Republic,* and the important difference between *nature* and *artifice* which it addresses, see Warnek 2005, 190.

38. In his book *Heidegger and Aristotle: the Twofoldness of Being*, Walter Brogan explores this tension between φύσις and τέχνη, nature and technological knowledge, writing that "when τέχνη handles a natural being for the sake of producing something, it produces something other than the being it found there.... The human being's way of bringing forth beings is not natural; it is based on a learned familiarity with what is and can be; it is learned" (Brogan 2005, 45). Brogan further notes that τέχνη is concerned not with the Being of beings, but with how a particular being can be *used* (Brogan 2005, 46). If one were to apply this understanding of the tension between φύσις and τέχνη to the problematic of naming in the *Cratylus,* one would see that a technological model of naming is fatally limited in its ability to bring the nature of a thing to light. In his *Chorology,* Sallis articulates the opposition between φύσις and τέχνη as it plays out within Plato's *Timaeus* (Sallis 1999, 15).

39. I thus disagree with Baxter that the tool analogy represents Socrates' "prescriptive ideal" for a rationally based theory of language (Baxter 1992, 48–49). Far from offering a prescriptive picture of what a language *should be* (but ultimately cannot fully be), Socrates has shown how a technological understanding of language traps human beings within the world of *mere* appearances, severing them completely from Being. Far from endorsing the technological view of language, Socrates will spend the remainder of the *Cratylus* attempting to overcome it.

40. For the most rigorous and thoroughgoing analysis of the importance of *use* (χρήσεται) in the *Cratylus,* see Gonzalez 1998.

41. See Sallis 1975, 215.

42. Indeed, throughout the Platonic corpus, one never finds an occasion where Socrates simply and straightforwardly lauds *his own* dialectical ability, nor calls *himself* a dialectician. It has been the history of Platonic scholarship, certainly not Socrates himself, that has typified Socrates as a dialectician. Given that the dialectician is always presented as one who *knows* (see *Phil.* 57e), it would hardly be surprising if Socrates—as he who knows only that he does *not* know—were to distance himself from such a person.

43. See Weingartner 1970, 18–19, who notes the extent to which Socrates' account of naming emphasizes the role of proper function: ". . . Socrates must be understood as giving an account of how naming should be done, *if* it is to be a perfect instrument for the enterprise of dialectic" (Weingartner 1970, 19; my emphasis).

44. Hermogenes, too, does not know. Some ten lines later, after Socrates has demonstrated that Cratylus' position must be correct, Hermogenes says, "I do not know how to answer you, Socrates," thereby announcing his ignorance.

45. On the limits of analogy here, see Gonzalez 1998, 69.

46. Socrates' use of this oath at this point in the text serves as a subtle reference to Hermes, who was often associated with the Egyptian dog-headed god Anubis. See Sachs 2011, 137n8.

47. See Kirkland 2007, 4 ff.

48. In his translation of the *Cratylus,* Fowler astutely observes that τραγικόν can mean both "goat-like" and "of the tragic," and suggests that the word here has both meanings. Though this is true, τραγικόν must be understood as denoting tragedy in both cases, for it is the tragic goat in particular which is meant by the word τραγικόν, rather than the αἴξ. Socrates is drawing attention not only to Pan's goat-like nature, but more specifically to his tragic character.

49. Λόγος is meant here in its most general signification. On the affinity between μῦθος and λόγος for early Greeks, one may turn, for example, to Martin Heidegger's *What is Called Thinking* (1968, 10). However, for those disinclined to reach for Heidegger in situations such as this, one need not go any further than a Greek dictionary (such as Liddell and Scott), in which the connection is clear.

50. See Stewart 1905, 2–3:

> [T]he Platonic Myth is not illustrative—it is not Allegory rendering pictorially results already obtained by argument. Of this the experienced reader of Plato is well aware. He feels when the brisk debate is silenced for a while, and Socrates or another great interlocutor opens his mouth in Myth, that the movement of the Philosophic Drama is not arrested, but is being sustained, at a crisis, on another plane. The Myth bursts in upon the Dialogue with a revelation of something new and strange; the narrow, matter-of-fact, workaday experience, which the argumentative conversation puts in evidence, is suddenly flooded, as it were, and transfused by the inrush of a vast experience, as from another world. . . .

51. See Sallis 1975, 15–16.

52. For example, it is fitting that in three famous Platonic myths—the so-called myth of Er from the *Republic,* the palinode from the *Phaedrus,* and the myth of the true earth from the *Phaedo*—Socrates concerns himself with describing regions not readily available to human experience: namely, what lies before birth and after death. Given the extent to which these regions are concealed from human experience, μῦθος, as a veiled mode of discourse—which is to say, a veiled mode of λόγος—is most appropriate.

53. Socrates will indicate this proximity in the *Phaedo* when he says that the story of the true earth cannot be *known* to be true, but ought to be *believed* nonetheless (*Phd.* 108d and 114d).

54. It should not go unremarked that Pan, like his father, is well known for his sexual salaciousness, and is frequently represented with a large and erect phallus.

55. One could say that the tragic life subsists on the fallacy of parts and wholes which haunts the *Cratylus.* See Sallis 1975, 185.

56. These are precisely those who take the part for the whole: they do not recognize the part/whole distinction.

57. One begins to see great meaning in Hermogenes' opening question to Cratylus about whether he wishes for Socrates to gather them up into the λόγος.

58. See Kirkland 2007, 6 ff.

59. See *Phil.* 50b; *Rep.* 394c–d.

60. See *Rep.* 395a10.

61. Yet again we see that what is at stake in the dialogue is both Hermogenes' inheritance and his ability to retrace Socrates' own journey of self-knowledge.

6. A Homeric Inheritance

1. See *Theaetetus* 152e5, where Homer is said to be a tragic poet.
2. As Rosenstock suggests, this line may indicate that Hermogenes' father Hipponicus is dead (Rosenstock 1992, 399). See also Ademollo 2011, 20. Cf. Nails 2002, 163.
3. Baxter suggests that it is due to the high fees charged by the Sophists (and, presumably, Hermogenes' poverty) that Hermogenes does not wish to look to them for knowledge concerning the correctness of names (Baxter 1992, 88). However, the text makes it quite clear that it is because he rejects (οὐκ ἀποδέχομαι) the teachings of Protagoras that Hermogenes scoffs at Socrates' proposal to turn to the Sophists (391c).
4. See *Theaetetus* 155d; see also Riley 2005, 39. Sallis argues that Socrates' mention of "wonder" marks the excessiveness of Homer's position regarding λόγος (Sallis 1975, 217). To add to this, the relationship between wonder and laughter, noted in the Introduction, should not go unnoticed here. In marking the wondrous character of Homer's wisdom concerning names, Socrates could just as well be marking its ridiculousness.
5. On Homer as the origin of Greek education and culture, see Baxter 1992, 113 ff.
6. Through his use of βούλομαι, Socrates has hinted that the example is as Hermogenes would wish, that it is to his liking. This serves to reinforce our previous claim that the account of language Socrates is developing is not his own, but belongs rather to Hermogenes. We shall return to the importance of βούλομαι in the following chapter.
7. See Sallis 1975, 219. See also Baxter 1992, 50.
8. As Joe Sachs observes, Hermogenes' response indicates his reticence to accept Socrates' conclusion (Sachs 2011, 169). See also Baxter 1992, 49.
9. Sedley believes Plato to have erred in his recollection of this Homeric passage. Further, Sedley refuses the possibility that the misquotation is a deliberate subversion of the argument on Socrates' or Plato's part, stating that "I cannot see what the point of the subversion would be" (Sedley 2003, 78). Rosenstock argues that the misquotation is indeed deliberate and is meant to raise questions about the nature of inheritance (Rosenstock 1992, 400). Ademollo, too, argues that it is deliberate, though for different reasons (Ademollo 2010, 154). Following Rosenstock, and against Sedley, I shall argue that the misquotation is indeed deliberate and subversive of the argument, and hope to make the precise point of such subversion clear.
10. Riley astutely observes Socrates' misquote (Riley 2005, 42).
11. See Sallis 1975, 220. See also Riley 2005, 43; Ademollo 2010, 162; Rosenstock 1992, 401. At the end of Book XXII of the *Iliad* (478 ff.) Hector's wife, while lamenting her husband's death, describes the terrible fate that likely awaits Ἀστυάναξ.
12. See *Acharnians*, 1220; also, *Birds*, 1255, where Pisthetaerus is threatening to rape the goddess Iris. See also Henderson 1975, 112.
13. This seems to be the meaning behind the title of Eubulus's play Ἄστυτοι, or "The Limp Ones" (circa third century BCE). See Henderson 1975, 112.
14. Hector's son Ἀστυάναξ was ridiculed on just this score by a third century AD writer, Strato of Sardis. See Swain 2007, 118.
15. See chapter 3.
16. It should be noted that this "clue" only applies to the last of Socrates' Homeric examples, which involved a discrepancy between what two classes of *humans* called a thing.

This clue has no immediately evident bearing upon the other examples, each of which involves a difference between a human name and a divine one.

17. See 384a8, and 406b8.

18. See Taylor 1960, 75. For Callias's appetite for the "wisdom" of the sophists, see *Apology* 20a.

19. See Proclus 2007, 28.29: "The man of knowledge demonstrates the methods of discovery to the learner, thereby imitating Hermes the Guide."

20. Further, that Hermogenes was present at the death of his friend Socrates (*Phd.* 59b) should already give us some grounds for believing that he came to walk the path of philosophy. Proclus refers to Hermogenes as a "Socratic" (Proclus 2007, 4.10).

21. Interestingly, Agis II was son of Archidamus, "ruler of the people."

22. A certain Iatrocles is mentioned in Plato's likely spurious 8th Letter (*Epist.* 363e), though nothing of substance is said of him. Another of the same name is mentioned by Lysias in his *Against Eratosthenes* (42.4). Demosthenes, too, mentions an Iatrocles without saying anything substantial about him. A certain Eupolemos is mentioned by Demosthenes in his *Against Macartatus* (43.7) as being friendly with Glaucon.

23. There is a certain militant aspect to Polemarchus evident from the very beginning of the *Republic* (*Rep.* 327c). However, as Joe Sachs notes in his translation, this aspect comes to be tempered by Socrates through their discussion (Sachs 2007, 28n3).

24. I.e., his relationship to his biological father and his relationship to his namesake Hermes are both in question.

25. This example also further indicates that Socrates is inspired by Euthyphro: for Euthyphro's concern lies precisely with what is beloved by the gods (*Euthr.* 7a).

26. See Rosenstock 1992, 403. As Joe Sachs observes (Sachs 2011, 171n14), Socrates' description of Orestes is reminiscent of Homer's description of the Cyclops at *Odyssey* IX.186–192.

27. See Sophocles, *Electra*, 504. See also Euripides, *Orestes*, 1024–1062.

28. See Hamilton 1942, 348.

29. See Pausanias, 8.4.10. According to some sources, Myrtilus is said to have been buried behind his temple at Pheneos. See Farnell 1909, V. 4. Also, according to Pausanias, it was to atone for the murder of Myrtilus that Pelops built the very first temple to Hermes in Peloponnese (Paus. 5.15.5). On the quarrel between Atreus and Thyestes, see *Statesman*, 268e.

30. According to pseudo-Apollodorus, e.3.1, the gods set Tantalus into a lake in Hades surrounded by beautiful and bountiful fruit trees. Whenever the accursed child-eater bent down to drink, the water would recede and dry up. Likewise, whenever he would reach, tantalized, for the fresh and nourishing fruit, the trees would pull their branches back in taunting reproach. During all of this the aforementioned stone hung above his head. See also Hamilton 1942, 347, who omits the presence of the hanging stone.

31. See *Frogs*, 1125 ff. During an argument about whose poetry is superior, Euripides criticizes Aeschylus' opening line of the *Oresteia* (now lost):

> Aeschylus: Hermes, lord of the dead, who watch over the powers. . . . Euripides: Well, look, you've got Orestes saying this over the tomb of his father, and his father is dead, right? Aeschylus: Yes, that's right. Euripides: Let's get this straight. Here is where his father was killed, murdered in fact by his own wife in a treacherous plot, and you make him say Hermes is *watching* over this?!

Euripides' complaint comes to deal precisely with inheritance (πατρῴῳν) (line 1148 ff.).

32. As Joe Sachs notes, Ζήνα is a form often used by poets (Sachs 2011, 173n19). See *Euthyphro,* 12a9.

33. It was in response to a prophecy that one of his sons would overthrow him that Cronus ate his children. See *Theogony,* 132–182, 453–506, 617–819.

34. See 406d. See also *Republic,* 378a.

35. See Sallis 1975, 221: "What the etymologies are beginning to make manifest is, not the things named, but rather the situation of the naming itself." Also: "The naming being carried on in the form of etymologizing is utterly oblivious to the proper being of the things named."

36. Aegisthus was born incestuously to Thyestes and Pelopia, and was later abandoned by his mother. It was Atreus, not knowing that the child was the offspring of his hated brother Thyestes, who took him in and raised him. Years later, Aegisthus killed his (step-) father Atreus at the behest of Thyestes. Later, in collusion with Clytemnestra, he slew Agamemnon as he returned home from the war. It is Hermes, in the *Iliad,* who foretells the revenge of Agamemnon's death: "The death of the son of Atreus [i.e., Agamemnon] will be avenged by Orestes" (*Odyssey* I.40; see also Hamilton 1942, 350).

37. *Hymn* IV.292.

38. This necessity is most clearly seen in the fact that scholarship has raised the question of the identity of this Euthyphro again and again.

39. See Diogenes Laertius II.29.

40. See Rosenstock 1992, 404.

41. See the Derrida quote above.

42. The question is whether λόγος, as inheritor of its father's *property,* inherited precisely this lack of property, this withdrawal.

7. What Words Will

1. Such a scene, though consequent to Protagoras's and Homer's views concerning λόγος, will eventually be associated by Socrates with the radical flux of Heraclitus (401d; 402b–c).

2. See 406c. See also 400b, 425d, and 426b.

3. See Sallis 1975, 244.

4. Ibid., 232.

5. On the limits of translation, see Gadamer 1989, 386.

6. See Fowler's introduction to his translation of the *Cratylus:*

> The dialogue cannot be satisfactorily translated, because the numerous etymologies cannot be appreciated without some knowledge of Greek; nevertheless it is interesting, even though the etymologies be not thoroughly understood. Some of them are manifestly absurd, and in some cases the absurdity is obviously intentional. (Fowler 1926, 4)

7. See Brumbaugh 1958, 502; Ademollo 2011, 182 ff. Baxter is good at observing the play, and suggests that one ought not read too rigid a pattern into the etymological section (Baxter 1992, 90).

8. The phrase τοῦ αὐτομάτου, which can mean "willfully" or "from out of oneself," here has the more colloquial sense of "by chance," as both Sachs and Reeve render it in their translations. (Fowler renders it as "haphazard.")

9. It is interesting to note that the sun (ἥλιος), at least, was not a *primitive* god only, for, according to Alcibiades in the *Symposium,* Socrates himself "held up his hands" (ἀνέσχεν) to Helios on a cold morning following a long night of contemplation (*Symp.* 220d).

10. See *Republic* 379a and 381d, where such an understanding is said to belong to the tragic poets.

11. See Sallis 1975, 239.

12. See ibid., 240. See also Baxter 1992, 89, 94: "The direction of the etymologies is firmly headed one-way toward the human and the flux-ridden; each stage takes us further along this path, with no reference back to the divine." Though I generally agree with this statement, I shall immediately argue against the final clause.

13. Sallis further notes that this descending order is all the more conspicuous when seen against the ascending order of the previous etymologies (Sallis 1975, 240), those pertaining to the house of Atreus. However, as was previously argued, this Homeric scene in which the gods are understood solely in human terms dramatically emphasizes the extent to which the human is trapped in the lower parts of λόγος so long as he adheres to the tragic view of language. In other words, even though the order of the etymologies in this section follows an ascending movement, the fact that they are offered from the tragic and mendacious realm of human beings transforms—indeed, one is tempted to say *translates*—the ascent into a tragic descent. Though the orders seem to be different, they both serve to underscore the limitations of the tragic view of λόγος.

14. As Rosenstock notes, "Words may point upward or downward—and it is the direction of the gaze, the direction of our *desire* for *ousia,* which is critical . . . " (Rosenstock 1992, 413; my emphasis).

15. As Sachs observes, the words ἐπισκοπεῖν (to examine or look into) and ἀναλογίζεσθαι (to gather up or produce an account) are both of enormous importance in Plato's *Theaetetus,* where Socrates attempts to account for the possibility of λόγος and knowledge in the face of radical becoming (*Tht.* 185b–186e; Sachs 2011, 177n29).

16. This passage should remind us of the *Theaetetus,* where the philosopher (i.e., Thales) is seen to have such an upward gaze (*Tht.* 174a).

17. See Baxter, who observes the extent to which Hermogenes helps dictate the order of the etymologies (Baxter 1992, 89). I am suggesting that Hermogenes' active role reveals his erotic commitment to the inquiry underway.

18. Though, in the case of ἀναψῦχον, ἀνα- means *again.*

19. See Pseudo-Apollodrous, *Bibliotheca* 1.15. See, more importantly, *Symposium,* 179d. See also *Republic,* 620a. After Orpheus failed to maintain a forward gaze and surrendered to his desire to turn around and behold his wife, it was Hermes who escorted her back down to Hades. See Grant and Hazel 1980, 206.

20. Orpheus is mentioned again at *Cratylus* 402b as being sympathetic to the doctrines of Heraclitus.

21. This move from human names to divine names structurally corresponds to the movement from the human lineage to the divine lineage that took place in Socrates' presentation of the tragic house of Atreus (see chapter 6).

22. As Sallis has argued, the account Socrates offers of the name Hestia dramatically serves as nothing less than an *invocation* of Being (Sallis 1975, 246).

23. As Sachs notes, Ῥεα is associated with ῥεῦμα (stream), and Κρόνος with κρουνός (a gushing spring) (Sachs 2011, 180n36).

24. See *Iliad* XIV.291; also, *Iliad* XIV.303.

25. As will be seen below, such refinement is characteristic of the tragic understanding of λόγος.

26. See Henderson 1975, 159.

27. Regarding Socrates' desire for the body, see *Charmides*, 154b ff.

28. Heath argues that Plato lifts the etymology for Hera from the first scene of Aristophanes' *Knights* (Heath 1888, 202).

29. It is of course Apollo to whom Socrates owes his philosophical mission. See *Apology*, 21a ff. See also *Phaedo*, 85b.

30. See Ademollo 2011, 175.

31. See also Sophocles' *Philoctetes*, 742.

32. One begins to see here a connection between the comic view and Socrates' own self-described philosophical posture as enunciated in the *Apology*. We shall return to this point in the final chapter.

33. For my thoughts concerning the dramatic date of the *Cratylus*, see my chapter 1.

34. It should be recalled that Socrates, in his first words of the dialogue, recited the ancient adage that "beautiful things are difficult" (384b). It is because of such difficulty that they must be courageous here.

35. See, for example, the beginning of Aristophanes' *Frogs*.

36. Sachs 2011, 190n55.

37. Hesiod, *Theogony*, 769.

38. See Grant 1980, 206. See also Brann 2004, 119.

39. See *Iliad* VIII.368 and *Odyssey* XI.623, where Cerberus is referred to simply as "the dog" (κύων). Joe Sachs, following Eva Brann, takes Socrates' swear to refer to Hermes (Sachs 2011, 137n8).

40. According to Pseudo-Apollodorus—whose account, it must be stressed, was offered several centuries after Plato's death—Heracles encountered a waylaid but alive Theseus upon his arrival in Hades. Upon seeing his friend, Heracles lifted Theseus from the chair of forgetfulness into which he had been placed, thus saving him from an eternity spent amongst the shades of Hades. According to this account, it is just after saving Theseus that Heracles fights and subdues Cerberus, sporting his lion-skin cloak the entire time (Pseudo-Apollodorus, *Bibliotheca*, 2.5.12).

41. The fact that this comes not long after the mention of Orpheus, famous for a nearly identical descent, bolsters this interpretation.

42. Socrates has called for a lack of cowardice (411a). At 415c, Socrates will examine the word "cowardice" (δειλία), stating that he should have examined it previously while considering the word "courage" (ἀνδρεία). We shall return to this below.

43. The humorous, and sexual, nature of this etymology should not go unnoticed.

44. On the mediate position of *daimons*, see *Symposium*, 202e ff.

45. The homophony between πλάττοντες and "Plato" suggests that Plato himself, the author of this comedy, has been rearranging letters like a tragic poet, concerned not at all with the truth, but only with the shape (πλάττοντες) of his mouth. A similar pun occurs at 415d.

46. That this is a playfully delivered insult is clear. What is less clear is whether there is a sexual sense to this insult. For the suggestion that references in Greek comedy to the mouth and flute-girls often carry a sexual connotation, see Henderson 1991, 184.

47. This quote is from *Iliad* VI.265, where a battle-weary Hector refuses his mother's offer of wine. Socrates is trying to stay sober, unlike the drunken tragic name-givers discussed above.

48. In between announcing that they must turn to the "loftiest heights" of their subject, and actually turning to an account of the words ἀρετή and κακία, Socrates quickly

inserts an etymology for the word "contrivance" (μηχανή) (415a). Such an insertion suggests that the accounts for the lofty words to come are mere (tragic) contrivances. Socrates will even come to employ a certain contrivance in the etymology for κακός: namely, the claim that it is of foreign origin (416a).

49. Socrates notes that they "seem to . . . have passed over a lot of other things as well" (415c; Sachs). This comment serves to mark the disorder and the *play* of the etymologies. Baxter sees this disorder as indicative of the extent to which Socrates, throughout the etymologies, is immersed in the world of appearances: "The conclusion to be drawn from this is that the disorderliness of the etymologies is to be taken at face value as far as the exact detail of the ordering goes; Socrates is enmeshed in the world of δόξα, as he is quick to stress, and so things are disorganized" (Baxter 1992, 90).

50. See also 414c for a similar play on words.

51. Διακεκροτηκέναι is translated by Sachs as "hammered away"; by Fowler as "knocked to pieces"; by Heath as "a vigorous shattering to pieces."

52. One could argue that the Socratic practice of philosophy, as articulated in the *Apology,* amounts to a hermeneutical matter: Socrates, in the face of the oracle given at Delphi and relayed by Chaerephon, sought to *interpret* the god's saying, rather than simply adopt it as true. We shall return to this in the final chapter.

53. The *eta* is added at the front of the word to make it aorist.

54. See, for example, 392a; 397a; 399e; 401a; 411d.

55. See especially 414c–d.

56. See Sallis 1975, 262.

57. Just before the conclusion of Socrates' long series of etymologies, Hermogenes tells him to "speak boldly" (ἀλλὰ θαρρῶν λέγε) (426b).

58. On the "ancient analogy" between ἔρως and λόγος, see Carson 1986, 49–52, *passim.*

59. The full Greek passage is as follows: οὐ μέντοι μοι δοκεῖ προφάσεις ἀγὼν δέχεσθαι, ἀλλὰ προθυμητέον ταῦτα διασκέψασθαι. Given that Socrates has intimated on several occasions that the investigation will be playful (see, for example, 406c), I have elected to follow Fowler's translation of ἀγών as "game" rather than the more conventional "contest" or "struggle." The phrase appears to be an idiomatic expression; see *Laws* 751d.

60. There is a homophonous play here between οἱ παλαιοί and οἱ πολλοί, "the many," who are often presented as knowing nothing worthwhile. See *Crito,* 44c–d.

61. See Gonzalez 1998, 79. Further, the word that one would use to explain this onomatopoeic effect would *itself* need to contain letters that bear an onomatopoeic relationship to their object (i.e., the name in question).

62. "And in the same way, the lawgiver appears to bring the rest of them to the task of making in letters and syllables a sign and name for each of the things there are, and to compose out of them the ones still remaining in imitation of those things themselves" (427c–d; Sachs).

8. The Tragedy of Cratylus

1. See Euripides, *Iphigenia Aulidensis,* 1142: "αὐτὸ δὲ τὸ σιγᾶν ὁμολογοῦντός ἐστί σου." Literally, "your silence itself is agreement."

2. See *Sophist* 264a, where thought (διάνοιαν), considered as a silent (σιγῆς) dialogue in the soul (ἐν ψυχῇ), is said to be capable of either affirming or denying. We shall return to this passage below.

3. See Sallis 1975, 215.

4. Ibid., 226.

5. Ibid., 216.

6. See Aristotle, *Metaphysics,* 1010a10 ff.

7. See Plutarch, *De garrulitate:* ὅταν ἐν συλλόγῳ τινὶ σιωπὴ γένηται, τὸν Ἑρμῆν ἐπεισεληλυθέναι λέγουσιν (502f). See also Guthrie 1950, 91; Huffington 1993, 126; Willis 1993, 145.

8. The word σμικρός occurs three times in as many lines (428a2–3).

9. See Sallis 1975, 187.

10. See Ademollo 2011, 319.

11. Socrates' statement that in reinterpreting what has been said one must try to look "forward and backward at once," though evidently referring to the *Iliad* (I.343; III.109), cannot help but bring the duplicitous Hermes to mind.

12. The infinitive μεταστρέφεσθαι, being in the present tense, has an aspect conveying continuous or ongoing action.

13. This may also be pandering to Cratylus's desire to teach, a desire indicated by his willingness to take Socrates on as a pupil (428b).

14. οὐκοῦν φῶμεν καὶ ταύτην τέχνην εἶναι καὶ δημιουργοὺς αὐτῆς. The Greek here is ambiguous: ταύτην could refer to instruction (διδασκαλίας) from the previous line (428e5), as Fowler assumes. However, context indicates that it is the *making of words,* and not instruction, to which ταύτην refers, as Cratylus's immediate mention of the νομοθέτας verifies (429a1).

15. Further, Socrates' use of painting as an analogy reveals the extent to which this technological view is one which sees name-making as a mimetic procedure, as a matter of using names to imitate reality. As already seen in previous chapters, such a view of language is essentially limited in its ability to make reality manifest insofar as imitations are always subject to the opinions and wishes of those who make the imitations.

16. The entire passage reads: Ἆρα ὅτι ψευδῆ λέγειν τὸ παράπαν οὐκ ἔστιν, ἆρα τοῦτό σοι δύναται ὁ λόγος; συχνοὶ γάρ τινες οἱ λέγοντες, ὦ φίλε Κρατύλε, καὶ νῦν καὶ πάλαι. The Greek here is unclear. Scholars and translators typically take Socrates to be saying that there are many who, like Cratylus, make the claim that it is impossible to speak falsehood (see Ademollo 2011, 327). However, the Greek could also mean that there are many who *speak falsely.* If the latter, Socrates would be making a joke by saying that Cratylus, in claiming false speech to be impossible, is now (νῦν) speaking falsely, as was Hermogenes earlier (πάλαι).

17. It could be the case, however, that even though *words* (as one part of λόγος) cannot be false, λόγος has some other false part. However, this possibility is never considered by Cratylus or the other interlocutors.

18. In this register, see Sallis 1975, 225.

19. Note that it is implicit here that for Socrates λεγεῖν, φαίη, εἴποι, and προσείποι all more or less *say the same,* despite their different syllabic arrangements.

20. On this, see Baxter 1992, 14, 184.

21. Such a position would also be hubristic in the extreme. If all names are true and perfect doubles of the beings they name—if, therefore, the names are beings—then the name-maker, in making names, would be making *beings:* that is, the name-maker would be a god.

22. Socrates here calls Cratylus ὦ γενναῖε, which Joe Sachs translates as "noble friend." More literally, it means "suitable to one's birth." As will be suggested at the end of this analysis, Cratylus will indeed prove himself to be suitable to his birth.

23. Since the word σκληρότης has both rough (i.e., *rho*) and smooth (i.e., *lamda*) parts, Socrates' word choice playfully hints at the dual nature of *logos* itself with its rough and smooth parts.

24. See, too, 427e, where Cratylus calls upon Hermogenes by his name.

25. See Ademollo 2011, 30.

26. This passage performs precisely what is seeks to convey. "Custom" (ἔθος) and "convention" (συνθήκης) are two different words that bring the same thing to mind: that is, despite their material differences, they more or less *say the same*.

27. See, for example, Anagnostopoulos 1973, 332; Keller 2000, 302; Sedley 2003, 147–148.

28. The suggestion is that any words that they would examine would belong to human λόγος, and would thus be subject to the limitations inherent in human λόγος.

29. For a similar account, see Ademollo 2011, 448.

30. See Sallis 1975, 296.

31. See Sallis 1975, 297. Socrates will come to say that he and Cratylus have reached the agreement that it would be better to discover beings through themselves than through words (439b). However, this is only a temporary agreement that Socrates makes precisely in order to underscore the hopelessness of such a situation.

32. On the extent to which the etymologies reveal the essential stability of Being, see Gonzalez 1998, especially 86–87.

33. Regarding the essential ambiguity of λόγος, see Rosenstock 1992, 412–415.

34. On the self-vitiating character of Cratylus's position, see Sallis 1975, 309.

35. As argued in chapter 3, ὀρθῶς also has the sense of uprightness or erection, as the English "correct" likewise suggests.

36. It should be noted that, as usual, Socrates poses this possibility *as a question*.

37. See Sallis 1975, 298–304, for an excellent interpretation of this dream.

38. Ibid., 303. Sedley also acknowledges the hypothetical nature of the forms (Sedley 2003, 165). It should here be insisted that there is no Platonic *theory* of forms within the *Cratylus*, or anywhere else. See Sachs 2007, 165.

39. Note the extremely comic description of this tragic condition.

40. See Kirkland 2007, 6–8.

41. See Aristotle's *Politics*, 1253a9 ff.

42. Kirkland 2007, 13.

43. For provocative passages in this regard, see *Phaedo*, 108b, and especially 101d.

44. See Sallis 1975, 304, who argues that Socrates' use of the dream image is meant in part to move Cratylus, who is stuck at the level of images, up to the recognition of the image/original difference.

45. One can imagine that Plato, in using this word, is suggesting a joke on the word for joking, σκώπτειν. Though no such word exists, one could imagine the word to be ἀ-σκώπτειν, which would mean something like "non-joking." The suggestion would be that Cratylus has an insufficiently playful attitude toward the inquiry into words.

46. See Ademollo 2010, 487.

47. See especially 406b and following, where Hermogenes is eager to hear Socrates' explicitly playful (παιδικῶς) etymologies of the names of the gods.

48. As mentioned in chapter 1, the *Cratylus* arguably takes place on the morning of the day on which the conversations of the *Euthyphro* and *Theaetetus* occur. (On this, see Allan 1954 and Sallis 1975.) If so, this would place the conversation in the *Cratylus* sometime in 399 BCE, the year Socrates was executed.

49. See Rosenstock 1992, 414.

Conclusion: The Comedy of the *Cratylus*

1. See Kirkland 2007, 8.

2. See Rosenstock 1992, 415: "Philosophy's task as it is embodied in the *Cratylus* is not to master the ambiguity of our discourse, but to let its uncanniness unsettle our assumptions about who we are and what is 'proper' to us."

3. See Sallis 1975, 51.

Bibliography

Ackrill, J. L. 1997. "Language and Reality in Plato's *Cratylus*." Pp. 33–52 in *Essays on Plato and Aristotle*, ed. Ackrill. Oxford: Oxford University Press.

Ademollo, F. 2011. *The Cratylus of Plato*. Cambridge: Cambridge University Press.

Allan, D. J. 1954. "The Problem of Cratylus." *American Journal of Philosophy* 75: 71–287.

Anagnostopoulos, G. 1973. "The Significance of Plato's *Cratylus*." *Review of Metaphysics* 27: 318–345.

Barnes. J., ed. 1984. *The Complete Works of Aristotle*. Princeton: Princeton University Press.

Barney, R. 2001. *Names and Nature in Plato's Cratylus*. London: Routledge.

Baxter, T. M. S. 1992. *The Cratylus: Plato's Critique of Naming*. Leiden, Netherlands: Brill.

Benardete, S. 1980. "Physics and Tragedy. On Plato's *Cratylus*." *Ancient Philosophy* 1: 127–140.

———, tr. 1984. *Plato's Theaetetus*. Chicago: University of Chicago Press.

———, tr. 2001. *Plato's Symposium*. Chicago: University of Chicago Press.

Bernal, M. 2006. *Black Athena: The Afroasiatic Roots of Classical Civilization*. Vol. III. New Jersey: Rutgers University Press.

Bloom, A. "The Ladder of Love." Pp. 55–178 in Benardete 2001.

Brann, E., E. Salem, and P. Kalkavage, eds. 2004. *The Music of the Republic: Essays on Socrates' Conversations and Plato's Writings*. Philadelphia: Paul Dry Books.

Brogan, W. 2005. *Heidegger and Aristotle: The Twofoldness of Being*. Albany: State University of New York Press.

Brown, N 1990. *Hermes the Thief: Evolution of a Myth*. Great Barrington, Mass.: Lindisfarne Press.

Brumbaugh, R. S. 1958. "The Order of Etymologies in Plato's *Cratylus*." *Review of Metaphysics* 9: 502–510.

Burger, R. 1984. *The Phaedo: A Platonic Labyrinth*. New Haven, Conn.: Yale University Press.

Calvert, B. 1970. "Forms and Flux in Plato's *Cratylus*." *Phronesis* 15: 26–47.

Carson, A. 1986. *Eros the Bittersweet*. Princeton, N.J.: Princeton University Press.

Cornford, F. M. 1909. "Hermes, Pan, Logos." *The Classical Quarterly* 3: 281–284.

———. 1937. *Plato's Cosmology*. Indianapolis: Hackett.

———. 1957. *Plato's Theory of Knowledge*. London: Routledge.

———. 1961. *The Origin of Attic Comedy*. New York: Anchor Books.

Cousin, V., tr. 1833. *Oeuvres De Platon* XI. Paris: Rey et Gravier.

Crudden, M., tr. 2001. *The Homeric Hymns*. Oxford: Oxford University Press.

Davies, J. K. 1977. "Athenian Citizenship: The Descent Group and the Alternatives." *The Classical Journal* 73: 105–121.

Demand, N. 1975. "The *Nomothetes* of the *Cratylus*." *Phronesis* 20: 106–109.

Derrida, J. 1981. *Dissemination*. Trans. Barbara Johnson. Chicago: University of Chicago Press.

Dillon, J., tr. 1993. *The Handbook of Platonism*. Oxford: Oxford University Press.

Dobrov, G. W. 2001. *Figures of Play: Greek Drama and Metafictional Poetics*. Oxford: Oxford University Press.

Dover. K. J. 1989. *Greek Homosexuality*. Cambridge: Harvard University Press.

Duvick, B., tr. 2007. *Proclus: On Plato's Cratylus*. Ithaca: Cornell University Press.

Edwards, J. B. 1918. "The *Euthydemus*." *The Classical Weekly* 11: 210–213.

Fagles, R., tr. 1990. *Homer: The Iliad*. New York: Penguin Publishing.

———, tr. 1997. *Homer: The Odyssey*. New York: Penguin Publishing.

Faivre, A. 1995. *The Eternal Hermes: from Greek God to Alchemical Magus*. Grand Rapids, Mich.: Phanes Press.

Farnell, L. F. 1909. *Cult of the Greek States, Vol. V*. Oxford: Clarendon Press.

Fowler, H. N., 1914. *Plato: Euthyphro, Apology, Crito, Phaedo, Phaedrus*. Cambridge, Mass.: Harvard University Press.

———, tr. 1926. *Plato's Cratylus*. Cambridge, Mass.: Harvard University Press.

Freydberg, B. 1997. *The Play of the Platonic Dialogues*. New York: Peter Lang Publishing.

———. 2000. "Retracing Homer and Aristophanes in the Platonic Text." Pp. 99–112 in *Retracing the Platonic Text*, ed. J. Sallis and J. Russon. Evanston, Ill.: Northwestern University Press.

———. 2008. *Philosophy and Comedy: Aristophanes, Logos, and Eros*. Bloomington: Indiana University Press.

Friedländer, P. 1969. *Plato*. Princeton: Princeton University Press.

Friedrich, P. 1978. *The Meaning of Aphrodite*. Chicago: University of Chicago Press.

Freydberg, B. 1997. *The Play of the Platonic Dialogues*. Peter Lang Publishing. Gadamer, Hans-Georg. 1989. *Truth and Method*. New York: Continuum Publishing.

Gibbs, L., tr. 2008. *Aesop's Fables*. Oxford: Oxford University Press.

Gonzalez, F. J. 1998. *Dialectic and Dialogue: Plato's Practice of Philosophical Inquiry*. Chicago: Northeastern University Press.

Gordon, J. 1999. *Turning Toward Philosophy*. University Park: Pennsylvania University Press.

Grant, M., and J. Hazel. 1980. *Lexikon der antiken Mythen und Gestalten*. Munich: Deutscher Taschenbuch Verlag.

Guthrie, W. K. C. 1950. *The Greeks and Their Gods*. Boston: Beacon Press.

———. 1981. *A History of Greek Philosophy VI: Aristotle, an Encounter*. Cambridge: Cambridge University Press.

Hamilton, E. 1942. *Mythology*. New York: Brown and Company.

Heath, D. D. 1888. "Notes on Plato's Cratylus." *Journal of Philology* 17: 192–218.

Heidegger, Martin. 1959. *Unterweg zur Sprache*. Pfullingen, Germany: Neske.

———. 1968. *What is Called Thinking?* Trans. J. Glenn Gray. New York: Harper and Row.

Henderson, J. 1975. *The Maculate Muse: Obscene Language in Attic Comedy*. Oxford: Oxford University Press.

Holowchak, M. 2003. "Wisdom, Wine, and Wonder-lust in Plato's Symposium." *Philosophy and Literature* 27: 415–427.

Hopkins, B. 2011. "The Unwritten Teachings in Plato's *Symposium*." *Epoché* 15: 279–298.

Huffington, A. 1993. *The Gods of Greece*. New York: Atlantic Monthly Press.

Hyland, D. A. 1995. *Finitude and Transcendence in the Platonic Dialogues.* New York: New York University Press.

Jowett, B. 2009. *Plato's Cratylus.* Rockville, Md.: Serenity Publishing.

Kahn, C. H., 1973. "Language and Ontology in the *Cratylus.*" In *Exegesis and Argument,* ed. E. N. Lee, A. P. D. Mourelatos, and R. M. Rorty, 152–176. New York: Humanities Press.

———. 1979. *The Art and Thought of Heraclitus.* Cambridge: Cambridge University Press.

———. 1996. *Plato and the Socratic Dialogue.* Cambridge: Cambridge University Press.

Keller, S. 2000. "An Interpretation of Plato's *Cratylus.*" *Phronesis* 45: 284–305.

Kerényi, K. 1976. *Hermes: Guide of Souls.* Tr. Murray Stein. New York: Spring Publishing.

Kirkland, S. 2007. "*Logos* as Message from the Gods: On the Etymology of 'Hermes' in Plato's *Cratylus.*" *Bochumer Philosphisches Jahrhuch für Antike und Mittelalter* 12: 1–14.

Lamb, W. R. M., tr. 1924. *Plato: Laches, Protagoras, Meno, Euthydemus.* Cambridge, Mass.: Harvard University Press.

———, tr. 1927. *Plato: Charmides, Alcidiades 1 and 2, Hipparchus, the Lovers, Theages, Minos, Epinomis.* Cambridge, Mass.: Harvard University Press.

Levinson, R. B. 1958. "Language and the *Cratylus*: Four Questions." *Review of Metaphysics* 11: 28–41.

Liddell, H. G., and R. Scott. 1996. *A Greek–English Lexicon, With a Revised Supplement.* Oxford: Clarendon Press.

MacKenzie, M. 1986. "Putting the *Cratylus* in its Place." *The Classical Quarterly* 36: 124–150.

Martin, T. R. 1996. *Ancient Greece: From Prehistoric to Hellenistic Times.* Princeton, N.J.: Yale University Press.

Modrak, D. 2001. *Aristotle's Theory of Language and Meaning.* Cambridge: Cambridge University Press.

Nails, D. 2002. *The People of Plato: A Prosopography of Plato and Other Socratics.* Indianapolis: Hackett Publishing.

Nightingale, A. 2000. *Genres in Dialogue: Plato and the Construct of Philosophy.* Cambridge: Cambridge University Press.

Nussbaum, M. 2005. "The Comic Soul: Or, This Phallus That is Not One." Pp. 155–180 in *The Soul of Tragedy,* ed. Victoria Pedrick and Steven M. Oberhelman. Chicago: University of Chicago Press.

Pangle, T. 1985. "The Political Defense of Socratic Philosophy: A Study of Xenopon's 'Apology of Socrates to the Jury.'" *Polity* 18: 98–114.

———, tr. 1988. *Plato's Laws.* Chicago: University of Chicago Press.

Plato. *Platonis Opera. Volume I: Euthyphro, Apologia, Crito, Phaedo, Cratylus, Theaetetus, Sophista, Politicus.* Oxford: Oxford University Press.

Proclus. 2007. *On Plato's Cratylus.* Trans. B. Duvick. New York: Cornell University Press.

Reeve, C. D. C. 1998. *Plato's Cratylus.* Indianapolis: Hackett Publishing.

Riley, M. 2005. *Plato's Cratylus: Argument, Form, and Structure.* Amsterdam: Rodopi B.V.

Rosen, S. 1968. *Plato's Symposium.* New Haven, Conn.: Yale University Press.

Rosenstock, B. 1992. "Fathers and Sons: Irony in the *Cratylus.*" *Arethusa* 25: 3.

Sachs, J., tr. 2004. *Plato: Theaetetus.* Newburyport, Mass.: Focus Publishing.

———, tr. 2006. *Aristotle: Poetics.* Newburyport, Mass.: Focus Publishing.

———, tr. 2006. *Plato: Republic.* Newburyport, Mass.: Focus Publishing.

———, tr. 2011. *Socrates and the Sophists: Plato's Protagoras, Euthydemus, Hippias Major, and Cratylus.* Newburyport, Mass.: Focus Publishing.

Sallis, J. 1975. *Being and Logos.* Bloomington: Indiana University Press.
———. 1995. *Double Truth.* Albany: State University of New York Press.
———. 1999. *Chorology: On Beginning in Plato's Timaeus.* Bloomington: Indiana University Press.
———. 2000. *Force of Imagination.* Bloomington: Indiana University Press.
———. 2004. *Platonic Legacies.* Albany: State University of New York Press.
———. 2005. "The Flow of φύσις and the Beginning of Philosophy: On Plato's *Theaetetus.*" Pp. 177–193 in *Proceedings of the Boston Area Colloquium in Ancient Philosophy,* ed. J. Cleary and G. Gurtler. Leiden, Netherlands: Brill.
———. 2008. *Transfigurements: On the True Sense of Art.* Chicago: University of Chicago Press.
Schleiemacher, F. 2010. *Introduction to the Dialogues of Plato.* Tr. W. Dobson. Whitefish, Mont.: Kessinger Publishing.
Scully, S., tr. 2003. *Plato's Phaedrus.* Newburyport, Mass.: Focus Publishing.
Sedley, D. 2003. *Plato's Cratylus.* Cambridge: Cambridge University Press.
Smyth, H. W. 1920. *Greek Grammar.* Cambridge, Mass.: Harvard University Press.
Steiner, A. 1915. "Die Etymologien in Platons *Kratylos.*" *Archiv für Geschichte der Philosophie* 22.2: 109–132.
Stewart, J. A. 1905. *The Myths of Plato.* London: Macmillan.
Strauss, L. 1964. *The City and Man.* Chicago: University of Chicago Press.
Suhr, E. 1967. *Before Olympos: A Study of the Aniconic Origins of Poseidon, Hermes, and Eros.* New York: Helios Books.
Swain, S. 2007. *Severan Culture.* Cambridge: Cambridge University Press.
Tanner, S. 2010. *In Praise of Plato's Poetic Imagination.* Plymouth, U.K.: Lexington Books.
Taylor, A. E. 1960. *Plato: The Man and His Work.* London: Dover Publishing.
Thomas, C. 2008. "Inquiry Without Names in Plato's *Cratylus.*" *Journal of the History of Philosophy* 46: 341–367.
van den Berg, R. M. 2008. *Proclus' Commentary on the Cratylus in Context: Ancient Theories of Language and Naming.* Leiden, Netherlands: Brill.
Warnek, P. 2005. *Descent of Socrates: Self-Knowledge and Cryptic Nature in the Platonic Dialogues.* Bloomington: Indiana University Press.
Weingartner, R. 1970. "Making Sense of the *Cratylus.*" *Phronesis* 15: 5–75.
West, T., and G. West, trs. 1998. *Four Texts on Socrates.* Ithaca, N.Y.: Cornell University Press.
Willis, R., ed. 1993. *World Mythology.* New York: Duncan Baird Publishers.
Wolf, U. 1994. *Platon. Sämtliche Werke Bd. 3: Kratylos, Parmenides, Theaitetos, Sophistes, Politikos, Philebos, Briefe.* Hamburg: Rowohlt Taschenbuch-Verlag.
Wood, A. 2007. "Names and 'Cutting Being at the Joints' in the *Cratylus.*" *Dionysius* 25: 21–32.
Zuckert, C. 2009. *Plato's Philosophers: The Coherence of the Dialogues.* Chicago: University of Chicago Press.

Index

S. Montgomery Ewegen is Assistant Professor of Philosophy and Classics at Trinity College.

www.ingramcontent.com/pod-product-compliance
Lightning Source LLC
Chambersburg PA
CBHW020402100426
42812CB00001B/167